MERRITT LIBRARY

951.9 PRA
Pratt, Keith
Everlasting F
history of Ko

Mer

D0406100

E~~verlasting~~ Flower

Everlasting Flower
A History of Korea

Keith Pratt

REAKTION BOOKS

Thompson-Nicola Regional District
Library System
300-465 VICTORIA STREET
KAMLOOPS, BC   V2C 2A9

This book is dedicated to my friends Lee Chaesuk and Chu Sangon,
who epitomize the very best qualities of the Korean people

Published by Reaktion Books Ltd
33 Great Sutton Street
London EC1V 0DX, UK

www.reaktionbooks.co.uk

First published 2006
First paperback edition 2007

Copyright © Keith Pratt 2006

All rights reserved
No part of this publication may be reproduced, stored in a retrieval system, or
transmitted, in any form or by any means, electronic, mechanical, photocopying,
recording or otherwise, without the prior permission of the publishers.

Printed and bound in Great Britain
by Biddles Ltd, King's Lynn

British Library Cataloguing in Publication Data

Pratt, Keith L.
    Everlasting flower : a history of Korea
    1. Korea - History
    I. Title
    951.9

ISBN-10: 1 86189 335 3
ISBN-13: 978-1-86189-335-2

1017770033

Contents

Preface   6
Maps: Early Kingdoms on the Korean Peninsula   8
      Modern Korea   9
Chronology of Korean History   10

Introduction   13

I The Creation of State Identity

  1 From Earliest Times to AD 668: Cultural Patterns in Flux   29
  2 Unified Silla, AD 668–936: The Building of Confidence   59
  3 Koryŏ, 918–1392: The Struggle for Independence   85
  4 Early to Mid-Chosŏn, 1392–1800: The Search for an
     Acceptable Orthodoxy   116

II A Century of Insecurity

  5 The Hermit Kingdom, 1800–64: Tradition at Work   153
  6 Incursion, Modernization and Reform, 1864–1905:
     Tradition at Bay   177

III A Century of Suffering

  7 Culture under Threat, 1905–45: The Colonial Era   209
  8 Partition and War, 1945–53: Return to Disunity   241
  9 Post-War Korea: Tradition and Change   264

Sources and Further Reading   308
Discography   313
Acknowledgements   314
Index   315

Preface

This is not the kind of in-depth study that comes from concentrated research and a well-earned PhD thesis. Rather, it is a personal impression of a country, formed over half a lifetime's subjective and loving (if sometimes frustrated) acquaintance with it. Originally I suggested 'The Role of Culture in the Evolution of Modern Korea' as a subtitle. The publishers thought this was too cumbersome, and they were probably right. It did have the merit of giving the reader some idea of what to expect, though it may have given an exaggerated idea of what I was aiming at. My approach has been to offer a series of snapshots of what seem to me to be important elements in the formation and development of the modern Korean state and its national psyche. I have tried to convey the pride that Koreans have in their country's ancient traditions and to explain the insistence they place on their nation's independence in the history of East Asia. For all the heritage they unquestionably share with China and Japan, Koreans emphatically proclaim that they and their culture are quite distinguishable from their neighbours and theirs. Nationalism is strong, in both North and South Korea. The world needs to understand it, though not necessarily to fear it: it shapes the character of the Koreans who live and work at home and abroad, and it drives the ideologies, economies and foreign policies of the two Koreas. It has been regularly apparent in the opening years of the twenty-first century, fuelling arguments, for example, over China's (successful) submission to UNESCO for World Heritage recognition of Koguryŏ sites in eastern Manchuria, and Japan's claim to sovereignty over the Tokto islands in the East Sea / Sea of Japan.

In writing the book I have consulted the Korean dynastic histories (*Samguk sagi*, *Koryŏsa* and *Chosŏn wangjo sillok*); early compendia such as *Samguk yusa*, Sŏ Kŏjŏng's *Tongguk t'onggam* (1484) and Han Ch'iyun's eighteenth-century *Haedong yŏksa*; Chinese dynastic histories and encyclopedias including the *Cefu yuankui*; and Xu Jing's *Gaoli tujing*. Some of the secondary sources that I have found particularly helpful will be found in the suggestions for further reading at the end of the book.

Transliteration of Korean terms and names follows the McCune-Reischauer system, except in the case of prominent figures and place names for which alternative usages are better known, and of individuals who prefer or preferred alternative spellings of their names. Chinese titles and names follow the Pinyin system.

A series of boxed Picture Essays illustrate subjects mentioned in the text and provide more detailed information.

Picture Essays and Charts

1	Portrait of Dong Shou	48
2	Grey stoneware jar	52
3	Grey stone funerary vessel	54
4	Funerary headware of King Muryŏng	56
5	Soapstone relief of a boar	60
6	Decorated roof-tile	70
7	Pagodas at Pulguk-sa	74
8	Temple bell from Sangwŏn-sa	82
9	Wooden mask	92
10	Confucian sacrificial music	98
11	Printing blocks for the Korean Tripitaka	110
12	Inlaid celadon jar	112
13	A page from *Sŏkpo sangjŏl Han'gŭl cha*	122
14	Building a turtle boat	134
15	Hwasŏng fortress	142
16	Chŏng Sŏn, *Manp'okdong*	148
17	Detail from a nectar ritual painting	156
18	Kim Hongdo, *Wrestling (ssirŭm)*	162
19	An eight-panel screen	166
20	Yi Hanch'ŏl, *Portrait of Kim Chŏnghŭi*	170
21	Independence Gate	186
22	A *Ŭigwe* screen	188
23	Map of Seoul	200
24	Kisan, *Chess Players*	204
25	The former Japanese Government-General Building, Seoul	214
26	Yi Insŏng, *One Autumn Day*	230
27	Yi Chungsŏp, *Family*	258
28	Taedong river, December 1950	261
29	Making long-stem bamboo pipes	281
30	Hwang Yŏngyŏp, *Human Being*	284
31	The Seoul Arts Center; The Whanki Museum	288
32	Song Shiyŏp, *The Sound of Creation*	294

Chronology of Korean History	10
Principal Events in Korea, 1945–50	242
The Korean War	250

Early Kingdoms on the Korean Peninsula

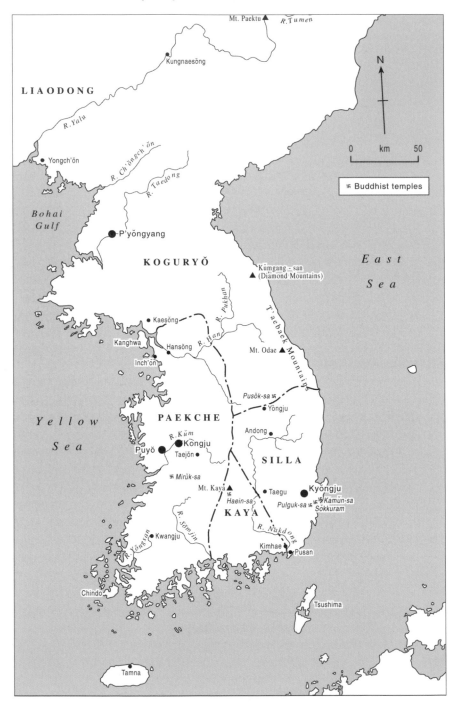

Modern Korea

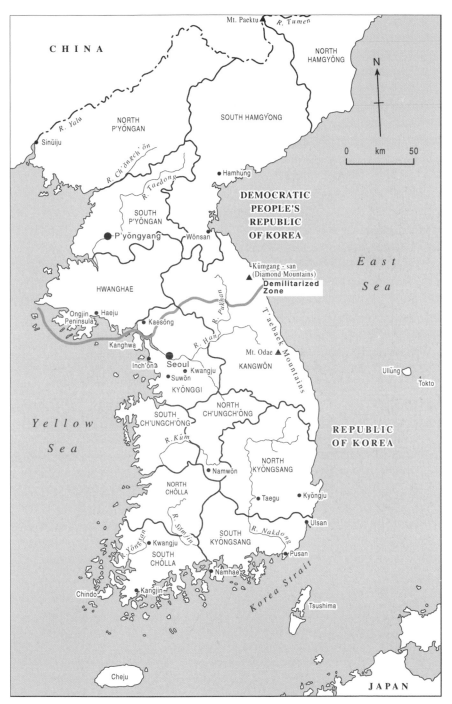

CHINA

Mt. Paektu

R. Tumen

NORTH HAMGYŎNG

N

SOUTH HAMGYŎNG

R. Yalu

NORTH P'YŎNGAN

Sinŭiju

R. Ch'ŏngch'ŏn

0   km   50

Hamhŭng

R. Taedong

DEMOCRATIC PEOPLE'S REPUBLIC OF KOREA

SOUTH P'YŎNGAN

P'yŏngyang

Wŏnsan

E a s t

Kŭmgang - san ▲ (Diamond Mountains)

S e a

HWANGHAE

Demilitarized Zone

R. Pukhan

Ongjin Peninsula

Haeju

Kaesŏng

R. Han

T'aebaek Mountains

Kanghwa

Inch'ŏn

Seoul

Kwangju

Mt. Odae ▲

Ullŭng

KANGWŎN

Suwŏn

Tokto

KYŎNGGI

Y e l l o w

NORTH CH'UNGCH'ŎNG

SOUTH CH'UNGCH'ŎNG

S e a

R. Kŭm

REPUBLIC OF KOREA

NORTH KYŎNGSANG

Namwŏn

NORTH CHŎLLA

Taegu

Kyŏngju

R. Sŏmjin

R. Nakdong

Ulsan

R. Yŏngsan

Kwangju

SOUTH KYŎNGSANG

Pusan

SOUTH CHŎLLA

Namhae

Chindo

Kangjin

K o r e a   S t r a i t

Tsushima

Cheju

JAPAN

CHRONOLOGY OF KOREAN HISTORY

± 6000 BC   Neolithic communities evolve on the Korean peninsula.
2nd m.   Development of agriculture
± 800   The Korean Bronze Age begins
± 500   Emergence of Old Chosŏn along the Taedong river basin
± 400   The Korean Iron Age begins
early 2nd C.   Wiman Chosŏn succeeds Old Chosŏn
108   Han armies invade Wiman Chosŏn; Chinese commanderies
               are set up across the north of the peninsula
early 1st C.   Formation of Koguryŏ around the upper Yalu and Tumen
               river reaches

AD
1st C.   Lelang develops as the principal Chinese commandery; rivalry
               grows with Koguryŏ
1st–3rd C.   The Proto-Three Kingdoms period. Silla, Kaya and Paekche
               emerge from the tribal federations of Chinhan, Pyŏnhan and
               Mahan in southern Korea
313–14   Chinese commanderies of Lelang and Daifang fall to
               Koguryŏ and Paekche
late 4th C.   Buddhism is accepted at the Koguryŏ and Paekche courts
527   Silla recognizes Buddhism
562   Silla mops up Kaya
660   Silla destroys Paekche with Chinese help
668   Silla conquers Koguryŏ with Chinese help, ending the 'Three
               Kingdoms' Period
676   Unified Silla expels the last Chinese troops from its soil
8th C.   Unified Silla prospers at the heart of flourishing East Asian
               civilization (China, Korea, Japan)
892   Later Paekche proclaimed by Kyŏn Hwŏn at Chŏnju
901   Kungye raises the standard of Later Koguryŏ at Kaesŏng
918   Wang Kŏn overthrows Kungye and proclaims the state of
               Koryŏ
935   Wang Kŏn enters Kyŏngju and reunites the country under
               the Koryŏ banner
11th C.   North-east Asia tolerates an uneasy balance between Khitan
               Liao rule in Manchuria, Song in China and Koryŏ in Korea
1122   Liao falls to the Jurchen Jin dynasty in Manchuria and
               northern China; Jurchen armies raid Koryŏ
1196   The Koryŏ court falls under control of military dictatorship
               led by the Ch'oe clan
1231–59   Mongol invasions establish foreign command over peninsula
1274, 1281   Unsuccessful Mongol attempts to invade Japan bring suffering
               to Korea
1368   Mongol power in East Asia collapses; Korean relations with
               the new Ming dynasty in China boost Neo-Confucianism
1392   Yi Sŏnggye leads the revolt against the Koryŏ court and
               founds the Chosŏn regime

1418-50	The reign of King Sejong the Great, marked by economic and cultural advances
mid-16th c.	Growth of factionalism, breaking into open rivalry in 1574
1592-8	Hideyoshi commands catastrophic Japanese invasions (*Imjin waeran*), which are repelled with Chinese assistance
1627, 1636	Manchu invasions; the Chosŏn court submits to the imminent (1644) Qing dynasty rulers of China
mid-17th c.	Genesis of the *sirhak* ('Realistic Learning') movement
1724-76	Reign of King Yŏngjo
1762	Death of Crown Prince Sado
1776-1800	Reign of King Chŏngjo
1785	The first Christian church is set up secretly at a house in Seoul
1811	Hong Kyŏngnae's rebellion reveals widespread discontent at maladministration
1864-1907	Reign of King Kojong
1864-73	The Taewŏn'gun rules as de facto regent
1866	Kojong marries his queen, Min; the *General Sherman* incident brings the USA to the Chosŏn court's notice
± 1880	Growth of the Self-Strengthening Movement
1882	The Treaty of Amity and Commerce with USA (the 'Shufeldt Treaty'), followed (1883-6) by treaties with eight European nations
1883	America appoints its first minister to Seoul
1884	The Revd Horace Allen arrives in Korea; the Kapsin Coup bares Sino-Japanese diplomatic rivalry on the peninsula
1885	Chinese and Japanese troops withdraw following the Treaty of Tianjin
1887	The first Korean legation in Washington is opened
1894-5	The Tonghak Rebellion sparks the Sino-Japanese War; success strengthens Tokyo's ambitions in Korea, displayed in the Kabo reforms
1895	The assassination of Queen Min drives King Kojong to sanctuary in the Russian embassy
1897	Kojong declares himself emperor of the Great Han Empire
1904-5	The Russo-Japanese War consolidates Japanese imperialist moves in North-East Asia
1905	The Protectorate Treaty gives Japan unprecedented powers in Korea
1907	Korea snubbed at The Hague Peace Conference
1910	The Treaty of Annexation inaugurates the Japanese colonial era
1910-18	Japanese Government-General conducts a Land Survey
1919	The March First Movement lifts the lid on Korean resentment at the Japanese occupation; Korean Provisional Government established in Shanghai
1926	The death of ex-Emperor Sunjong sparks new independence demonstrations
1929	The Kwangju Incident heightens anti-Japanese tension
1931	Japan launches military aggression in Manchuria

1932	Japan creates the puppet state of Manzhouguo in China's three north-eastern provinces
1937	The Japanese invasion of China proper begins
1940	Koreans are forced to take Japanese names
1945	Liberation is followed by division along the 38th parallel: North Korea comes under Soviet influence, the South under the American Military Government (-1948)
1946	The Autumn Harvest Uprising
1948	
(Feb.)	The DPRK forms the Korean People's Army
(April)	The Cheju Rebellion
(May, August)	Elections held in South and North fail to form a pan-Korean government
(Dec.)	National Security Law enacted in the ROK
1948–60	ROK's First Republic, under Syngman Rhee as president
1948–94	Kim Il Sung rules the DPRK
1950	Outbreak of the Korean War
1953	The Korean War ends in stalemate; an armistice divides the land along the DMZ
1965	ROK–Japan Treaty of Basic Relations
	The Soviet Union supplies the DPRK with an experimental nuclear reactor
1971	Launch of the New Community Movement (Saemaŭl Undong)
1972	Introduction of the Yusin Constitution
1979	Assassination of President Park Chung Hee
1980	The Kwangju massacre
1988	Start of the ROK's Sixth Republic, moving in the direction of democratic reform
	Seoul Olympic Games
mid-1990s	Famine in North Korea leads to World Food Programme aid
1996	Ex-Presidents Chun and Roh convicted of treason and other crimes
1997	International Monetary Fund intervenes to counter ROK economic collapse
1999	DPRK admits inspectors from the International Atomic Energy Agency
2000	Summit between President Kim Daejung and Chairman Kim Jong Il
2002	Korea and Japan co-host the football World Cup

Introduction

Early European mapmakers showed Korea as an island off the north-east coast of China. The Jesuit priest Martino Martini got it right in his Chinese atlas published in Vienna in 1653, but to this day some Westerners still find it a bit of a mystery. Its name may not immediately conjure up an image of the shape, size, or even the exact location of the peninsula whose situation at the far eastern end of the Eurasian land mass makes it one of the most strategically sensitive small countries in the world. In the past, some people have likened it to a rabbit, facing China with its ears pointing north-eastwards towards the Russian frontier; others to a dagger, pointing away from China in the direction of the Japanese island chain. More often it has been described as a bridge or pathway between its two better-known neighbours – not a very long path, just some 600 miles from top to bottom, a distance that an army could cover in a few weeks. Even the water splash in which it ends, and that separates it from the Japanese island of Kyūshū, is no wider than that between Wales and Ireland, and in its middle there is a convenient stepping stone to help the traveller over, the island of Tsushima.

Since 1948 the Korean peninsula has been divided into the Democratic People's Republic of Korea (DPRK) in the north and the Republic of Korea (ROK) in the south. An estimated 23 million people live in the DPRK and a further 48.25 million in the ROK. The partition, roughly along the 38th parallel, is a political one, not following any ancient or logical pattern, either ethnic or topographical. It gives the DPRK rather more than half the surface area, 47,300 square miles to the ROK's 38,000. Both have major rivers – the Tuman (Tumen), Amnŏk (Yalu), Ch'ŏngch'ŏn and Taedong in the North, the Han, Kŭm and Nakdong in the South – which open up access to the interior and have been well used by friend and foe alike since neolithic times. The North is more mountainous and has greater mineral resources, whereas the South benefits from richer agricultural land. Running across the top of the peninsula, the Changbaek range forms the backbone of the mountains. From its highest peak, Mount Paektu, the Tumen and Yalu rivers flow east and west respectively into the East and Yellow seas. In winter they freeze hard, the whole region is deep in snow, and the barrier between Korea and China looks impenetrable. Yet where there's a will there's a way: in January 1836 the first Western missionary to enter Korea, Father Pierre Maubant, secretly stole over the frozen Yalu. And to present-day Korean refugees intent on migrating in the opposite direction neither rivers nor mountains are a real deterrent. Southwards from the Changbaek Mountains, like the rabbit's backbone, runs a chain containing the famous Diamond Mountains, Kŭmgang-san. Beloved for centuries by artists, poets and philosophers, they were the first destination to be offered to South Korean tourists when the North tentatively cracked open its door in 1998.

The West watched this experiment with interest, but not so very long ago Europeans and Americans had seen little relevance to their own lives in the concerns of East Asia. Then came World War Two and Pearl Harbor, the Chinese civil war and the attack on HMS *Amethyst*, the Korean War and the sacrifices of United Nations troops. Memories of the nineteenth century's so-called yellow peril were revived, and to a 'free world' in the grip of Cold War, the implications of communism in China carried added danger. Later in the twentieth century fear gave way to grudging respect, and as 'tiger' economies boomed in Japan, South Korea, Taiwan, Hong Kong and Singapore, the British prime minister, Tony Blair, was among those suggesting that the West might have something to learn from East Asia's traditionally linked systems of social organization and business management. But admiration soon turned to caution. As European economies faltered in 2002, commentators advised that lessons should be learned from the spectacular Japanese financial collapse in 1997; as South Korean *chaebŏl* conglomerates began to waver, even European drivers of Kia and Daewoo motor cars grew anxious; and, to put the cap on it, in early 2003 Kim Jong Il, 'Dear Leader' of a country defined by President George W. Bush as part of an 'axis of evil', talked up a nuclear crisis while famine stalked his land, and even President Kim Daejung's 'sunshine' policy of accommodation with his difficult neighbours failed to win American support. The pendulum of political interest swings fast, but never again will the West write off the nations of East Asia as irrelevant to its own future. What happens in and between the DPRK and the ROK matters to us all.

Like Europe, East Asia has a long history that has seen close alliances and bitter wars. Nowadays a sense of regional integrity is developing, born of economic imperatives, in which respect for the contributions of all member states is acknowledged. But there is still a long way to go. The People's Republic of China (PRC) hankers after reunion with the Republic of China (Taiwan), by force if necessary. The Korean War remains unfinished, with hostilities between the states on either side of the Demilitarized Zone (DMZ) halted only by an armistice. And neither China nor Korea is satisfied that Japan has made sufficient apology or reparation for the way it victimized and humiliated their people from 1895 onwards. Political tension among these five states often runs high, with the USA, Russia and the European Union ever ready to give commands, advice or offers from the touchline. At the very heart of this vital region, politically, economically and culturally, is Korea. And paradoxically, a proper picture of its nationalist spirit is essential to understanding the prospects for an integrated East Asian unit. We need to know what makes Koreans feel different from their Chinese and Japanese neighbours, as well as what they have in common. Almost the first thing my teacher of Korean musical history, Professor Lee Hye-ku, said to me in 1972 was: 'You must not come here as so many Westerners do, just expecting to find a repository of Chinese and Japanese civilization. Of course our culture has been overlain by theirs and we can still see signs of that, but what you must also look for are the native traditions of the Korean people underneath.' So we have to recognize Korean distinctiveness in cultural as well as political terms, to see how its leaders have identified Korean best interests, and to identify the artistic tastes and skills of which they were and still are proud. The key to understanding modern Korea lies in understanding what the land meant to its people in the past.

Korea has gone by many names, official and unofficial, in the course of its history. 'Korea', and its earlier spelling Corea, can be traced back to Marco Polo's attempt to transliterate the name that he was familiar with at the time of his sojourn in thirteenth-century East Asia. The Chinese often referred to a neighbouring country by the title of its ruling dynasty, and Marco Polo made Koryŏ, 'High and Beautiful', into Cauli. Early Koreans themselves were happy with the rather prosaic Dongguk, 'Eastern Country', until in 1897 the newly self-styled emperor and former king, Kojong, upped the nation's image when he proclaimed the Great Han (Taehan) Empire. Echoes of that name still resound through present-day South Korea, the 'Great Han Republic' Taehan Min'guk. Nineteenth-century Western sobriquets, like Hermit

Kingdom and Land of Morning Calm, were popular if misleading. Among twentieth-century literary epithets one drew attention to the mountainous backbone running down the peninsula by referring to it as Cheyŏk, 'Plaice Country', and the poem adopted by the Republic of Korea for its national anthem in 1948 quotes a contemporary name, 'Hibiscus Land' (*Kŭnyŏk*), when it sings of 'Thirty thousand leagues of mountains, streams and deathless flowers'. (The hibiscus, which Koreans call the everlasting flower, is the national flower of the ROK.)

However I try to define and explain Korea, I do so as an outsider. I can strive to make my assessment as fair and objective as possible, given that I am observing the country and its people from the other side of the world and that I view all history and culture – my own just as much as others' – with Western, and far from agreed, preconceptions and prejudices. But from within East Asia, the picture of Korea is liable to look quite different. Over the centuries, the Chinese, the Japanese, and especially the Koreans themselves, have all seen Korea in a different light, reflecting their own assumptions and priorities. To the imperial Chinese court, from the Han dynasty (206 BC–AD 220) to the Qing (1644–1911), the peninsula was one of the closest parts of *tianxia*, 'all under Heaven', for which the emperor accepted theoretical responsibility on behalf of Heaven. It was the most cooperative partner in the so-called tribute system, which formed the basis of the Chinese worldview in imperial times. In return for the benefits of Chinese civilization and the offer of military protection, the rulers of vassal states pledged their (similarly equivocal) allegiance to the Dragon Throne and undertook to send it regular gifts. Educated Koreans and Japanese knew very well what forms of etiquette the Chinese preferred and were quite capable of performing them when required, on sending seasonal greetings to the imperial court, for example, or entertaining visiting Chinese embassies. To the Chinese it was only natural that Korea's intelligentsia should learn and copy superior Sinic etiquette and culture, even if its lower-class majority understood little of these arcane rites and led their own daily lives differently. As far back as the Han dynasty, the classic Chinese geography, the *Shanhaijing*, had used the flattering term 'country of gentlemen' in possible reference to the peninsula.

The Japanese regarded Korea in more pragmatic terms. For centuries before direct shipping lanes were established with China, it was the route via which they obtained the fruits of mainland cultures and economies. The stepping-stone island of Tsushima had a mixed population of Koreans and Japanese and was governed by a Japanese *daimyō*. Both sides benefited from trade, and relations were often cordial. Twice in their history, however, Japanese leaders used Korea as the pathway towards what they hoped would be continental domination, and with shattering effect. The first attempt was from 1592 to 1598, when the armies of Toyotomi Hideyoshi invaded and partially occupied the peninsula. The second followed events in the late nineteenth century, which resulted in the Japanese colonization of Korea in 1910 and prepared the way for the invasion of China. Both stemmed from the vision of a pan-Asiatic sphere under Japanese leadership in which Korea would play a largely anonymous role. The first period saw the widespread destruction of buildings and works of art, a foretaste of the attempt by colonizers in the second to deal a fatal blow to Korea's cultural individuality. Chinese foreign policy-makers might have contented themselves that all states were 'under Heaven' and that by extending Chinese influence over as many as they could, the emperor's soldiers, diplomats and scholars were distributing Heaven's bounty widely across this one big family. Yet although their books did sometimes record an interest in the habits of what they called the 'barbarian' races, they themselves did not really expect to change the lives of ordinary Koreans, Vietnamese, Burmese, Japanese or central Asian tribesmen. It was up to local rulers to pass on what they learned of ideal Chinese behaviour. The twentieth-century Japanese colonial administration, however, went further, by annexing Korea and then trying to impose Japanese ways on the whole of its society. Its anthropologists set out to justify the occupation on the postulated grounds that the peoples of eastern Siberia, Manchuria and Korea shared common ethnic roots with Japan. Koreans began to find out what it meant to be newly recognized but undervalued members of Japanese society.

Dominated by China on one side and periodically harassed by Japan on the other, Koreans themselves have long been used to assessing their part in regional structure. Nationalism coloured much of their writing on this theme in the later twentieth century, and we get inklings of its presence in two earlier periods also. The first was in the twelfth and thirteenth centuries, when the scholar-official Kim Pusik compiled a comprehensive history of Korea, the *Samguk sagi* ('History of the Three Kingdoms'), and the monk Iryŏn complemented this rather orthodox account with a collection of legends and folk tales. Compiled around 1285, he called it *Samguk yusa* ('Additional Material on the Three Kingdoms'), and it has given pleasure to its readers for many centuries. One of its tales is that of the semi-divine Tan'gun, whom Iryŏn credited with laying the state's foundations as far back as the third millennium BC. In the days of the mythical Chinese emperor Yao, he wrote, the supreme god Hwan'in allowed his son Hwan'ung to descend to earth. Ung took with him 3,000 attendants and three talismans that his father had given him, and landed under a tree on T'aebaek Mountain. (It is not certain where this was. There is a T'aebaek in modern Kangwŏn province, but this is an unlikely contender. Mount Myohyong, north of P'yŏngyang, has some supporters, but most opinion favours Mount Paektu.) There he turned a female bear into a woman called Ungnyo, 'Bear Woman'. When the tiger with which she shared a cave was unable to keep the strict rules that Ung had set them in order to become human, Ung married the woman himself. They bore a son, Tan'gun, who established Ko Chosŏn, 'Old Chosŏn' (Ch. Gu Zhaoxian), and its capital at Asadal ('Holy City'). When Tan'gun had ruled for 1,500 years, the Chinese king Wu, founder of the Zhou dynasty, enfeoffed a man called Kija (Ch. Qizi) as the first king of Chosŏn. Thereupon Tan'gun withdrew and became a mountain god. (So for those who still believe this story the implication is that their own progenitors were descended from a she-bear. Fossilized flora and fauna from Korean palaeolithic sites do certainly include bones of bear among those of many other wild animals.) We shall never know how old the Tan'gun tradition already was in Iryŏn's day, but his was the first literary mention of a hare that has run and run to the present, and shows no sign yet of being stopped. Tan'gun studies are still popular in nationalistic Korean circles, especially in the DPRK, though others rubbish their validity.

The second suggestion of incipient nationalism came in the eighteenth century, when Korean scholars of the *sirhak* ('Realistic Learning') conviction, shaken by the Japanese and Manchu invasions and the fall of China's Ming dynasty, began to reassess their country's needs as objectively as they knew how. In the process they re-examined Chinese and Korean historical records and came up with two better authenticated alternatives to Tan'gun as founders of their kingdom, the aforesaid Kija, and Wiman (Ch. Wei Man). Both were apparently of Chinese origin and had founded Chinese-style statelets to set the peninsula on its historical path. Kija was said to have been an honourable relative, perhaps a nephew, of the decadent last Shang king, who had fled to the north-east at the time of the Zhou conquest in ±1045 BC. What was believed to be his tomb was discovered near P'yŏngyang (but is now thought to date from no earlier than the twelfth century AD). Wiman was identified as a military commander in the north-east Chinese state of Yan who deserted early in the second century BC to the P'yŏngyang area, establishing his capital at Wanggŏmsŏng. Neither story can be corroborated archaeologically, but what matters is that Chinese literati – and thus later Korean historians – clearly linked the statelet of Zhaoxian with early events in the shaping of their own country. *Sirhak* researchers were in fact endorsing the claim established by Yi Sŏnggye in 1392 to his dynasty's legitimacy through lineal descent from Chinese origins. In Confucian terms this kind of authentification was a priority, and Kija was set to become the most important political symbol of the Chosŏn dynasty. He was credited not only with stimulating economic progress but also with a wide range of cultural innovation representing all that China most respected, covering writing, poetry, divination, rites and music. As for Wiman, the *sirhak* scholar Yi Ik (1681–1763), who was deeply interested in scientific historiography, accused him of being an alien, but some modern Korean historians have turned him into an ethnic north-easterner, a Dongyi; made him an erstwhile Ko Chosŏn bureaucrat; and so lifted the stigma of being a foreign usurper from his shoulders: he too has been authenticated into the origins of modern Korea. Their Confucian upbringing meant that educated Koreans accepted the pro-Chinese bias of their forebears uncritically, and even *sirhak* advocates were unable to break wholly free of this inclination. But whereas the Sinicized literati had previously spurned the oral traditions and native skills of ordinary people, converts to *sirhak* now began to look at them afresh, and to bring fresh qualities with unique Korean features to their art, literature and music.

In all three countries of East Asia written records are profuse: those from China date from the first millennium BC; the earliest Korean sources come from the Unified Silla period (AD 668–936), and the Japanese from the eighth century AD. They comprise government records and unofficial critiques, the collected writings of scholars, diaries, travellers' tales, eyewitness accounts and documentary monographs, biographies and hagiography, fact and fiction, songs, prose and poetry. They range from ephemeral jottings to multi-volume encyclopedias. They cover history, geography, economics, philosophy and religion, the arts and aesthetics. Because communication across the region was quite easy, people from all three countries had plenty to say about each other. Comparison of their writings should, one might think, make it fairly easy for modern scholars to find answers to their questions. But of course, the reverse is true. So much writing includes a comparable amount of prejudice and imagination on the part of the races and individuals who produced them. And even though today's scholars may apply scientific research to confirm or refute literary records, and archaeologists are frequently unearthing fresh evidence, the suspicion of politically motivated partiality, whether Chinese, Korean or Japanese, still hangs over the interpretation of history. The 'horse-rider theory', for example, that the Japanese Yamato kingdom was founded by Eurasian steppe horsemen who crossed the straits between AD 250 and 400 is no longer accepted. But in 1994 Wontack

Hong claimed that Yamato was certainly established by mounted cavalry, namely Paekche warriors descended from Puyo tribespeople: it was an ironic, and unproven, counter to earlier Japanese attempts to justify colonial dominion on the grounds of shared ethnicity.

The prehistory of the peninsula and of what we know today as Manchuria still holds many an undisclosed secret. Centuries of fighting and industrial development have destroyed archaeological and historical remains; that said, excavations have so far failed to reveal any evidence of cultural or political development corresponding to the supposed discrete states of Tan'gun, Kija or Wiman. It would mean a lot to Koreans to be able to blow away the haze that hangs over their origins and establish the true story of early state formation on the peninsula, especially if that were to confirm a measure of ancient independence in relation to China and to lay to rest any lingering doubts about a Japanese ethnic relationship. But, in the words of Hyung Il Pai,

> the original Korean race . . . cannot be extrapolated from the archaeological record using concepts of race and national identity formed in the late nineteenth and early twentieth century . . . [T]he pursuit of nationalistic causes has overshadowed the more important goal of developing a coherent methodology for interpreting the prehistory of the Korean peninsula.

The Chinese, Koreans and Japanese long ago settled into a tolerable triangular relationship, each developing strong pride in their own characteristics and traditions. Recurrent migrations led to ethnic and cultural mixing, which nevertheless failed to blur the edges of their respective nationalist spirits. Like most neighbours they had their occasional differences, some of them serious, but on the whole the three states traced a pattern of coexistence that survived until the mid-nineteenth century. Then, as outsiders arrived from Europe and America with new ideas and recommendations for modernization, new interpretations of nationalism also developed, and the traditional order in East Asia began to change. Whether nationalism is, in the words of James Palais, either 'a blessing [or] a curse' usually depends on the point of view of the commentator. Its worldwide evolution after the nineteenth century came in response to imperialism and colonialism, but even within a single country it has assumed varied, sometimes complex, forms, and these have been neither unchanging in nature nor constant in strength. Three kinds of nationalism have stirred Koreans since the late nineteenth century, reflecting and restoring a people's damaged pride.

Political nationalism

The publication on 7 April 1896 of the first newspaper to be written entirely in the Korean *han'gŭl* alphabet, *Tongnip Sinmun* ('The Independent News'), was part of the nationalistic response to the Japanese-inspired Kabo reforms, and one of the positive outcomes of the Patriotic Enlightenment Movement (Aeguk Kyemŏng Undong). In July that year the Independence Club was founded and took the lead in organizing demonstrations against the reforms. As tension rose, such signs of Korean chauvinism were quickly suppressed, but the passage of time failed to quench the spirit behind them, and feelings of antipathy towards foreign-imposed institutional change, however needful from a modernizing point of view, fuelled racial hostility up to and beyond the Japanese Annexation in 1910. The public declaration of Korean independence on 1 March 1919 made a statement that would not be forgotten and which the occupying regime could never ignore.

After Liberation in 1945 anti-foreignism turned against America and the USSR, but the Korean War and the Armistice in 1953 brought a fresh focus for political nationalism. The number one rival now became the regime across the DMZ, each side claiming the right to rule the whole peninsula. Legitimacy became the first objective of political nationalism as both North and South found that they were dependent on foreign support, and anti-foreignism was relegated to second place. The DPRK could not afford to offend either the USSR or the PRC and trod a careful line in foreign policy, while its regimented and manipulated people turned out on regular occasions to voice their unanimous and wholehearted love and support for their 'Great Leader' Kim Il Sung. In the South, gratitude for continuing US military and economic protection was tempered by popular resentment at America's persistent record of backing autocratic and oppressive regimes in Seoul. For their part, as the ROK strove to recover from the past and look to the future, successive presidents from Park Chung Hee to Kim Daejung prioritized economic targets as proof of their nationalist credentials.

While the hoped-for reunification remained afar off, scholars in both North and South began to re-examine history to see how it could help their particular regime's bid for pan-Korean legitimacy. Political and social theorists had traditionally believed that the key to earlier misfortunes and current policy was to be found by examining the past and seeing where their predecessors had gone wrong. In the 1950s, as a result of their leaders' reliance on the Soviet Union, China and the United States, neither regime's historians could occupy the moral high ground by accusing the other of returning to traditional great-power sycophancy and surrendering recently won independence. Instead, both sides turned back to ancient history to try and prove that it was they who had inherited the right to rule. Foundation myths came back into fashion: whilst both sides gave official approbation to Tan'gun, the DPRK could lay better claim to his ancestry by virtue of his association with Mount Paektu, where it said it had discovered his tomb, while the ROK played up its supposed descent from Wiman.

Minjung *nationalism*

Koreans traditionally expected life to be a battle, against either oppression from their superiors or the effects of natural disasters. Even so, the hardships and exploitation they suffered after 1910 were exceptional, and, to make matters worse, the rest of the world seemed impervious to their cries for help. So the sudden Japanese capitulation on 14 August 1945 was greeted with delight and optimism. But hopes of sovereignty restored were cruelly dashed, and the post-Liberation separation of North from South even prompted comparison with the divisions of the Three Kingdoms or Koryŏ period. Politically, the two new republics began by instituting systems that were not too dissimilar, in that they each showed an instinctive inclination towards the imperial Chinese system of military-backed autocracy paying lip service to satisfying popular needs. People in the ROK soon saw through this. As a succession of militaristic regimes, beginning with that of Syngman Rhee in 1948, showed scant regard for the interests of ordinary Koreans, a groundswell of resentment began to voice the mood that had been growing for half a century. In time this would be known as *minjung* ('populist') nationalism. Its peak of frustration is identified with the army's infamous and bloody gunning down of demonstrators in Kwangju in 1980, but in truth both the nature of that protest and the level of the authorities' response give a misleading impression of *minjung* nationalism. Instead, as a gathering rumble of discontent at the old order of aristocratic elitism (in the late Chosŏn), the cruelty of alien conquerors (the Japanese colonial era) and the corrupt government of military dictatorship (the early ROK), it appeared in a variety of social, religious, literary and artistic forms. Sometimes violent, yet never iconoclastic, it showed that the Korean people, like the Chinese during the Civil War of 1946–9, were at last prepared to stand up.

The dividing line between political and *minjung* nationalism looks thin. Both expressed frustration at political repression; both involved demonstrations. But whereas those who led the way with the former tended to be members of identifiable groups – Chosŏn literati, students, socialist activists, converts to communism – capable of defining their targets in specific terms, the point about *minjung* nationalism was that it involved all kinds of people, many of whom would not have understood or used political arguments but who knew that their time was coming. Challenging the passive Confucian viewpoint that history is made and led by the rulers, members of all classes united to affirm more and more what the historian Sohn Pow-key of Yŏnsei University had written in 1970, that 'the people played the major role in historical development'. Fresh attention was paid to the recent history of popular movements, especially the Tonghak Rebellion and the partisan militia known as *ŭibyŏng* ('justice fighters'). Politically, such views hinted at an interest in democracy, something of which neither Korea nor its traditional mentor China had had any experience, and which the military dictators resisted with every means at their command.

Cultural nationalism

The Japanese moved quickly against political opposition after 1910, but were less concerned by signs of remanent Korean nationalism in cultural form. They encouraged art and archaeology – both because they now said it was part of their own heritage and because cultural activities provided opportunities for collaboration that some Koreans were prepared to accept – endeavouring all the while to weigh the delicate balance between those activities that might stimulate Korean nostalgia for a vanished past against those that would promote feelings of ethnic association with Japan. At the same time, they saw artistic activity under their own control as an anodyne way of channelling the younger generation's emotions. Some Koreans were fooled, but many more were not, and subtle ways were found for painting, music and literature to sustain the sense of Korean difference.

After 1945 Korean historians hurried to publish books correcting what they saw as the distortion of history due to traditional Chinese-style scholarly attitudes and Japanese take-over attempts. 'It is said that Korean histories should outgrow dynastic-centered description of history, correct historical facts that were distorted by government-patronized scholars during the Japanese colonial rule, and be written from an objective point of view. I entirely agree with this', wrote Han Woo-keun. Objectivity, of course, is monotonously impossible for historians to attain. The authors of one of the new texts, Sohn, Kim and Hong, desiring to 'present an easy-to-read and interpretative Korean history' and hoping that 'the reader will find the true picture of Korean history in this book', began by lamenting their partitioned country. 'The need for the Korean people to lift such an unhappy division through the consolidation of national power', they wrote, 'is paramount. For this national goal we, the Korean people, have continuously attempted to build up our own power. These self-motivated efforts, throughout Korean history, have always been successful.' The reader of the present book must judge just how well supported this claim is.

As I visited South Korea through the 1970s and '80s I encountered all three forms of Korean nationalism. I breathed the tear gas fired against students demonstrating over what they saw as Park Chung Hee's pro-Japanese policies. I witnessed the anti-Soviet outrage when Russian jets shot down KAL Flight 007 in September 1983. I listened to peasants' objections to aspects of the Saemaŭl Undong ('New Community Movement'), and to townspeople's resentment at the continued use of curfew. Before it opened in 1974, I toured the Suwŏn Folk Village, a didactic reconstruction of Chosŏn-dynasty society that sanitized the past and remains popular to the present day. Most of all, it was music that brought home to me the unique richness of the Korean cultural heritage, although, to my surprise, public appreciation of it was more equivocal. I studied *kayagŭm* (zither) and *p'iri* (oboe) at the National Classical Music Institute and began to research into musical history, activities that most Koreans regarded as abstruse and curious. I was unable to read modern Korean, and I could manage only because traditional musical scores and primary historical sources were written wholly in Chinese characters (*hancha*), and even modern academic books still partly so, despite Park Chung Hee's endorsement of *han'gŭl*. The government periodically issued revised lists of *hancha* that were officially acceptable for everyday use. Most Koreans' musical taste preferred Western pop or classics. The opening of the grand Sejong Cultural Center in 1978 was accompanied by a major arts festival. The Main Hall boasted a 98-rank, six-manual pipe organ, with 8,098 pipes arranged in the shape of Korean *kŏmun'go* zithers hanging from the wall, and seating for audiences of 4,200. The mayor of Seoul, Koo Ja Choon, spoke of his hope that its citizens would 'develop a deeper and more meaningful appreciation of and concern for the preservation of our traditional arts'. Yet throughout the whole seventeen-week festival only one performance of traditional Korean music was given in the Main Hall. There were, it is true, a few evenings of music and dance newly composed by Koreans, but the overwhelming majority of events were of Western music by Western performers. They were well attended and warmly applauded. Traditional Korean music was given in the Small Hall, with a seating capacity of just over 500. One concert consisted of a brilliant performance by a virtuoso *taegŭm* (flute) player, who sat on the floor at the edge of the stage. It was quite short and there was no interval. When it was over he got up, made a slight bow to the sparse audience, which responded with a brief handclap, and walked off. Of course, this was an alien environment for a musical performance of this kind and a lengthy ovation would have been out of keeping with Korean tradition, but the fortunes of Korea's own musical glory did seem to be lagging. Post-war writers of poetry and stories had not been slow to extol the Korean heritage. Nor had painters, looking for ways of proclaiming their independence from traditional Chinese subjects and forms while at the same time trying to avoid paths that would lead them too close to Western modernism. Yet most musicians, with such a unique resource of national culture at their command, had apparently succumbed to Beethoven and Beatlemania.

Times have changed, and in the past twenty years the Korean traditional cultural situation has been transformed. Nowadays nobody uses Chinese characters, except for writing shop signs, book titles or entries in calligraphy competitions. Any definition of Korean national pride would be bound to emphasize the unique *han'gŭl* alphabet. It is commonplace for children to learn Korean instruments as well as the piano, violin, trumpet, etc; and by working with Western colleagues traditional musicians have made international reputations as both performers and composers. Confident now in the strength and sophistication of their own musical heritage, they have struck out beyond preservation and restoration, the primary aims in the 1970s, and seen it develop. Perhaps they took heed of a comment made at the Durham Oriental Music Festival in 1979. Chinese and Koreans had been invited to give concerts of their traditional music. Audiences found pieces in the PRC programme to be unimaginatively Westernized, but at least comprehensible, whereas the Korean performances fell strangely on the ear. The group from Beijing, who for ideological reasons in 1979 were unable to express any appreciation for what they called *gudai yinyue* ('ancient music'), convened a seminar to discuss what was meant by 'traditional' music. Tradition, they said, must be an evolving process; addressing the Koreans, they asked: 'Why are you so backward?' Perhaps some of the Koreans took it to heart. *Backward* is not an adjective that anyone would use nowadays in a definition of South Korean culture.

The twenty-first century has witnessed continuing exhibitions of nationalism, defending what Koreans see as their rights against both Chinese and Japanese remanent imperialism. Chapter One describes the rise of Koguryŏ as one of the first kingdoms in what is now Manchuria and North Korea. In 2003 a fierce argument was stirred up when China applied to have archaeological sites at Ji'an, on its side of the border, recognized by UNESCO as a World Heritage Site. South Korea mounted an intense campaign against what it interpreted as a move to claim Koguryŏ as part of ancient China. Since at that time neither China nor Korea existed in their modern geopolitical senses, the dispute proved nothing other than the strength of today's sense of Korean nationhood, and it was academics rather than ordinary citizens who were most aroused by it. Two years later the protests were more widespread when Tokyo reiterated its ownership of the small Tokto or Takeshima islands. The year 2005 had been designated Korea–Japan Friendship Year, more in hope than celebration, but possession of these islands had long been disputed, and the year was less than three months old when anti-Japanese demonstrations erupted on the streets of Seoul. Nationalism haunts many an old battlefield.

I

The Creation of State Identity

From Earliest Times to AD 668: Cultural Patterns in Flux

This chapter summarizes the evolution of the earliest social and political units on the Korean peninsula, and the appearance and growth of the three kingdoms that are eponymous with the first historical period in Korean history. It outlines the early interaction between the Chinese mainland and the Korean peninsula, and explains the pride that modern Koreans feel in the cultural aspects of this early age.

About 400,000 years ago *homo erectus* took possession of a cave at Hukwuri, near P'yŏngyang in northern Korea. Further south, his relatives set up homesteads at Kŭmgul on the Namhan river, and at Sŏkchang-ni near the Kŭm river in South Ch'ungch'ŏng province. In due course these creatures died out or moved on, leaving behind them stone tools, hand-axes and the bones of the fauna on which they preyed, including elephant, tiger, bear, rhinoceros, boar, monkey, bison, deer and horse. Later, *homo sapiens sapiens* also left remains in both northern and southern Korea. Among those that have been ascribed to the middle palaeolithic (100,000–40,000 BP) is a site at Suyanggae, in North Ch'ungch'ŏng, which yielded evidence of workshops with anvils and hammer stones. An upper (late) palaeolithic site carbon-dated to 21,000 BP, also at Sŏkchang-ni, includes a dwelling for up to ten people, part of a hunting community that used axes, knives and scrapers.

Neolithic sites are more plentiful, and are again distributed from top to bottom of the peninsula. Clusters of settlements have been found along the coast and in river valleys of the north-east (Yalu), north-west (Tumen), west (Ch'ŏngch'ŏn) and south (Nakdong). The earliest to be C14-authenticated are on the east coast at Osanni, Kangwŏn, and suggest that northern and eastern Korea may have been settled by tribes from southern Siberia from about 6000 BC onwards. Remains from Amsa-ri, near Seoul, date from around 3000 BC and show signs of influence from the Liaoning direction, where the

Hongshan culture of 3500–2000 BC and the Xiajiadian, carbon-dated to 2500–1500 BC, stretched along the Bohai corridor and may have contributed to the development of Korean settlements. Neolithic villages were grouped in small clusters and practised mixed hunting, gathering and fishing economies. Mussels, clams and oysters formed a staple part of people's diet, and bones and artefacts were well preserved underneath the shells that they threw away. Nowadays their rubbish dumps bear the rather grand name of shell mounds and are valuable sources of information for archaeologists. Villagers lived in semi-subterranean dwellings with a central hearth. At Osanni and other north-eastern locations, and then down the west coast as well, they learned to make thin, flat-bottomed pottery vessels, decorating them at first with incised patterns and with lines pinched into relief. From about 5000 BC, at sites between the Ch'ŏngch'ŏn and Han rivers, they began to produce conical containers and to put geometric patterns on their wares with a toothed scraper (*chŭlmun*, 'comb pattern'). Comb patterns spread to other parts of Korea and continued to adorn ceramic wares until the Bronze Age, but around the beginning of the second millennium BC a new style of hard-fired, undecorated (*mumun*) pottery appeared, associated with upland locations away from the coast and not unlike that found in some parts of Heilongjiang province in China. Xiajiadian artefacts included stone and pottery pieces similar to those of the Korean *mumun* phase (though Korean sites have not revealed the pottery tripods that were common in Chinese neolithic assemblages). *Mumun* came from farming communities that cultivated rice and used semi-lunar knives to reap cereal crops, and the fact that they made polished stone swords and stone arrowheads might mean that they had to defend themselves against human enemies as well as wild animals. Some archaeologists believe that they had also begun to domesticate pigs. The origins of rice cultivation on the peninsula seem to coincide with the beginnings of upper Xiajiadian culture, and traces from Hunamni, Kyŏnggi province, have been scientifically dated to 1200 BC. (Claims presented in 2000 that burnt rice grains from Sorori, North Ch'ungch'ŏng province, had been dated to 15,000–14,000 BP are still disputed.) Communications were easy around the littoral, and if sailors were unhappy about sailing direct from the Shanghai delta or the Shandong peninsula they could hug the coast around the bay with relative ease. It may have been by one of these routes that rice first reached Korea.

Death rituals already assumed a degree of formality in neolithic communities. They buried the deceased in pits, jars or stone cist tombs, and from about 1000 BC onwards also began to lay a big single stone, or dolmen, horizontally over the tomb. Some nearby cultures in Manchuria and Siberia did the same, but there are said to be more than 30,000 dolmens in Korea, the most in any country in the world, and such weight of numbers argues that the practice originated there. Dolmen burials come in different styles, some of them evidently regional. Many stones are found singly, others in groups or in lines, and some are linked by a pavement. The heaviest weigh as much as 232 tonnes, and some have mysterious egg-shaped depressions on top that have yet to be satisfactorily explained. To ease the passage of the body into its next life personal effects were buried with it, including pottery, bronze daggers, *kogok* curved bead jewellery and curious spoon-shaped implements sometimes decorated with a carved human face. These are so far among the first examples of Korean figurative representation, though *chǔlmun* sites have yielded a small number of primitive efforts at shaping human figures from clay and faces from shell, which have been put forward as possible signs of fertility rites. A bone flute in P'yǒngyang National Museum is dated to *c.* 2000 BC and may have come from a *mumun* dolmen tomb. Precious grave goods like these suggest the appearance of social stratification.

Generally, dolmens are associated with the transition from the late neolithic into the Bronze Age. (North Korean archaeologists, who have been suspected of allowing adherence to political rather than academic considerations to guide their judgement on the antiquity of Korean civilization, believe that some of their 'pavement sites' date back as far as 2000 BC.) Bronze weapons, arrowheads, shields and mirrors went into dolmen tombs. They were presumably valuable possessions, and may have been acquired through trade. The Bronze Age came rather late to Korea. The first remains date from around the beginning of the eighth century BC and seem to be linked with Upper Xiajiadian culture. Later, second-century BC stone moulds from the Yǒngsan river valley in the far south-west suggest, but do not prove, the possibility of Chinese influence from the direction of the Yangzi delta. Exactly when Koreans first began to make bronzes for themselves is unclear, but it was some time before the fourth century BC. Once they had started, they were not slow to learn and develop their own styles. In Shang China, the possession of bronze was a symbol of royal power, and it may have had a special connotation in Korea too, for bronzes are not found in village settlements. Korean creations included a distinctive version of the Manchurian mandolin dagger (*sehyǒng tonggǒm*), featuring a blade with a shaped waist; a halberd more slender than contemporary Chinese examples; and mirrors with two carrying loops instead of the usual Chinese one, decorated with geometric patterns on the back. Mouldings on Chinese mirrors incorporated a definite cosmic element not found on Korean mirrors, and were apparently made in clay rather than stone moulds.

Korean bronze casters made a unique eight-armed rattle of small bells. Today it is part of the shaman's ritualistic paraphernalia, and this may have been its original function. Geometric patterns and animal motifs found in rock art from south-east Korean locations, especially at Pan'gudae near Kyŏngju, have been interpreted – not without arousing some scepticism – as shamanistic designs with Siberian overtones. The designs themselves cannot be dated precisely, and shamanism was so widespread, in China as well as Siberia, that no one can say when it entered Korea and from where. The *Guanzi*, a Chinese miscellany of materials probably compiled by Liu Xiang (79–8 BC), says that it was powerful in Yan, the Zhou dynasty statelet that stretched around the Bohai coastal plains from somewhere north of the Shandong peninsula to the far side of the Liaodong peninsula.

Yan was the most northerly of the late Zhou inter-state federation, and beyond it moved the tribes that the Chinese disparagingly called the Dongyi ('eastern barbarians'). The Chinese built walls to try to minimize contact with them, but these were no barrier to either raiding armies or the peaceful exchange of trade. The Xiongnu, for example, were feared and despised by the Chinese, yet archaeological finds in Inner Mongolia show that they had learned much from their contacts with the northern statelets and were far from unsophisticated. Chinese authors probably used the conglomerate term Dongyi loosely to include some or all of the tribal confederations of horse-raising nomads of Inner Mongolia, the Xianbei and Wuhuan, members of the Tungusic Ye and Mo (Kor. Maek) tribes from along the Yalu river, and the Puyŏ tribal unit of the Sungari river. The Ye and Mo may have migrated down to the Yalu basin from their homelands above the Sungari river some time after the eighth century BC. In 1913 the Japanese anthropologist Siratori Kurakichi linked them together as the Yemaek and recognized them as the ancestors of the historical Korean kingdoms of Koguryŏ and Paekche. Others saw them as founders of a statelet around the northern and eastern flanks of Yan that bore the name Zhaoxian (Kor. Chosŏn, 'Morning [or Early] Freshness'). Exactly how and when that statelet came into being is unclear, but in the twentieth century it became linked to the earliest Korean foundation myths. Some Korean historians identified its predecessors with the people of Ko Chosŏn ('Old Chosŏn'), said to have been founded by Tan'gun. The possibility thus arose that the ancestors of their own race were to be found among the Dongyi.

Probable though it seems that the ancestors of today's Koreans arrived on the peninsula via Manchuria, and that a statelet known as Zhaoxian / Chosŏn did exist somewhere in or beyond the Liaoning region controlled by Yan, these stories do not shed any definite light on the foundation of the first proto-Korean state or states. The earliest literary records are too scrappy and were too subject to later manipulation for a convincing understanding of ancient history. Twentieth-century Japanese scholarship debunked the Tan'gun myth on the basis of its late origins, but nationalist Korean historians fought back. Among them Sin Ch'aeho (1880–1936), intent on proving Korea's ethnic origins independent of either China or Japan, identified shamanistic and topographical elements in the story and determined that Tan'gun's empire had stretched as far north as the Amur river and south to Liaodong and Korea. Another great Korean nationalist, Ch'oe Namsŏn (1890–1957), not only argued in favour of the myth but even went so far as to claim that it showed the origins of a cultural sphere extending from Japan in the east as far as Asia Minor in the west. A more moderate but equally unsubstantiated interpretation came from Yi Kibaek, who proposed Tan'gun as the founder of a Dongyi cultural sphere. Thus, what had started life as a legend proved under conditions of colonial occupation to be so attractive a palliative that it began to acquire a veneer of historical respectability. That process has since been taken to its limits by historians in the DPRK, anxious to prove not only that their regime has inherited a ruling mantle of unimpeachable antiquity, but also that their political philosophy of *juche* ('self-reliance') is equally well founded. Under their patronage Tan'gun has been turned into the unquestioned historical progenitor of the Korean people and creator of the Korean state. The Dear Leader Kim Jong Il is said, quite incorrectly, to have been born on Paektu-san ('White-headed Mountain'). Koreans everywhere recognize this 'holy mountain' as a national symbol, and in the context of rival political claims to leadership of a reunified country the implications of a new 'semi-divine' birth on its slopes would be obvious. If North Koreans could travel freely within their own country, or if North Korea figured prominently on the international tourist itinerary, it would without doubt prove to be the number-one attraction in the country. Perhaps the groundwork for tourism was being laid when, in 1993, DPRK archaeologists announced that bones found in a tomb at Kangdong-ŭp, Kangdong-myŏn, had been electronically tested and dated to 5001 BP. They were hailed as the remains of Tan'gun and his queen.

As the second century BC dawned, the inhabitants of the region we know as Manchuria were a mixed bunch. Yan had erected two lengths of wall, the more easterly of which stretched across the Yalu river, to defend itself from the Dongyi. When Yan fell to Qin in the 220s BC, these were incorporated into the First Emperor's Great Wall of China and formed part of the new nation's north-eastern boundary. For the next century or more, imperial China showed little interest in political or military activity beyond it. To Liu Bang, founder of the Han dynasty in 206 BC, the questions of how far Chosŏn stretched, how firm its political authority was, and whether its relations with the troublesome Xiongnu tribes made it a potential ally or enemy of China were all matters as uncertain as they mostly still are to modern historians. The year after his death in 195 BC, a new capital was founded at Wanggŏmsŏng, near modern P'yŏngyang, by Wei Man (Kor. Wiman). In modern terms Wiman Chosŏn, as we call the state he ruled, was neither Chinese nor Korean. Its population came from both west and east (and very probably north, too), and saw ample opportunities to profit from trade in both directions. For a long time Han enjoyed peaceful relations with Wiman Chosŏn and with tribes beyond it in southern Korea. Until, in 109 BC, Wiman's grandson King Ugŏ killed an envoy from Emperor Wudi and threatened to interrupt communication between southern Korea and the Han court. Then, the Martial Emperor's response was unequivocal. Han armies swept north across Manchuria into northern Korea, destroyed Wanggŏmsŏng, and in 108 BC set up four commanderies. This turned out to be a defining date in north-east Asian history. Of the four, Lelang (Kor. Nangnang), centred on the restored site of Wanggŏmsŏng in the Taedong valley, and Xuantu (Kor. Hyŏndo), filling erstwhile Yemaek lands north of the Yalu, were the most important; in 82 BC they absorbed Zhenfan (Kor. Chinbŏn) and Lintun (Kor. Imdun), extending south from Lelang to the Han river valley and east to the coast respectively. Lelang flourished under the command of the Chinese Gongsun clan, and for a long time lived in comparative peace. Its fortress, T'osŏngni, on the southern bank of the river, was a source of Chinese economic and cultural influence across the peninsula and remained an impregnable symbol of Chinese regional authority for more than 400 years. By contrast, Xuantu came under increasing pressure from the central Manchurian tribal confederation of Koguryŏ, and in 75 BC had to be relocated further westwards.

Later myth claimed that Koguryŏ had been founded by a skilful archer and horseman, born from a miraculous egg near Bear Mountain on the Yalu river about 59 BC. His name was Chumong, and he also became known as King Tongmyŏng. (To demonstrate that 'North Korean' Koguryŏ was older than 'South Korean' Silla, Kim Il Sung had DPRK historians push the date of its foundation back to 277 BC. On his orders, archaeologists discovered Tongmyŏng's tomb near P'yŏngyang in 1974, and a mausoleum was built there.) The actual origins of Koguryŏ are obscure. Its inhabitants were probably descended from people based further to the north, perhaps in the Songhua river heartland of Puyŏ or in the lands of the Yemaek. Their first capital on the Yalu was at Hwandosŏng, and from there they already posed a threat to Lelang. The stage was set in fact for the great love–hate relationship that would dominate the Sino-Korean drama for more than two millennia. In the first century AD the Koguryŏ leader assumed the title of king (*wang*), an honour previously bestowed by the Han emperors on their own designated regional representatives. That notwithstanding, the Chinese had no reason to anticipate any impending challenge to the success of Lelang. They were wrong.

Han officials sent to work in Lelang were expected to collect tribute for shipment back to Chang'an, raise taxes and organize corvée labour. They were helped by Chinese families who had lived in Wiman Chosŏn for generations and by a native elite that seems to have been formed before the Chinese arrival. They rewarded collaborators with titles, seals and luxury goods including gold, silver and silks. Characters inscribed on some of their seals suggest that these people were able to use the Chinese script. Wealthy local families lived, as they would later be buried, in great style. They wore Chinese-style bracelets, earrings of silver and glass, bronze belt-hooks and tortoise-shell hairpins. They ate off lacquered dishes and drank from cups of wheel-made, hard-fired grey pottery, more advanced than products from native areas. Into the grave with them went bronzes, jades, lacquerware, chariot fittings, tools and weapons that included the highly valued Chinese crossbow. So too did Chinese coins, collected as status symbols rather than currency, for trade was conducted by barter. It was probably knife-coinage from Yan that first introduced the Koreans to iron in the third century BC. Its revolutionary effects were not confined to social-status marking. The appearance of iron ore in southern Korea alerted both Chinese and Japanese to the region's economic possibilities, and the production of iron harness, weaponry and armour began to turn peninsular armies into formidable forces.

Early in the third century AD it became clear that the days of the Han were numbered in China, and Liaodong came under increasing attack from Koguryŏ. A counter-campaign mounted by the Gongsun leadership around AD 209 forced Koguryŏ to relocate its capital across the Yalu to Kungnaesŏng, but all the Chinese commanderies in Korea lay north of the Han river and expatriate officials on the peninsula must have felt exposed. In 220 Cao Pi formed a new imperial administration in Luoyang, took the dynastic title Wei and removed the Gongsun overlords from Lelang. When he mounted a successful attack on Koguryŏ in 238, Chinese authority over Manchuria and the northern half of the peninsula seemed secure again. Native and Chinese refugees alike fled south of the Han river into a region that many of them already knew from trade and diplomatic contacts. Once this had been the polity of Chin. Our knowledge of its history or territorial extent is limited, but during the third century AD it was superseded by three tribal confederations, Mahan in the south-west, Pyŏnhan in the central south and Chinhan in the south-east (the so-called Samhan, 'Three Han'). Their economic power rested primarily on mixed agri-culture, including dry cereals, rice and silkworms, and their ability to supply iron. All three paid tribute to Lelang, and their leaders enjoyed Chinese luxury goods. Evidence suggests that these southerners prac-tised shamanic religion, including divination with bones. According to the Chinese history *San guo zhi* (*Wei zhi*), they had no horse-riding skills: if so, it did not deter them from mounting occasional attacks on Lelang. Perhaps they sensed a future in ships rather than horses, for their iron was already being traded around the southern coasts. On the other hand, the *Wei zhi* was probably wrong. When Paekche, Mahan's successor, donated horses to the Yamato court in AD 404, it already shared with its neighbours in Koguryŏ a reputation for mounted archery.

Across the straits the proto-Japanese civilization called Wo (Jap. Wa) by Chinese writers was on the brink of transition from the Yayoi (300 BC–AD 300) to the Kofun (AD 300–700) period. While its consoli-dation into a centralized state was still far off, the first kingdom of Yamato was taking shape at the end of the fourth century AD. Textual references tell of 'Wa' envoys to both Korea and China, and even if some of these were no more than enterprising adventurers or even coastal merchants blown off course, it was the genesis of a diplomatic triangle that would dominate the region for centuries to come. Japanese ships were as yet unable to sail directly across the sea to the Chinese coast, and Koreans profited from Yamato diplomats stopping off on Korean soil on their way to the Middle Kingdom. Rulers in northern and southern Korea quickly appreciated the advantages of exchanging formal missions with both neighbouring countries. For the time being, however, their eyes were fixed more on the north than the south. The remaining years of Chinese dominion on the peninsula were numbered.

Far from being cowed by the Wei challenge in AD 238, Koguryŏ was back with an offensive against Lelang in 247. At the same time another commandery, Daifang, which had been carved out of Lelang's southern counties in AD 204, also came under threat from the newly rising kingdom of Paekche. An assault on Lelang in 313 finally tipped the scale, and by 314 both commanderies had capitulated.

THE THREE KINGDOMS PERIOD

The Korean peninsula was now entering a crucial period. Hardened by harsh climate and mountainous terrain, Koguryŏ's uncompromising approach to military and diplomatic activities confirmed it as the strongest power in the region. In AD 427 King Changsu moved its capital southwards from Kungnaesŏng to a site near modern P'yŏngyang. There it confronted Paekche, which, having consolidated its position within the territory of Mahan, had, like a cuckoo in the nest, overthrown it in AD 369. Down in the south-east, Saro, one of twelve Chinhan tribal units, emerged as the front-runner that would eventually form the kingdom of Silla. And in the far south, tribes that had formerly belonged within the confederation of Pyŏnhan now took shape as Kaya. Two of its territories acquired special prominence. They were Tae ('Great') Kaya around modern Koryŏng and Pon ('Original') Kaya along the lower Nakdong river (modern Kimhae).

The process of state formation was not yet complete and competition between the rising powers was fierce. There was no concept of fixed territorial boundaries and the range of the states' dominion was fluid. Koguryŏ and Paekche each moved their capital cities twice; Silla was unusual in the ancient East Asian world in that it preserved its seat of government in the same place for perhaps as long as seven centuries, calling it Saro in the proto-Three Kingdoms period and Kyŏngju from AD 503 onwards. Pragmatism and self-interest ruled, and warfare was frequent as alliances were made and broken with apparent disdain. Peasants struggling to farm the valleys through which armies marched and counter-marched, or local officials of towns called on to switch allegiance to their latest overlords, must sometimes have felt utter bewilderment, and may neither have known nor cared to which kingdom they belonged. Merchants up and down the peninsula struggled to keep their businesses going. To legitimize and strengthen their positions, tribal leaders propagated claims of supernatural elements in the foundation of their states, and claimed shamanistic powers for themselves to ward off natural disasters and boost harvests. Political ideas across the peninsula were confused, but were starting to be driven by the search for ultimate unification and stability. In Silla, political decisions were sanctioned in the course of rites honouring the dynastic founder.

Meanwhile China too was fractured, as a succession of non-Chinese regimes ruled the north and five Chinese dynasties the south. The capitals of those in the north were located at Datong, Luoyang, Ye and Chang'an, while all five southern courts ruled from Nanjing. Envoys journeyed between the two Chinas, the three Korean kingdoms, Kaya and Japan in search of aid and trade. Koguryŏ was the kingdom in most frequent contact with a Chinese court, generally – as its geographical situation dictated – the northern one. It matched persistent diplomacy with military confrontation, and was used to suffering heavy casualties. Paekche launched the second-highest total of missions, mainly by the dangerous sea route to Nanjing. Silla, being the most remote, dispatched the fewest. The reunification of the Middle Kingdom by Sui in AD 589 and the revival of active Chinese involvement in the Three Kingdoms' rivalry led to a noticeable increase in the overall frequency of missions: Paekche, for example, which according to an aggregate of those listed in Korean and Chinese sources sent 123 missions during the period AD 372–660, did so most often from the early sixth century AD, and annually from 624 onwards. No single text provides a complete record of diplomatic encounters, and often it is only those rated as unusually important that get a mention. The sentences referring to them are terse to the point of off-handedness, and sometimes pose more questions than they answer. We are not always told whether envoys went with specific purposes or what they took as gifts, though items of gold- and silverware were prominent among them, and Paekche seems to have sent plenty of 'shining armour'. The Chinese treated them all as tribute-bearing missions, even if requests for military aid should really be seen in a different light from the ritual offering of congratulations on the accession of a new emperor or the announcement of a new king.

A record of embassies underlines the bureaucratic imperative for undertaking the risky journey from one country to another. As the Chinese invested vassal rulers and their hangers-on with grand-sounding titles, robes and seals, so in turn the Korean courts began to adopt Chinese rites and ceremonies, and to follow the official dress code of the Chinese courts. The Koguryŏ and Paekche courts officially accepted Confucianism in the fourth century AD, and among the Chinese texts studied by their scholars the *vade mecum* of Chinese etiquette, *Liji* (Kor. *Yegi*, 'Record of Rites'), was prominent. Koguryŏ opened a Confucian Academy in AD 372; three styles of Chinese calligraphy were copied (Ch. *kaishu* / Kor. *hyesŏ*, regular script; *lishu* / *yesŏ*, clerical script; and *xingshu* / *haengsŏ*, running script); and scholars needed live contacts with Chinese colleagues in order to keep their ideas fresh. The benefit would be felt in the efficiency of a government's man-management system, and by impressing Chinese ambassadors if and when they should arrive.

It was not only students of Confucianism who needed to charge their batteries from Chinese sources of inspiration. The newly established and growing Buddhist communities in all three kingdoms had to maintain pastoral and study links with their parent bodies, the holy mountain regions in northern and southern China. The monk Sundo is said to have introduced the new religion to P'yŏngyang in AD 372 while presenting a request from the Eastern Jin court for an alliance against the Murong Xianbei state (called Former Yan) in Manchuria; a Serindian monk, Malananda, brought it to Paekche's Hansŏng (modern Seoul) in AD 384; and Kyŏngju, which must already have heard of Buddhism from its two neighbours but where it had to overcome the strongest opposition from shamanic interest groups, accepted it in AD 527 after the monk Ich'adon had dramatically sacrificed his life. The courts were well used to the idea of bolstering secular rule with an aura of spiritual authority, and Buddhism, so they were led to believe, could perform miracles to defend the state. Commoners responded to royal edicts encouraging them to accept the new religion, adding it to their customary shamanistic practices. The Korean courts understood too that patronizing Buddhism would impress on the Chinese leaders that they shared their ideas and appreciated their aesthetic taste. Now, as monasteries, pagodas and Buddhist statuary sprang up around the three Korean capitals, craftsmen joined scholars in moving around between the states. In AD 541, when King Sŏng of Paekche asked the Nanjing court for Buddhist texts and teachers of the *Shijing* ('Book of Odes'), he also requested artisans, perhaps to help build and decorate his new palace in Sabi. Twelve years later, it was Paekche architects who supervised work on Silla's great Hwangnyŏng ('Yellow Dragon') temple.

Korean scholars and artisans were welcome in Wa. Professional scribes introduced Chinese characters there in AD 405 and probably monopolized their use for some time after that. King Sŏng of Paekche is credited with introducing Buddhism into Japan, via either a mission sent in AD 538 or another in 552 that presented the Yamato court with gifts of gold and copper Buddhist images, ritual objects and sutras. The Koguryŏ monk Hyeja crossed the sea in 595 to work as tutor to Prince Shōtoku. Craftsmen who emigrated in 588 to build Asukadera, Japan's oldest temple, also introduced the art of tile-making. Shortly afterwards the monk Kwallŭk earned a reputation in Nara as a teacher of the calendar and geomancy (*p'ungsu*). An early seventh-century Buddhist triad at Hōryū-ji is inscribed with a name similar to that of the craftsman who made two of the silver bracelets found in King Muryŏng's tomb, though whether it was made in Paekche or Japan is impossible to tell. The first Paekche seamstress had been sent to Yamato in AD 403, just after a considerable influx of migrants, and Chūgū-ji preserves a piece of embroidery finished in 622 by local needlewomen under the supervision of Paekche teachers. The resident Korean community in Japan included many examples of occupational groupings, and the number of asylum-seekers rose when Paekche finally succumbed to Silla and Tang forces in 660.

Ancient history the world over is enlivened by larger-than-life heroes and villains. As states and empires were formed, it was only natural that men (and sometimes women) of character, ambition and organizing ability should seize their opportunities and make names for themselves. Feared and respected in their lifetime, they would be immortalized by biographers and hagiographers for their achievements and the standards they set. Nowhere was this truer than in China and Korea, where Confucianism held up exemplars for emulation and anti-heroes as warning lessons. None of the three kingdoms is lacking in heroic figures. For the most part they comprise the kings under whom they took shape, developed and flourished. Three stand out: Kwanggaet'o of Koguryŏ, Muryŏng of Paekche and Pŏphŭng of Silla. Kwanggaet'o (r. AD 391–412) extended Koguryŏ's territory until it covered nearly two-thirds of the peninsula and most of Manchuria as far as the Sungari river. He looked southwards too, sending troops to assist Silla to repel a Yamato fleet attacking the coast in league with Paekche in AD 400. When he died, his son Changsu had a memorial stele erected next to his tomb at Kungnaesŏng. It measured 6.34 metres and weighed 37 tonnes, and on it 1,775 Chinese characters carved in *yesŏ* script related the legend of Chumong and gave an account of the great king's exploits. Despite its size, the stone was lost for many centuries. When it was rediscovered in the early 1880s, a rubbing taken by a Japanese soldier was used as evidence to support the idea that Yamato had once colonized southern Korea. Examination of the stone today shows that the reference to Kwanggaet'o's victory in AD 400 is indecipherable: some Koreans believe that it was deliberately defaced, perhaps during the colonial period.

By the third quarter of the fifth century Koguryŏ power was irresistible, and after vain appeals to Northern Wei China for help, King Kaero of Paekche (r. AD 455–75) was forced to abandon his capital at

Hansŏng. Before killing himself on the banks of the Han river, he managed to evacuate his court southwards to Ungjin (modern Kongju). It was there that his second son Sama came to the throne in AD 501 and was buried in 525. His posthumous title is Muryŏng ('Military Peace'), and the *Samguk sagi* depicts him as a handsome and imposing man. He was one of the first architects of a Paekche revival, securing his northern border with a series of fortresses, creating an irrigation system and forming an alliance with the court in Nanjing that led to the dedication of a new temple in Ungjin to the Liang emperor Wudi. According to some accounts, Muryŏng had served as a Paekche feudal ruler of Wa, a *tamno* king. Others even claim that he was born on Kyūshū to the sister-in-law of an earlier *tamno* king. The luxurious contents surrounding him in his tomb certainly confirm a taste for both Japanese and Chinese style.

Throughout Muryŏng's reign, Paekche lived in peace with its eastern neighbour Silla. There, the major innovations of his contemporary ruler Pŏphŭng (r. AD 514–40) included an administrative code of 520 which introduced the *kolp'um* ('bone-rank') system of political and social stratification, strengthened the central authority of the state and adopted Chinese court dress. He promoted irrigation schemes in conjunction with powerful landowners, and formally recognized Buddhism in 527. Hitherto shamanism had been predominant in Silla, but as a system it lacked a holistic structure and its rites and claims differed even from village to village. Buddhism's advocates had probably impressed on Pŏphŭng how much progress Koguryŏ and Paekche had made since they adopted the new religion, and argued that it could help to cement society at a time of potentially unsettling upheaval. Exactly what that society made of the consequent ban on the killing of animals (AD 529) is a matter for conjecture. Pŏphŭng himself, however, was evidently a sincere convert to the faith, for at the end of his reign he withdrew to a monastery (and his wife to a nunnery). As a pivotal date in the interrelationship of history and culture it would be hard to over-exaggerate the significance of 527. It coincides with the beginning of Silla's emphatic rise to political supremacy over Kaya, Paekche and Koguryŏ, its identification as the tributary state that Chinese courts had eventually to treat with most respect, and its cultural transformation in less than two centuries from back-marker to front-runner on the peninsula.

The pacifism we think of today as a characteristic of Buddhism is all very well, but could it have served these kings of ancient history as well as their great armies and generals did? When 305,000 of Sui Yangdi's soldiers poured over the Yalu and Salsu (Ch'ŏngch'ŏn) rivers in 614, bent on retribution for the disaster two years earlier when only a fraction of an even bigger army destroyed by Ŭlchi Mundŏk managed to struggle home through the mud, the defence of the Koguryŏ capital relied on the same general. The *Samguk sagi* says, as we might expect, that he was 'self-possessed, brave and resourceful'. (The second-highest military award for bravery in South Korea today is the Ŭlchi medal.) It also makes a point of commending his ability to write, the inference being that he had more than basic literacy. As P'yŏngyang was besieged, Ŭlchi composed a poem of supposed surrender, which he sent to the commanders of the weary Chinese armies. It read:

> Your divine plans have plumbed the heavens;
> Your subtle reckoning has spanned the earth.
> You win every battle, your military merit is great.
> Why then not be content and stop the war?

Fearing a trap, the Chinese rejected the offer, but when it was repeated, their exhaustion got the better of them and they withdrew in a hollow square. This was the chance Ŭlchi had been hoping for. His own soldiers rushed out and chased the Chinese right back to their own frontier town in Liaodong, a distance of some 150 miles, in less than 48 hours. According to the *Samguk sagi*, only 2,700 reached home safely. Ŭlchi Mundŏk's renown is rivalled only by that of Silla's outstanding general, Kim Yusin, whom we shall meet in chapter Two.

The laconic nature of textual references to these trans-regional exchanges does little to suggest the human stories lying behind them. We can only guess, for example, what it felt like for the girls periodically sent as brides to foreign courts, for the crown prince of Paekche when he was dispatched to the Yamato court as a hostage in AD 397, or for a Silla prince who experienced the same fate in 402. What emotions might these two have felt when they were sent home after eight and sixteen years respectively in Japan? We may only wonder whether the eighteen Koguryŏ musicians, kept to play at the Sui emperor Yangdi's court in Chang'an, were victimized after Ŭlchi's victories. And what mental turmoil might thousands of Chinese prisoners of war have felt before they rejected the chance of repatriation from Koguryŏ in 618? Was the roving Silla ambassador Kim Ch'unch'u (d. 661) immune to nerves as he criss-crossed a region tense with war, visiting Koguryŏ, Yamato and Tang China? Held hostage in Koguryŏ after failing to persuade its military dictator Yŏn Kaesomun to switch allegiance from Paekche, he had to be rescued by a military task force. In 648 he was off again, this time in search of help from China, whose own attack on Koguryŏ had been repulsed at Anshi, in Liaodong, three years previously. Up till then Emperor Taizong had evidently tried to treat the Three Kingdoms with a degree of even-handedness, and had even shown that he had a human side. We catch a glimpse of it in 631 when he returned two beautiful female musicians sent by Silla as tribute, saying that 'the pleasures of music and sex cannot be compared with the love of virtue'. In 641 he had ceremonially mourned the death of the Paekche king Mu. After Anshi he spared 14,000 Koguryŏ prisoners of war and even sent them presents as a mark of respect for their brave defence of their city, though thousands more were marched back to slavery in Chang'an, where their uncompromising reception showed that the emperor was no wimp. To be on the safe side, Koguryŏ sent him two beautiful women in gratitude for sparing so many captives. Taizong sent them home too, sympathizing with their grief at being separated from their families. Ch'unch'u may well have wondered what to expect from his risky venture, and hoped that the benevolent side of the Son of Heaven's character would prevail. In the event his journey turned out to be pointless, for Taizong was dying. But the Kim family's involvement with China did not end there. Ch'unch'u's son Kim Inmun, a noted calligrapher, was sent to Chang'an in 651 to serve in the imperial bodyguard, and later became assistant commander of the large Chinese force that campaigned against Paekche. Ch'unch'u himself saw off two rivals to become King Muyŏl on the death of Queen Chindŏk in 654. When he too died in 661, Emperor Gaozong sent an envoy to Kyŏngju with imperial condolences. Seven years later, when Tang assisted Silla again in the final destruction of Koguryŏ, the relief in China must have been profound.

CULTURAL CHARACTERISTICS

Craftsmen across the peninsula all used the same materials – clay and stone, silver and gold, bronze and iron, jade and ivory, wood and lacquer. But regionalism was strong, and as they developed their own tastes and skills, their work exhibited different characteristics. In Koguryŏ the style of art reflected the outlook of a border people toughened by a harsh climate, rough terrain and frequent border clashes. That of Paekche was imbued with a gentler nature, perhaps a reflection of its creators' sincere Buddhist convictions. Until its somewhat dramatic conversion to Chinese ways in the sixth century AD, Silla, the kingdom most remote from outside influence, showed the least sign of artistic sophistication, though treasures in the National Museum of Korea at Kyŏngju show that it was collecting high-quality goods from abroad. Among them are a superb Scythian dagger sheath of intricately worked gold and red agate from the vicinity of the tomb of King Michu (r. AD 262–84), and a beautiful phoenix-shaped Chinese glass vessel found in the fifth–sixth-century AD Hwangnam tomb.

The influence of Han culture, so widely admired and imitated during the commanderies period, did not disappear promptly with the colonists in AD 313–14. Some Chinese residents, anyway, lived on in Koguryŏ, and the adoption of Confucianism and Buddhism presented the Three Kingdoms with intellectual and cultural imperatives for keeping direct lines of contact with China open. But both philosophies also provided a stimulus to independent cultural progress. The Korean stone stupa, for example, a structure placed within the grounds of a temple to hold holy relics (*sarira*), texts or offerings, evolved from the substantially larger Chinese pagoda of wood or brick, which was a building rather than a monument. The Korean model usually had just three or five shallow, tapering storeys, though one at Mirŭk-sa, near the Paekche capital at Sabi, had seven or nine granite storeys when it was built around AD 600.

Many of the surviving examples of early arts and crafts come from tombs. Excavation of these began during the Japanese colonial period, and even though few had been unmolested, they still preserved a capacity to amaze. The most elaborate were those of the ruling classes in and around Lelang. At first they comprised subterranean wooden chambers, until in the third century AD brick or stone tombs containing one, two or three chambers became fashionable. These were built above ground and covered with protective earth mounds. Some 1,500 cover the river delta to the south-east of P'yŏngyang, and future grave robbers were doubtless grateful for these giant molehills. Inside, domed ceilings and walls and floors were lined with decorated bricks. The coffins of rich occupants might be encased within an outer casket, extravagantly and colourfully decorated. More than one member of a family might occupy the same tomb, and the burial goods they took with them into the next life were usually piled in a side chamber. In the Tomb of the Painted Basket, a double-chambered burial from *circa* AD 100, lay the three coffins of a man, a woman and a child. The man had a dagger at his side and leather shoes on his feet. Three rolls of yellow silk were found, apparently those referred to in the inscription on a wooden tablet indicating that he was a high Lelang official. A low curved-leg table of partly lacquered wood was large enough to host a banquet, and other burial goods included gold, silver and tortoiseshell jewellery, and statuettes of horses, chariots and human figures. The eponymous basket was of lacquered wickerwork with brightly painted figures on the sides, and a wall painting showed a number of horse-riders.

Approximately 10,000 Koguryǒ tombs are known. While the elite emulated Chinese fashion, furnishing them with gold and silver objects, jewellery, jade, lacquered goods, ironware, bronze ritual vessels, coins, silks and wooden figurines, and decorating them with tiles, bricks and paintings, ordinary people would expect to finish their days in an earth-pit grave, perhaps unblessed even by the protection of a wooden coffin. They did, however, try to afford better for village leaders, whose status entitled them to be buried with the traditional Korean bronze dagger and who sometimes aspired to take imitation, or even authentic, Chinese goods with them.

A local habit in Paekche was to use jar coffins (two urns laid head to head at the rim) for the interment of young persons or the second-ary burial of cremated bones. Typical grey earthenware examples have been found at Yǒngam, in the far south-west. As in contemporary Japan, some 'double-urn' burials took place in cemeteries, and were covered by earth mounds shaped like keyholes. Without doubt the most famous Paekche tomb, and the most revealing single example of the value that Paekche placed on its overseas contacts, is that of King Muryǒng. Its rectangular vaulted chamber, lined with decorated bricks and entered through an arched access protected by a stone animal, had lain undisturbed from his burial in the eighth moon, 525, until it was excavated in 1971. A stone inscription recorded the king's entombment at the end of the 27-month mourning period, and that of his queen four years later. It called him the 'Great General and Pacifier of the East', and among the treasure-trove of goods surrounding the lacquered coffins were royal regalia of native style, as well as valuable items imported from China.

On the far side of the peninsula, Silla buried the dead in single or double wooden coffins surmounted with piles of earth, so that the distinctive mounds arising from the fields around Kyǒngju looked no different from those seen outside P'yǒngyang. Then came wooden chambers, and from around AD 300 – in a distinctive custom that some archaeologists have linked with the Siberian region – royalty were also protected inside the mounds by stones. The wooden chamber was faced with stones and further encased within piles of boulders before the enveloping earth was heaped over it. This, and the absence until the mid-sixth century of an entrance tunnel, helped to deter robbers, even if the weight of rock was liable to cause eventual implosion on top of the coffin. Stone chambers were introduced only in the late Silla period. Their excavation, beginning in the 1920s, revealed some of Korea's greatest historical treasures and earned them their modern sobriquets, including Gold Crown Tomb, Silver Bell Tomb, Decorated Shoes

Tomb and Heavenly Horse Tomb (so-called after the painting of a galloping horse on a birch-bark saddle-flap). A gourd-shaped double mound from the mid-fourth to mid-fifth century AD may be the first example of a Silla royal tomb. Officially known as Hwangnam No. 98 North and South, the names of its occupants are unknown and it is commonly called the Husband and Wife Tomb. The northern mound, over the queen's burial chamber, is higher (23 m / 75 ft) than its neighbour (22 m / 72 ft), perhaps indicating that she was the senior partner. Her tomb contained a gold crown, that of her consort a gilt-bronze crown. Gold belts, sword pommels and items of jewellery are the earliest known examples of Silla goldwork. Among other objects in the chests of burial goods were rare examples of Chinese pottery, Sassanian silver and Roman glass. A pit inside the king's mound was filled with iron weapons. In accordance with shamanistic ritual a horse, wearing a full set of harness and stirrups, had been sacrificed near the top of each mound to assist the royal partners to rise into their next life. Dramatic, colourful and noisy, the funerary rites must have been tinged with suffering too, for alongside the king's coffin lay the skeleton of a fifteen-year-old girl. Until King Chijŭng banned human sacrifice in AD 502, Silla royalty, like their neighbours in Kaya and Wa, took living aides with them into the next life.

Painting

Murals found in the tombs of all three kingdoms provide virtually the only extant examples of early Korean painting. The majority, and the most detailed, come from Koguryŏ and include portraits, scenes of social activity and religious symbols. Much later, Korea would be able to claim genre painting as one of its most distinctive forms, and the Koguryŏ murals give a foretaste of this. More than 70 are concentrated around P'yŏngyang. The entertainments illustrated in Dong Shou's fourth-century AD tomb (Picture Essay 1) – music, dance and wrestling – are encountered again in Changch'ŏn-ri No. 1 tomb at Kungnaesŏng, where an elegant lady is pictured with a zither, and in the Tomb of the Wrestlers and Tomb of the Dancers of the fifth to sixth century AD. The red phoenix, blue dragon, white tiger and green-black entwined tortoise and snake – the sa sin mythical guardians of the four cardinal directions in Chinese and Korean folk religion – fly around the ceilings of many early tombs, but by AD 500 come down to occupy whole walls. In the sixth century AD Buddhist deities also offer their protection.

Investigation of painted tombs is far from complete. Archaeologists of the DPRK announced two major discoveries in 2002. One, at

Saenal-ri, South Hwanghae province, was from the Lelang period. Its brick walls were covered with geometric patterns and remnants of the four mythic animals. The other, a 7.6-metre-long suite in typical Koguryŏ style at Songjuk-ri, Yŏntan county, they dated to the early fifth century AD. It comprised an entrance passage, reception chamber, connecting passage and coffin chamber. The floor had been covered with mud and spread with charcoal before being whitewashed. The walls were of trimmed limestone, neatly whitewashed, and painted with murals showing a procession, a hunt, soldiers and domestic scenes. Huge red pillars were painted in the corners of the chambers to create the impression of a dwelling house.

Music and poetry

To the definers of contemporary fashion – the Chinese – the arts that mattered most were the skills of the brush, especially poetry, and the moving but fleeting notes of music. Koreans who could read and write were thoroughly familiar with the Chinese sense of aesthetic priorities and used Chinese characters. Not surprisingly, the earliest claim in relation to a Korean poetic tradition is associated with royalty. As far back as 17 BC King Yuri of Koguryŏ is reputed to have composed the Song of Yellow Birds, a legendary ditty whose origins are actually unknown:

> Yellow birds play around,
> Male and female together.
> How painful that I'm alone.
> Whom do I return home with?

Another piece of supposedly royal poetry was by the Silla queen Chindŏk (r. AD 647–54), who according to the *Samguk sagi* embroidered it herself and sent it to the new Tang emperor Gaozong in AD 650. His father, Taizong, had sent her a gift of books on her own accession. The poem began flatteringly (and quite untruthfully):

> When great Tang began its glorious work,
> And the plans of the eminent emperor prospered,
> Fighting stopped and men donned robes of peace,
> Civil rule resumed the heritage of earlier kings.

What kind of verse was enjoyed by ordinary people is unknown, but it would have been sung, and we know more about musical performance than we do about literary creation. Music accompanied court

1 Portrait of Dong Shou

In 1947 a tomb was excavated near the mouth of the Taedong river. Although it was in the vicinity of P'yŏngyang, an inscription showed that it had been built later than the Chinese evacuation of Lelang and before the establishment of the Koguryŏ capital there. In it were buried Dong Shou (Kor. Tongsu), who had died in AD 357, and his wife. According to the tomb's inscription, consisting of 68 characters in ink, Dong had been a general in Yan (Liaodong) who had fled to Koguryŏ in AD 336 and risen by 343 to administer territory in former Lelang and Daifang. Historians are unsure whether he was one of the many Chinese bureaucrats who stayed on after the fall of the commanderies, or whether the inscription represents a piece of self-aggrandisement on the part of a local *parvenu*. Supporting the latter argument is the fact that the tomb is of Koguryŏ rather than contemporary Han style. Built of stone slabs, it consists of a central chamber with a corbelled ceiling supported on eighteen columns, an antechamber and two side rooms. It was covered with an earth mound.

The most remarkable feature of Dong Shou's tomb is its elaborate painted murals. They remain the oldest known Korean examples of the Chinese habit of decorating the walls with pictures of the deceased, scenes from his life and the pastimes he enjoyed. In this case the antechamber and side rooms are painted to represent Dong Shou's household. Besides portraits of Dong, his wife and their attendants, the artist has included corners of their household such as the kitchen, coach house and stables. The master sits cross-legged under a lotus-topped canopy, its curtains drawn up. He is wearing a Chinese-style silk robe, with a bow at the bottom of a v-neck, and an official hat, and holds a feathery fan. The attendant on his right is holding a writing brush, and the one on his left a scroll. His wife sits apart under a canopy of her own, also waited on by servants, with her hands hidden inside her long wide sleeves. Entertainment is provided by two groups of musicians, a dancer and two wrestlers. The group accompanying the dancer is playing a zither, a lute and a long vertical flute. Two of the musicians in the second group are playing the long horn (*kak*), which, like the banners borne by the men on either side of the doorway into a side room, do not appear in Han representations of entertainment scenes. It is unclear whether the wrestlers, who are some 5 metres away, form part of the same picture: if so, we may wonder whether domestic entertainment in fourth-century Korea had diverged away from the more relaxed, genteel type of entertainment seen in Han pictures.

On one wall of the central chamber is painted a grand procession of some 250 people. Dong rides in an ox-drawn carriage, flanked on either

Portrait of Dong Shou, wall-painting from Anak No. 3 tomb, P'yŏngyang, Hwanghae province, *c.* AD 357.

side by lines of armed foot-soldiers and horsemen. Although the tomb was in a poor state of preservation when discovered, it is possible to reconstruct details of the iron armour and plumed helmets worn by the footmen and the lamellated coverings on the horses. Small military-style bands march and ride to front and rear of the carriage. The 'front band' (Ch. *qianbu*, Kor. *chŏnpu*) consists of two drums and a bell, each carried by two men on shoulder poles and played by a third. The four men of the 'rear band' (Ch. *houbu*, Kor. *hupu*) ride line abreast. They play a small inverted bell struck with a hammer (*yo*), a small horn (*ka*), pan pipes (*so*) and a double-bodied drum. This is one of the best illustrations anywhere of Han dynasty *guchui* ('banging and blowing') music.

Koreans on both sides of the DMZ are immensely proud of the Koguryŏ tomb murals. In Seoul, a full-size reproduction of Dong Shou's portrait occupied a prominent position inside the entrance to the former National Museum premises in the Capitol Building (Picture Essay 25).

ceremonies and banqueting, merry-making, seasonal festivals, work in the fields, prayer in the temples and marching to battle. (Tang armies captured musicians from both Koguryŏ and Paekche in the early seventh century AD.) By Queen Chindŏk's time the Silla administration had a dedicated music department (the Umsŏngsŏ), and it is likely that the other two kingdoms did as well. Texts mention seventeen instruments played in Koguryŏ. They included two kinds of zithers (Picture Essay 2), harps, lutes and flutes, one set of pan pipes, three sizes of oboe, one mouth organ, three drums and a conch shell. Identification of some of these instruments, and details of their appearance, can be problematic. Most of them were also used in Chinese music and some had originated further west across central Asia. One of the zithers may have been the native *kŏmun'go*, said to have been modelled on a Chinese *guqin* received by King Changsu (r. AD 413–91) from the Eastern Jin court. Its strings were stretched over a series of fixed bridges and played by striking with a short wooden plectrum.

We know of seven instruments used in Paekche, among which the predominance of flutes and lutes suggests music milder in tone than that of Koguryŏ. Five of them are seen on a beautiful gilt-bronze incense burner found on Mount Pongnae in 1993, depicting immortals on a holy mountain. Musicians from both Paekche and Silla crossed the sea to Japan. One was Mimaji of Paekche, who had learnt music, dance and masked drama in south-east China, and who emigrated to Japan in AD 612. (In the 1970s the Cambridge musicologist Lawrence Picken found evidence in Japan enabling him to reconstruct the lilting tunes of seventh-century China, which must also have been hummed and whistled in Korea.)

Manual arts

As for the quality of the three kingdoms' pottery, sculpture and metal-work, we can make up our own minds on the basis of hard evidence. Plenty of early pottery survives. Among the grave goods buried as status indicators, at least one native earthenware pot of a rough, porous type known as *hwabunhyŏng* was frequently included. According to Hyung-il Pai, 'How and why such a vessel became the only grave offering of clearly native production placed among items of Han origin is a difficult question . . . We can assume that it could easily have had a ceremonial use or symbolic value . . . The popularity of these pots is evident, since most Han Lelang burials have at least one *hbh* pot.' *Wajil*, grey, hard-fired earthenware dating from around the year dot, shows signs of Chinese influence, and the use of 'Kimhae' stoneware, the precursor of porcelain, fired at temperatures higher than 1,000 °C, seems to have been associated with the introduction from southern China of the *long* ('dragon') ascending kiln about the fifth century AD. Pottery was made for utilitarian rather than artistic purposes, and plentiful and varied though it was, it did not attract the research sponsorship and production facilities that Chinese courts lavished on it. (In King Muryŏng's tomb the only ceramic vessels – a white ewer, a jar and five lamps – came from Liang, and not one from Paekche itself.) Yet utilitarian or not, artistry certainly helped shape many of the pieces that went into the kilns. Potters in Kaya and Silla produced a stylishly perforated kind of base of their own design. Some examples were free-standing and were used as a rest for containers; some were integral to lamps or wine pourers, and made in familiar shapes such as horses, boats, carts, houses and straw sandals. Nowadays, individual works of art from the Three Kingdoms period are treasured as a source of national pride, and Korean authors hail them as 'the most genuinely indigenous of all Korean art forms'. Copies of the stone warrior seen in Picture Essay 3 are on sale in many an antique shop in Seoul's Insadong, and although China has numerous ceramic horsemen, it has nothing of such character.

When it comes to originality in metal craftsmanship, the crowns and girdles found in the Three Kingdoms tombs rate as some of Korea's greatest national treasures, unrivalled in East Asia (Picture Essay 4). Bronze casters created superb gilt-bronze images of the Buddha, as well as plentiful supplies of mirrors, daggers, harness jingles, and belt-hooks. And ironsmiths, developing their techniques with furnace and anvil, fashioned superb sets of armour and weaponry.

By the end of the Three Kingdoms period, skylines across the peninsula were dotted with thousands of dolmens and tomb mounds, while fortresses, castles and city walls on the one hand, and temples, pagodas and Buddhist statues on the other, contrasted the yang and the yin in contemporary public architecture. Only a fraction remains visible today: Hideyoshi's invasion (1592–8) and the Korean War (1950–53) bear much of the responsibility for that. Nevertheless, what time and man seem to have obliterated, archaeology has begun to recover. Tombs, as we have seen, have yielded their treasures. The remains of the stone ramparts behind which Paekche and Silla sheltered their courts and administration can be seen at Wiryesŏng in south-east Seoul and Panwŏlsŏng near the centre of modern Kyŏngju. One of the chain of fortresses built in AD 375 around the Paekche capital Hansŏng, at Mount Isŏng, appears to have been taken over subsequently by Silla.

2 Grey stoneware jar

Korea's unofficial national instrument is the *kayagŭm*, a half-tube zither with twelve strings of twisted silk. The player seen facing us on this jar sits cross-legged on the floor and rests the right end of the instrument on his knees. He plucks the strings with his right hand and depresses them with the left, below the movable bridges over which they are stretched. The version of the *kayagŭm* used in court music is distinguished by two 'ram's horns' at the bottom end; the smaller, lighter one seen in ensembles and solo performance was developed originally for folk music.

Kayagŭm means 'zither of Kaya'. According to the *Samguk sagi*, it was invented by King Kasil of Kaya, who ordered his musician Urŭk to compose twelve tunes for it, saying that 'different countries have different languages, so why should their music be the same?' Kasil is otherwise unheard of, perhaps because Kaya was soon swallowed up by Silla, at whose court Urŭk sought sanctuary in AD 551–2. There King Chinhŭng provided him with accommodation and sent him Chuji, Kyego and Mandok as students. These three revised his twelve tunes into five new versions for use at the Silla court. The name 'zither of Kaya' stuck, and although the number of strings subsequently increased, the instrument is still recognizably the same as it was some 1,500 years ago. The shadowy Kasil gets the credit for inventing it, and on stylistic grounds the jar illustrated here, decorated with figures (*t'ou*) of whom one plays a zither, must date from around his time. But literary and artistic references, pottery figurines and the remains of a zither itself, discovered in 1997 in Kwangju and dated to ± 1 BC, prove that zithers were already known in Korea. In Koguryŏ, Wang Sang'ak is believed to have developed the Chinese zither into another typically Korean version, the six-stringed *kŏmun'go*. So exactly where Kasil's inspiration came from, and why he should have tried to produce another member of the zither family, remain unknown. Perhaps it was all a matter of Kaya pride. The fact that the zither seen here also has six strings may indicate that Kasil copied the number of Wang Sang'ak's strings, or it may be simply that the potter did not know how many strings the *kayagŭm* actually had. There is no doubt, however, that what we see *is* a *kayagŭm*: the ram's horns make that quite certain. Together with the *kŏmun'go*, the five-stringed *pip'a* lute and three flutes, it quickly established itself as part of a popular ensemble known as *samhyŏ samjuk* ('three strings and three flutes').

A substantial repertoire of musical tunes existed. Silla alone is said to have had 185 pieces for the *kayagŭm*, some of them Chinese. Music was popularly believed to have magical, quasi-religious powers and the

Grey stoneware jar decorated with human and animal figures, late 5th to early 6th century AD, Kyŏngju, height 34.2 cm.

roughly shaped human and animal figures applied around the neck of this vessel suggest that it was used in fertility rites. Two figures are seen having sexual intercourse, while the zither player is evidently a pregnant woman. When King Chinhŭng sent Kŏch'ilbu to attack Koguryŏ *circa* AD 553, he ordered Urŭk and his student Imun to play music. We do not know what sort of music it was. Perhaps it was part of a sacrificial performance intended to stir up the spirits' sympathy; perhaps it was something more meditative, to help the king take his mind off the possible fate of his minister.

3 Grey stone funerary vessel

The character of this figurine might incline one to think that the swift skill admired by Han soldiers in the cavalry of the Mongolian and Manchurian barbarians had been lost by the time this form of warfare descended from the plains onto the Korean peninsula. Yet Koreans prized the horse, even if it was unable to match the buffalo as a domesticated animal in their mountainous and riverine terrain. The strutting mounts on the wall of Dong Shou's tomb seem to have learnt their stuff from numerous Warring States and Han Chinese predecessors, and Koguryŏ armies made good use of cavalry. The sight of mounted, armoured warriors riding to war must have been depressingly familiar to peasants trying to till their fields.

Tombs in Lelang and beyond contain gold, bronze and iron fittings for horses and chariots. Quantities of iron armour for soldiers and their mounts have been discovered in southern Korean tombs, especially in the Kaya and Silla regions, and a fifth-century AD glazed pottery figure from Kimhae shows a Kaya warrior dressed for battle in armour and helmet, carrying a shield and a spear. His horse is protected by a heavy blanket scored to show that it was made of iron or leather plates. Although no buried chariots themselves, or even miniature versions of them such as those found in China, have yet been discovered in Korea, the deceased were evidently assumed to need horse-drawn transportation in their next life. Remains of sacrificial horses are found in Silla tombs. About the same time as the potter was shaping our mounted warrior, another artist was decorating two pairs of birch-bark saddle-flaps to be put with four saddles into a royal tomb. The tomb, one of the best known in Kyŏngju, is called Ch'ŏnma-ch'ong ('Heavenly Horse Tomb'), for he painted on them a horse, reminiscent of the famous Han dynasty bronze 'flying' horse found in Gansu province. Experts have noted Scythian-style decorative elements in this unique example of Silla painting. If it did indeed inherit a centuries-old central Asian tradition attributing supernatural powers to fleet-footed horses, it was a remarkable survival. Bronze belt buckles adorned with a horse are found in tombs all over Korea and in Kofun Japan. Some are finely shaped and decorated, others more crude. According to Lisa Bailey, they too 'reflect the influence of the Scythian animal style, especially of the Ordos region; they also convey a Chinese sense of plasticity', and Koreans obviously loved them too.

Silla laws specified what kind of saddles and trappings members of different *kolp'um* ('bone-rank') classes might use: openwork metal decoration on some saddle-plates followed a pattern used in fourth-century AD Liaoning. The equestrian figure seen here is one of a pair discovered

Grey stone funerary vessel in the shape of a mounted warrior, Gold Bell Tomb, Kyŏngju, 5th–6th century AD, 23.5 × 29.4 cm.

in 1924 in the Gold Bell Tomb in Kyŏngju. The cup on its back and the spout on its chest indicate that it was a pouring vessel used in some kind of funerary rite, and the headgear of the rider and the stirrups – introduced to Korea in the early fifth century, perhaps via the Xianbei confederation – identify him as a warrior. Neither he nor his mount, however, is dressed in battle armour.

4 Funerary headwear of King Muryŏng

Kings of the three kingdoms and Kaya all wore gold crowns. We do not know when or how often they did so: excavated examples are not robust, and may have been made specially for their owners' journey into the next world. Those of Silla and Kaya consisted of a complete circular headband, decorated with designs of punched dots and hung with gold discs and comma-shaped jade *kogok*. Five uprights were fastened to the inside of the headband on the Silla crowns, rising like stylized trees or antlers above the wearer's head. More discs – found also on similar crowns from first-century AD Bactria and third- to fifth-century AD eastern Mongolia – and *kogok* dangled from the side branches. Like the headband, the 'trees' were cut from sheet gold. They were particularly elaborate on the Silla crowns, branching out and carrying further gold and jade adornments, and likenesses have been found with shamanic headdresses from earlier Scytho-Siberia. This suggests that the Silla king, bearing supreme religious as well as political power, took part in shamanic ceremonies. The decoration on Kaya crowns was less elaborate, and in Koguryŏ and Paekche artistic inspiration came from China rather than Siberia. Here royalty wore silk caps, onto which were fastened openwork gold ornaments.

The opening of King Muryŏng's tomb at Kongju in 1971 provided unparalleled evidence about elite artistic taste in Paekche. The 62-year-old king and his queen, aged about 30, had been laid to rest surrounded by hundreds of precious objects that showed the importance attached to Paekche's contacts with southern China and Yamato Japan. The design of the tomb was contemporary Chinese, the main chamber being entered through a tunnel in a south-facing hillside, lit by green glazed lamps placed in wall niches. Signs of the hold that Buddhism had taken on the kingdom were everywhere. The walls were covered with moulded bricks bearing lotus patterns. Ornaments on the couple's crowns – the king's a flaming lotus and the queen's a lotus surmounted by a palm leaf – are further allusions to the faith. A silver and gold wine cup with a stand and cover is richly decorated with lotus in a landscape setting. The royal heads rested on lacquered wooden pillows between pairs of wooden phoenixes, the queen's pillow elaborately painted with animals and lotus flowers. A string of Liang-dynasty Chinese coins was placed on her epitaph stone as payment to the earth spirits for the purchase of the land, and the sole pottery vessels were Chinese. Among other treasures in the tomb were silver plates, which evidently covered the two ends of a zither, and bronze chopsticks, some of the earliest known in Korea.

The architectural style of Muryŏng's tomb spread from Paekche to the Japanese islands. Many of its treasures, including the crowns them-

Gold decoration from the funerary headwear of King Muryŏng, 5th to early 6th century AD, Kongju, 30.7 × 14 cm.

selves, the spiked gilt-bronze shoes and some of the jewellery, are matched by similar pieces found in southern Japan, especially in the richly furnished Fujinoki tomb of the late sixth century AD in Nara, where a mirror bears exactly the same inscription as one in Muryŏng's tomb. Most, if not all, gilt-bronze crowns found in Japan are said to have been made in Korea.

Here, archaeologists found an inkstone, an iron plough, numerous clay and iron figurines of horses, and an inscribed wooden tablet from the sixth century referring to an attack by Koguryŏ forces. Back to light, too, have come the foundations of the city walls at Kungnaesŏng, fine buildings from the next Koguryŏ capital at P'yŏngyang and the long perimeter wall of a new conurbation begun nearby on Mount Taesŏng in 552, punctuated by 20 gates.

No walls or gates told the traveller that he had passed from one state into another, but inscribed monuments were set up with an eye on territorial claims and historical approbation alike. Four inscribed stones marked the tours of inspection that the Silla king Chinhŭng made to the northern, southern and western regions of his country between 555 and 568. On the last of these, erected at Maun Pass, the king stated: 'I have inspected the territory under my jurisdiction and inquired into popular feelings. I intend to encourage by rewards the loyal and the trustworthy, the sincere and the talented, those who apprehend danger and those who fight with valour and serve with loyalty.' It was a pronouncement worthy of the Son of Heaven himself, demonstrating the sense of responsibility that would help Silla royalty to triumph in the momentous challenges of the next century.

Iron Age Korea was now playing a part on a wider international stage. The three kingdoms all recognized China's role as hegemon of the East Asian region, but they themselves were taken seriously at Chinese courts and in Japan. All these states were jockeying for position, and although the Sui and Tang restoration of unity strengthened the hand of the Middle Kingdom, Korea and Japan were now more than bit players. If, in cultural terms, the continuing Chinese influence proved to be a major catalyst for change and development, and

> if the acceptance of certain agreed-on common standards for elite East Asian higher civilization did tend to promote a degree of cultural convergence throughout the region, this may have acted as little more than a modest counterbalance to an opposing natural process of seemingly inexorable diversification . . . The resulting fusion generated several distinctively and gloriously new civilizations [Charles Holcombe].

CHAPTER TWO

Unified Silla, AD 668–936: The Building of Confidence

At a time when Anglo-Saxon England was divided into the kingdoms of Northumbria, Mercia and Wessex, Silla's victories over Kaya, Paekche and Koguryŏ established the first period of unified rule across the Korean peninsula. This chapter introduces the civilization of Unified Silla. It emphasizes that although Chinese political influence was strong across the East Asian region, Korea played a crucial part in managing communications around the Yellow Sea, and in transmitting culture from the mainland to the Japanese islands.

'SERVING THE GREAT'

According to today's popular image in Korea, it is a military figure rather than King Munmu (r. 661–81) who symbolizes the country's new-found unification and independence. The equestrian statue of Kim Yusin (595–673) that guards his tomb in Kyŏngju – a modern reinforcement for its ancient spiritual protection (Picture Essay 5) – has an emotional impact on many of those Koreans who see it. No matter to them that Silla had needed Tang help to overcome Paekche and Koguryŏ, or that resistance from both kingdoms persisted for several years and made unification precarious. No matter that the inhabitants of Koguryŏ north of the Taedong refused to accept Silla rule and established a rival kingdom. His indeed was the military glory and it was well deserved. Kim Yusin was an aristocrat, the son of a prince of Pon Kaya. He must have been well educated, for he was a member of the elite group of Silla youth known as *hwarang*. Why and when this organization came into being is uncertain. By the time Yusin joined it in his mid-teens, it was probably devoted to educational, cultural and moral training, and reflected both Buddhist and Confucian ideals. Serious though its patriotic aims and objectives may have been, its activities seem to have been far from dull: members went on visits to holy mountains, learned martial arts and music, painted their faces and wore bejewelled shoes. Whether or not *hwarang* received military training, as was once thought, and whether or not Yusin received divine

5 Soapstone relief of a boar

In agricultural societies such as Korea's, heavily dependent on the weather and accustomed to flooding, drought and other natural disasters, the study and interpretation of the heavens was essential. So was reliance on spirits to guide and guard the virtuous. Astronomy and astrology were indistinguishable. Han China associated twelve animals with the divisions of the sky covered by the planet Jupiter in its twelve-year circuit around the sun, and with the so-called earthly branches that combined with ten celestial stems to form a sexagenary timing and dating system. The animals – six wild and six domesticated – were the rat, ox, tiger, hare, dragon, snake, horse, ram, monkey, cock, dog and boar. Each was believed to exert some influence over events during the period of its ascendancy, whether two-hourly periods of the day, monthly portions of the year or five annual occurrences through the 60-year cycle. They were also associated with a direction. The first animal in the sequence, the rat, commanded the north; the last, the pig, the north-north-west. By Sui and Tang times the creatures were widely used for decorating bronze mirrors, memorial tablets and tomb sculptures.

Unified Silla decorated and protected the tombs of royalty and other important figures with carved stone figures of the zodiac animals, placing them around the retaining wall of an earthen tumulus and facing the direction they each represented. Such figures assumed greater prominence in Korea than in China, and good examples survive in the Kyŏngju area. Zodiac animals were finely sculpted, usually in relief or less commonly in the round. Their heads are set on human bodies and legs; they are clothed and carry weapons to defend the tomb. A set of the three-dimensional figures, approximately 1.15 metres high, surrounded the tomb of King Sŏngdŏk. Befitting someone of his repute, General Kim Yusin's tomb was guarded not only by the twelve animals, all wearing civilian clothing, but also by three smaller plaques showing the horse, boar and rat dressed in the armour of the *sa ch'ŏnwang*, the four guardian kings often seen protecting the entrance to Buddhist temples. These figures had been finely sculpted in soapstone and are exceptionally well preserved. The fourth has been lost.

Soapstone relief of a boar from the tomb of Kim Yusin, late 7th–early 8th century, Kyŏngju, height 40.8 cm.

assistance, as the early Koreans themselves believed, he turned out to be a brilliant commander. It was he who, at the age of 65 and nearing the end of a distinguished career, led the Silla army in a two-pronged land and sea assault with Chinese troops, which shattered Paekche in 660. The following winter he took relief supplies of 1,500 tons of grain to a Tang army vainly besieging P'yŏngyang. Then, when the Chinese gave up and retreated home, his suffering soldiers had to fight their own way back through the snow to Silla. Yusin was too old and too ill to take part in the final campaign against Koguryŏ, but even left at home, said King Munmu, he had the psychological effect of a strong wall.

Tang assisted again when Koguryŏ was eventually crushed in 668, but sentiment came second to Kyŏngju's new sense of national integrity, and in 676 the Chinese found their own armies being driven out, at least as far as Liaodong. A strong warning was being sent out about Korean independence in the wake of the country's newly won unification. Kings Muyŏl (r. 654–61) and Munmu came from the Kim clan, as had the last twelve monarchs of pre-unification Silla and as would all but three of the 27 monarchs of the Unified Silla dynasty. Much of the credit for this remarkable continuity that served Korea so well should go to King Pŏphŭng, whose *kolp'um* system of social and political stratification had put a sort of ring fence round his clan's authority. By his decree in 520, kings of Silla were to be drawn from the topmost category known as *sŏnggŏl* ('sacred bone'), and from Naemul (AD 356–402) onwards that had meant kings with the Kim surname. Strict lineal descent was broken in the first half of the seventh century and thereafter *sŏnggŏl* status withered away, but royal members of the Kim clan from the second category, *chin'gŏl* ('true bone'), managed to hold on to the succession, and even allowed the royal Kims of Kaya to integrate with them after 532. Third rank in society belonged to the *tup'um* ('head rank'), the aristocracy from which members of the government and military officers were drawn. *Kolp'um* rules were being flouted by the ninth century, but much later, in Chosŏn times, the reminder that class distinction had mattered in antiquity made the gentry's adoption of Neo-Confucianism – characterized by social hierarchy and male domination – all the easier.

Actually, even in the Unified Silla, the assumption that social inequalities were inevitable and proper did not guarantee that everyone was happy about them. The peasantry, living in small farming communities under village headmen, had to surrender a proportion of their produce in tax and were liable for labour duties. To them, anyone with any authority belonged to a world apart, and was treated with a mixture of fear, awe and, frequently, loathing. What they could not be expected to appreciate was that even for those within *kol'pum* ranks, privilege was far from synonymous with security. When the royal clan eventually lost its 'sacred' tag it became simply *primus inter pares* and could be challenged by other noble clans. The scope for political rivalry and intrigue was almost unlimited, from inside the Kim clan just as much as from outside. Two monarchs took particularly decisive action to strengthen their position. In 651 Queen Chindŏk abolished the old Hwabaek Council of Nobles, headed by its president, the Sangdaedŭng, and replaced it with the Chipsabu Chancellery under a chief minister, the Chungsi; and thirty years later King Sinmun (r. 681–92) purged his opponents and stamped his own authoritarian mark on the administration. In place of the previous army of six *bu* divisions, which may have been associated with the aristocratic power bases of old Saro society in the valleys around Kyŏngju, he created a non-conscript army. Efforts to curb the power of the aristocracy met with only partial success, however, and throughout the rest of Korean history relations between monarchs (or presidents) and their officials would continue to be tension-filled.

However preoccupied with domestic issues they might be as they set course across uncharted political and social waters, the early kings of Unified Silla could not but take into account the likely attitudes and responses of the Son of Heaven to their policies. At first they had good reason for apprehension. They had broken a solemn oath, sworn by representatives of Silla, Paekche, Koguryŏ, Tamna (modern Cheju island) and Japan with Emperor Gaozong himself on China's holy Mount Tai in 666, to keep the peace on the peninsula. They had resisted the emperor's efforts to restore a Chinese commandery system in Korea and install King Munmu as 'governor-general of Kyerim', and in 676 had fought off Tang forces intent on replacing him with his brother, Kim Inmun. And when the garrison of 20,000 Chinese troops installed in P'yŏngyang was expelled that same year, it was plain that Gaozong's plan had flopped. It was touch and go, but the emperor's decision not to launch a fresh invasion of Korea in 678 narrowly avoided the unedifying spectacle of a pro-Buddhist Son of Heaven going to war against a vassal state itself in the grip of Buddhist fever.

Inexperienced at handling political unity, let alone the pressures of becoming an independent Premier League state, the rulers of Unified Silla had not only to create a modus vivendi with the Middle Kingdom and the Japanese court at Nara, but also learn to cope with a rival in Manchuria. This was Parhae, the creation of an erstwhile Koguryŏ general, Tae Ch'oyŏng, who after serving in the Tang army at Chengde (Jehol) had fled north-eastwards. There, in modern Jilin province, he rallied around him an alliance of tribal peoples, including Malgal, Yemaek and many of the inhabitants of former Koguryŏ territory north of the Taedong river. He took the title King Ko (r. 699–719) and established his capital at Sanggyŏng ('Superior Capital'). Almost inevitably, he modelled his court on Chinese patterns, proclaiming the name Parhae (Ch. Bohai) in 713. In dealings with Japan, however, the new administration called itself Gaoli (Jap. Korai, Kor. Koryŏ), claiming legitimacy through supposed descent from the ancient Koguryŏ rulers of Manchuria, and so much of that former kingdom's territory did it command above and below the Yalu that some Korean historians treat the period of its existence as one when the peninsula was still divided, rather than unified under Silla. They call it the Nambuk Sidae ('North–South Period'). Parhae acknowledged Tang suzerainty and traded with China, Korea and Japan. It reached the pinnacle of its power under King Tae Insu (r. 818–30), and although some may have breathed a sigh of relief when it fell to the Mongolian Khitan under the leadership of Yehlu Abaoji (872–926) in 926, the days of Silla itself were by then numbered.

But all that lay in the future. Fortunately, the failure of China's imperialist ambitions on the peninsula didn't impair the gradual warming of the Tang–Silla relationship. Partly this reflected Chinese relief and respect for the firm creation of authoritarian rule in Kyŏngju. Partly it was a mark of the Middle Kingdom's self-confidence through the early eighth century, the heyday of 'Great Tang', when curiosity about other lands and tolerance of foreign communities in their midst gave the main Chinese cities a distinctly cosmopolitan air. And eventually, as China faced hostility in central Asia from Tibetans and Arabs and suffered revolt by one of its own military commanders, An Lushan, in 755, it marked gratitude for Silla's continued support during the court's temporary exile to Sichuan. Credit for these good relations belongs also to the sound judgement of the early kings. Munmu had dispatched the first recorded tribute from post-unification Silla in 675. Sinmun reorganized government systems along Chinese lines, adopted Chinese court dress and set up a Confucian Academy. In 686 he asked China for books on Tang ritual. His son Hyoso (r. 692–702) was a convinced Buddhist, and when he died the Empress Wu had the palace gates in Chang'an shut for two days as a mark of respect. The death of his younger brother Sŏngdŏk (r. 702–37) brought forth a fulsome letter of respect from Emperor Xuanzong. His reign represented the high point in Tang–Silla relations, and the emperor, posthumously investing him with the title of Senior Guardian to the Heir Apparent, honoured his country with the ancient epithet of *junzi zhi guo* ('Country of Gentlemen'). Two of his sons went to the Middle Kingdom, one as a student at the Imperial Academy, the other to become a Sŏn monk and eventual abbot of a monastery in Chengdu. He contributed troops to help defend Dengzhou, in Shandong, against Parhae attacks in 734. Arguably, it was Sŏngdŏk who brought the tribute system as close as it ever came in almost two thousand years to fulfilling Chinese expectations of it.

The tribute system was known as *shida waijiao*. The phrase *shi da* (Kor. *sadae*) means 'serving the great', and when the Chinese Confucian philosopher Mencius coined it in the fourth century BC he envisaged the vassal being overawed into compliance with the suzerain's wishes. To imperial China's neighbours, however, it offered a means of flattering the region's superpower into possible approval and support for their own designs. It meant sending missions conveying New Year and birthday greetings, acknowledging imperial accessions and deaths, announcing important events at the vassal court, presenting tribute, and then in return looking for or even requesting Chinese largesse or assistance. Silla dispatched such delegations in 63 years of the eighth century, sometimes more than one a year. The system meant considerable expenditure on both sides. If the cost of setting up travelling parties weighed heavily on the tributary state, their reception could not afford to seem parsimonious. The Tang government opened a hostel in Dengzhou to accommodate groups arriving from both Korea and Parhae, which tried to outdo Silla with the size and frequency of its embassies. In 731 the 120 men of its embassy each took home a gift of 30 rolls of silk. When parties from Silla and Parhae arrived more or less simultaneously, they were treated and gifted on an equal footing, but as time went by Parhae developed an edge. In 775 it obsequiously sent four lots of tribute, and by the early ninth century was dispatching considerably more than Silla, whose envoys were faced with the more difficult journey. It is impossible to estimate the cost of the tribute system in real terms for the historical records are frequently imprecise about amounts of goods sent, referring simply to 'gold and silver objects', 'textiles', etc., but all sides were out to impress and the Tang court was undoubtedly open-handed with gifts of silks, teas, ritual vessels, Buddhist images and so on. For its part, it was happy to receive goods of economic value. Korea was renowned for high-quality gold and silver goods and for brass with heavy copper content. Its ginseng was superior; it was a source of drugs including the physic nut *latropha jampha* and bezoar; and seafoods and pine seeds were on its list of tributary foodstuffs. Chinese scholars prized its *tak* mulberry paper, first perfected in the early eighth century AD, and among the books it sent were Buddhist sutras. But the Chinese court also appreciated rarities. Silla sent a miniature horse in 723 and five more in 730, the same year that Parhae sent 30 full-size horses. Both sent hunting birds, and Silla also managed to come up with peacocks and walrus ivory, but it doesn't appear to have matched the Parhae gift in 777 of eleven Japanese dancing girls.

If human tribute strikes us as objectionable, we should remember that both Tang and Silla were slave-owning societies (if not to the extent familiar to us in ancient Greece and Rome). A corollary to the likely fate of the Japanese girls, which was enslavement, was the taking or sending of what are sometimes described as official hostages. The Chinese encyclopedia *Cefu yuankuei* (AD 1013) devotes a separate section to this system, which according to a memorial of 825 had already affected more than 200 men of Silla to date, and details of its operation suggest that rather than offensive it was at worst unfortunate, at best quite desirable. Those so detained were often members of foreign royalty, sometimes leaders of embassies. An enforced stay in the Chinese capital probably came as no great surprise; it could lead to signal advancement, and might even be accepted as a favour. Kim Inmun, son of King Muyŏl, had spent several years in the imperial bodyguard when Emperor Gaozong appointed him as second-in-command of 130,000 Chinese troops sent to help Silla's campaigns against Paekche and Koguryŏ in the 660s. Hostages might be housed, clothed and allowed to study in the Chongwenguan Confucian Academy in Chang'an, established by Emperor Taizong in 639 for students from tributary states. On occasions the Silla court actually requested permission for boys or young men to enter China for study purposes. If and when they were eventually sent home, their experience could be put to good use. The Chinese dynastic history *Xin Tang shu* identifies natives of all three Korean kingdoms among the 8,000 students enrolled in the Academy, and reports an edict of 715 commanding that all visiting foreigners should receive Chinese education. They were set examinations and might then be awarded official posts. In the ninth century 88 men of Silla, including members of the royal clan, are said to have achieved this. The length of time a hostage might spend in China was imprecise. Men marked out by particular distinction might be allowed to return to Korea as assistant commissioners accompanying Tang missions. In 820 Prince Kim Sasin, now holder of a post of lower-fifth rank at the Tang court, memorialized the throne requesting permission to be sent with the next embassy to his homeland. Less sanguine perhaps was

Prince Kim Yunpu, who memorialized in 836 that although he had had three jobs of up to sixth grade and twice gone home as assistant commissioner, he had now been detained for 26 years. On occasions the Korean court asked for the return of those it felt had been in China long enough, but some hostages died before enjoying the opportunity to see their homeland again.

Economic stringency in the early ninth century reflected a serious copper shortage in China, prompting an imperial commissioner to warn that supplies from Parhae and Silla must be safeguarded. Foreigners were blamed for undermining the fortunes of Great Tang, and warlordism increased. Wealthy Koreans exercised considerable power over the Shandong peninsula, where political control fell into the hands of a family of Koguryŏ descent, headed between 806 and 819 by Yi Sado. A junior military commander in the army that helped to suppress this over-mighty foreign subject was another Korean, Chang Pogo. This man's burgeoning career reflects not only the breakdown of central authority in the Middle Kingdom, but also Kyŏngju's own growing financial and control difficulties. On leaving the army he patronized the Buddhist faith and established a power base of his own in Shandong, as well as building up a considerable navy on the island of Ch'ŏnghae (modern Wando) off the south-west Korean coast. The Bohai gulf was a lawless area. Pirates were seizing people in Silla and selling them as slaves in China. When Chang's ships swept the seas clear of this menace and rendered them safe for trade, the Silla court made him a garrison commander of 10,000 men on Ch'ŏnghae, both in gratitude and to gain his loyalty. Using his strong links with the Korean community in southern Japan, he completed a powerful economic triangle between the three countries and monopolized the international trade in ceramics. He was, in fact, the kind of supra-national entrepreneur with whom we are familiar today, and in the difficult period following the economic crisis of 1997 the Samsung Corporation invoked his spirit by establishing a Chang Pogo Foundation to examine ways of encouraging creativity in international commerce. But the man it dubbed the 'King of Maritime Trade' had actually turned out to be an over-mighty subject. In 839 he was involved in a plot that put a lesser royal, Kim Ujing, on the throne as King Sinmu. Although he was rewarded with a military title, tax-collecting rights and even an official residence in Kyŏngju, the nobility resented this social upstart, and when the king died just four months later, Chang's position was dangerously exposed. He was assassinated in 846.

Today's holidaymakers in Kyŏngju head for the Bomun Lake Resort. Mostly they stay in or around the glitzy, fun-fairish area near the hotels at its south-east corner, but if they walk along its western shore – showered by cherry blossom confetti from lines of pink trees shimmering in the spring sunshine – they pass by a wooded hillside. In 1988 a stone monument was discovered recording the construction here in AD 552 of Myŏnghwalsan, a fortress built to protect the ancient capital of Saro. Another name for Saro had been Kyerim ('Cockerel Forest'), after the legend that a white cock crowed when Alchi, founder of the Kyŏngju Kim clan, was discovered in a golden box in a forest, newly born from an egg. (Three eggs in an iron cauldron, discovered among funerary items in the Heavenly Horse Tomb, are believed to be a reference to this myth.) In time Saro became Kyŏngju, but to its inhabitants it was Kŭmsŏng, the 'Golden City', a pun on the name of the Kim ('Gold') clan, which besides exerting tight control over the opulent capital made the name of Silla reverberate around north-east Asia. Reminders of its proud history confront visitors round almost every corner in Kyŏngju, dubbed an 'open-air museum' by more than one modern guidebook.

Sports teams, we all know, play better against more illustrious competition: it is not so much imitation as inspiration. And in confronting the glorious civilization of China in the early eighth century, both Korea and Japan raised their game. They laid out rectilinear cities on a grid plan – Sabi (Puyŏ) in the sixth century, Kyŏngju in the seventh and Nara in the eighth – showing their admiration for the greatest city anywhere in the contemporary world, the Tang capital of Chang'an. It *was* imitation, of course, though not in any spirit of sycophantic subordination. Rather, the Koreans and Japanese were demonstrating that their skills were not inferior to those of the Chinese. Kyŏngju's new cityscape took shape under King Munmu. Measuring approximately 4.3 kilometres north–south by 4.5 kilometres east–west, it was divided like Chang'an into squares (*bang*), or wards. The standard measurement for a *bang* seems to have been 140 by 160 metres, enough for more than 100 households. Whether there were just 36 of them or 1,360, as modern experts and the *Samguk yusa* have respectively claimed, is still to be resolved, as are other features of the city's ground plan. Much, however, has become clear about this teeming metropolis of around one million inhabitants, which drew foreigners from as far afield as the Middle East and Japan. It was located on a broad plain, just below the point at which tributaries from the surrounding hills flowed into the Hyŏngsan river. One of the builders' first tasks was to dig an artificial lake to help the drainage of the site, using tools supplied from the nearby iron furnace. It was called Anapchi ('Ducks and Geese Lake'). The job was finished in 674 and turned to good advantage as an attraction within the crown prince's new Eastern Palace. Partial remains excavated in the 1970s show what a magnificent complex it must have been (Picture Essay 6). Partying was frequent: one of the games that went well when the wine was flowing freely was forfeits, played with an octagonal die of polished wood on whose faces were written penalties such as 'Drink three cupfuls in one go', 'Sing one verse of *Wolgyŏng*', 'Empty away two cupfuls' and 'Let all other players hit you on the nose'.

Anapchi is one of the stops on the bus tour of Kyŏngju taken by today's tourists. Were it not for Kim Yusin's leadership in the unification wars things might have turned out quite differently for Munmu, and the old general would no doubt have been a guest of honour at the Eastern Palace's inauguration had he not died the previous year. It is fitting, anyway, that the bus should pay a respectful visit to his tomb, as it does to a memorial – of quite a different kind – to another of the monarchs he served. Three things distinguish Queen Sŏndŏk (r. 632–47): she was the first of three queens to rule Silla in their own right; she gave particular encouragement to Buddhism; and she ordered the building of Asia's oldest surviving observatory, Ch'ŏmsŏngdae ('Reverently Observing Stars Platform'). Completed in 634, it is now a star itself, ready to face the battery of cameras pouring off the bus. The circular building, shaped like a flask with a concave neck, stands on a square base and is 8.8 metres high. It is constructed of 365 stone blocks in twenty-four courses, twelve below and twelve above a single, south-facing window. On top are two hollow squares, each made of four blocks. To the present day, experts are intrigued as much by the symbolism and mathematics of its design as by the concern for astronomy that it reflects.

Close by the observatory, in Tumuli Park, 20 great mounds mark the resting places of Silla royalty. Here the curious now stop for a peep inside the Heavenly Horse Tomb, where replicas of the burial goods are laid out for public scrutiny. Among them are a golden crown, a silver belt, gilt-bronze shoes, an iron sword, spear and axe, and, of course, the saddle-flap painted with the galloping steed that gives the tomb its name. Then, suitably awed, it's back through the trees to the bus, to be whisked away into the southern hills and to amazement of a different kind. The P'osŏkchŏng ('Abalone Stone Pavilion') buildings where the Silla court once entertained itself at parties have gone, leaving just a granite channel shaped something like an abalone shell winding under

6 Decorated roof-tile

The Silla court called its beautiful artificial lake Wŏlchi ('Moon Lake'), though nowadays it is known by the name it acquired in the Chosŏn period, Anapchi ('Ducks and Geese Lake'). It was set in landscape designed to imitate Wushan, a scenic and holy mountainous region in China, and stocked with exotic flora and fauna. Rocky islands created in the lake were decorated as retreats for the Daoist Immortals. The Eastern Palace was a worthy setting in which to impress visiting embassies. So far the foundations of 28 buildings have been found, the largest of which was Imhae-jŏn ('Sea-side Pavilion'). Here more than 1,000 guests could sit down to state banquets, entertained by music and dance from both Korea and China. Ice was brought from a nearby stone icehouse, still extant. Here too the last king, Kyŏngsun, entertained his rival Wang Kŏn in 931 and surrendered the throne to him in 936.

Archaeological investigations begun in the 1970s have unearthed more than 30,000 utilitarian items from the bed and vicinity of the lake, including a wooden boat, farming implements, armour, stirrups, glass and crystal beads and polished bone ornaments. More than 24,000 tiles have been found. A few of them are rectangular, and would have been mounted vertically at the gable end of a descending corner ridge. Korean tile-makers had perfected their art by the seventh and eighth centuries AD, and decorated the circular end-tiles of roofs with hundreds of different moulded designs based on the lotus, floral and cloud patterns, deva spirits, dragons, and real and imaginary birds and animals. From an enormous (182 cm) tile moulded in two halves, discovered on the site of Hwangnyŏng-sa in 1976, the faces of elderly men laughed out. Mythical creatures such as the phoenix and the unicorn offered power and protection to the building beneath. Forty-one rectangular tiles discovered at Anapchi, glazed green and brown, were decorated with fierce masks that glared forth from high up on the palace buildings, frightening away evil spirits. The face seen here has been described in general terms as that of a monster or ogre, reminiscent of the ancient Chinese *taotie*. Close inspection, however, shows that between its horns the creature carries the *yŏŭi-ju* ('As you wish') jewel seen in depictions of the dragon and the bodhisattva Kwanseŭm, and that from either side of its jaws waft strands of cosmic energy, or *ki*. Its intentions therefore seem to be active as well as reactive, and Kang Woo-bang identifies it as a dragon dedicated to fighting fire.

Decorated earthenware roof-tile (*ch'imi*) from Anapchi, 8th century, Kyŏngju, 33.7 × 28.5 cm.

an ancient elm. Not much to look at, but there's more to it than meets the eye. Scholars in Korea, Japan and China all enjoyed a game that required players to compose a poem before a cup of wine, floated down a stream, reached the point where they were sitting. What made the P'osŏkchŏng 'race-track' different, according to experiments conducted by modern hydraulic specialists, was that as water flowed through the channel, twists along its irregular course created planned vortices where a cup would be trapped and its rate of progress made unpredictable. Players seated at each point would try to compose a poem, or to drain the cup, before it was whisked away again. While King Kyŏngae and his family, members of the Pak clan, were relaxing here in 927, or perhaps were absorbed in prayer at the shrine, they were taken unawares by the fearsome general Kyŏn Hwŏn, a Kim-clan supporter. The women were raped, Kyŏngae was killed, and the Kims reoccupied the throne in the bloodiest of circumstances.

An important visitor being shown around Kyŏngju in the Unified Silla period would probably have gone to just these same places. In addition, he would surely have visited the country's greatest temple, Hwangnyŏng-sa ('Yellow Dragon Temple'), which graced the suburbs of the city close to the Eastern Palace. It was begun in AD 553 and completed sixteen years later, and subsequent renovation and extensions gave it a Golden (image) Hall with a 16-foot (4.8-m) Sakyamuni statue, a lecture hall, a pagoda, a bell pavilion (for the great bell cast in 754), a sutra pavilion and surrounding domestic quarters and cloisters. The Mongols destroyed it in 1238 and it was never rebuilt, but modern excavation of the foundations shows that it was eight times as large as Pulguk-sa, and more than 20,000 artefacts have been recovered from the site. Across the road from it still stand the lower three levels of another pagoda, belonging to Punhwang-sa ('Eminent Emperor Temple'). Built of stone cut to look like brick, it was finished in 634, the same year as the Ch'ŏmsŏngdae observatory. The upper storeys (seven or nine in number) have fallen in and made entry by the four doorways impossible. The famous monks Chajang (seventh century) and Wŏnhyo (617–686) both stayed in Punhwang-sa, and it may have been from here that Chajang planned the construction of Hwangnyŏng-sa's own nine-storeyed pagoda, finished in 646. It was made of wood, without the use of nails, by 200 Paekche workmen under the supervision of the architect Abiji, and is estimated to have been 80 metres (262.5 ft) high. The two temples were closely linked and both received royal patronage. Their pagodas were of similar elevation, but whether or not they were planned to balance each other, one of wood, the other of stone and brick, is unknown.

Symmetry and proportion are evident in the layout of many Korean temple complexes, including Pulguk-sa ('Buddha Land Temple'), which stands some 10 miles south-east of Kyŏngju. Like the Hwangnyŏng-sa bell, its building was a project authorized by King Kyŏngdŏk (r. 742–65), whose reign marked the apogee of Unified Silla culture. It was begun in 751 to replace an earlier temple called Hwaŏm Pulguk-sa, dating from King Pŏphŭng's time, and took seventeen years to complete. For all that today's temple is much smaller than it was then, many Koreans would not hesitate to name Pulguk-sa if asked for the most famous symbol of Unified Silla. Wherever tourism in Korea is advertised its picture appears, blocks of softly coloured granite, white marble balustrades, grey tiles, sandy courtyards and *tanch'ŏng* ('five-coloured') woodwork, nestling into the lush background of pine, bamboo and fruit trees up the Toham-san hillside. The silence and calm that once enfolded it have gone. Visitors no longer climb up to the front gate by the steep two-tiered staircase, the so-called Azure Cloud and White Cloud bridges, but crowd in through a side gate. Once inside they jostle to be photographed before the main Buddha hall, Taeŭng-jŏn. The courtyard in front of it is bisected by a stone path from the front gate, halfway along which stands a simple stone lantern of Silla date, and on either side a soaring granite pagoda (Picture Essay 7). Both date from 756 and are thought to have been the work of the Paekche craftsman Asadal. Though dissimilar, they were meant to complement each other as yang and yin (Kor. *ŭm*). The one on the right, Tabot'ap ('Many Treasures Pagoda'), represents the Buddha Prabhutaratna. It is 10.5 metres high and elaborate in design; its sister on the left, Sŏkkat'ap ('Sakyamuni Pagoda'), is the Buddha Sakyamuni. It is 8.3 metres tall and simpler. Although it is not unusual to find relics and treasures hidden inside stone pagodas, great excitement accompanied the discovery inside Sŏkkat'ap of the world's oldest extant block-printed text, a page of the Pure Light 'Dharani Sutra', in 1966.

The style, proportions and materials of Korean temple buildings imitated those of contemporary China, and were in turn replicated in Nara Japan by Korean and local architects. They are to be seen, for example, in Tōdai-ji, the centre for the Avatamsaka school developed by the Silla monk Simsang from 740 onwards. Much of what we see today at Pulguk-sa is not really so ancient. The buildings first ordered by the chief minister Kim Taesŏng (701–774) had been ravaged by fire more than once before being destroyed by the Japanese in 1593. They were reconstructed in the eighteenth century, fell into disrepair in the Japanese colonial period, and were restored to their present excellent

7 Pagodas at Pulguk-sa

Cremation came to Korea in the seventh century AD as a new form of committal to the next life. Although not everybody preferred it, King Mumnu opted for it as a means of saving expense when he died (a priority that had not marked his lifetime's enterprises), and ordered his ashes to be buried at sea so that his dragon spirit could protect his kingdom. Ashes were one of the items that might be buried beneath a stone pagoda, where they would become part of the *sarira* ('relics') of a holy man and worthy of veneration. According to the *Samguk sagi*, the first *sarira* were received by King Sŏng in AD 549, from Liang. In modern times many *sarira* items of great value have come to light. The receptacle inside which the treasures were placed was frequently itself an item of fine craftsmanship. From a stone pagoda at Kamŭn-sa of ± 682 comes a gilt-bronze box decorated with four musicians standing around a miniature stupa and playing a flute, a phoenix-headed lute, a drum and cymbals. Concealed inside the box was a small crystal bottle containing the *sarira*. By this time gold was being supplanted by bronze and silver, so the discovery of a late seventh-century gold Buddha from Nawon-ri, Kyŏngju, was particularly rare. Just as valuable, though in a different way, were copies of the scriptures, containing the words of a Buddha and counting as a physical manifestation of his presence. They too were buried as *sarira* items.

Outstanding among the treasures found inside the Sŏkkat'ap stupa when it was opened in 1966 was a block-printed edition, 6 metres long by 6.65 centimetres high, of the Pure Light 'Dharani Sutra' (*Mujujŏnggwang tae-darani-gyŏng*). Printed on paper, half of it had crumbled away, but the remaining half was in good condition. It had been carved out of twelve wooden blocks, each containing up to 63 lines of eight-character text. The sutra had been translated from Sanskrit into Chinese in Chang'an by Mi Toxian between 680 and 704, precisely the period when the Empress Wu (623–705) invented eight new characters. Though they were quickly abandoned after her death, four of them appear on the Sŏkka scroll. Pan Jixing suggests a printing date for it of 702, and Kim Songsu claims that a text dated 706 found in a stone pagoda at Kuhwang-dong, Kyŏngju, is written in the same hand. Clearly the sutra was printed before the year of its concealment, 751, and even this would make it the world's oldest extant example of a printed text. Where it was printed is uncertain. Chinese scholars have argued for Luoyang. Certainly, it is just the kind of gift that could have reached the

Tabot'ap and Sŏkkat'ap stone pagodas at Pulguk-sa, AD 751, Kyŏngju, heights: Tabot'ap 10.5 metres, Sŏkkat'ap 8.3 metres.

Silla court from the Chinese capital during, say, the reign of King Sŏngdŏk and been regarded as sufficiently precious to be buried as part of Pulguk-sa's inaugural ceremonies. But Koreans also claim the credit for it, pointing out that Kyŏngju was quick to adopt other reforms instituted by the empress, such as her short-lived calendric revision (695–700), and may well have used the new characters. They also believe that the mulberry-bark paper (*tak chongyi*) on which the sutra was printed was invented in Korea for special use in the eighth century if not earlier. Whichever is right, no one really doubts that block printing emanated first from China, perhaps well before the Sŏkka Sutra was produced, and it seems highly likely that Kyŏngju craftsmen soon learned how to print texts for themselves. Spreading the Buddhist message was a powerful incentive to progress.

condition only in the 1970s. Along the way, efforts were made to honour the past by recreating the temple as far as could be remembered or deduced from descriptions, and those today who imagine that they can feel what it was like when it flourished as a haven of Silla religious experience may not be so far off the mark after all.

CULTURAL DEVELOPMENTS

The tribute system was the inter-state manifestation of Confucianism. It was hierarchical: it emphasized China's supremacy and its right to expect formal acknowledgement from tributary states of their subordinate status. It was ritualistic: it established a complex pattern for sending and receiving missions and the ceremonial behaviour that accompanied their exchange. It was text-dependent: the documents carried by Chinese envoys to vassal courts were couched in high-flown language full of allusions to the Confucian Classics, and a signal mark of imperial grace was permission for a vassal state to use the Chinese calendar. As Mencius had anticipated, culture could refine and pacify: Unified Silla genuinely seemed to enjoy Chinese literature, music and dance, architecture and sculptural forms, and it became Tang's most compliant vassal state.

Despite its early affirmation of political autonomy, Korea admitted China's undeniably paramount authority in matters of Confucianism and of Buddhism. The former had bureaucratic, literary and social appeal, the latter visual and spiritual. Native Korean interpretations of each philosophy would soon appear, but for the moment Koreans were happy enough to learn from what their neighbours had to offer. The centralized civil and military administration at Kyŏngju showed the court's admiration for Chinese models. The Ministry of Rites supervised the Confucian Academy (T'aechakkam) and appointed scholars to teach the Confucian Classics: among its treasures were portraits of Confucius and his disciples brought back by Sŏngdŏk's son when he returned from the Imperial Academy. Courses lasted nine years, and students were aged from 15 to 30. Some may have been taught by Sŏl Ch'ong (c. 660–730). Son of the great monk Wŏnhyo by a widowed Silla princess, Sŏl earned his position as trusted adviser to King Sinmun by telling him the story of the peony, perhaps the first recorded parable in Korean literature. The king of flowers, it went, was seeking a companion. Given the choice between a beautiful and seductive young woman – a rose – who offered physical comforts, and a dowdy, limping old man – a pasque-flower – the wavering king accepted the latter, though not without a certain amount of persuasion. It was, of course, the correct Confucian decision.

Very little of what the early Koreans wrote has survived. Just 25 ancient poems, called *hyangga* ('country songs'), have been preserved in the *Samguk yusa* and elsewhere, and of these only a few with apparent *hwarang* connections may date from the Silla period. Luckily, however, some of the work of Ch'oe Ch'iwŏn (857–*c*. 910) has survived. Ch'oe was sent to China at the age of eleven and entered the Imperial Academy. Six years later he passed the civil service examination and worked for the Tang administration until 885, rising to the rank of censor. He is best known today for his poetry, but his prose was also so effective that, according to Yi Kyubo, his denunciation of the Chinese rebel Huang Chao terrified this fearsome warlord into submission. He returned to Korea at the grand old age of 27 and became vice-minister for war.

Music ranked highly in the Confucian definition of culture. Thirty thousand foreign musicians were kept at Emperor Xuanzong's court, Koreans among them. In Korea itself, Chinese music and dance was known as *tangak* ('Tang music'), in contrast to their own and that of non-Chinese foreigners, which was called *hyangak* ('country music'). Seven Chinese instruments (a lute, zither, two flutes, mouth-organ, pan pipes and waist drum) are carved on a stone Amitabha stele of 637 now in the Kyŏngju National Museum, and the Unified Silla ensemble also incorporated the *tang-p'iri* oboe. A poem of 751 by Yuan Jie (719–772) entitled 'Ode to the Eastern Barbarians' compliments Koreans on trying to preserve authentic, old-style Chinese courtly music in preference to what Yuan regarded as the inappropriate styles then supplanting them. Ch'oe Ch'iwŏn linked the introduction into Korea of Buddhist chant, *pomp'ae*, and its associated dances with the return of the monk Chinkam from China in 830, but they almost certainly came earlier. The source of much of the new music and dance lay to the west, and Ch'oe composed a group of five poems about entertainments of central Asian origin, which he would have seen at the Tang court. The first is inspired by circus acrobats, the last by a masked lion dance:

> Brandishing their bodies, swinging their arms,
> They vigorously roll their golden bells.
> The bright moon rolls and the stars shine
> As even the whales dance in the calm sea waves.
>
> Your mane is worn and piled with dust
> From the sea of sand that you have crossed.
> A shaking head, a brandishing tail,
> You are the lion, king of all beasts.

Much circumstantial evidence about the development of early society and government comes from the *Samguk yusa*. When it came to writing a good book, Iryŏn knew a thing or two. His stories are full of miracles, mystery, sex and humour, and historians continue to draw on them, despite their frequent lack of historicity, for the insight they give into the colourful, superstitious and often dangerous lives led by inhabitants of the Three Kingdoms and Unified Silla. Great land-owning monasteries dominated the countryside and influenced governments, and the monk's brush flies most prolifically when it comes to describing Silla Buddhism. It is here, for example, that the secret of Wŏnhyo's improper paternity is given away. According to Iryŏn, he was so overcome with remorse at breaking his vow of chastity that he shed his monastic robes, made a mask out of a gourd and toured the countryside converting villagers in droves to Buddhism with his singing and dancing. In the bawdy, masked dance drama (*t'alchum*) that is a popular feature of present-day traditional Korean culture, one of the standard figures of fun is the dissolute dancing monk. The historical Wŏnhyo, however, was certainly no comic turn. He was the first of Korea's own great Buddhist thinkers, as well as a great popularizer of the religion among people of all classes. After abandoning an initial plan to visit China with Ŭisang in 650 he returned to Kyŏngju, where he read as many Mahayana texts as he could and became renowned for his commentaries aimed at unifying their variant traditions. In Punhwang-sa, Hwangnyŏng-sa and elsewhere he lectured and wrote on 'Harmonizing the Debates between the Ten Schools', and the sect that he founded, Pŏpsŏng-jong, was later known as Chungdo-jong ('The Middle Way School'). It was one of the group of Five Teachings (*O-gyo*) of Silla Buddhism that emphasized study (*kyo*) and doctrinal orthodoxy.

Ŭisang was the founder of Hwaŏm-jong ('Flower Garland School'), another of the *O-gyo*. He accompanied a Tang envoy returning to China and stayed there, studying, until prompted to return to Korea in 670 by uncertainty about the fate of his recently united country. No doubt he had sensed China's expectation of a Korean welcome for the restoration of Chinese rule, a kind of return to the 'Lelang spirit'. But he may also have heard of local resistance to the establishment of a Chinese garrison in P'yŏngyang. Perhaps he hoped that by spreading the lessons he had learned from his long analysis of the 'Flower Garland Sutra' (*Hwaŏm-gyŏng*) he could help to resolve tension. In any event, Hwaŏm-jong turned into one of Korea's principal Buddhist sects. The Chinese monk Fazang wrote to Ŭisang from Chang'an in 692,

More than twenty years have passed since we parted, but how could affection for you leave my mind? Between us lie ten thousand miles of smoke and clouds and a thousand folds of land and sea; it is clear we will not see each other again in this life. How can I express, adequately, how I cherish the memory of our friendship? Owing to the same direct and indirect causes in our former existence and the same karma in this life, we were fortunate; we immersed ourselves in the great scripture, and we received its meaning by special favor granted us by our late master. I hear with even greater joy that you have, on your return to your native country, elucidated the Flower Garland Sutra, enhanced the Dharma realm, and arisen from causation unhindered. Thus Indra's net is multi-meshed and the kingdom of the Buddha is daily renewed; you have widely benefited the world.

China was the centre of gravity of the Buddhist world, attracting pilgrims even from India itself. Those arriving from Silla could stay first at a Korean monastery on the Shandong peninsula before venturing inland. One of those who went even further, to south Asia, was the sixteen-year-old Hye Ch'o. Inspired by an Indian acquaintance to embark on his own voyage of exploration to the source of the Law, he sailed from Guangzhou to the Ganges delta, and spent some four years touring holy sites before returning overland to a monastery in Chang'an in 728. There he began his life's work of study and translation, and his journal, discovered at Dunhuang in 1909, stands alongside those of the Chinese pilgrims Faxian (*fl.* 399–416) and Xuanzang (600–664) as a valuable description of early medieval India and its religion.

The *O-gyos*' preference for learning and exegesis in the search for enlightenment distinguished them from the Sŏn (Ch. *Chan*, Jap. *Zen*) persuasion, which may have reached Korea in the late seventh century. The very kernel of Sŏn belief, that fundamental truth is inexpressible and that its apprehension may result from a state of mental readiness as much as acquired learning, rendered it liable to local particularism. Through the ninth century discrete sects developed in various geographical locations, supported by their neighbourhood gentry. They are known as the Nine Mountain Schools (Kusan-mun). In the tenth and eleventh centuries Sŏn lost ground to the Pure Land (Ch'ŏntae) School, but Chinul's great twelfth- to thirteenth-century syncretic creation of Chogye-jong, in which enlightenment assumed primacy over cultivation, gave it fresh impetus, and it remained the dominant element in Korean Buddhist teaching through the difficult period of the early

Chosŏn. Evidence of its continued vitality comes in very different forms, including the composition by the monk Sŏsan (1520–1604) of one of the most famous original Buddhist texts by a Korean, *Sŏn-ga kwigam* ('Sŏn School Tortoise Mirror'), and the significant part played by monks in anti-Japanese resistance during the Imjin wars.

We have already encountered two dominant aspects of Korean Buddhism, monasticism and scholarship. Two more, artistry and an affinity for the countryside, were evident in the hills around Kyŏngju, where Thomas Merton's assertion in *The Seven Storey Mountain* that 'the artistic experience, at its highest, [is] actually a natural analogue of mystical experience' was vividly corroborated. Hundreds of stone statues, pagodas and temples were carved and built high across the forty-something valleys of the sacred Namsan mountains. If those that are portable have now been removed to the National Museum for safety, dozens still remain, a reminder if one were needed of that epithet 'open-air museum'. Silla's sculptors excelled themselves, and attained the peak of perfection in the Sokkuram ('Stone Cave Hermitage') grotto. Here, in a cave dug from the hillside high above Pulguk-sa, facing east towards the rising sun, the temple's architect Kim Taesŏng planned a UNESCO World Heritage Site. Its central figure is a white granite Sakyamuni Buddha, more than 3 metres high, seated in the lotus posture. A mood of transcendent tranquillity takes precedence over naturalism. The head is outlined dramatically against a nimbus carved on the wall behind him. Beneath the beehive hairstyle a crystal jewel marks the centre of his forehead. The eyes, nose, mouth, ears and three rolls of flesh at the base of the neck are carved with perfect symmetry. The folds of his robe sweep tightly across his chest from left shoulder to right breast, leaving his right shoulder bare. His left hand lies in his lap in the contemplative gesture and the right points down to the earth in the earth-witness *mudra*. The hem of his robe is arranged over his lower legs with careful artistry. The image is both formal and unostentatious, and its impact is all the greater for it. Carved in relief out of the cave walls around the Buddha are fifteen attendant bodhisattvas. The Sokkuram grotto dates from the mid-eighth century, simultaneously the apogee of Tang artistry. If the works of Silla craftsmen betray their awareness of Chinese models and taste, what they created in stone and bronze proclaims native Korean prowess.

Artistry of a different kind shines forth from numerous stone pagodas and memorial stelae. For whatever reason – and according to Nancy Steinhardt 'we cannot explain why . . . China and Japan have so few stone pagodas and Korea has so many' – architects made this form of construction a characteristically Korean treasure. While by no means unique to the Unified Silla period, it dominated the plastic arts at this time when government and society were so imbued with the Buddhist faith. The Korean stone pagoda is usually square in form, although a small number are lantern-shaped, bell-shaped or octagonal. Three, five or more tapering storeys stand on a square pedestal. Generally, each of them is a solid block of stone, although the lowest may comprise supporting pillars or three-dimensional figures of protective bodhisattvas, monks or lions. Between each storey projects a canopy. Early pagodas are unadorned and achieve their effect through perfect balance and simplicity. Those of the eighth and ninth centuries are more elaborate, their stone faces adorned with delicately carved relief figures of guardian deities, flying devas and musicians, along with lotus emblems and wispy clouds.

Another glorious feature of temple layouts were their bronze bells (Picture Essay 8). The best-known Silla example hangs today under an open-air pavilion in the grounds of the National Museum at Kyŏngju, and every day, on the hour, visitors cluster round it and wait expectantly to hear its doleful note. (They do not need to stand so close, for these days it comes from a sound-reproduction system nearby, and even when it was rung 'live' it is said that the sound could be heard 40 miles away. If this were ever true, which is highly doubtful, it must have been when it hung in its original surroundings at Pongdŏk-sa.) Great bells of this sort were rung before morning and evening services to call the faithful in from the countryside. Today's visitors have probably heard or read the story that when this particular one was being cast, it was so large that it cracked repeatedly and could not be rung. Until, that is, 771, when the master of the foundry threw his own three-year-old daughter into the molten metal to appease the dragon spirit in charge of fire and metal. Then the new bell tolled beautifully, ringing out with a mournful note sounding like a child's cry, 'Emi! Emi!' ('Mummy! Mummy!'). This is another of Iryŏn's legends, although the same tale of a sacrificial child was linked with the Seoul city bell cast in 1396, and its connection with the Pongdŏk-sa, or Emille, bell seems to have become common knowledge only since 1945. In fact, the fame of the latter should not depend on eschatology and voyeurism, for the skill of Silla metalworkers deserves better recognition. The bell is 3.36 metres (11 ft) high, 2.2 metres (7 ft 6 in.) in diameter, and weighs 18.9 tonnes. Commissioned by King Kyŏngdŏk in honour of his father, Sŏngdŏk, its side bears a long dedicatory inscription eulogizing his preference for education and skill over gold and jewellery, and his efforts to encourage virtue in farmers and merchants. Four devas with censers kneel on cushions, surrounded by a delicate tracery of ribbons and lotus fronds.

8 Temple bell from Sangwŏn-sa

Temple bells are one of the glories of traditional Korean craftsmanship and reached their artistic apogee in the Unified Silla period. They were Korea's special contribution to the 'international' phase of Buddhism, which prompted the sponsorship of enormous works of art in China and elsewhere. Three things distinguish them from their Chinese counterparts: an elaborate suspension knob incorporating a hollow acoustic tube; four panels of nine studs placed immediately below the band around the top; and decoration on the walls of the bell comprising pairs of flying devas and circular lotus patterns, which also mark the points for striking the bell. Ornamental bands encase the stud panels and encircle the top and bottom rims of the bell. The devas, which show similarities with the same kind of spirits fluttering around the walls of caves in Dunhuang and elsewhere, frequently carry censers, musical instruments or gifts of food to present to the Buddhas. Until the ninth century they fly with their knees drawn up under them; thereafter they also sit cross-legged on seats of clouds.

The Emille bell is the largest surviving example of the genre, but the oldest is one cast for Sangwŏn-sa temple on the holy mountain of Odae-san, Kangwŏn province. A story in the *Samguk yusa* says that the monk Chajang went on pilgrimage to the shrine of the bodhisattva Munsu (Manjusri) in China, and was told by a dragon in a vision that he would find 10,000 Buddhas on the mountain. Climbing Odae-san in AD 643 he saw nothing for the thick fog, but on his way down he met Munsu in person and was prompted to found the temple (646) and set about organizing the Yul-jong (Vinaya) sect.

The bell was cast by order of a nobleman's wife, Hyudori. Two pairs of matching devas, kneeling on wispy clouds, adorn its sides. They carry a *konghu* harp and a *saeng* mouth-organ, familiar instruments in Tang and Unified Silla ensembles, though the harp later disappeared from use in Korea and the style of the mouth-organ would undergo many changes in future centuries. The devas wear thin, loosely draped dresses fastened with a circular brooch at the waist, and bangles on their wrists. Their hair is tightly coiffeured on top of their heads, and swirling ribbons and tassels stream out around and behind them. Musical devas continued to adorn bells, and the walls and ceilings of temples, in later ages. By modern times they had grown used to carrying almost every kind of musical instrument, but in deference to the Neo-Confucian sense of propriety, they had also learned to fly much more heavily clad.

Bronze temple bell from Sangwŏn-sa, Odae-san, Kangwŏn province, 725, height 1.7 m.

Bands of floral arabesque ring the top and bottom edges and surround the four stud panels. The bell is one of Korea's best-loved National Treasures.

When I first saw Kyŏngju I felt as if I was taking a step back into the past. Pulguk-sa was in the process of restoration and still fronted with market gardens instead of today's parking lots and tourist shops. The country road along which I walked to get there from the town was almost deserted. On the way I stopped to rest in a grove of pine trees. They shaded the tomb mound of King Sŏngdŏk, buried in 737 and still guarded by the remains of twelve zodiacal animals in military uniform. The silence was numinous and all-embracing. Nearly thirty years on from that visit in 1978, the public-relations people have done a good job: Kyŏngju hotels are full of tourists; the Namsan hills are full of climbers; buses and taxis queue up outside Pulguk-sa; sightseers throng the temples and gawp at the tomb mounds. Yes, Kyŏngju deserves its popularity, though silence is now regrettably hard to come by. Among Koreans, this city is a symbol of pride in what is widely seen as the first ever period of unified Korean rule, and across the southern half of a peninsula divided since 1953 the concentration of so much political and cultural glory in one place is a source of tangible inspiration. How far that is wholly appropriate is another matter, for Unified Silla's domain never did incorporate the full territorial extent of the Three Kingdoms, and some of its subjects remained unhappy at what they saw as division into northern and southern regions. So by all means let us acknowledge Silla's success, but let us notice too that across the top of the wider picture loomed the first manifestation of what would prove to be a persistent threat to Korea until modern times: a rival regime in Manchuria. And let us not forget either that if Kyŏngju could boast 267 years as capital of Unified Silla, its successor, Kaesŏng, would have many more, 457 to be precise, as the seat of Koryŏ government. Today, that historic city lies within the frontiers of the DPRK.

CHAPTER THREE

Koryŏ, 918–1392:
The Struggle for Independence

The veneer of unity that the Koryŏ dynasty guarded for nearly five centuries concealed mounting problems for the royal Wang clan, which surrendered control first to its military leaders (1170–1258) and then to the Mongols (1231–1368). This chapter shows how Korea tried to steer a difficult diplomatic path through intensifying inter-state rivalries. It reveals the tension at court between Buddhism and Confucianism, and shows how both were identified with important aspects of cultural progress.

The early Middle Ages had been a glorious period in the history of East Asia. The civilization of Tang China, Unified Silla Korea and Nara Japan matched – outshone even – that of any other part of the contemporary world, and drew ambassadors, pilgrims, scholars and merchants from as far away as South Asia and the Middle East. But the dawning of the tenth century proved calamitous, as one great ruling clan after another fell. Tang was the first to go in 906. The name given to the short but intense spell of disunity that followed in China, 'Five [northern] Dynasties and Ten [southern] Kingdoms', says it all; and when re-unification came in 960, relief exceeded even resentment at the Song dynasty's tough new laws. Parhae went in 926, absorbed into Abaoji's growing Khitan empire, which eventually extended across southern Manchuria and parts of northern China: it showed its presumptuous challenge to Chinese regional domination by taking a dynastic title, Liao. Refugees poured into northern Korea, among them the heir to the Parhae throne. But metaphors of frying pans and fires spring to mind, for in Korea too armies were on the march and halcyon days of stability under the Unified Silla had gone. The tyrannical rebel Kyŏn Hwŏn declared himself ruler of Later Paekche at Chŏnju in 892, and an aristocratic soldier-monk, Kungye, followed suit by proclaiming Later Koguryŏ at Kaesŏng in 901. The latter was dispatched by one of his own military commanders, Wang Kŏn, in 918. The Unified Silla government in Kyŏngju hung on until Wang's army approached the gates in 935, and then negotiated reasonable surrender terms. Later

Paekche was mopped up the following year, and the brief but unpleasant period known as the Later Three Kingdoms was over.

Wang Kŏn named his new regime Koryŏ ('High and Beautiful'), a deliberate evocation of ancient Koguryŏ. But rather than harking back to a time when the peninsula was divided and China dominated the region, the new king had to look to the future. As three new powers – Song, Liao and Koryŏ – competed for territory and status, north-east Asia embarked on a long and unsettled period when fluidity, rather than the traditional Sinocentric hierarchy, characterized the international political system, and when asylum seekers would troop from state to state in search of sanctuary and a peaceful life. In Korea, the task confronting Wang Kŏn, or King T'aejo ('Great Forbear') as he is usually known, was to ensure that his country recovered its unity, strengthened its identity and confirmed its right to political independence.

THE TENTH CENTURY

Today, Kaesŏng lies a short distance north of the DMZ in the DPRK. It is a modestly sized town of some 200,000 inhabitants that has suffered badly in time of war because it lies between Seoul and P'yŏngyang. Many of its old buildings and monuments have been destroyed. The Museum of London is working with the Korean authorities on a long-term archaeological rescue project, but the instinctive aversion of the DPRK regime to international tourism means that, in stark contrast to the situation in Kyŏngju, historical sites currently on show reflect little of the town's former glory. In 2004 it attracted publicity only as the site for a modest joint DPRK–ROK manufacturing venture turning out iron pots and kitchenware, a symbolic reminder, perhaps, of the role that iron wares played in the much earlier economic fortunes of the peninsula. (By 2005 work had begun on developing a wider DPRK/ROK industrial park outside the town.) A thousand years ago, thanks to the efforts of T'aejo, Kaesŏng was one of the region's major cities, a magnet drawing people from across Asia.

T'aejo's family came from the north-western island of Kanghwa, far from the Silla capital in Kyŏngju, and was in trade and shipping rather than government. Having triumphed over both Kyŏn Hwŏn and Kungye, yet still little more than chief of 'a confederation of warlords', he had to tread a thin political line, satisfying his own supporters, placating those of the regimes he had deposed and deterring an immediate challenge from the direction of either Manchuria or China. By taking the name Koryŏ, T'aejo challenged the assumption by the erstwhile leaders of Parhae, and their recent conquerors the Khitan, that *they* were the true heirs of Koguryŏ and might lay claim to its former lands. On the other hand, his own claim to current political legitimacy derived from King Kyŏngsun's surrender to him at Anapchi in 935, that is to say, in succession to Silla, the former conquerors of Koguryŏ. If this anomaly made the legitimization of his position look uneasy, the disorder into which he had helped to throw the country threatened to undo the progress made under Silla.

T'aejo took positive measures to secure his position. Showing a glimpse of statesmanship, he rewarded Kyŏngsun's capitulation by granting him a title superior to that of any Koryŏ nobles and recruiting former Silla officials into his own government. They had, however, to uproot themselves from their old power base in Kyŏngju and move to his new capital in Kaesŏng. He married a queen from the royal Kim line of Silla and took a further 28 wives from the ranks of powerful noble families, an astute political move aimed at diverting possible dissidence among them as well as ensuring the birth of an heir. He ordained that appointment to official posts must be on ability and integrity. When, by 934, his own observations showed that local magnates, drawing their income from stipend villages, were still exploiting and oppressing the poor and weaker members of society, including the women, he reiterated the importance of effective rewards and punishments and chastised them.

As King T'aejo grew old not all the *sŏngju* ('castle lords') who had helped bring him to power would surrender their territorial privileges, not even to gain a royal father-in-law: only when King Kwangjong (r. 949–75) freed many of their slaves did the throne manage to break the grip of these warlords and their private armies. In 943, conscious of his approaching end, T'aejo issued a set of Ten Injunctions (*Sip hunyo*), principles and practical considerations for the future conduct of government. The opening statement, Number One, affirmed the importance of Buddhism to the fortunes of the kingdom. The Sixth, on the other hand, reminded his successors that they must not neglect the ancient spirits of mountains and rivers, and the last was a reminder of the importance of studying history and the classics as a guide to the present. This, T'aejo's final testament, gave balanced encouragement to Buddhism, shamanism and Confucianism, and when his tomb and the surrounding area were excavated prior to the rebuilding and opening of his mausoleum to the DPRK public in 1994, a gilt-bronze statue of the king was discovered that reflected his eclectic beliefs. Seated like a deified Buddhist image, he wore a royal crown decorated with symbols of hills, clouds and the sun and moon. Nearby were placed a number of curved official belts adorned with beads. Among the paintings on the walls and ceiling of the tomb were the blue dragon, the white tiger and symbolic pictures of pine, bamboo and plum blossom.

By the time the sixth king, Sŏngjong (r. 981–97), set up the Altars of Earth (sa) and Harvest (jik) in Kaesŏng in 991 the status of the city was well established. P'yŏngyang, Seoul and Kyŏngju were designated northern, southern and eastern capitals respectively, but it was Kaesŏng, the central capital, that really forged ahead. It was an administrative, educational and religious centre, the location of the only permanent markets in the country and the destination for incoming foreign missions. Where court ritual and ceremony – the official face of Confucianism – were concerned, even Liao envoys commented on the excellence of its (Chinese) style. But the strength of Confucianism really flowed from the conviction with which scholar-officials allowed it to influence their public and private lives, and that was a matter of lifelong learning. Korean scholars took their education seriously. When illness detained the Chinese refugee Shuang Ji in Kaesŏng during 958, he made good use of his time by helping King Kwangjong to set up a civil service examination system. Two syllabi tested knowledge of Chinese texts, one (chinsa) of literary works, the other (myŏnggyŏng) of the five Confucian Classics. Both would lead successful candidates into the higher echelons of the bureaucracy, and offered members of powerful country families the chance of a legitimate way into government. A third degree, chapkwa, was more practical, and covered law, mathematics, medicine and divination. The cause of education was advanced still further by King Sŏngjong and his minister Ch'oe Sŭngno (927–989). In 992 the king founded the National University (Kukcha-gam), successor to the Silla king Sinmun's T'aehakkam in Kyŏngju and predecessor of modern Seoul's Confucian Academy, Sŏnggyun-gwan. A hundred years later, leading scholars had established a dozen independent schools (sŏwŏn) of their own that would rival it, creating a bifurcation into state and private sectors that is still a characteristic of Korean higher education. (More ominously for the interim, the foundations had been laid down for the growth of factions around the private academies that would bedevil politics in the Chosŏn era.) The state system was subsequently given a responsive boost by King Injong (r. 1122–46), who set up schools in rural areas (hyanghak) as well as in the capital (kyŏnghak). Their purpose was to train young men in a particular, Confucian, mindset and to identify future officials. If we are minded to criticize the immediate objective, however, we miss the point: the Korean literati were well aware of the broader value of training minds, and those who preferred a different ideological path could always follow the one leading to the monastery doorway.

A good deal of the credit for Sŏngjong's Confucianizing reforms goes to Ch'oe Sŭngno. He had known all five of the Koryŏ kings to date, and was critical of those who came after T'aejo for not living up to the founder's expectations. He stressed the importance of the king behaving towards his subjects in accordance with the humane principles laid down in the *Book of Changes* and the *Analects* of Confucius. Urging the king to follow Chinese example more closely, but not slavishly, he made proposals for strengthening central government authority with a system modelled on the Song government in Kaifeng. The resultant structure, which tried to cover both civilian and military matters and to guard against excessive royal autocracy, was neither simple nor permanent. It included a Privy Council (Chaech'u), three Chancelleries, a Censorate and Six Boards, of Personnel, Revenue, Rites, War, Punishments and Works. In addition, both Sŏngjong and Hyŏnjong (r. 1009–31) followed up Ch'oe's ideas for extending central control into the countryside, where twelve provinces were created in 983 and prefects and magistrates began to check the power of the castle lords.

Politicians and religious leaders invariably take liberties when they reinterpret their sources of inspiration, and in urging Sŏngjong to revive T'aejo's principles as a means of improving government morality and effectiveness, Ch'oe was no exception. In particular, he sought to curb the powers of the Buddhist community with a forthrightness that might have offended the dynastic founder. T'aejo knew that he must acknowledge his need for transcendental support. Although he had adopted 'Award from Heaven' (*Ch'ŏnsu*) as his reign title in 918, Korean kings, unlike Chinese emperors, did not generally bolster their position by claiming a heavenly mandate for their actions. Pragmatic considerations might mean the inevitable pursuit of Confucian measures, but even Confucians felt some empathy with Buddhism, which continued to claim pole position in religious observations at court. The royal clan provided Buddhist leaders, and Buddhist rites were observed across society and across the country. Numerous artists and craftsmen benefited from its patronage. T'aejo would have been foolish to upset the status quo, and his First Injunction charged that 'The success of every great undertaking of our state depends upon the favour and protection of Buddha. Therefore, the temples of both the Meditation and Doctrinal schools should be built and monks should be sent out to those temples to minister to Buddha.' He went on, however, to warn that the uncontrolled proliferation of temples risked wasting energy and resources. In 982 Ch'oe Sŭngno, shifting the emphasis, said that Buddhism should attend to people's spiritual needs, while Confucianism looked after the affairs of state.

Most people found that shamanism satisfied their spiritual needs as well as Buddhism, and would have seen no point in trying to separate them. The court patronized three festivals as state events. Yŏndŭnghoe was the lantern-lighting ceremony that lit up the whole dark country on the fifteenth day of the first moon, in the depths of winter. By contrast P'algwanhoe, on the fifteenth day of the eleventh moon, was the harvest festival, and village communities turned it into an exuberant, raucous event. The court's celebrations reflected both native and imported traditions. Itinerant entertainers, *kwangdae*, brought in the culture of the countryside (Picture Essay 9), while Chinese dances added a more sedate touch. Among new ones introduced at the commemoration of 1073 was a choreographed version of the Chinese ball-throwing game *p'ogurak*, still performed today as a *tangak* dance at the National Center for Korean Traditional Performing Arts. As T'aejo had anticipated, the early Chosŏn rulers did later cancel the observation of P'algwanhoe and Yŏndŭnghoe. But they continued to observe and sponsor a third festival, one of exorcism and celebration that marked the end of an old year and the beginning of the next. This was *narye*, dating from early Koryŏ, when the programme often included the Silla masked dance *Ch'ŏyong*. Ch'ŏyong was the son of the dragon that cared for the East Sea, and the reputed son-in-law of the Silla king Hŏn'gang (r. 875–86). According to the *Samguk yusa* version of his tale that was later sung,

> Under the moonlight of the Eastern Capital
> I revelled late into the night.
> When I came home and entered my bedroom
> I saw four legs.
> Two legs were mine,
> Whose were the other two?
> The person underneath was mine,
> But whose body was taking her?
> What should I do?

His decision, in fact, was to forgive his wife's seducer, the God of Sickness, who in gratitude promised to avoid any household displaying Ch'ŏyong's portrait on the doorpost. The *Ch'ŏyong* dance remained a firm favourite at the Chosŏn court and was depicted in pictures of banquet entertainments throughout the dynasty.

China still called many of the intellectual shots across the region, but in political terms Kaesŏng had to show that it was going to be nobody's lackey. T'aejo's Fourth Injunction read:

In the past we have always had a deep attachment for the ways of China and all of our institutions have been modelled upon those of Tang. But our country occupies a different geographical location and our people's character is different from that of the Chinese. Hence, there is no reason to strain ourselves unreasonably to copy the Chinese way. Khitan is a nation of savage beasts, and its language and customs are also different. Its dress and institutions should never be copied.

As a gesture of sympathy for the people of Manchuria, many of whom were related to his own, T'aejo had ostentatiously allowed a present of 50 camels sent by Liao in 942 to starve to death. But his government still pursued diplomatic contacts with its Chinese neighbours. It accepted official calendars as signs of investiture from Later Tang, Later Jin, Later Han and Later Zhou rulers, and adopted Chinese court dress in 956. The year after the introduction of the new examination system, four books on filial piety were sent to China. No sooner were the new Song rulers installed in Kaifeng in 960 than King Kwangjong sent officials asking them for Chinese musicians and instruments, and the following year, as a gentle reminder of Korea's own literary and religious reputation, he sent the Ch'ŏnt'ae monk Ch'egwan with copies of Buddhist books reputed to have been lost during the chaos in China.

In the first 32 years of the Song dynasty Korea sent twenty embassies to Kaifeng and received sixteen in return. But neither traditional admiration for Chinese culture nor willingness to show a degree of cooperation added up to automatic Korean compliance with China's expectations. When China asked for Korean help in attacking Liao, which was threatening tributary communications in 985, King Sŏngjong approved but failed to send it: so perhaps it came as no surprise when the Korean ambassador Wŏn Uk's plea for Chinese aid against the Khitan in 993 was ignored. This left Kaesŏng patently uncertain over which 'great' was currently the one to serve. Six missions left for China between 994 and 1003, but off to the Liao capital in Shangjing (modern Harbin) also went precautionary singing girls, eagles and maps, and, rather more pragmatically, 20 students to learn the Khitan language. As a sign of which way it thought the wind was blowing, in 995 Koryŏ adopted the Liao calendar.

To meet the Khitan threat, Sŏngjong reformed the military system. All commoner males between 15 and 60, with the exception of government officials and monks, were liable for military service (though evasion was commonplace). Drawing on professional soldiers from hereditary military families, Sŏngjong created two guard armies and six

9 Wooden mask, 14th–15th century

Tourists in modern South Korea enjoy masked dance performances as an amusing spectacle. Koreans value them also as an ancient cultural form with origins lying far back in the Three Kingdoms period. Some derive from *sŏnang* ('guardian spirit') plays associated with seasonal and fertility rites. Others, *sajagye*, revolved around worship of the lion as a bodhisattva and came from central Asia, perhaps in the Unified Silla period. In the Koryŏ, a further category of plays and acrobatic entertainments was known as *sandae togam*. In early Chosŏn it was managed by a government department of the same name. Masked dance was associated then with humorous entertainment, especially social satire, and this is the form in which the plays are usually presented today. They have no story line and comprise a series of boisterous, often bawdy sketches, which, while reflecting the Neo-Confucian norms of society, mock corruption and debauchery in all walks of life.

Masked dance drama was popular across south, central and eastern Asia. Its traditions disregarded frontiers, and performers crossed from both Paekche and Silla to Japan. The Tang court enjoyed it. A painting in the Shōsōin Treasury shows an itinerant entertainment troupe in the eighth century. Low-class actors called *kwangdae*, which was perhaps a name for their masks, passed easily in and out of the Koryŏ court. A group known as *sŏllang* put on masked dance shows at the P'algwanhoe festival and may have been descended from the *hwarang* of the Silla period. Masked performances of the Ch'ŏyong tale are said to have originated in the ninth century. The Chosŏn court played it for visiting envoys in the hope that the masks would frighten away evil spirits before their journey home. Nevertheless, the moralistic atmosphere of the court periodically gave *sandae* players a hard time, and they must have developed a phlegmatic attitude to changes in their fortunes. A painting dated 1623 in the National Museum shows them performing *Ch'oyŏng* at a banquet; King Injo expelled them from court in 1634; and we see them back again performing for the Society of the Elderly and Brave (*Kiyŏnghoe*) in 1720.

Craftsmen made masks from whatever materials came easily to hand, including gourds, wood, bamboo, clay and paper. They gave them features caricaturing the figures they represented and painted them brightly and humorously. The Hahoe Mask Museum at Andong preserves more than 200 examples from different regional cultures. One of these is that of Hahoe itself, where the set of plays put on for the Pyŏlsin ritual festival on the fifteenth day of the first moon is listed as an Intangible Cultural Asset. Nine Hahoe masks (National Treasure no. 121) date from the late Koryŏ or early Chosŏn period and are the oldest extant examples in

Wooden mask, 14th–15th century, Hahoe, North Kyŏngsang province,
22 × 21.6 cm.

Korea. They represent a scholar, aristocrat, bride (seen here: her half-closed eyes indicate shyness and the small mouth her relative silence), widow, monk, female flirt, butcher, busybody and fool. Deeply carved from alder wood and preserving traces of lacquered decoration, five of the masks have separate and movable chins. Their deep-set eyes and long noses were a suggestion to the historian Kim Won-yong of foreign influence.

divisions to defend the capital and border. Those serving in the five provincial and three county armies shared farming among their duties, but despite the promise of land as reward, their status was little better than that of the peasantry with which their numbers were often made up. The top brass in the military council (Chungbang) found themselves inferior in practice to civilian administrators in the Privy Council, with which they were supposedly on a par. But when the Khitan invasions tested the system in the eleventh century they found it wanting, and by the twelfth century malcontents at home were showing up its weaknesses still further.

THE ELEVENTH CENTURY

Kaesŏng's caution appeared justified when, after decades of fighting, China finally succumbed in 1005 and signed a peace treaty at Shanyuan agreeing to pay Liao annual tribute of silver and silk. Emboldened by this, the Khitan found King Mokchong's message of congratulations unconvincing, and in 1010 they mounted a major invasion across Koryŏ's northern boundary, the line of the Yalu and Tumen rivers. Strong resistance was led by Kang Kamch'an (948–1031). As magistrate of Hansŏng he was said to have summoned a marauding 100-year-old tiger, severely chastised it and placed restrictions on its future lifestyle. Now he defeated a 100,000-strong Liao army at Kŭiju. But this tiger fought back, and 'cut the Sino-Korean umbilical cord with fire and sword' (Rogers) by sacking Kaesŏng. Koryŏ too began paying tribute to Liao, and in 1033 tried to protect itself by starting a defensive wall that eventually stretched some 350 miles inland from the mouth of the Yalu river, along a line that lay well to the south of the border.

Despite this inauspicious beginning, the eleventh century gradually saw the working out of a pragmatic relationship around the East China Sea. In mixed culture zones like the Manchurian border regions, geopolitical frontiers and questions of national identity meant less than survival and prosperity. State-controlled markets operated and maritime trade flourished irrespective of political tensions. When a merchant, Huang Zhen, brought a message to Kaesŏng from Emperor Shenzong in 1068 indicating China's willingness to reopen diplomatic relations suspended since 1030, the Koreans were happy to respond. They sent a request for physicians, painters and sculptors, and the Korean government built a hostel for Chinese envoys so luxurious that it was later turned into a royal palace. The first to use it, in 1078, was An Dao, whose two specially built vessels, dubbed 'divine ships', carried gifts of clothing and textiles, belts, tea, teapots, silver vessels, bowls, wine warmers, horses, riding crops, musical instruments and candles. The Koreans promptly sent back gifts of gold, silver, rice, clothing, belts, horses and saddles. During the 'golden age' of Song–Koryŏ relations that followed, China sent its neighbour large and costly quantities of textiles, tea, drugs and books. The acerbic Confucian official Su Shi warned against the security risk of supplying books and maps to the Koreans, who might pass vital information on to the Khitan. He also complained about the expense of entertaining Korean visitors while China continued to send tribute missions of its own to Shangjing, though it seems likely that the balance of trade in official gifts stood economically in China's favour. Making inter-governmental and personal gifts was a valuable way of exchanging luxury and cultural items, foodstuffs and medicines across the region.

Books transmitted to Korea in this way included titles on history, philosophy, *belles lettres*, ritual and music, and in 1101 the *Taiping yulan* encyclopedia. Buddhist texts were widely exchanged between Song, Liao, Koryŏ and Japan. King Munjong's fourth son, the monk Ŭich'ŏn (1055–1101), took thousands of missing titles with him to China in 1085. That he was no mere delivery boy, but a true biblio-phile, is evident from nearly 5,000 books he collected from China and Japan to incorporate into his *Supplementary Tripitaka*. Returning from China in 1086, he devoted himself to drawing together the doctrinal and meditation schools into a revived form of Ch'ŏnt'ae. He lay the foundation for the subsequent blending of the two streams by Chinul (1158–1210), and Chinul's school, which he named Chogye after the Guangdong monastery of the great sixth patriarch Huineng, was set on a permanent footing by one of the greatest Korean Buddhist lead-ers, T'aego (1301–1382). Today's Chogye-sa in Seoul, headquarters of the religion for millions of South Koreans, was formerly known as T'aego-sa.

THE TWELFTH CENTURY

If the triangular relationship around the Bohai gulf was not entirely relaxed, it was at any rate tolerable, at least until another threat loomed over the northern Manchurian horizon. Then, as Aguda led the Jurchen from the Sungari region into the furthest Liao territories, warning bells rang in both Kaesŏng and Kaifeng. Koryŏ troops took delivery of their first gunpowder weapons in 1104 and may have used them as General Yun Kwan (d. 1111) campaigned against the Jurchen in 1107, building nine new fortresses around Hamju in the north-west. In 1110 Emperor Song Huizong, anxious perhaps to stiffen Korean resolve, sent King Yejong a message honouring him with the title of 'true king' (Ch. *zhen wang*) and absolving him from feudal obligations. But then, as Aguda nailed his colours to the mast and assumed imperial appurtenances of his own, Huizong's apprehension got the better of his political judgement. In an attempt to take charge of events, in 1114 and 1116 he sent Yejong two huge gifts of musical instruments (Picture Essay 10), asking the Koreans to bring Jurchen representatives to him to discuss an anti-Liao alliance. Yejong refused the Son of Heaven. It was true that Koreans did not like the Khitan, even if the court did watch entertainments put on for it by Khitan refugees, and although they denounced the Jurchen as barbarians, they took into account that these people also claimed descent from Koguryŏ and seemed well on the way to wresting Huizong's heavenly mandate from him. Neither did his successor, King Injong, want to be seen as Huizong's puppet, and nor at this stage did he want to promote an alliance that could threaten Korea. His hesitation was warranted: Aguda's forces overwhelmed both Liao and northern China, and as the Chinese court fled Kaifeng in 1126 and Huizong was taken captive to Manchuria, Kaesŏng pledged submission to the new Jurchen regime, the Jin ('Golden'). Injong was persuaded by his father-in-law Yi Cha'gyŏm that this was the new interpretation of 'serving the great'. It was a decision that did not meet with general approval, and the monk Myoch'ŏng raised an unsuccessful rebellion, but thereafter Koryŏ–Jin relations settled into an acceptable routine, and annual embassies were swapped for almost a century.

To foreign courts, Kaesŏng was no doubt synonymous with Korea. And indeed, it was not just the capital, but also home to a considerable percentage of the Korean people. Contemporary estimates numbered its residents at around 1.5 million, out of a total population of no more than five million. Although this was very likely an exaggeration, there is no doubt that the metropolitan area already dominated the peninsula and was the place to which all would-be social climbers had to migrate, just as Seoul set the pace across South Korea in the second half of the twentieth century. We have an eyewitness account of it, written by a 32-year-old Chinese scholar, Xu Jing, who accompanied an embassy to Kaesŏng in 1123. The reports filed by his predecessors must have whetted his curiosity about the Korean court, and despite tight surveillance and limitation on his movements, he built up his own broad picture of life in the capital and its surrounding country during his month-long stay. Many of the ceremonies he saw and the habits of the literati he met would have made him feel at home. His hosts, Kim Pusik among them, shared his interest in art and music, and if the Koreans were anxious to pick their visitors' brains, Xu was just as skilful at gathering information from them. On his return to China he wrote a book, the *Xuanhe fengshi Gaoli tujing* ('Illustrated Account of the Xuanhe [year] Embassy to Korea'), which he presented to the emperor. Its 40 chapters covered such things as towns and cities, gates, palaces, clothing and headgear, transportation, weapons, customs, women and slaves, and were divided into about 300 subsections. Rather than a continuous prose description, the text was written in the form of extended captions to the illustrations. The pictures were later lost, but the notes survive. As well as pointing to instances where Korean procedures imitated the Chinese, such as, for example, the king's personal testing of successful *chinsa* candidates on their ability to compose *shi* or *fu* poems, Xu also noted aspects of daily life that he found different and interesting. He was impressed by Koreans' cleanliness, but shocked by their habit of mixed bathing in streams. He commented on their habit of book-collecting, which had led to the creation of excellent libraries (and shortly afterwards he may have been distressed to hear that some of them had been burnt during a failed rebellion by Yi Cha'gyŏm in 1126). One section was devoted to Korean ships. Arriving in two 'divine ships' of their own off the mouth of the Han river, the Chinese were met by ten or so official boats and carried ashore in 'guest boats'. Xu's was about 100 feet (30.5 m) long and manned by a crew of 60. It contained five rooms, and its beautifully appointed main pavilion had a high ceiling covered in silk decorations. Fine though it sounds from his description, Xu's comments on Korean shipping in general are less than complimentary, raising the possibility that he was telling his imperial dedicatee what he thought he might wish to hear. Koreans had, in fact, long dominated East Asian maritime trade, even out of Nanjing. Very soon, however, Chinese seagoing and shipbuilding were to receive a fillip from the Song court's move to Hangzhou, at which point Korean ship-owners began to be cut out of the profitable route between China and Japan. Although evidence suggests that there were Koreans among the crew of a merchant ship that sank off the south-west coast of Chŏlla in 1323, its cargo of more than 20,000 pieces of celadon and other porcelain wares, recovered from 1976 onwards, contained just three Korean vessels.

As the Chinese embassy was carried to Kaesŏng, Xu would have had a chance to observe the countryside. Theoretically all land belonged to the state, and villagers worked on large estates to provide income for the landlords who were entrusted with it. These included members of the royal clan, aristocratic families rewarded with prebend lands for military or political service, government departments, local officials,

10 Confucian sacrificial music

To medieval Koreans, music was either 'elegant' (*aak*), 'Chinese' (*tang-ak*) or 'native' (*hyangak*). Most of their instruments were familiar elsewhere in East Asia, and despite the names of the categories, Chinese tunes turned up in all three. But local traditions were strong and imported tunes were quickly Koreanized, even those of *tangak* and *aak* that Emperor Huizong sent in 1114 and 1116 respectively in an effort to overawe the Korean court with the splendour of Chinese ceremonial culture.

To traditional Confucianists, music was a vital component of government. It still is to the communist government in today's North Korea, and to many South Koreans the performances accompanying the sacrifices to the royal ancestors at the Chongmyo Shrine and to Confucius at the Confucian Academy (Sŏnggyun-gwan) – survivors of those unique and splendid gifts in the early twelfth century – mean more than just an occasion reconstructed for tourist cameras. The participants in the rites, including descendants of the last royal family at Chongmyo, honour their ancestors and spiritual forebears with ancient liturgy and authentic respect. Though revised in the Chosŏn period to suit Korean ideas and taste, and watered down nowadays in length and format to satisfy contemporary time schedules and stamina, they still provide a thrilling glimpse into the arcane, colourful and rich tapestry of medieval East Asian ceremonial. In China itself these rites were discontinued after the fall of the Qing dynasty, but in Seoul they survived the end of the monarchy and outlasted the colonial period, a tribute to Confucian powers of spirituality and a gentle hint at regime continuity.

Huizong's gift in 1114 comprised 167 beautiful instruments, 10 volumes of music and 10 more of performance instructions. The instruments included sets of iron slabs (*panghyang*), lutes, zithers, harps, flutes, oboes, mouth-organs, ocarinas and drums. The music was a splendid contribution to the *tangak* music and dance already known in Kaesŏng, and King Yejong had it performed three times before the year was out. Two years later, encouraged by this reception and also by the request in 1115 for five Koreans to study ritual (*li*) and Confucian ceremonial (*ya*) in China, Huizong dispatched 428 instruments, a truly amazing gift. Physically and logistically, the job of loading and transporting them, not to mention the bulk and weight of the accompanying vestments for officiants, musicians and dancers, must have been formidable. Whether they made the journey by land or sea is not clear – either would have been dangerous – but all seem to have arrived intact. Among them were 20 sets of bells (*p'yŏnjong*) and 20 of stone chimes (*p'yŏn'gyŏng*). Even today, bell sets are 1.7 metres and chimes 1.5 metres in height, and in 1116 they can have been no smaller or lighter. Along

Confucian sacrificial music, Sŏnggyun-gwan.

with other instruments such as the wooden tiger (ŏ) and tub (ch'uk), they were supposedly unique to *aak* (Ch. *yayue*). This underlines another outstanding feature of the donation. Never before had this refined music, reserved solely for Chinese imperial sacrifices, been offered to a 'barbarian' ruler. In his growing anxiety to counter the rivalry of the Jurchen, Huizong could not have dreamed up any greater flattery. Korean kings throughout the Koryŏ and Chosŏn dynasties, accepting its transcendental powers, continued to perform the music as an imprecation in the national interest.

magistrates and Buddhist monasteries. Many of these treated the land as if it were their own, and lax oversight by the court permitted the growth of a new class of powerful landowners deriving income from unauthorized activities and sources, some of which later involved collaboration with Mongol overlords. Free farmers were able to rent 'people's land', provided that they could afford to pay taxes and labour dues. These might be lower than the rents demanded by landlords, but rulers were well aware that resentment at the perceived injustices of the land tenure system posed dangers, and periodically they made attempts at reform. A land survey led Chŏng Tojŏn (d. 1398) to put forward proposals in 1389 that resulted in the confiscation and redistribution of estate lands under the Rank Land Law (kwajŏnpŏp), one of Yi Sŏnggye's first measures as founder of the Chosŏn dynasty.

Xu complimented the Koreans on weaving silk, even if they were not, he believed, so good at breeding the worms, and he observed that Korean tea was bitter compared with Chinese varieties. He was unfairly critical of Korean notions of health care, which he wrongly believed had relied mainly on shamanic rites and exorcisms until a big Chinese donation of doctors and medicines had arrived in 1079. His claim that Kaesŏng didn't have many shops also seems surprising, though he may have been judging it against Kaifeng, which was a major regional entrepôt. Certainly, Kaesŏng merchants in the Chosŏn period had a reputation for efficiency and determination that must have dated back to the Koryŏ. The central market was managed by the Kyŏngsi-sŏ, which fixed prices, opening hours and rules of operation. Metal coinage had been introduced by King Sŏngjong back in 996, and copper cash like that of the Chinese – circular with a square hole in the middle for threading on a string – had been produced by a mint set up 1097. When this turned out to be unpopular, a new issue in 1102 was promoted by the opening of an official tavern in the capital. But people were conservative and still preferred to barter, using cloth as the chief exchange commodity: in 1114 one bolt of cloth was the equivalent of eight pecks (tu) of rice. Pace Xu Jing's disparaging and possibly face-saving comment on the number of its shops, Chinese, Khitan, Japanese and Arab merchants headed for Kaesŏng: the Muslim owner of a dumpling shop was even immortalized in the first verse of a popular song, Ssanghwajŏn (banned in 1490 on the grounds of what the Neo-Confucian authorities deemed to be its lewdness). What Xu said was, however, more correct with regard to rural towns in general. Although P'yŏngyang and Hansŏng (Seoul) had permanent marketplaces, local and provincial trade elsewhere consisted mainly of periodic fairs for delivering routinely needed goods such as medicinal herbs and drugs, and for obtaining items that would fetch a good profit when traded abroad, like horses.

Just three years after Xu Jing's embassy, in 1126, trouble came to Kaesŏng, when the chief minister Yi Cha'gyŏm, threatened with dismissal, burned down seventeen-year-old King Injong's palace. Nine years later, when Injong rejected Myoch'ŏng's advice that the chances of recovering old Koguryŏ territory now in Jin hands would be stronger if he rebuilt it in P'yŏngyang and moved the capital there, the charismatic monk rebelled. Loyal Confucian ministers summoned Kim Pusik from Kyŏngju to head an ad hoc army, and the spirit of Ch'oe Sŭngno might have been heard cheering it on to victory. The Confucian regime clung on to the reins of power until 1170, but Injong's successor Ŭijong (r. 1146–70) brought relations between civil and military authority to an impasse. This hedonistic monarch's preference for aesthetics over economics was symbolized by a new pavilion in the palace grounds, which he had roofed with expensive celadon tiles. He treated army officers degradingly, and when Kim Pusik's son set fire to General Chŏng Chungbu's beard, the latter had had enough. He staged a coup that overthrew Ŭijong, killed some of the Confucian leaders and ushered in a 'military period' that preserved the monarchy and the dynasty, but reversed the traditional superiority of civilian bureaucracy over military command.

The new climate had some of the characteristics of a banana republic (or of the contemporary Japanese shogunate), the generals competing with each other while maintaining a pretence of deference to civilian authority. Twenty-five years of administrative chaos then followed until the Ch'oe clan came to the fore, and over four generations maintained what has come to be known as the Ch'oe dictatorship (1196–1258). Choosing the kings and sheltering behind a façade of continued royal legitimacy, Ch'oe Chunghŏn, Ch'oe U, Ch'oe Hang and Ch'oe Ŭi ensured that actual military control was implemented by a largely civilian bureaucracy qualified by exam success. Confucian tradition was already so inherently felt in Korean government circles that even usurpers like Chunghŏn afforded more comfort to bureaucrats trained in its scholarly ways than to Buddhist apologists, whom he condemned. At the same time he pledged to improve conditions for the long-suffering peasantry. Evoking the memory of Wang Kŏn, he presented the king with Ten Injunctions, saying that

> If the people are destitute, how can sufficient rent be collected?
> The local officials are sometimes dishonest and corrupt; they
> seek only profits, thereby injuring the people. The slaves of

powerful houses fight to collect land rents, making the people groan in anxiety and pain. Your Majesty should select good and able officials and appoint them to the provinces to prevent the powerful families from destroying the people's property.

But it didn't happen, nor did Chunghŏn's own autocratic behaviour provide any sector of society with real encouragement: his own was perhaps the most obvious example of those 'powerful families' he criticized for enriching themselves through extensive landholding. Uprisings of peasants, soldiers and slaves occurred repeatedly throughout the late twelfth and early thirteenth centuries. Elite Patrols (*Sam pyŏlch'o*) protected the Ch'oe clan's security, and individual leaders within it were supported by large bands of personal retainers who owed them strong allegiance. But in the end it was not domestic discontent that undermined Ch'oe chances of continuing power, but Koryŏ's first experience of the frightening military machine of the Mongols.

THE THIRTEENTH CENTURY

In the medieval as in the modern world, diplomatic exchanges opened up more than commercial opportunities, and were used for political and military intelligence gathering. Perhaps, as the twelfth century wore on, the spies failed to appreciate what they heard about developments across central Asia. Perhaps peace around the Bohai gulf bred complacency. Perhaps Korean politicians were too absorbed in serious domestic upheavals. Whatever the reason, nobody – neither the Chinese nor the Jurchen nor the Koreans nor their own distant relatives the Khitan – spotted what the Mongols were up to, and it was to cost them all dearly. By 1206, when a gathering of pastoral nomad chieftains swore allegiance to Chinggis Khan, they were well on the way to building one of the greatest empires the world has ever seen. Using a combination of brilliant cavalry skills, which both Jurchen and Khitan may once have shared but had lost after years of settled existence, and divide-and-rule tactics, which the Chinese themselves had customarily employed to control the barbarians, they took control of large parts of Manchuria. They forced the Jurchen to evacuate their capital from Zhongdu (modern Beijing) to Kaifeng (1215), suppressed any hope of Khitan irredentism and gave the Koreans notice that they, the Mongols, would now expect the greatest quantities of tribute.

By the time Chinggis Khan died in 1227, his armies commanded central Asia and had advanced as far west as the Crimea. The three sons and a grandson among whom his territories were divided, far from being satisfied with what they got, continued his expansionist policy. In 1231 the new supreme khan, his third son Ögödai, launched the first of several attacks on Korea. Bands of peasants, slaves and monks put up brave resistance, but Kaesŏng fell without much of a struggle and the Mongols felt confident enough to withdraw the bulk of their troops, leaving behind garrisons in the main towns and administrators to liaise with Koryŏ local authorities in running the country. Chinggis and Ögödai had used widespread massacre in their conquest of western Asia. Kublai, elected khan on his brother's death in 1259, switched attention to the east, and while he certainly didn't go soft, he realized the need for a more accommodating approach to such a civilized region. In Korea cooperation was particularly desirable, since he saw the kingdom as a launch-pad for invasions of southern China and Japan, and for such a venture Korean nautical expertise would be indispensable. The Korean response, however, was mixed. Banking on the Mongols' dislike of the sea, the court, the government and their servants and slaves had taken refuge in summer 1232 on the island of Kanghwa, near the mouth of the Han river. There the nobility maintained their accustomed lifestyle and could perhaps have tolerated the status quo indefinitely, had not the Elite Patrols continued to fight the invaders, supported by peasant and slave units. Although the Ch'oe dictatorship presented no real threat to Mongol supremacy, its continued intransigence prompted five further invasions. The worst of these came in 1253–4, when, says the *Koryŏsa*, more than 200,000 Koreans were taken prisoner and the number of dead was too great to count. It was during this campaign that Kyŏngju's wonderful pagoda at Hwangnyŏngsa was destroyed. Only when the last of the military leaders, Ch'oe Ŭi, was assassinated in 1258 was the court able to affirm its desire for peace, King Kojong deciding that collaboration was the sole option. Even then, the *Sam pyŏlch'o* fought on from new bases on Chindo and Cheju islands, and only after 12,000 Mongol troops had successfully attacked them on Cheju did the court return to Kaesŏng (1270). By then, Kublai Khan's new capital at Khan Balek (Dadu, modern Beijing) was well on the way to completion. As his Chinese dynastic title Yuan ('Beginning') proclaimed, it was supposed to be the start of a new order in East Asia.

The Mongols were exacting overlords. From Korea they required lavish tribute and royal husbands for Mongol princesses. Since 1239 they had expected the Korean crown prince to reside as a hostage in Liaodong, where he was awarded the title King of Shenyang and 'ruled' over the Korean population. The first to be so invested was Wang Sun, who was actually not the crown prince but who had been sent as a decoy and remained undetected for years. When Kojong died in 1259 his son was en route to the Mongol capital at Karakorum ('Black Camp') in western Mongolia. Earlier that same year Möngke Khan had also died and his brother Kublai was himself journeying northwards to Karakorum for the election of a new Great Khan. The two men met and began a long personal friendship, which the modern historian Ki-baik Lee (1984) sees as sycophantic. Both the new Koryŏ king, Wŏnjong (r. 1259–74), and later his son, Ch'ungyŏl (r. 1274–1308), who took Kublai Khan's daughter as the first Mongol queen of Korea, were willing to travel long distances for personal consultations with the Great Khan.

Kublai's appetite for conquest was still unsated, and he now demanded Korean military assistance. Japan was slipping into a long period of weakened imperial authority and military disunity. The Kamakura shogun Tokimune unwisely managed to offend Kublai by refusing to switch diplomatic recognition from Southern Song Hangzhou to Dadu, and needed to be taught a lesson. Given the Mongols' poor seafaring qualifications, Koreans would have to play a significant part in the invasion that Kublai now ordered. Korean yards built more than 700 ships, and according to the dynastic history *Yuan shi*, 14,600 of the 23,000 soldiers who sailed in them in November 1274 were Korean. The fleet was the largest ever to threaten the Japanese coasts, yet its attack was a failure. Its planned sailing was delayed by Wŏnjong's death in June; Japanese resistance on Kyūshū took the invaders by surprise; a great storm arose to hamper them; and by the time the retreat was sounded some 13,500 men had perished.

The Great Khan was not to be denied, and the Japanese failed to help their cause by murdering two of his envoys in 1275. Even China was unable to resist his cavalry, and when Hangzhou was captured from the last Song emperor in 1279, he gained access to the shipbuilding yards of the Yangzi delta. There he ordered 200 more ships, planning that they should transport 100,000 soldiers from the port of Quanzhou to link up with 40,000 Chinese, Mongols and Koreans aboard a further 900 vessels sailing from Korean ports. He invited King Ch'ungyŏl to Dadu to discuss his plans, and a Korean, Hong Ta'gu, was put in overall command of the naval expedition. Once more things went wrong. The yards could complete only 50 new ships, and unsuitable river vessels had to be commandeered. Setting sail in June 1281, the fleets failed to liaise; the Japanese again resisted valiantly; and a typhoon forced the attackers to abandon their assault. Tens of thousands died, the Mongol mantle of invincibility lay ruined, and the tale of how the imperial ancestors had intervened to protect them with a 'divine wind' (*kamikaze*) entered Japanese mythology. Even though the *Yuan shi*'s claim that the fleet consisted of 3,500 ships may be exaggerated, hundreds of wrecks could await discovery off Kyūshū, and in 2002 underwater archaeologists excavated the first of them. More than 230 feet (70 m) long, it had been built in Fujian, and among its rich store of well-preserved artefacts were crossbow bolts, arrowheads, leather armour and a Mongol helmet. Especially significant was the discovery of a ceramic bomb filled with gunpowder and iron shrapnel, ancestor of the mortar bomb and harbinger of modern warfare. (The first recorded use of a mortar bomb in Europe comes in 1357, in Italy.)

New measures, introduced as Kublai pressed ahead with his attempt to create a multi-national empire, make it clear that neither friendship nor obsequiousness strengthened the Koryŏ hand. The word *ch'ung* ('loyal') had to be incorporated into kings' titles (Ch'ungyŏl was the first of six so named); government ranks were given new, provincial-style titles; and the court was required to adopt Mongol dress. Korean historians see these as more than just a cosmetic exercise, rather as a demotion of the country to son-in-law status. Then, seeking a spiritual authority recognizable by Tibetans, Chinese, Koreans and Japanese that would authenticate his temporal powers, Kublai developed a theory claiming to have inherited universal Buddhist supremacy from his grandfather Chinggis Khan. He took as his spiritual adviser the Tibetan Grand Lama 'Phags-pa, giving him authority over the Buddhist community throughout the Mongol empire. At his request 'Phags-pa also devised a new alphabet for writing all the languages of the empire. It had 42 letters and was based on Tibetan script. In Korea, where it arrived in 1273, it was used until the fall of the Mongol dynasty in 1368, but scholars brought up to revere Chinese characters were never going to take it seriously. On the other hand, genuine cultural sharing did take place in Dadu. The court acquired Korean musical instruments. Korean artists met Chinese calligraphers and painters whose work they admired and whose tastes and styles influenced their own. Artisans of different nationalities were brought together. A ten-storeyed pagoda commemorating a royal wedding in 1348 was built at Kyŏngch'ŏn-sa by Chinese and Korean craftsmen, exemplifying one of the more acceptable Korean duties within the confederation. Today, it stands in the National Museum of Korea.

THE FOURTEENTH CENTURY

Royal supremacy did not rise like a red phoenix with the court's return to Kaesŏng in 1270. Life in the capital was still dominated by powerful families that had cooperated with the Mongols and accumulated lands during its absence on Kanghwa, and now saw a chance to enter government. They lacked the traditional aristocracy's respect for the scholar-bureaucrat, and the literati, who had been reduced to following orders during the military period, sensed that the time had come for them to reassert Confucian principles and influence policy. Neo-Confucianism was already well established as the major political and social philosophy in China, where the crystallization by Zhu Xi (1130–1200) of early Song thinkers' ideas into a practical lifestyle was gaining wide acceptance. An Hyang (1243–1306) brought a complete set of Zhu's works from China and set up a state fund for Neo-Confucian education in 1304. Despite having many friendly contacts with China, he was a Koryŏ loyalist. So was Yi Saek (1328–1396), one of those who encouraged King Kongmin (r. 1351–74) to introduce reforms aimed against the Mongols and their collaborators, and even to take military action against them in the north. Now Kongmin may deserve his reputation as a gifted painter and calligrapher, but as a statesman he was not skilful enough to carry through tricky reforms. And when, with assistance from a former Buddhist monk, Sin Ton, he tried to do just that, sacking ministers of state, returning expropriated lands to their original owners and freeing many slaves, he threw the court and literati into a state of turmoil. It was not simply a question of whether or not to go on 'serving the [Mongol] great', or just scholarly sour grapes at the success of the *nouveaux riches* families. Rival cliques formed; intrigue filled the air; and the attitudes of Buddhists and Neo-Confucians, once reasonably tolerant of each other, began to polarize. Allegiance to the Koryŏ dynasty itself was wavering.

An erstwhile monk turned rebel leader, Zhu Yuanzhang, administered the *coup de grâce* to the Mongols in China and brought their dynasty to an end there in 1368. The ultimate beneficiary of this service in Korea was Yi Sŏnggye (1335–1408). Although he had served Koryŏ well as an army commander, frustration finally led him to drive its last king into exile and execute several members of the royal family. His move was the culmination of the anguish suffered by men of principle at the turn of events from Kongmin's reign onwards. Even so it did not meet with universal approval. The young master of the Confucian Academy, Chŏng Mongju (1337–1392), had devoted his career to putting his principles into action. He set up local schools to teach Neo-Confucian morality and a granary to issue relief rations in times of hardship; he carried out diplomatic missions to the Ashikaga shogun in Japan and Zhu Yuanzhang's new, and strongly Confucian, Ming court in Nanjing; he admired Yi Sŏnggye and felt, like him, that the Koryŏ court's excessive commitment to Buddhism was the root cause of corruption in public affairs. But unlike Sŏnggye he chose to stand by it. His sense of loyalty drove him in fact to martyrdom, for he plotted against Sŏnggye, and in the very year that the latter accepted the royal insignia of a new dynasty, Chŏng was assassinated on the Good Bamboo Bridge in Kaesŏng by agents of Sŏnggye's son Pangwŏn. Yi Sŏnggye affirmed his country's allegiance to the Ming dynasty. It was a Confucian step: whether it was a step forwards or backwards is debatable.

CULTURAL DEVELOPMENTS

Wang Kŏn's dynasty managed to survive for more than four centuries. Although his testamentary advice about the value of Buddhism had, on the whole, been heeded, it had been inadequate to prevent the nation's political fragility being exposed by enemies from outside and within. In cultural spheres, however, the Koryŏ bequeathed lasting memorials to its people's imagination and intellect that its founder could have been proud of.

Books were a matter of importance and status. In 1135 Kim Pusik received an order from King Injong to compile a history of his country. He would have understood the political agenda. He had recently suppressed Myoch'ŏng's revolt in P'yŏngyang. What his book would be expected to do was to justify the Koryŏ regime's own overthrow of its predecessors two centuries earlier, and to explain how Unified Silla had been the rightful conqueror of Paekche and Koguryŏ back in the seventh century. That way, the legitimacy of his own king's authority and dedication to peace would be affirmed, and those like Myoch'ŏng who advocated expansion northwards into Manchuria would be silenced. Kim himself was descended from Silla aristocracy, and he might also have welcomed a chance of boosting his own ancestors' image. Though now officially retired, he had access to books in the court library at Kaesŏng and was probably able to draw on a team of official researchers. Taking Sima Qian's first general history of China, the *Shiji*, as his model, he compiled basic annals (*pon'gi*) for each of the three kingdoms – twenty chapters for Silla, ten for Koguryŏ, six for Paekche – a set of monographs, and a collection of 50 biographies. In keeping with his objectives he didn't stop in 668, as the title of his book might imply, but covered the Unified Silla period as well, and submitted the complete work to Injong in 1145. What the king read was a text edited in accordance with Confucian principles. It was factually objective – at least, as far as Kim and his team could make it so – but it provided a moralistic account of history. Its content had been selected with Kim's idea of the king's requirements in mind. It omitted whatever Kim and his fellow bureaucrats thought it unnecessary for their king to know about. Its coverage concentrated on matters of concern to the literati and neglected more popular affairs, and drew on Chinese accounts of the period for information on specialist subjects as far apart as music and astronomy. The king, of course, knew this full well, even if today's users need to make the appropriate allowances. Yet even with this proviso, and the reservation that some of its dates are inaccurate, the *Samguk sagi* remains invaluable as a source of information about early Korean history.

Iryŏn's aims, when he drafted the *Samguk yusa* 140 years later, were different. His book was a deliberate attempt to supplement the Confucian-oriented selection of information in the *Samguk sagi* with Buddhist stories, most of which emanated from Silla. He tells how Buddhism arrived in Koguryŏ and Paekche, and writes about such topics as pagodas, famous teachers, hermits, exorcisms and filial devotion. He briefly introduces Old Chosŏn, Wiman Chosŏn, Lelang, Puyŏ, Koguryŏ, Paekche, Kaya, the Samhan polities and other smaller tribes in a section entitled 'Strange Events'. And among the foundation myths he tells is his account of Tan'gun's birth, perhaps a call for Koreans in troubled times to put aside rival claims about whether Koryŏ was descended from Silla or Koguryŏ, and unite under the banner of a still older founder figure.

Scholars across East Asia had long prized Korean paper and brushes. Now, men of Koryŏ went on to even more significant achievements in book production. Fonts of characters for movable-type printing were first made from clay, but, finding these too fragile, craftsmen experimented with metal type. Monasteries took the lead, casting the pieces in their forges, so it may be no coincidence that the world's oldest surviving example of a text printed with movable metal type is a Sŏn book dated 1377, *Pulcho chikchi simch'e yojŏl*, now in the Bibliothèque Nationale in Paris. Early efforts were inferior in quality to sheets printed from hand-carved wooden blocks such as those preserved in Haein-sa (Picture Essay 11), and fine block-printed editions never lost their appeal. Nor did printing mean the end of fine calligraphy. Sutras continued to be beautifully written and painted on blue or white paper under the auspices of the court's Offices of Gold and Silver Letters. Indigo dye protected mulberry paper against worms, so the choice of coloured paper was not simply a matter of aesthetic preference.

The first mention of metal type comes in the collected works of Yi Kyubo (1168–1241), who commissioned a printing of Ch'oe Yunni's *Sangjong kogum ye* ('Codification of Ancient and Modern Rites') of

1162. Twenty-eight copies were produced on Kanghwa between 1234 and 1241. Yi gained his first official post when he was nearly 30, but he was not really a political animal. He preferred literature, music, painting and drink – not necessarily in that order: devotion to zither-playing and heavy drinking made him, he said, a disciple of the old Chinese poet Tao Qian (AD 365–427). Despite a Confucian upbringing, he was open about his Buddhist sympathies, and wrote optimistically about the saving potential of the Tripitaka edition of 1236. Although his forthrightness made him enemies and he experienced a period of exile, he eventually rose to the post of Sangguk, Chief Minister. Perhaps James Scarth Gale's assessment of him in the 1920s as 'the greatest scholar and statesman that Korea had yet seen' is exaggerated, but as a writer alone he deserves a place on a pinnacle. He was a fine prose-writer of everything from official documents to essays on literary history, and he composed widely in his preferred medium of verse. One of his best-known pieces is an account of Chumong's Koguryŏ foundation tale, which despite its length is lyric rather than epic, and combines elements of myth and tribal history. In contrast, little poems like 'The Frog' show why his poetry has been likened to that of the great Chinese Li Bai (AD 701–762), and earned him – like Li – a reputation as an emotional poet:

> No angry words or fierce looks cross your eyes,
> And yet at times your stomach swells with fire.
> Proud of the music of your band you sing,
> And yet, uncharmed, we turn our ears away.

The arts of the brush were rated more highly than those of the hands, but their ceramics earned Koreans a high reputation across the region. Potters probably worked with immigrant Chinese teachers, but the interruption to contacts with northern China in 1127 proved to be an incentive, driving the Koreans on to show their self-reliance. Both countries now excelled in ceramic production, and if Koryŏ artisans turned out less in variety and overall quantity than their neighbours, they ceded nothing in aesthetic quality or technical skill. Xu Jing was complimentary about Korean celadons, but he didn't mention their white porcelain, inspired perhaps by Chinese Ding wares, or the black vessels they made by underglaze painting with iron. Neither did he see the later copper-red underglaze painting or the famous inlaid celadons (Picture Essay 12), which only appeared after his visit and which nowadays epitomize Korean cultural innovation. Chinese kilns produced so much celadon that it was used as ballast by sea-going

11 Printing blocks for the Korean Tripitaka

Printing blocks for the Korean Tripitaka, 1236, Haein-sa, North Kyŏngsang province.

The idea of art and religion serving the interests of statesmen and government is perfectly familiar to us. Had it not been for the authority and sponsorship of rulers, the West would lack many of its greatest buildings, monuments, statues and paintings, and the glories of the King James Bible would have been unknown. East Asia offers plenty of analogous examples. The tribute system provided countless opportunities for the skills and artistry of China's craftsmen to be admired beyond its frontiers, while Buddhism, ironically turned into the handmaid of many a ruling class, provided an internationally recognizable visual language. Blue and white porcelain from Jingdezhen adorned the courts of Middle Eastern potentates, while great works of Buddhist statuary looked down on their sponsors from Afghanistan in the west to Japan in the east. The Mongol leaders, commanding an empire that also transcended former national frontiers, were quick to exploit both tributary communication and religious imagery.

In times of trouble, rival sides in Asia were accustomed to invoke spiritual aid from Buddhist deities, just as they did in the West from the Christian God. So while the Mongol leadership espoused Lamaist Buddhism, Koreans believed that a complete woodblock printing of the scriptures, a scholarly and expensive undertaking, would earn them divine protection. King Hyŏnjong had initiated such a project in 1010 when the Khitan threatened, and the resulting Great Canon (*Koryŏ Changgyŏng*) took 40 years to finish. The 6,000-volume set and its plates were stored in Puin-sa, near Taegu, together with a 4,740-volume supplement (*Sok Changgyŏng*) compiled by Ŭich'ŏn at the end of the century. The Mongols burned them there in 1232. Better luck awaited the Korean Tripitaka (*Koryŏ Taejanggyŏng*), even if it too failed to fulfil its strategic objective. Still believing in the redemptive power of the scriptures, King Kojong's court assembled a team of monks in 1236 to begin a fresh carving, based on the best available editions of more than 1,500 Chinese, Khitan and Korean texts. Its 81,258 blocks of magnolia wood, measuring 65 by 24.5 by 6.5 centimetres and weighing 3.5 kilograms, each contained 23 lines of fourteen characters. They were completed in 1251 and lacquered. When, despite them, the Mongol general Jalairtai returned less than two years later to inflict worse mayhem than ever before, the Tripitaka was safe on Kanghwa, where it stayed until the late fourteenth century. Then it was moved, first to Seoul and finally to the mountain security of Haein-sa. Here, in 1488 a special library was built for it where the slatted wooden walls protected the blocks in an airy environment, safe from the ravages of temperature and humidity, to the present day.

12 Inlaid celadon jar

Chinese potters evacuated to Korea during the turbulent tenth century AD passed on to local craftsmen their enthusiasm for new wares and techniques. Potters from northern China seem to have settled in central Korea, while evidence from the south-west indicates the presence of still larger numbers of immigrants from south-east China. There, a ceramic production centre grew up in a pleasantly wooded area around Kangjin, Chŏlla Namdo province. The rich reddish soil contained high iron levels; abundant stocks of timber and flowing water were available; and finished wares could conveniently be shipped up the west coast to the capital. 'Dragon kilns' snaked up the hillsides. One at Sadang village, first excavated in 1964, was 7 metres (23 ft) long.

Two elements were essential for celadon manufacture: special glazes containing a small amount of iron oxide, and a reduction firing temperature of 1,100–1,200 °C. The colours spread across a spectrum from yellowish olive green to a pale grey-blue, and were prized for their likeness to jade, with its associated powers of longevity. Koreans called their best shades 'kingfisher-coloured'. Decoration was added by moulding, incising or underglaze painting, and a delicate glaze crackle was also used. Lotus, peony, chrysanthemum, willow, cranes, clouds and ducks featured among the designs, joining with purity of form, stylistic range and colour to achieve aesthetic brilliance. Then, from around the middle of the twelfth century, what many Korean experts regard as the acme of beauty was reached, the development of inlay (*sanggam*). By cutting out the design and infilling it with white or black slip, Koreans perfected a technique unknown in China. The supremacy that this gave them, however, was short-lived, and in less than a hundred years a growing heaviness in form and lack of originality betrayed an industry depressed at the Mongol invasions and lacking in inspiration.

The Koryŏ court wanted as much celadon as it could get, not only for its intrinsic beauty but also because its purity was associated with Buddhism. Not that this restricted its use: all kinds of goods, utilitarian as well as ritualistic, spread widely across the country. The National Museum, for example, owns a stoneware hourglass drum refreshingly painted with a swirling floral pattern in brown iron oxide under a celadon glaze, a special technique giving it a Chinese *cizhou* effect. A cup and saucer set, the cup standing on a raised perch in the middle of the saucer, was a distinctively Korean shape, and tables were graced by celadon dishes, cups and wine pourers. Scholars stood celadon vases and brush-holders on their desks and used celadon water-droppers shaped in animal or human form. They specially liked the high-necked, narrow-waisted Korean version of the *meibyŏng* ('plum blossom') vase. Women

Inlaid celadon jar, 12th–13th century, height 42 cm.

kept cosmetics in celadon boxes, and laid their heads at night on celadon pillows. (Osaka Municipal Museum has one in the shape of two lions.) Buddhist monks performed rites using celadon censers and *kundika* water sprinklers, and collected alms in celadon bowls. Xu Jing describes an incense-burner covered by a crouching lion, perhaps the very piece discussed by Gompertz on page 306, as 'the most distinguished of all their wares'.

junks. The Koreans may not have matched that, but their output was still plentiful. Wandering along country paths in Sadang, near the site of the Koryŏ kilns at Kangjin, in 1978, I realized that I was walking on a pavement of broken shards. Stooping to pick up pieces, I found that they were fragments of inlaid celadon. They had lain there and been trodden underfoot since somebody had discarded them, perhaps 600 years before.

In the history of Koryŏ we see many of the elements that would characterize and shape Korean politics and society through succeeding centuries: the rise of Neo-Confucianism, with its emphasis on lineage and male dominance; respect for education, examinations and literary record; an imbalanced social hierarchy, notwithstanding a degree of social mobility; the dominance of civil leadership, prompting the occasional military backlash; the throne's struggle to control the aristocracy in the capital (*yangban*) and hereditary families in the country (*hyangni*); political factionalism; crises originating in Manchuria; tensions over land issues; recurrent peasant uprisings; the popularity of Buddhism, especially in lower-class society; and the patronage of shamanism by all levels of society. And if a whiff of medievalism hangs over the attempt to bolster the dynasty by writing up the Tan'gun myth or by carving the Tripitaka woodblocks, the cool aplomb with which Yejong handled Emperor Huizong's cultural hegemonism seems thoroughly modern.

By no means was Koryŏ the beginning of the modern era, but Korea had without doubt turned the corner from antiquity and begun to experience the demands of nationhood. There is irony here. Our own age is consumed by the quest for progress, often into an unknown future. In the Sinocentric world admired by *yangban* scholars, advance from antiquity was seen as retreat and decline. The past represented a Golden Age, and reforms sought to turn the clock back towards what could be deduced of it from classical texts. Emperor Huizong called the music he sent to Yejong in 1114 'new music'. What he meant by this was not something like the difference between plainsong and polyphony, or the leap from Tallis to Monteverdi. It was, paradoxically, the latest in a series of attempts by Chinese court musicologists to recreate the supposedly perfect ceremonial music of antiquity, the Zhou, Shang and Xia dynasties, in the hope that Heaven would be pleased to hear it again and send blessings to the Middle Kingdom. According to Huizong, 'caring for fine rites and making music is really our first duty when it comes to governing the country and regulating the outside world', and his accompanying message to Yejong in 1116 quoted, a bit tactlessly, the well-known saying from the *Shijing* that there was nothing like music 'for changing the evil customs of a place'. What was actually new about his music, first heard in Kaifeng in 1107, was that it used a scale devised by a 90-year-old Daoist, Wei Hanjin, based on units of measurement derived from the length of the emperor's third, fourth and fifth fingers. If it sounded weird to the Koreans they were too tactful to say so, and performed it throughout the year. After that, as visits from Chinese envoys dried up, they probably allowed it to become Koreanized with some relief.

In China, no serious reforms were proposed without an attempt to validate them by citing historical or canonical precedent. Korean politicians were not so tightly circumscribed, although we have seen how heavily the imperative of legitimization weighed upon Wang Kŏn, how Kim Pusik followed Confucian principles in his positive use of historiography, and how, in Iryŏn's *Samguk yusa*, Buddhist scholarship also acknowledged the value of stories from earlier times. History, as Ch'oe Sŭngno reminded King Sŏngjong, offered heroes to emulate and warnings of pitfalls to be avoided, and if the new king learned the lessons of his five predecessors, he could stand in relation to T'aejo as Tang Xuanzong had done to his ancestor Taizong. None of this meant that society stood still, either in China or Korea. Inventions and innovations aimed at settling immediate problems contributed to longer-term developments: changes in ceramic decoration were tried and met with approval; improvements were made to printing methods; land was occasionally redistributed and slaves freed. But not because any of these were perceived as steps towards a permanently changed world. To look forward into the unknown, to base policy on predictions of new and as yet untried circumstances, was not part of the Sinocentric way. Even the object of peasant revolt was to restore happier times past, not to revolutionize the basis of socio-political thinking about the future.

CHAPTER FOUR

Early to Mid-Chosŏn, 1392–1800: The Search for an Acceptable Orthodoxy

The Chosŏn (sometimes referred to as the Yi after the name of its ruling clan) can be divided into three periods: from 1392 until the Japanese invasions of 1592–8; from the early seventeenth century until the arrival of the Western powers in the 1860s; and the age of modernization and reform preceding Japan's seizure of Korea in 1910. In the last of these three, Korean leaders proved less resistant than Chinese to the idea of accepting foreign assistance to restore their country's fortunes.

In the political and social spheres, Confucianism triumphed over Buddhism as orthodoxy, though Buddhism continued to enjoy widespread popular adherence. Both philosophies influenced the arts. The Korean literati greatly admired and imitated the cultural tastes of their political suzerains the Chinese, but after the cataclysm of the Japanese wars they also opened their minds more widely to native and European traditions. In the fine arts they still preferred East Asian styles and forms, but in the later nineteenth century the impact of Western culture was noticeable in town planning, architecture, medicine and patterns of religious belief.

It was 1392. In Christian Europe Richard II was king of England, while in western Asia the Scourge of God, Tamerlane, was trying to recreate the great empire of his supposed ancestor Chinggis Khan, building tall towers out of the skulls of his massacred opponents – two men with quite different views on the sovereignty of the ruler, sharing only an exalted concept of his entitled independence. The contemporary portrait of Richard preserved in Westminster Abbey suggests that he brought sensitivity to his understanding of divine kingship, and throughout 1392 he handled his opponents at home and abroad with quiet diplomacy. But the bust of Tamerlane in the State Historical

Museum in Moscow, reconstructed from the skull unearthed from his tomb in Samarkand in 1941, shows a man of uncompromising, ruthless determination, one whose enemy Ibn Arabshah described as fearless, cunning and awe-inspiring. As things turned out, neither the Plantagenet kingdom nor the Timurid empire would last very long. But across the world in East Asia, Yi Sŏnggye was inaugurating a dynasty that would still be ruling Korea long after the Turkic Muslim's own empire had gone, the British had put paid to the Mughal dynasty founded by his descendant Babur – even after the Victorian age in Britain itself had come and gone. Twenty-five kings of the Yi clan reigned throughout the Chosŏn dynasty, the longest in Korea's history. They too believed in their divine mandate, although their Confucian concept of royal responsibility to Heaven and Heaven's people was quite different from anything that inspired Christian, Muslim or Mongol kings, princes and governors. Yi Sŏnggye had his portrait painted more often than Richard, 26 times it is said, but no original or early copy survives. A nineteenth-century picture shows him standing, feet apart and hands across his stomach, wearing a blue robe embroidered with five-clawed dragons and a confident, thoughtful expression.

Credit for laying the foundations of the enduring Chosŏn oligarchy goes to the early kings and to the elite class of Confucian ideologues, the *yangban* (or *sadaebu*), that served them. The civilization they shaped bears so many signs of their admiration for China that un-suspecting observers may be deluded into believing that Korean and Chinese society and culture were to all intents and purposes one and the same, yet through the second half of the long period covered in this chapter the *yangban* enjoyed, and depicted via their arts, an outlook on life that was capable of reinterpreting rather than blindly imitating the Chinese example they admired. (The same went for lower-class artists: they too enjoyed painting landscapes and flower-and-bird studies like the Chinese, but the results were often strikingly different.) Hae-jong Chun points out that genuine cultural interchange might have been all the greater had it not been for the tributary relationship, which limited contact to officially approved occasions at court and frontier locations. But nowhere, of course, was free trade yet a recognized concept, and across East Asia diplomatic relations between nations of unequal standing all followed the Chinese tributary pattern. Despite the loyalty it still felt to the deposed Ming regime, the Chosŏn court established trib-utary relations with the Qing after 1644 for reasons of both diplomatic and cultural pragmatism. And coming effectively second in the inter-national hierarchy, it tried to maintain a superior / inferior relationship with Japan and the Ryūkyū kingdom. The educated men hand-picked to go on foreign missions valued meetings with local scholars, and despite the nasty taste left by memories of Hideyoshi's vainglorious exploits, diplomatic links between Seoul and Edo soon restored vital contacts between Korean and Japanese literati and artists with a shared interest in Chinese literature, philosophy and art. (Berlind Jungmann has shown, for example, how the Korean interpretation of Chinese literati painting, *namjŏnghwa*, helped to influence the development of the Japanese *nanga* style.) But intellectual pleasures could not hide economic difficulties. Missions were large and expensive. Tributary goods required by China tended to fall into the luxury category, especially gold, silver, textiles and animal skins, and far outweighed the economic value of the imperial largesse dispensed in return. Hae-jong Chun stresses the serious drain this constituted on Korea's tax silver, only partially mitigated by acquisitions made privately by members of tribute embassies. James Lewis points too to the 'enormity of the [economic] burden' laid on Korea by official trade with Japan. Cotton played such an important part in this that in 1486 the Ministry of Revenue had to raise the cloth tax to counteract the effects of the half-million *p'il* being exported each year in exchange for Japanese copper and tin. In the southern ports ships were also loaded with cotton and ginseng for dispatch to the Ryūkyūs, from where incoming vessels brought a wider range of goods, but in smaller quantities – gold, copper, cinnabar, swords, aromatics, medicines (including pepper, which was used as a form of currency exchange) and sharkskins. From the mid-seventeenth century rice supplanted cotton as Japan's number-one desideratum, and substantial gifts of ginseng added further to the costs of outfitting an embassy.

THE KINGLY WAY I

It was time for a change in 1392, and Song Neo-Confucianism, which Korean scholars first encountered in late thirteenth-century Dadu, promised a restoration of higher moral values and leadership qualities, as well as an end to the economic power of the Buddhist community. The new Ming authorities embraced it strongly, and political elites in Kaesŏng also saw its potential. So when Yi Sŏnggye claimed the title of king, he laid aside some personal respect for Buddhism and did so on a Neo-Confucian ticket, expressing his intention of restoring proper relations between the ruler and his people, and acknowledging Korea's need of China's approbation. The distinguished scholars Yi Saek and Chŏng Mongju contested his right to overthrow the Koryŏ rulers, but among his supporters, Yi Saek's pupil Chŏng Tojŏn proved one of the most valuable. He helped legitimize his master's usurpation of the throne by talking up Chosŏn's link with Kija. It was on his advice that Yi Sŏnggye had broken up large estates belonging to Koryŏ nobility and the Buddhist community in 1390, redistributing land among his own officials, government agencies, schools and Confucian shrines. He expressed reservations about the Buddhist monk Muhak's choice of a site on the northern banks of the Han river as the best location for a new capital, but once the argument was settled and the palaces and city walls built, in 1394 he organized the transfer of the capital from Kaesŏng to Hanyang (Seoul). He attacked Buddhism, especially for those beliefs that encouraged individualism to the detriment of social activities. He laid the basis for a revised legal system based on the Ming code, introduced the long-established Chinese *shi lu* (Kor. *sillok*) system of court record-keeping and dynastic-history compilation, and began work on the official history of the Koryŏ period. It was completed as *Koryŏsa* in 1451 after many false starts. (The *sillok* of the Chosŏn dynasty were published in 1933–4 by the Japanese colonial government, 1,893 volumes of primary historical material that have no parallel anywhere in the world.) Nevertheless, Yi Sŏnggye's abdication in 1398 unleashed a very un-Confucian battle for the succession among his four sons. One, Pangsŏk, was murdered, and Chŏng Tojŏn met the same fate for supporting him. When Yi Sŏnggye himself died, ten years later, he was canonized as King T'aejo ('Exalted Ancestor'), the temple name of the founding emperors of the Song, Liao, Jin and Ming dynasties in China. It was appropriate for one who had inaugurated an intense period of Sinicization. The course he charted, redirecting Korean politics and scholarship along a path firmly in parallel with China's, would have a profound influence on Korean society. And however ambivalent some of his compatriots might later feel about their obligations to the Middle Kingdom, the Dragon Throne would consider itself entitled to claim Korean allegiance so long as Yi T'aejo's descendants occupied the palaces of Seoul. In 1403 Emperor Taizu approved the title of the dynasty, Chosŏn, with its implications of links with ancient China. He dispatched symbols of investiture to King T'aejong and accepted Korean tribute in return. Korean literati immersed themselves in the study of Neo-Confucian books. The importance of education and examinations in the Confucian classics was reiterated. Magistrates were ordered to act in accordance with Neo-Confucian principles. A new warmth filled relations between the two courts.

Yi Sŏnggye's concept of kingship may have been no less autocratic than Richard's or Tamerlane's, but he and his descendants, whatever their exaggerated ideas about their heavenly mandate and the king's rights and privileges, owed their continued possession of the throne as much to an acceptable balance of power with their nobility as to any mutually agreed concept of royal prerogative. The complex system of bureaucracy that constituted the country's central administration constrained their potential for autocracy, and the fact that they could be held personally responsible to the Chinese emperor for the conduct of their national policy gave ministers an argument against their excessive arrogance. Not all kings were thus deterred, however, and everybody – whether commoner, minister or relative – took care to approach them with an exaggerated show of respect and awe-filled deference. They themselves understood just how difficult, time-consuming and exhausting were the demands of acting in accordance with unimpeachable Confucian etiquette. Sitting on top of the social and political pyramid was not a comfortable perch. Neither was it easy to fend off family and political rivals and follow the middle way exalted in the Confucian Classics. Equity and equality didn't come into it: pragmatism showed that it was more important to satisfy the *yangban* than merchants or slaves, just as in foreign and economic relations an expensive show of deference towards China must be maintained, with the hope of compensation at the expense of Japan and the Ryūkyūs.

If the Chosŏn tree set deep roots in T'aejo's time, its first heavy fruition was unquestionably enjoyed in the reign of the fourth king, his grandson Sejong (r. 1418–50). Not for nothing is he frequently referred to as 'the Great'. No early portraits of him exist, but modern depictions reveal a self-confident, generous nature, and the hagiography that surrounds him in Korea today paints a picture not only of a true polymath but of one born before his time, an example fit to inspire genuine social and technological progress. The list of his interests and achievements, though not quite endless, certainly makes impressive reading. It is corroborated by an extraordinarily detailed set of *sillok* for his reign, faithfully recording eyewitness accounts of everything he said and did over 32 years on the throne. On their basis alone he fully deserves the statue that looks down on today's visitors crossing the grounds in Seoul's Tŏksu Palace. One of his first moves, in 1420, was to found a research centre charged with seeing what intellectual and institutional lessons could be learned from China, the Chiphyŏn-jŏn ('Hall of Assembled Worthies'). Consisting of about twenty of his most promising young scholar-officials, it studied legal, historical, literary and cultural topics. An interest in all aspects of agriculture, from the raising of silkworms to land taxation and from improvements in irrigation to the keeping of meteorological records, is attributed to his concern for the ordinary people. He had newly devised rain gauges distributed around the country, and is credited with encouraging the invention of improved sundials and water clocks. A book of practical advice entitled *Nongsa chiksŏl* ('Plain Words on Agriculture') was researched and published in 1429, and Sejong took personal charge of an experiment on palace land designed to learn lessons about crop management in bad weather. In 1444 he reduced the harvest tax from 10 to 5 per cent, and commanded local officials to help farmers maximize food production: a dramatic improvement was reported. He sponsored research into medicine at home and abroad, particularly the study of native herbs as a branch of agriculture. The result was a 56-volume pharmaceutical encyclopedia published in 1433 and entitled *Hyangyak chipsŏngbang* ('Compendium of Native Prescriptions'), followed by another in 1445, in 365 volumes, called the *Ŭibang yuch'wi* ('Classified Collection of Medical Prescriptions'). Sejong promoted medical education, aiming to benefit the common people – even women and prisoners – as well as the nobility.

Integral to educational measures commissioned by Sejong were improvements in metal-type printing and the quality of fonts. Both bronze and lead fonts were used (the latter to print books in large typeface for the assistance of the partially sighted), although wooden block-printing was preferred for books required in multiple copies. Sejong appreciated literature. His statue shows him seated, holding the book *Hunmin chŏng'ŭm* ('[For] Instructing the People, Correct Sounds'). This was a primer devoted to popularizing the *han'gŭl* alphabet, recently invented by either the Chiphyŏn-jŏn or the king himself. *Han'gŭl* was really intended as a step towards widening literacy in Chinese characters, but the masses did not take to it and the literati had no need of it (Picture Essay 13). Its time would not come until later.

Although Sejong was intent on keeping rites and ceremonies at court up to the best Chinese standards, he acknowledged the value of preserving local customs out in the country. In both environments music and dance were of vital importance. Marketplaces shook to the strident notes of the *t'aep'yŏngso* (a double-reed oboe with a wooden stem and conical metal bell), complicated rhythms on the *changgo* hourglass drum, and the shouts and clapping of excitable spectators, while at court royal sacrifices, diplomatic events and social occasions took place to the strains of more esoteric melodies. The notes of *aak* and *tangak* had to be perfectly modulated and produced. They had to be complemented by the slow, smooth movement of dancers and regulated, stately actions of officiants. To achieve the purest possible ritual performances, Sejong ordered the reform of court music. The work was entrusted to Chŏng Inji, minister of personnel, rector of the

13 A page from *Sŏkpo sangjŏl Han'gŭl cha*

The announcement of the completion of King Sejong's alphabetic project comes in the *Sejong sillok* for the end of the lunar year 1443. Two years later the book *Hunmin chŏng'ŭm* ('Correct Sounds for Instructing the People') was unveiled, along with an explanatory document by Chŏng Inji and colleagues from the Chiphyŏn-jŏn entitled *Hunmin chŏng'ŭm haerye*. This guide, 'Explanations and Examples', reassured numerologically concerned Neo-Confucian readers that the consonants were divided into five groups corresponding to the Five Elements, the five tones of the musical scale (velar/wood/la, lingual/fire/do, labial/earth/fa, dental/metal/sol, laryngeal/water/re) etc.; that the combination of three basic vowels represented Heaven, Earth and Man and produced eight more (matching, for example, the eight sounds, *p'arŭm*, into which musical instruments were classified); and that all vowel sounds together were either yin or yang. Letters were grouped into squares consisting, at maximum, of an initial consonant, a single or combination vowel, and a final consonant. The shape of the letters and their arrangement into squares may have been derived from the Tibeto-Mongol *'phags-pa* script. Today, 24 of the original 28 letters are still in use.

One of the first books to be printed in the new script was *Yongbi ŏch'ŏn ga* ('Songs of Dragons Flying in the Heavens'), a paean of 248 poems written by scholars of the Chiphyŏn-jŏn in praise of Sejong's ancestors, notably King T'aejo. Published in 1447 in Chinese characters and Korean *han'gŭl*, it is still regarded as one of the great classics of early Korean literature, and one way and another, Sejong could surely have done little more to recommend use of his script. (Except, that is, to abandon its primary purpose of promoting literacy in Chinese characters among ordinary people: that was quite enough to condemn it in the eyes of the upper class.) Although some *sirhak* scholars used it in the eighteenth and nineteenth centuries, the pejorative name *ŏnmun* ('vulgar script'), coined for it in 1444 in a critical knee-jerk memorial by Ch'oe Malli, stuck right down to the twentieth century. Only then did the nationalist phonetician Chu Sigyŏng (1876–1914) invent the modern name *han'gŭl*, which, like the script itself, caught on as a symbol of Korean separateness amid the culture of the greater Japanese empire. Like Chinese, *han'gŭl* was written in vertical lines and read from right to left. Calligraphers still sometimes write it like this, though for all practical purposes it is now printed horizontally from left to right. The example shown here is from the 'Life of Sakyamuni in Detailed Sections, with *Han'gŭl* Translation'. The original version, in Chinese characters, was reissued by Crown Prince Sejo at the request of his father, King Sejong.

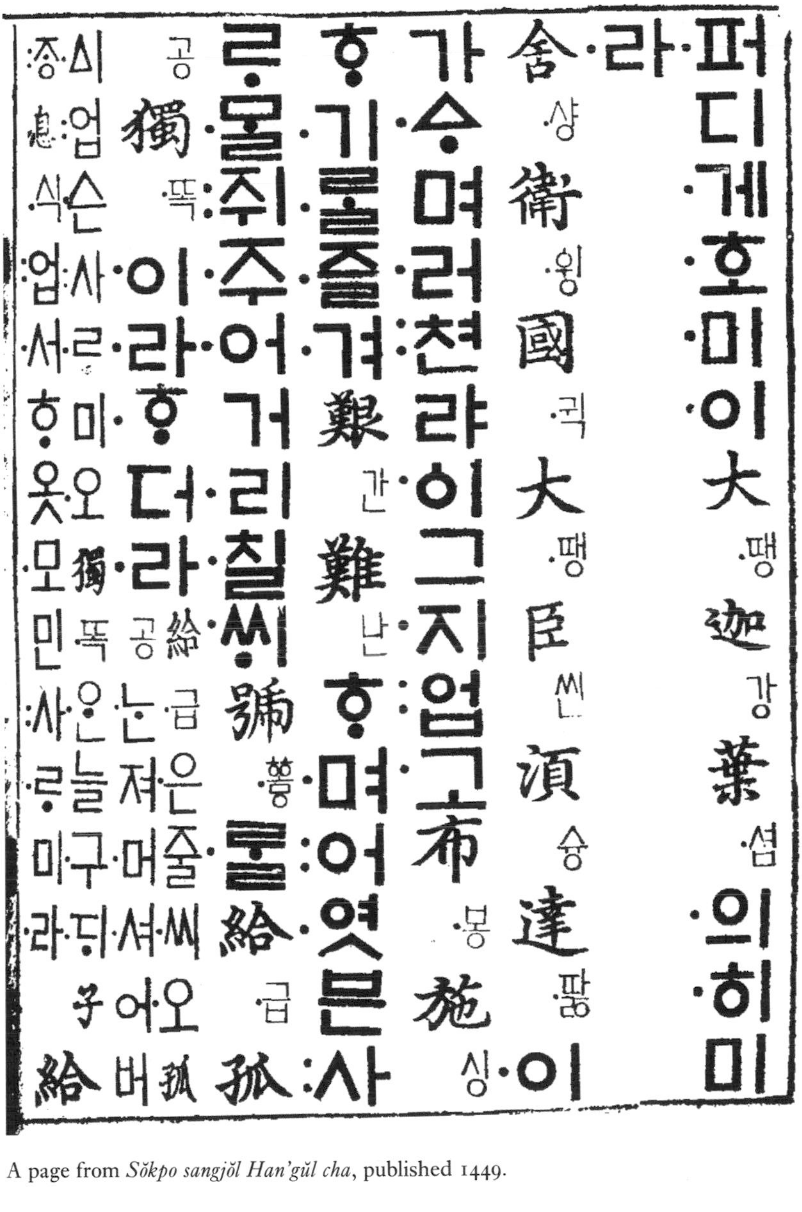

퍼디·게호미·이大땡迦강葉셥·의·히미

·라舍샹衛윙國귁大땡臣씬須슝達땁施씽·이

가·숭·며·러쳔·라이그·지업·고布봉·며·어·엿·븐·사

ㅎ·기룰·뎌艱간難난ㅎ·며

르·몰쥐주·어거·리·칠씨歸뽕·롤給급

獨똑·이·라ㅎ·더·라

공獨똑

죵息·업·식·손·업·사·서·루ㅎ·미·옷·오·모·민·사·루미·구·라·듸·라子給버孤孤:사給

A page from *Sŏkpo sangjŏl Han'gŭl cha*, published 1449.

Confucian Academy and author of a postscript to the *Hunmin chŏng'ŭm*, and to a fifth-grade junior official named Pak Yŏn. New tunes performed in 1433 were deemed acceptable (though they were certainly not a genuine restoration of ancient Chinese ones as was the intention), and Pak was promoted. His musical notations for the song cycle *Yongbi ŏch'ŏn ga* ('Songs of Dragons Flying in Heaven') were appended to the *Sejong sillok*, using the new and advanced notational system *chŏngganbo*. But the most lasting memorial to his scholarship and to Sejong's encouragement of music came later, in the encyclopedia *Akhak kweibŏm* ('Musical Studies Guide'), which was compiled and published by command of King Songjong (r. 1469–94) in 1493. This remains the most valuable source of information on traditional Sino-Korean music. Intended for scholarly use, it appeared in Chinese characters, and ironically, given Sejong's legacy, no complete translation into *han'gŭl* was made until 2000.

A paragon of virtue indeed was King Sejong the Great! Yet however much we may approve his forward-looking measures, he was, of course, a man of his own age and not of ours. He confirmed the execution of an official's wife for committing adultery; he supported an official who divorced his wife for failing to bear him a son; and he approved an order that *yangban* women should not be allowed out onto the streets of the capital in daytime. Committed to his grandfather's political philosophy out of filial respect and from genuine conviction that Neo-Confucianism would benefit all classes of society, Sejong accepted as corollary that Buddhism undermined social and economic interests. His predecessor T'aejong had defrocked more than 80 per cent of monks on charges of unregistered ordination, confiscated huge amounts of Buddhist land and slaves, and dissolved more than 70 per cent of the monasteries. Sejong approved, but nevertheless recognized that the country's deep-rooted commitment to Buddhism, evident even at court, was not going to go away in a hurry. He tried to hasten it on its way: he commanded that its seven schools should be reduced to just two, Sŏn(jong) and Kyo(jong), ordered the closure of still more monasteries and introduced a ban on monks from outside Seoul entering the city, an interdict that would survive right down to the late nineteenth century. But he turned a blind eye to some continuing observances, even attending them himself, and he patronized the leading monk, later known as Hamhŏ (1376–1433), who sought to find common ground in the teachings of Buddhism and Confucianism. Nor was he unaware that Buddhism still oiled the wheels of international statecraft: the ambassador Pak Sŏsaeng told him in 1429 that as official presents, books about the faith were valued highly in Japan, and throughout the fifteenth century the Chosŏn court continued to send copies of Buddhist scriptures requested by the Ryūkyū authorities.

If the Confucian ideal of a sage king, someone to emulate the mythical Chinese heroes Yao and Shun, was in practice unattainable, Korea seemed to have found a fair substitute in Sejong. He was one of the world's great monarchs, so great in fact that his successors in the fifteenth century were bound to pale in comparison whether or not they tried to live up to his example. Indeed, though both Sejo (r. 1455–68) and Sŏngjong (r. 1469–94) were cultured men who encouraged literary projects such as the compilation of *T'ongguk t'onggam* ('Complete Mirror of Korea') and *Akhak kweibŏm* respectively, what sticks in the public memory is that Sejo was an usurper who killed his seventeen-year-old nephew Tanjong to forestall any possible restoration attempt, and that Sŏngjong's accession at the age of thirteen came thanks to the machinations of his maternal grandmother, Sejo's queen Yun. Herein lies the crux of Chosŏn's longevity and the fallibility of the Korean monarchical system. While society as a whole allowed a man to take concubines, it denied their offspring (known as *sŏŏl* or *sŏja*) the rights due to the sons of his legal wife. In the case of the succession to the throne, on the other hand, the preservation of the male lineage was deemed of great importance. Not only might the rule of primogeniture be waived in favour of a younger son or another male relative if the king's eldest son seemed unfit to be heir apparent – thus enabling the ruling clan to hang on to the throne longer than was the case in European monarchies – but sons borne by royal concubines might also be eligible, especially if their relatives could muster enough political clout. The potential for rivalry and intrigue is obvious.

No political system – be it despotism, oligarchy or democracy – is static, no institution – whether monarchy, state council or parliament – perfect as its agent. Around the world, ideologies ranging from Christianity and Shintō to Confucianism and Marxism-Leninism have been called in to lend credence to rulers' *modi operandi*, yet in the end people's perceptions of what they can expect from their leader have often been determined as much by the latter's character as by constitution or philosophical creed. That said, if the monarchy was the foundation of British political life and symbol of its statehood and nation for almost one and a half millennia, as has been claimed, no less was true in Korea. The roots of the Korean national monarchy lay far back in the Silla Council of Nobles, the Hwabaek, from whose ranks a king was chosen. The king afforded Unified Silla in its prime a measure of self-respect in relation to both China and Japan. Through much of the Koryŏ period the monarchy was weakened by the power of great *yang-*

THOMPSON-NICOLA REGIONAL DISTRICT LIBRARY SYSTEM

ban and *hyangni* families in the capital and the countryside, opening the way for military and foreign domination. Yet it survived, and by pinning Neo-Confucian colours so firmly to the mast, the early Chosŏn kings managed to combine principle and pragmatism, and restore to the institution an authority authenticated by the weight of ancient scriptures; a command over the education of all those who aspired to enter the government; a glamorized ritual that was replicated in every magistracy across the country and in households where the senior male worshipped the spirits of his ancestors; and respectability in the eyes of the Chinese court.

NEO-CONFUCIANISM IN ACTION

Like other -isms, Confucianism has meant many things to many people. To the leaders of the Three Kingdoms, it was a means of underpinning their authority as state formation progressed. To upper-class Koreans in the Unified Silla period it was a framework for personal study and a pattern for civic development. To men in the Koryŏ period it still spoke of desirable virtues, of loyalty, respect and determination, even if they were now more attracted by Buddhism's offer of personal salvation, not to mention its practical inducements such as money-lending and bargains at jumble sales. Neo-Confucianism – a Western name for what the Koreans knew simply as 'scholarly teaching' (*yugyo*) or the Way (*Do*) – had evolved as a new breed of thinkers in tenth- and eleventh-century China, anxious to lift that country out of the doldrums into which it had fallen and to recapture imagined ancient glories, realized that the old Confucian Classics were now well past their sell-by date. They took them down, dusted them off and re-examined them in the light of Buddhist metaphysics. This took them into realms of debate about hitherto unconsidered existential topics, until Zhu Xi pulled their cosmological speculations together and codified their newly identified principles into practical rules for political and social harmony. Most important of these was the assertion that, just as the cosmos was ruled by the Supreme Ultimate (Ch. *tai qi*, Kor. *t'aegŭk*), so was the state ruled by an absolutist monarch and the lineage or family by its patriarchal head. Autocracy and hierarchy must rule if the chaos represented by Khitans, Jurchens and, later, the Mongols was to be overcome.

The introduction of Neo-Confucianism to Korea gave fresh hope to those who were unhappy about the dominance of Buddhism at their own court, men like Chŏng Mongju, Yi Saek, Yi Sungin, Chŏng Tojŏn and, of course, Yi Sŏnggye. And the leaders of the new Chosŏn regime studied and accepted Zhu Xi's teachings on everything from state protocol to the interpretation of history, until the man they called Chuja, 'Master Zhu', became the symbol of orthodoxy, and his prescriptions for successful conduct in both public and private life, everything from passing examinations to running a household, sacrosanct. The education system took his commentaries on the Four Books and the Five Classics as its basis. They exalted the Three Bonds and Five Relationships (*samgang oryun*): bonds of subject to ruler (loyalty), children to parents (filial piety) and women to men (hierarchy), and relations between ruler and ministers, fathers and sons, elder and younger brothers, husbands and wives, and friends and associates. No educated person, or even perhaps many of the uneducated majority, was unaware of the rules he laid down for proper conduct in family life in his *Chuja-garye* ('Zhu Xi's Domestic Rituals'). These put special emphasis on the so-called Four Rites, *sarye*, the celebration of capping (see p. 158) and marriage and the observance of mourning and ancestral worship. It took some time for long-established Buddhist and shaman rites, such as those connected with weddings and funerals, to fall into line with patterns originating in China, and in the countryside they sometimes never did. But in Chosŏn Korea standardization of social organization and behaviour came to be the first meaning of Neo-Confucianism. So precise were its hierarchical prescriptions that they inevitably resulted in discrimination, for example against wives in cases of marital breakdown, widows not allowed to remarry, sons of secondary marriages barred from the regular examinations, and merchants facing constraints on enterprise lest their profit-making challenge the leadership status of scholars. Sometimes the rules were applied even more strictly than they were in China, and upward social mobility into the literati class was even more difficult.

In the fifteenth century some scholars, objecting to the rewarding of aristocratic 'meritorious subjects' (*kongsi*) with government posts, formed groups dedicated to high standards of official probity and concern for the interests of the peasantry. They were known as country scholars (*sarim*). Although they did not altogether eschew public service, some did shun official advancement and take to the countryside to pursue social improvements via their own lines of intellectual contemplation and research, a way of life that was, ironically, not so very different from the Buddhist practice of eremitism that Neo-Confucian apologists condemned as detrimental to the interests of society. Out of their tradition came the first great Korean speculative philosopher, Yi Hwang (1501–1570), the man whose name, says Michael Kalton, marks 'the advent of maturity in Korean Neo-Confucian thought'. Retiring from public life in 1549 and taking the brush-name T'oegye ('Return to the Valley'), he devoted his remaining years to metaphysical speculation based on the works of Zhu Xi, on which he became the first Korean to express constructive criticism. In particular, he pondered over the great Chinese debate about the cosmic dualism of principle (*i*) and matter (*ki*) and its contribution to the workings of the Supreme Ultimate, the Neo-Confucian equivalent of the Dao. Closely related to principle was the question of inherent nature, and to matter and force that of physical energy, or to put it another way, every human individual was made up of mind and body. From there stemmed discussion of human nature, and for T'oegye consideration of Four Beginnings and Seven Emotions. The Four Beginnings had been identified by Mencius as benevolence, righteousness, propriety and wisdom, and the Seven Emotions by the *Liji* as happiness, anger, sadness, fear, love, hatred and liking. T'oegye concluded that the Four Beginnings arose from principle and the Seven Emotions from matter, and to his mind the spiritual took precedence over the (more ambiguous) physical. In 1561 he began a long correspondence with a younger scholar, Ki Taesŭng (brush-name Kobong, 1527–1572), in which the greatest philosopher of the next generation, Yi I (Yulgok, 1536–1584), later participated. Yulgok himself, having dabbled at first with the idea of becoming a monk, had finally embarked on a successful career in official service, rising to the very top of the government before dying at the identical age when T'oegye had made his own momentous break with public life, just 48. Kobong and Yulgok argued that the relationship between *i* and *ki* was one of mutual dependence rather than superiority and inferiority, and that, for the scholar, practice was as vital as abstract analysis in pursuit of self-fulfilment. As this Four-Seven Debate, as it is known, rumbled on, so widely did the controversy spread that the 'study of nature and principle' (*sŏngnihak*) constitutes a second meaning of Chosŏn Neo-Confucianism.

In 1542 Chu Sebung, the county magistrate at Sunhŭng, North Kyŏngsang, opened a private academy dedicated to the memory of the Neo-Confucian scholar An Hyang, who had lived nearby. The court did nothing to discourage the subsequent proliferation of similar *sŏwŏn* ('writing courtyards'); indeed, it granted royal charters to many. By 1600 nearly one hundred had been established, and by the end of the eighteenth century there were over four times as many. They acted as centres for academic debate, provided communal facilities for ritual and cultural occasions, and collected and published books. (By the 1860s they also represented aristocratic privilege and a fiscal liability, and when they stimulated too much independent argument over political and economic matters, the Taewŏn'gun closed down all but 47 of them.) A proposal from T'oegye led to the Sunhŭng academy being awarded the royal title *Sosu sŏwŏn* ('Transmitted Cultivation Academy') in 1550, but by then T'oegye himself was already disillusioned with political service. What he disliked about it was the rise of sectarian rivalry and political prejudice. He would have grieved to see how, soon after his death, it erupted so violently that to later observers factionalism – over matters of ritual as well as rivalry for official preferment – came to represent a third meaning (or at least, trait) of Neo-Confucianism. We saw how in Sejong the philosophy had the capacity to bring the best out of a ruler. But the axiomatic linkage between political and moral issues meant that whilst it certainly generated scholarly discussion, tolerance was not one of its hallmarks, and the bigotry and prejudice of its competing cliques evoked the kind of terror experienced by contemporary Catholics in Elizabeth I's England or Puritans in Carolingian times. Bloodthirsty purges of political and scholarly rivals and dissenters, worthy of Tudor or Stuart England at their worst, were instituted by or in the name of the king. Korean scholars traditionally called them *sahwa* ('scholars' disasters'), though Western historians today prefer Ed Wagner's term 'literati purges'. Those in the fifteenth and early sixteenth centuries reflected confrontations between merit subjects, grateful for royal patronage and thus responsive to centralized rule, and *sarim* scholars, defending the principles of Neo-Confucianism less subjectively and favouring local control over the new wealth produced by the agricultural revolution. After the mid-sixteenth century sectarianism and rivalry over political appointments were more to blame. Twelve major *sahwa* occurred between 1453 and 1722, and even afterwards an atmosphere of suspicion and fear frequently hung over courtiers, and executions and banishment were ordered on the flimsiest of grounds. Not even kings themselves, or their relatives, were exempt from the machinations of spies, whistle-blowers and cut-throat partisans. Indeed, they were at the very heart of them, since the whole web was woven around the throne, the succession to it and the power of noble families to control it. Neo-Confucian absolutism expected constructive criticism of the ruler's behaviour via the Censorate, but made no legal provision for organized opposition. Since it also demanded the utmost loyalty of all men to their ancestors and kinsmen, the ruthlessness of inter-lineage competition was intensified and a quiet life was hardly to be expected.

For some experts a dispute over official appointments in 1574 marks the first appearance of factionalism (*tangjaeng*), but its origins actually lay some way back: nine of the twelve *sahwa* in fact preceded it. Most of those purged were *sarim*, who fell at the hands of the *hun'gu* ('meritorious and conservative') group. One who died was Cho Kwangjo. As a member of the Censorate he had proposed a simplification of the examination system, publication of *han'gǔl* translations of the Confucian Classics and the creation of village assemblies (*hyangyak*), but thanks also to his efforts to control the *hun'gu* he was framed, condemned and executed by judicial poisoning in 1519, aged just 37. The year 1574 saw two alignments – of gentry residents in western Seoul, who supported the advancement of Sim Ǔigyǒm, and those in the eastern quarters who backed Kim Hyowǒn – and through the remainder of the century these expanded the scope of factional arguments as they threw their allegiance behind Yulgok and T'oegye in the Four-Seven Debate. The Easterners (Tongin) held the upper hand, but in 1589 they fell out among themselves over the appointment of the heir apparent and split into Southerners (Namin), followers of T'oegye, and Northerners (Pugin), who preferred the philosophy of another *sarim*, Cho Sik (1501–1572). Confusion was compounded through the 1590s, the decade that saw the Japanese invasions, until, in 1623, by which time the Northerners were divided into no fewer than five factions, it was the turn of the Westerners (Sǒin) to seize the whip hand. But they too were bifurcated by now, and the story of the next sixty years concerns the fortunes of their Meritorious and Hardline factions, who dominated the government up to and after 1649 respectively. Then in 1683, after yet another argument over the nomination of a crown prince, this time for King Sukchong (1674–1720), four principal factions emerged. They were two parties of Westerners – the Noron ('Old Teaching') and Soron ('New Teaching') – the Southerners and the Lesser Northerners. Dignified by the appellation Four Colours (*sasaek*), these would survive and control government affairs until the second half of the nineteenth century.

In 1762 the execution of Crown Prince Sado split the ruling Noron party into Principle (or Dogmatist, Pyǒkp'a) and Realist (Sip'a) divisions, and the latter also recruited broad-minded scholars from the ranks of the Southerners. The Realists were the political face of the *sirhak* movement, men – Neo-Confucians, indeed – who were prepared to consider reshaping the mould of Sinocentric thought and behaviour and to try out whatever ideas might be best for their country, whether they came from China, from their own native traditions or even from Europe. Some questioned the unchallenged authority of Zhu Xi's orthodoxy and investigated the rival teachings of Wang Yangming (1472–1529), which many Chinese scholars preferred for the scope they afforded for individuality. Long-accepted historical sources were re-examined as a fresh guide to government; new studies were launched into areas as diverse as astronomy, geography, education and military affairs, as well as the implications of Western science and religion introduced to China by the Jesuit missionaries. One of the most eminent Realists was Chŏng Yagyong (Tasan, 1762–1836), at one time a favourite of King Chŏngjo and a would-be social reformer. His writings covered everything from the principle-matter debate to history, from music and mathematics to social order and good government. He studied the role of technology in agricultural improvements and submitted a report on rural poverty in Kyŏnggi province. He investigated the reasons for bureaucratic corruption, defended the poor against unjust capital punishment and reflected on Mencius's justification of rebellion against oppressive leadership.

In the fifteenth century Neo-Confucianism had encouraged innovation, and in the eighteenth it provided the ideological support for a social, political and economic renaissance. In the intervening period factions multiplied because it tolerated no other political parties or groupings, and in later times its heritage might be described as equivocal. Signs that its long command of political processes through the Chosŏn had prevented any system of organized opposition from developing among the government's critics were evident during the twentieth-century colonial period, when anti-Japanese groups at home and abroad proved unable to work together in the common cause, and again in post-military-era South Korea, when Kim Daejung and Kim Young Sam failed to unite in 1987 to challenge Roh Tae Woo. On the plus side, some Western observers saw Neo-Confucianism as the work ethic and social cohesiveness that drove South Korea's remarkable economic success in the late twentieth century. International recognition, such as Michael Robinson's view that 'in the main, traditional Confucian values have supported Korean economic growth', flattered Koreans, who in the 1960s and '70s had been in the habit of blaming Neo-Confucianism for everything from their unhappy experience of authoritarianism to class conflict. A wave of enthusiasm for its potential swept through the ranks of younger scholars, at least until the financial crisis of 1997 restored a sense of balance. It was a far cry from the traditional anti-commercial ethos propagated by early Confucians, but it showed that modern Confucians still respected both education and the profit motive.

THE JAPANESE WARS

Political arguments cost Korea dearly during the 1590s. Hideyoshi Toyotomi, the warrior who had only recently unified Japan, harboured greater ambitions: his attention was focused on the Dragon Throne in Beijing, no less. Korea would provide his pathway, and might even be his ally were King Sŏnjo to accept the sanctimonious and threatening proposals he sent him in 1590. Sŏnjo quite properly refused to join his campaign, but his ministers disagreed over whether the Taikō was a real threat or not. Kim Sŏng'il, leader of the predominant Tongin faction, refuted dire warnings of danger from Yu Sŏngnyong, of the Sŏin faction, and as late as the first month of 1592 a plea from the vice-minister of war, Song Yingchang, for the training of defensive troops went unheeded. While the Koreans prevaricated, Hideyoshi assembled more than 156,000 men around Nagoya (some say as many as a quarter of a million), over five times the complement of the Spanish Armada that had recently threatened England.

The fleet carrying the vanguard army used the island of Tsushima as its launch pad. Regarded by Koreans as their own but controlled by the Japanese Sō clan, Tsushima had long been a troublesome pirate lair. In an effort to control it, earlier kings had authorized trade via the ports of Pusan (Tongnae county), Chep'o (Ungch'ŏn) and Yŏmp'o (Ulsan), and in 1419 King Sejong had sent an expedition against it. Japanese communities grew up in the three ports, but after rioting by immigrants in 1547 Pusan was designated the sole point of entry and exit. (Frustrating though this was to merchants on both sides, the order remained in force until 1876.) It also became the way in for the First Division of the Japanese army, the 7,000 men of the Christian *daimyō* Konishi Yukinaga, who went ashore on the twelfth day of the fourth month (4m/12d), or 23 May 1592. The Catholic faith that many of them professed had been acquired from Jesuit missionaries over the preceding 43 years. So had the Portuguese-style iron helmets, plate armour and long arquebuses they took into battle. Pusan and Tongnae castles were swiftly taken, with furious slaughter of defenders and civilians alike, and the way was clear for the next wave of soldiers to land. Korean resistance was totally inadequate. In the words of their own commanders, 'our forces . . . are nothing more than [an] ill-trained rabble ignorant of combat', while the leadership itself was rent by rivalries. The Koreans were hopelessly outclassed in numbers, strategy, equipment and morale. Instances of great heroism notwithstanding, bows and arrows and primitive muskets were no match for samurai swords and arquebuses. The losers were beheaded, thousand upon thousand of them. Konishi's army entered Seoul on 5m/3d, just 20 days after landing at Pusan. It met no resistance because the court had already fled in the direction of P'yŏngyang, taking the royal ancestral tablets with it. Hideyoshi was exultant at the apparent fulfilment of his plans, and planned to embark for Korea the following spring. But unlike the army, the Korean navy was well armed with cannon and mortar and arrow-launchers, and less than a week after the fall of Seoul a fleet commanded by Admiral Yi Sunsin destroyed 37 Japanese ships off Kŏje island. In follow-up engagements in early July the armoured turtle-boat (*kŏbuksŏn*) made its appearance (Picture Essay 14). Hideyoshi's rejoicing was premature.

The Korean king appealed for Chinese assistance. Beijing harboured doubts about Korea's loyalty and sought to bring about an armistice, but by the time Sŏnjo reached P'yŏngyang the Wanli emperor had already approved the sending of aid, and when the court evacuated again as far as the border town of Ŭiju the first rescue mission was dispatched. It was far too small and Konishi's army easily ambushed and massacred it at P'yŏngyang. But Yi Sunsin's command of the west coast meant that Konishi failed to receive essential supplies, and as his rival the Buddhist general Katō Kiyomasa forged much further ahead into Hamgyŏng province, Japanese lines became greatly over-extended. Support for the Korean regular armies came from two unexpected sources. Bands of guerrillas, estimated to number 22,000 nationwide, attacked Japanese camps and destroyed their supplies. Many of the resistance fighters were former slaves, pressed into service when the war came and now providentially liberated by the destruction of their registration documents. And thousands of monks, answering a call to resist the invader from the Sŏn grand master Sŏsan (1520–1604), a poet and calligrapher now in his seventies, formed themselves into effective and morale-boosting units.

In January 1593 more Chinese assistance arrived, as the Ming general Li Rusong crossed the frozen Yalu at the head of around 48,000 cavalry and foot-soldiers, with cannon drawn on carts. This time it was they who out-thought and out-fought the Japanese, and the recovery of P'yŏngyang after a great battle marked a turning point in the war. The Japanese lost up to 13,000 men, and on 20 May surrendered control of Seoul as well. The city's few remaining inhabitants, said chief councillor Yu Sŏngnyong, looked like ghosts. When Sŏnjo returned to his ruined capital in November, he found only parts of the Tŏksu Palace habitable. In July 1593, as the Japanese fought their way back to the south coast, the final battle went their way at Chinju. Sixty thousand defenders and inhabitants were massacred, though a surprise Korean heroine, a *kisaeng* named Non'gae, earned immortality by embracing General Keyamura Rokusuke on top of a cliff and then toppling both of them to their deaths in the river below. The story may be apocryphal, but a memorial to her can still be seen in Chinju. The battle was

14 Building a turtle boat

People in south-eastern Korea danced to express their joy at what Admiral Yi did for them during the *Imjin Waeran* ('Black Dragon Japanese Struggles'). Their folk dance, *Sŭngjŏnmu*, now with words extolling his moral leadership and sense of loyalty, is still performed by the National Center for Korean Traditional Performing Arts. Incense burns to his spirit in shrines near the spots where he was born and died. In a modern age when tension between Korea and Japan is never far below the surface, Yi Sunsin remains an undoubted National Hero Number One. Ironically, until 1968 there was no focus in the capital for nationalistic respect to be shown to him. Then, in a prime example of Confucian hero exaltation, Park Chung Hee gave the great opponent of imperialism an officially sponsored boost to his reputation by unveiling Kim Saejung's commanding bronze statue of him. Its pose demonstrates the Confucian qualities of determination and loyalty, and its location, in the centre of Sejongno and in direct line south of Kwanghwamun, could not be more significant. Unfortunately, such is the density of the traffic that whistles past it that tourists tend to ignore it.

In the Yŏngsan War Memorial, however, they take their time over another dramatic memorial to the great admiral, a big (1:2.5) reconstruction of the *kŏbuksŏn* turtle boat with which his name is inescapably linked. According to an eighteenth-century description there were two versions of the design, one dating from the fifteenth century and the other from the late sixteenth. Yi Sunsin, then Left Navy Commander for Chŏlla province, and the naval architect Na Taeyong completed their own reconstruction of the earlier one only a matter of days before the Japanese armada arrived. The flat-bottomed ships were built on planks 10 centimetres thick. Seven courses of similar-sized beams made up the sides, which tapered from 34.6 metres in length at deck level to 20.6 metres at the keel. The maximum height measured 6.6 metres, including 2.3 metres from keel to gunwale. The figurehead was 1.3 metres tall and 91.5 centimetres wide at the mouth. A turret stood at the creature's tail. Two sails provided extra propulsive power to assist the 20 oars.

The ship was entered through a single opening in the convex protective decking, its 'turtle-shell'. Covered in vertical iron spikes to repel boarders, the roof may also have been clad with interlocking hexagonal iron plates as protection against fire-arrows. Below decks there were two levels, the upper one divided into 24 compartments, which included the captain's cabin and sailors' accommodation. Smoke poured frighteningly from the dragon's mouth, where four cannon were concealed, and from the stern. It is estimated that one vessel could transport up to 160 men and that its potential range was more than 100 miles in a day, but rather

An artist's impression of the building of a turtle boat.

than being a long-range transport vessel its greatest novelty was as a battering ram that could withstand collision with wooden boats and force its way into the midst of an enemy fleet with terrifying fire power. It was, according to Yu Sŏngnyong, 'so fast and nimble that [it] looked like a spinning spindle'.

The turtle boats played a significant part in Admiral Yi's victories but were few in number. Most of the ships under his command were open-topped *p'anoksŏn*, warships driven by rowers below deck while the fighting men attacked from behind raised gunwales above them. *P'anoksŏn* carried cannon of four sizes, shooting balls of iron or stone and raining three-metre-long burning arrows down on enemy heads. The captain commanded operations from a raised castle. The concept of the turtle boat evolved from this kind of design.

a warning that the Japanese were not yet to be written off. They built a string of castles (*wajō*) along the Kyŏngsang coast, and while ships bore many exhausted and relieved samurai away from Korea, 43,000 men were left to garrison them, an ominous reminder that Hideyoshi was used to getting his way. In the meantime, the war was temporarily suspended.

Almost from the beginning the Chinese had sought peace, and had opened truce talks in the spring of 1593 without consulting their Korean allies. In June negotiators purporting to come from Emperor Wanli accompanied Japanese troops leaving Pusan, and after an audience with Hideyoshi in Nagoya returned with his exorbitant demands. These included marriage to a Chinese princess, the restoration of trade and the ceding of southern Korea to Japan. No mention was made of his hankering after the Chinese throne, and in a letter to his wife, to whom he pretended that his retreating troops were coming back from Korea as victors, he wrote that if he got what he wanted he would now leave China and Korea alone. Wanli himself was told that Hideyoshi would surrender in return for enfeofment as the 'king' of Japan, and when the Ming envoy Yang Fangheng eventually sailed to carry out this investiture in October 1596 but made no mention of Hideyoshi's conditions, the wrathful *daimyō* once more unleashed his forces. This time, in August 1597, many hundreds of ships (perhaps even 1,000) carried more than 120,000 men, and the second invasion began with the odds firmly on Japan's side. Meanwhile, a review of military systems carried out by Yu Sŏngnyong, despite pinpointing the inadequacy of Korean armaments and the inappropriateness of exempting the large slave class from recruitment, had not led to significant improvements. And worse, Yi Sunsin, who had been raised to Supreme Commander of the Three (Southern) Provinces only in September 1593, had been falsely impeached by his jealous rival Admiral Wŏn Kyun and deprived of his command, narrowly escaping execution. Success in the first naval battle of the new campaign went to the Japanese, and once more the samurai poured ashore at Pusan.

Their first great victory, at Namwŏn in late September, was also one of the most bloodthirsty in the whole six-year trauma. Despite the arrival of a supporting Chinese army under General Yang Yuan, the Japanese Army of the Left took huge numbers of heads, sliced off their ears and noses, and sent them home to Hideyoshi as trophies. After that Chŏnju fell without a fight, and there Katō Kiyomasa's Army of the Right, which had taken a more easterly route, caught up: the road to Seoul lay invitingly ahead. But once more the dependence of advancing troops on west-coast sea lanes for their supplies was demonstrated. A swiftly reinstated Yi Sunsin saw off 133 Japanese ships at Myŏngyang, just north of Chindo, on 9m/16d (26 October), and the Japanese army, rather than confront the strong Korean-Chinese defence of Seoul without adequate provision, swung away east and south. On its way towards Ulsan and the hoped-for safety of the *wajō* it passed through Kyŏngju, destroying the historic Pulguk-sa. Ulsan turned out to be no safe haven, for the Japanese were outnumbered by the Koreans and a strong Chinese force, but after terrible suffering on both sides relief arrived to lift the siege and complete a surprising, if hollow, Japanese victory. And at the other, western, end of the line of *wajō* the allies received another salutary shock. Here stood Sach'ŏn and Sunch'ŏn castles, sheltering 10,000 and 13,000 Japanese respectively, and in Sunch'ŏn harbour some 500 Japanese ships awaited evacuation orders. Both castles should have been taken by the numerically superior allies, yet Sach'ŏn brought slaughter to more than 30,000 Chinese soldiers, and Konishi Yukinaga's defence of Sunch'ŏn again showed that the Chinese were brave but less than adept at scaling walls with ladders or siege machines, and they paid another heavy price. Even so, the final victory was Yi Sunsin's, as his ships destroyed the Japanese vessels attempting to escape the Sunch'ŏn trap. But in the Noryang strait opposite Namhae island he was killed by a bullet, a bitter-sweet but fitting end to a distinguished and active military career. Ironically, his invisible rival Hideyoshi had gone before him on 8m/18d, not heroically in battle, not through any dramatic act on the part of the Koreans or their Chinese allies, but 'peacefully, at home, after a long illness'. His grand escapade, in fact, had never taken him beyond Japan's shores.

Eyewitness accounts give an idea of what all sides had been through. 'Wounded men were abandoned, while those who were not wounded but simply exhausted crawled almost prostrate along the road ... Even men who were normally gallant resembled scarecrows on the mountains and fields because of their fatigue, and were indistinguishable from the dead.' After any savagely fought war, survivors declare 'never again'; yet one day, Koreans and Chinese *would* endure similar agonies as they fought side by side. A Chinese report from Korea in 1953 recorded: 'Our soldiers frequently starved. They ate cold food, and some had only a few potatoes in two days. They were unable to maintain their physical strength for combat; the wounded could not be evacuated.' It is tempting, indeed, to see parallels between aspects of the *Imjin Waeran* ('Black Dragon Japanese Struggles') of 1592–8 and the Korean War of 1950–53: China confronting its enemies on Korean soil; the swift and devastating marching of armies up and down the country; the suffering inflicted on the land, the people and the buildings; the terrifying use of 'human wave' battle tactics by the Chinese; the barbarity of soldiers on both sides; the futile peace negotiations in which Korean interests, if represented at all, were subordinated to those of other combatants; the long-lasting psychological trauma that each war induced. Of course, history never does really repeat itself. In the seventeenth century recovery seemed to come quite quickly: the country had escaped the colonization Hideyoshi dreamed of and the partition he proposed to China, and trade and diplomacy were soon restored. Post-1953, the Korean peninsula appeared to fare worse. But things would never be the same again after either war.

The Chosŏn population, which had shot up from 5.5 million in 1392 to perhaps 14 million in the sixteenth century (at the end of which the English, by way of comparison, numbered some 4 million souls), is said to have slumped to around 11 million by the mid-seventeenth. This may in fact reflect the loss of census records during the war, but destruction had engulfed palaces and hovels alike, and disease and despair followed. In 1624 a *yangban* rebel leader, Yi Kwal, drove King Injo out of Seoul, and three years later a fresh wave of invaders, the Manchus, marched in to break up the Korean-Chinese alliance and demand Chosŏn allegiance. Injo's prevarication brought them back in 1636. Most of the court fled to Kanghwa, but the king and Crown Prince Sohyŏn, unable to escape from the southern fortress outside Seoul, knelt in the snow and acknowledged Manchu suzerainty. Manchu preoccupation with their coming invasion of China meant that the kingdom was spared a repetition of its worst experiences with the Mongols; but the fact that this time the Ming were in no position to help prompted the *yangban* to re-evaluate the Middle Kingdom as a default source of protection for their own nation's interests. Some did remain steadfast in their loyalty to China; some opted to reinterpret their Neo-Confucian inheritance in a Korean context; and some, witnessing the spiritual and intellectual novelties introduced by Jesuit missionaries in China, decided that Catholicism and European science could serve their country too. (Ironically, it was Prince Sohyŏn who brought books on Western learning back from Beijing in 1644 after serving a period as a hostage.) Its evident victory against Hideyoshi notwithstanding, the position of the Ming dynasty too was undermined. Although the Koreans had provided its armies with food and horses during the wars, the cost of an unprecedentedly high level of support for a tributary contributed to its economic decline, and the losses endured by its top-quality north-eastern army units encouraged the Manchus in their war preparations: like Korea, China still had more battling and suffering to come. Peace did at last settle on Japan, and when Tokugawa Ieyasu (1542–1616) established his family's rule he satisfied a long craving for stability. Japanese soldiers, already inured to unspeakable horrors after centuries of civil war and merciless killing, had even so described Korean battle areas as a manifestation of hell. That their compatriots stood to gain from new skills brought to Japan by the many artisans taken there as prisoners, especially ceramic craftsmen, must have come as scant consolation.

THE KINGLY WAY II

The seventeenth and eighteenth centuries were a golden period for monarchy worldwide. They had their victims (Kwanghae [Korea] forced into abdication, 1623; Charles [England] beheaded, 1649; Louis [France] guillotined, 1793), but their luminaries shine out the more significantly in contrast – Louis XIV and XV, George II and III, Peter and Catherine of Russia, Kangxi and Qianlong of China. Korea, too, could boast two outstanding kings. If Yŏngjo (r. 1724–76) and Chŏngjo (r. 1776–1800) could not share contemporary rulers' taste for empire-building, they could nevertheless participate fully in an age of brilliant cultural creativity, even extravagance.

After an uneasy start (in 1728 Yi Inchwa led Soron extremists in an unsuccessful rebellion against the Noron-dominated government), Yŏngjo's was the longest reign in all Korean history. The king, showing an evidently genuine interest in the lives of ordinary people, would go to meet them at the palace gates, and visit the Chongno market to listen to merchants' stories. Concern for the poor and the abandonment of too much agricultural land underlay the introduction of a grain-loan system and the optimistically named Kyunyŏkpŏp ('Equal Tax Law') measure in 1750. The halving of the cloth tax, used to finance the army, was welcome, but the measure had only limited success because the yangban's traditional tax exemption meant that farmers now had to shoulder the burden of an extra harvest levy. Determined to rid the court of the political feuding and personal animosities that had marred his father's, Sukchong's, reign, Yŏngjo lambasted and lectured factional leaders, erected a stele honouring t'angp'yŏng '[peaceful] harmony' at the Sŏnggyun-gwan Confucian Academy and closed down some 300 unauthorized sŏwŏn for promoting partisan politics. He allowed the Noron to consolidate power that they would never again lose; in return, they accepted his demand that there should be no victimization of the Southerners, though acute rivalry did persist. It promised so well; so it is ironic that nowadays Yŏngjo's own intransigence is blamed for splitting the Noron into Dogmatists and Realists, and sad that the explanation for this links him in the minds of many people with a story of cruelty and death rather than with efforts to alleviate suffering. The issue concerned his treatment of his son, Changhŏn (1735–1762), who grew up to be a severe disappointment to his father. In accordance with custom, he was nominated regent when he was married in 1749 at the age of fifteen. It should have been auspicious, but in the later words of his wife, the Lady Hyegyŏng, 'it was a sad, sad day'. By 1759 his eccentric behaviour had become so unacceptable that Yŏngjo replaced him as heir apparent with his grandson, Changhŏn's son, rendering Changhŏn's titles of crown prince and regent all but empty. Thereafter Changhŏn went from bad to worse, drinking heavily, falling into fits of uncontrollable violence, wandering the city streets, bringing prostitutes into the palace and killing anyone who displeased him, until he was eventually deemed by the king and his physicians to be mad. When he refused to take poison, his father had him shut up in a rice chest, where he died in agony after eight days in the sun. Members of the Noron were divided, the Dogmatists approving and the Realists secretly criticizing the lengths that the king had gone to in defence of the succession. JaHyun Kim Haboush's view is that a modern psychoanalyst might interpret the behaviour of Changhŏn – or Crown Prince Sado ('Pondering Grief') as he was quickly renamed by a now remorseful Yŏngjo – as reaction against paternal rejection, when as a child he was denied regular access to his father in accordance with Neo-Confucian concepts of princely upbringing.

If Yŏngjo's memory is tarnished by this story, that of his grandson King Chŏngjo shines all the brighter because of it. Concerned for the welfare of the poor, he distributed grain to the most needy, accepted their petitions, tried to protect abandoned children and abolished the office that hunted runaway slaves. (His ambition to abolish slavery altogether was still unfulfilled when he died at the age of 49. Its defenders in Korea were as entrenched as William Wilberforce was finding them in the Western world.) According to a memorial by Minister Pak Chega (1750–1815), he would 'consult even such lowly people as grass and reed cutters' in the event of trouble. By encouraging improvements to dams and irrigation he helped stimulate food production and the value of cash crops. Known as a fair judge, he had the national law code revised in 1784. Periodic orders for parties and gifts honouring the over-sixties, -seventies and -eighties showed his interest in the elderly, and caring for his own sick grandfather (and suffering badly himself from boils) deepened his knowledge of medicine. Admitting the popularity of Buddhism, he approved the building and rebuilding of temples, though still not within the walls of Seoul. He even founded one himself, Yŏngju-sa, near Suwŏn, a hint of moral and spiritual turmoil in the mind of one who was not just a diligent Neo-Confucian but the exemplar par excellence of its principal virtue, filial piety. In the course of his reign Chŏngjo paid 70 processional visits to royal tombs dotted around Kyŏnggi province, and as they totted up we begin to see how obsessed he was with trying to expunge his own sense of guilt at his father's death. In 1789 he re-buried him at a geomantically auspicious site on Mount Hwa, south of Seoul. To guard it – and to strengthen his own position against rival political factions – he began to build a new castle-city, Hwasŏng, and when complete he stationed half of his new central army, Changyongyŏng ('Stout and Brave Garrison'), in it (Picture Essay 15). He never got round to transferring the whole court there, but he paid annual visits to his father's tomb, staying in a specially built detached palace (*haenggung*) and keeping a check on the monks' performance of rites for his father's soul at Yŏngju-sa. A royal excursion such as this was a large and expensive undertaking that needed careful planning: a detailed picture of the visit of 1795, on which Chŏngjo also took his widowed mother to celebrate her 60th birthday, shows a procession of more than 6,100 people and 1,400 horses.

In his award-winning novel *Everlasting Empire* (*Yŏngwŏnhan chekuk*), Yi Inhwa depicts Chŏngjo as a commanding but far from secure figure, a sensitive man forced to plot and intrigue to keep control of his feuding ministers; anxious, like Yŏngjo, to harmonize their rival factions and, like the *sirhak* scholars, to modernize his country, yet convinced of the truth of its Neo-Confucian heritage and unsympathetic to the Catholic converts who associated with *sirhak* within the Pukhak ('Northern Learning') group; a king rumoured to have died by a poisoner's hand. Actually he probably had skin cancer, but what undoubtedly fuelled the regicide theory was the fact that his sudden death followed immediately after he had taken a leaf out of the Chinese Son of Heaven's manual by proclaiming himself the earthly embodiment of the Heavenly Principle, thereby affirming his dedication to the concept of benevolent despotism. T'oegye's interpretation of the *Book of History* had said that such a ruler could understand the past, anticipate the future and govern the present in accordance with Heaven's will, and the fearsomely scholarly Chŏngjo was devoted to restoring the primacy of the ancient Confucian Classics. To the Dogmatists, who preferred Yulgŏk's concept of the sage king working alongside his scholarly ministers, this implicit downgrading of orthodoxy as embodied in the works of Zhu Xi might have been the last straw. Throughout Chŏngjo's reign they had filled most of the top government posts, the

15 Hwasŏng fortress

Hwasŏng fortress, Suwŏn, Kyŏnggi province.

Construction of the castle at Hwasŏng began on the slopes of P'aldal ('Eight Directions') Mountain in the first moon of 1794 and was completed in the eighth moon of 1796. It was, in fact, an expansion of the 340-roomed detached palace of 1789 into a fortified township of 5.75 square kilometres, now containing 576 palace rooms, gardens and pavilions, altars, military garrisons, an archery range and home farms to keep the inhabitants fed and comfortable in the event of siege. Hwasŏng means 'Flowery City', and it was also known as Susŏng ('City of Trees'), both names indicating the pleasant place it was intended to be as a residence for a court that, as it turned out, never fully arrived. Background research was carried out in the royal library to compare Chinese and Japanese construction methods with early Korean castle-building. Final details of the construction work under the direction of Ch'oe Chegong and Cho Simtae were recorded in the nine-volume *Hwasŏng songyuk ŭigwe*. It reveals that 70,000 workmen were employed, and were rewarded with rice, beans and medicines. They included 642 stonemasons, 295 plasterers, 335 carpenters and 11,820 decorators. The stone and brick walls were designed by Chŏng Yagyong, whose interest in Western machinery, learned in China, stood the builders in good stead. He is credited with constructing and using the first crane ever seen in Korea.

Soldiers of the Changyongyŏng kept guard from watchtowers and could fire from slit windows. Their stationing at Hwasŏng was not merely a defensive measure. The Military Training Command (Hullyŏn Togam), first established by Yu Sŏngnyŏng during the *Imjin Waeran*, commanded five armies around the capital, including the Royal Guards (Ŏyŏngch'ŏng). Chŏngjo, concerned about the dominance of the Dogmatist group among its officers in Seoul, purged them; he replaced the Royal Guards with an enlarged Inner Palace Guard, and created a new 20,000-strong command at Hwasŏng, a personal response to a potential military challenge to his authority.

Today, close by the mausoleum that Chŏngjo built for Prince Sado, are those of Lady Hyegyŏng and of Chŏngjo himself with his wife. The castle was extensively damaged during the Japanese colonial period, but rebuilding began in 1996 and is scheduled for completion by 2010. Tourists can still walk the walls of the city, which bears the modern name Suwŏn ('Watery Fields') and is a UNESCO World Heritage Site.

only Southerner to hold high position being Ch'oe Chegong (Pon'am, 1720–1799). Now, perhaps, they saw their power in danger of slipping away.

THE ARTIST'S CALLING

The Dogmatists saw their Sinocentric world outlook challenged by *sirhak* ideas and their political and economic security threatened by Yŏngjo's and Chŏngjo's reformist measures. Take the traditional Neo-Confucian dislike of commerce, for example. The central market that Xu Jing had come across in Kaesŏng had evolved into Six Licensed Shops (*yuk ŭijŏn*) in early Chosŏn Seoul: in return for rent paid in goods, the government leased premises in its main street, Chongno, to merchants dealing in thread, silk, cotton cloth, ramie and hemp cloth, fish and paper. As money spoke, independent traders began to challenge the authorities and rival the licensed shopkeepers. In the seventeenth century, when fiscal policy shifted away from collection in kind and the need for currency increased, even some *yangban* families saw the opportunity for profit, shook off their suspicion of trade and forged insider deals with these authorized monopolists. More people became town-dwellers, education expanded and merchants traversed the country with essentials and luxuries. Book sales rose. Those printed with metal type were too expensive for ordinary folk, and cheaper plates of wood or clay were used for titles in popular demand, especially love stories. The *sirhak* advocate Pak Chega memorialized in favour of greater maritime trade in 1786 so that 'books and pictures from all over the world might be procured, and thus the obstinate and narrow-minded views of our local scholars might be shattered without attacking them directly'. Wholesale and retail marketing developed, and guilds were formed. In 1762 Yŏngjo's government removed some of the licensed traders' privileges, and in 1791 Chŏngjo approved a further boost to private commerce with the Commercial Equalization Act. Three market areas were now permitted in Seoul, in Chongno and inside the great East and South Gates, and provincial towns large and small also boasted regular markets. *Yangban* families with links to the old monopolists started to lose out, and began to associate with craftsmen like furniture makers, seal-carvers, jewellers and weavers, who were also breaking free of earlier controls and producing new ranges of artefacts for private buyers. In the markets, commoners clamoured for cheap and colourful examples of folk arts to brighten their homes.

The cultural profile of the age was inevitably affected by all of this. It was not only private *yangban* patronage that encouraged wider manufacturing of craft goods, but the court too, with its splendid rituals, banquets and receptions. According to JaHyun Kim Haboush, it saw itself as the true inheritor of the 'spiritual heirship to the now defunct Ming imperial house', a claim that, even if it was too impertinent to express in so many words, was hinted at by the appearance in throne rooms of screens painted with the sun, moon and five peaks, symbolic of the ruler's sacred power. At any rate, it was a piece of self-deception that had to be lived up to, *vide*, for example, the swift order for the replacement of ritual instruments when they were destroyed by fire in 1744. But delusion or not, it did not simply result in the aping of Chinese cultural features. Both Yŏngjo and Chŏngjo encouraged *sirhak* ambitions, the former by commissioning Hong Ponghan's great ency-clopedia *Tongguk munhŏn pigo* ('Korean Reference Materials'), the lat-ter by setting up the Kyujang-gak Library and Research Centre in the Kyŏngbok Palace. (We are reminded of Kangxi's research academy, the Meng Yang Chai ['Studio for Receiving Cultivation'], and George III's great book-collecting habit.) Here Chŏngjo personally taught young scholars. His own writings, all hundred or so volumes of them, may not have occupied much space amid the 100,000 in the entire collection, but they showed his devotion to the classics and his interest in law, medical science and military arts. He was also more than competent as an artist and calligrapher. What he did not approve of, however, as a dedicated classicist, was the lighter, less allusive style of writing adopt-ed by Pak Chiwŏn (Yŏnam, 1731–1805) in *Yŏrha ilgi* ('Jehol Diary'). This record of Pak's visit to Beijing with an embassy in 1780 reflected the intellectual curiosity of the *sirhak* scholar. For some it represents the beginning of modern Korean literature, though others see this in the *Biography of Hong Kiltong* (*Hong-giltong-jŏn*), reputedly the work of Hŏ Kyun (1569–1618).

The cultural parameters of the *yangban*, though still fixed on Chinese models, were expanding. From studios like those of Chŏng Ch'ŏl (Songgang, 1536–1594) and Yun Sŏndo (Kosan, 1587–1671) came *sijo*, three-line poems that were ideal for evoking Koreans' love of nature and the whole gamut of their emotions. The first major anthol-ogy, however, *Ch'ŏnggu yŏngŏn* ('Songs of the Green Hills', 1728) was compiled by a *chungin* (see p. 154), Kim Ch'ŏnt'aek, and was followed by Kim Sujang's *Haedong kayo* ('Songs of Korea', 1763). The brush, hitherto the archetypal symbol of the invisible cords tying scholars to their Chinese sources of inspiration, now became an instrument expressing distinctive Korean aspirations. Female writers tried out the potential of *han'gŭl*, and painters discovered real-life subjects on their own doorsteps.

The voice followed the example of the wrist, and *yangban* with time to spare mastered the singing of long and difficult Korean songs, *kasa* and *kagok*. I looked for visual evidence of Chosŏn music-making on a research trip to Korea in 1983, when it became clear that although it was not a subject of particular interest to painters (less so than to those in China, for example), when it did appear its style and content were likely to be distinctively local as well as stereotypically Chinese. Surviving examples of early Korean painting of any kind are extremely rare. For this, Hideyoshi's men frequently get the blame, though pictures, of course, may have perished in fires at any time over the centuries, and others may yet turn up in tombs or be awaiting recognition in private collections or antique shops. What we know about Korean artists of the Koryŏ and early Chosŏn, however, is that they strongly admired and imitated Chinese painting styles. An P'yŏng (1418–1453) alone had a great collection of works by Chinese masters going right back to Gu Kaizhi, including 26 pieces of calligraphy by Zhao Mengfu and 17 pictures by Guo Xi. An Kyŏn's (b. 1418) still-extant *Dream Journey to Peach Blossom Spring* clearly reflects his admiration for the great Song dynasty landscapist. Pictures of the seventeenth century and onwards are not in such short supply, and among them I found music illustrated in predictable settings, scholars playing the zither, ox-herds playing flutes, performances appreciated across water or in the moonlight: all standard Chinese stuff. Chosŏn artists were adept at producing paintings virtually indistinguishable from those of their Chinese role models. Those engaged by the Court Painting Office, the Tohwa-sŏ, produced such things to order. Though few in number – Yŏngjo doubled their ranks to 30 in 1746 – some of them still rank among Korea's best painters. Most were poorly paid and looked down on by court officials, who as amateur artists themselves took pride in following the more individualistic style of the Chinese literati. In fact, the Tohwa-sŏ was not as stylistically constrained as the Imperial Painting Academy was in China. Its members were versatile enough to paint in both Northern (Academy) and Southern (literati) Chinese styles, and to produce Korean *sehwa* (New Year paintings) depicting symbols of longevity, the Daoist Immortals, mythical guardian figures and the ever-popular Korean tiger. One of the greatest Korean painters of all time was Chŏng Sŏn (Kyŏmjae, 1676–1759). Although he was an excellent landscape painter in the Chinese style, Kyŏmjae's reputation as the most influential artist of early modern times really stems from his innovative move to break away from idealistic landscapes (*kwannyŏm sansu*) and create a distinctive technique for rendering the actual sights he saw as he left the Tohwa-sŏ to take up an official post at Ch'ŏngha,

North Kyŏngsang province. Through his fifties he developed 'true-view landscapes' (*chin'gyŏng sansu*), making bold use of chopped axe-cut strokes and dots to portray granite outcrops, rushing waterfalls and sunlit glades amid thick forests, set against a background of razor-sharp mountain peaks (Picture Essay 16). He painted locations close to home outside Seoul, high up in the Diamond Mountains, and across on the east coast. His pioneering approach was in keeping with the inspiration of the *sirhak* movement, and where he led other artists followed, in Korea and, later, Japan. Not all could really capture the essence of the Korean landscape as successfully as he, but one who did, and managed like Kyŏmjae to execute both Chinese and Korean styles, was the scholar-artist Kang Sehwang (P'yoam, 1713–1791), whose album of sixteen *Scenic Spots around Songdo* (Kaesŏng) adopted an even more impressionistic style than Kyŏmjae's.

Moved as I was by Kyŏmjae's landscapes, what caught my attention was a ten-panel screen attributed to him, recording the magistrate of Tongnae county greeting Japanese envoys at Pusan. Musicians accompanied the official procession and provided the entertainment in the Guest House outside the walls of the Japan House (*Waegwan*). Painted some time between 1710 and 1758, this kind of detailed documentary record was in the same vein as the informative album leaves illustrating accounts of banquet entertainments given for the court's Society of the Elderly and Brave (*Kiyonghoe*), a kind of over-seventies club honouring distinguished officials that originated in King T'aejo's Office for the Venerable Aged (*Kirosŏ*). Several well-preserved and colourful examples of this art form date from the sixteenth century, and are the forerunners of the *ŭigwe* books and screens seen in Picture Essay 22. They clearly illustrate the size and range of musical ensembles and show the perennial popularity of masked-dance entertainment, especially the *Ch'ŏyong* dance sequence.

Kyŏmjae was not the only artist renowned for painting in both Chinese and Korean styles. Asked who was Korea's greatest painter, most Koreans would surely name Kim Hongdo (Tanwŏn, 1745–post-1814). Like Kyŏmjae, he was a member of the Tohwa-sŏ, until he so impressed King Chŏngjo with the portrait he painted of him that he was made a county magistrate. And for him, as for Kyŏmjae in similar circumstances, that marked the beginning of a kind of enlightenment, for although he was a first-rate painter of landscapes and flower-and-bird studies in the best of Chinese traditions, of Daoist Immortals and Buddhist deities (he is said to have provided the altar painting of Buddha still to be seen at Yŏngju-sa), and of court receptions on the grand scale, it was the people he met in the countryside doing ordinary

16 Chŏng Sŏn, *Manp'okdong*

Buddhists and Daoists in China and Korea identified particular mountain areas in both countries as holy. In these remote, difficult areas they built monasteries, temples and hermitages to be close to the abode of the Immortals, and poets, philosophers and artists sought inspiration in their beauty and solitude. The Diamond Mountains (Kŭmgang-san) earned their name because their myriad vertical peaks evoked the image of the diamond-hard Buddhist thunderbolt (*vajra*).

Artists attuned to the ideas of the Southerners' faction in the mid-Chosŏn period took the view that a picture should show the inner spirit rather than the outer form of a subject, and tended to paint in an idealized style. Those of the Noron persuasion preferred realism. Chŏng Sŏn (Kyŏmjae) could do both, and painted the Diamond Mountains many times both from imagination and from life. The title of this album leaf, which he wrote and signed above the centre at the left of the picture, literally means 'Ten Thousand Waterfalls Ravine', and is the name given to a famous spot where many rivers and streams converge. Needle-sharp peaks jostle for position in the distance, a feature of Kŭmgang scenery that folk artists loved to exaggerate. The dark mass looming above the lighter granite column in the centre of the picture takes its name from the blue crane, which is said to live here. The word *dong* carries connotations of habitation by fairy-like creatures, rather as 'grottoes' does in English. Something has caught the attention of the two scholars standing with their servant on a sloping rock, and they point towards the nearby grove of eight pine trees, but any conversation must be difficult against the sound of the rushing streams pouring down into the whirlpool to their right.

The poem in the top-right corner, chosen by Kyŏmjae to complement the subject, is by the great Chinese artist Gu Kaizhi (AD 344–405?):

A thousand cliffs compete in elegance,
Innumerable streams strive to flow,
Grass and trees thrive luxuriantly,
Clouds well up in coloured splendour [trans. Roderick Whitfield]

Its calligraphic style perfectly matches the brushwork of the picture, and creates a sense of an essentially vertical composition made up of many horizontal strokes, the yin and the yang in harmony. T-shaped trees and dotted clumps of vegetation are characteristic of Kyŏmjae's style, with rapid, rhythmic strokes conveying a strong sense of energy, dark wash suggesting the great bulk of rock faces, and an overall bluish wash adding mistiness to the scene.

Chŏng Sŏn, *Manp'okdong*, undated, ink and light colours on paper, 33 × 22 cm.

jobs, like washing clothes, tiling a roof, ploughing a field or teaching a class of schoolboys, whose pictures would cause him to be so honoured by modern generations. Nor was it all work: he painted popular forms of entertainment, too: a pair of wrestlers, a band of musicians and a dancing boy, and a rather untidy scholar with *pip'a* lute and a somewhat bemused expression. In Tanwŏn we see the sudden maturing of a genre-painting tradition that had first appeared on the walls of tombs in the Three Kingdoms period, visual evidence of a great artist's pride in being Korean.

Much the same may be said of his contemporary Sin Yunbŏk (Hyewŏn, 1758–*c*. 1820), from whose brush, incidentally, came the most careful and detailed study to date of a *kŏmun'go* zither, being strung by a courtesan. Hyewŏn's fame rests more exclusively on his genre paintings, especially those concerned with entertainment in its broadest sense, from the whirling excitement of female sword dancers to a pair of gentlemen dallying with *kisaeng* beside a lily pond, even to young monks spying on girls bathing in a stream. On the whole, Tanwŏn found his subjects among the *yangban*, and daringly poked fun at them, especially where sexual mores were concerned. The lifting of a corner of the curtain around the personal life of the straight-laced Neo-Confucian gentry delights us, who in today's moral climate see nothing erotic in the *kisaeng* leaning over the side of a boat, lifting her rear towards the gentleman standing behind her. But eighteenth-century society, however familiar it was with such behaviour, feigned shock to see it so advertised, and Tanwŏn was expelled from the Tohwa-sŏ. The kind of occasions the *yangban* preferred to be recorded were those that celebrated the auspicious events in a man's life and career. Most important of these were his first birthday, coming of age, marriage, passing the *chinsa* (doctorate) degree, appointment to an official post and 60th birthday. These, along with pictures of the subject with his children and grandchildren, or on his wedding anniversary, often formed the topic of screen panels, and were known as *p'yŏngsaeng-do* ('whole life pictures'). A formal portrait was needed for placing in a memorial hall alongside his ancestors' tablets, but *p'yŏngsaeng-do* were not at all formal, and so many circumstantial details of surroundings, bystanders and the like went into them that they may be classified as a type of genre painting. In them, for example, we see how, for all their Sinicized cultural elitism, the *yangban* enjoyed the acrobatics, masked drama and puppetry provided by *kwang-dae* performers.

II

A Century of
Insecurity

CHAPTER FIVE

The Hermit Kingdom, 1800–64: Tradition at Work

This chapter illustrates aspects of the way of life that Korea's leaders were anxious to protect, as the century wore on and unwelcome signs of challenge to their own interpretation and guardianship of it appeared.

SOCIETY AND CULTURE

Chŏngjo had no time for Catholicism and no more had any of the next three kings, Sunjo (r. 1800–34), Hŏnjong (r. 1834–49) and Ch'ŏlchong (r. 1849–64). At the turn of the century several thousand Christian converts in and around Seoul bore witness to six years of undercover work by a Chinese missionary, Father Zhou Wenmu. It was an era when ghastly prison conditions, excruciating torture and legal execution ended the lives of people in many parts of the world, either for daring to contradict the ideologies of the ruling class or for much lesser misdemeanours: think of France at the time, for example. The Korean response to unorthodox and potentially disruptive beliefs was no exception, and conditions in its jails were indescribably awful. A few Catholics had already died for their faith before the first widespread persecution took place in 1801, when 300 martyrs suffered ritual execution as a warning to others. Zhou Wenmu was among them. The twelve-year-old king Sunjo's marriage in 1802 brought some relief, since his new wife's clan, the Kims from Andong, had already been touched by *sirhak* ideas, and to exploit this half-opening a French bishop and two priests were moved from South-East Asia, the first Western clergy assigned to Korea. By the time they slipped separately across the frontier from Manchuria in 1836, however, Sunjo had died, and early in Hŏnjong's reign the Chos of P'ungyang got the better of the Andong Kims and revived the persecutions. In 1839 all three Frenchmen were executed, along with at least 140 Korean converts. The establishment that hunted Catholics down was not concerned about protecting their souls from heresy. Rather, it saw them as traitors.

They had (unsuccessfully) sought French military protection in 1801, and their shocking behaviour in denouncing the Neo-Confucian ancestral rites as idolatrous, even smashing up the tablets honouring their family spirits, was an affront to upper-class beliefs. This foreign ideology that proclaimed its recognition of individualism and promised salvation through self-denial and sacrifice threatened both the political and the social order. (Way back, Buddhism had faced the same accusations from Confucians in China and Korea, but Buddhism now had a long tradition behind it and was tolerated – outside Seoul at least – for the sake of its communal roles and functions [Picture Essay 17].)

The *yangban* class, the combined 'two groups' (Ch. *liang ban*) of civil and military power, had taken shape in the late Koryŏ and early Chosŏn period, and by mid-Chosŏn was synonymous with political and social leadership of the country. It was distinguished by education in the Chinese Classics, a lifestyle worthy of the Chinese literati and pride in the genealogies of its member clans. To make sacrificial offerings to their ancestors was an important duty for senior males, and the Catholic stance seemed to represent defiance of their authority. Many of them were rich landowners. They were exempt from regular military and corvée duties and paid less tax than others. To their inferiors they represented unimaginable privilege; they were 'stars in heaven'. They themselves, however, were only too conscious that posts could be lost and shame and poverty encountered through political disfavour, disputes over ethical standards, intrigue and slander, or downright incompetence. At least they were spared the threat of rivalry from beneath: upward mobility into their class was virtually impossible barring exceptional royal favour. Even the small but significant class of *chungin* ('middle men') functionaries could not anticipate it. These included the court's architects, interpreters and artists, the magistrate's tax gatherers and accountants, the community's doctors and astronomers. The *yangban* depended on their skills. They did not hesitate to take *chungin* girls into service, although any offspring resulting from mixed unions were labelled *sŏŏl*, stigmatized and denied *yangban* rights and privileges. Some *chungin* boasted family genealogies of their own and had passed their own examinations (*chapkwa*), but the fact that their education was in practical subjects rather than the classics demeaned their status.

The bulk of the population were *sangmin* ('common people'). They were the food growers, the street traders, the miners, the builders, the soldiers, those identified in Confucian theory as the foundation of the state yet still to see much benefit from it. They were not, however, the lowest members of society. Into the sub-class of *ch'ŏnmin* ('base people') fell public entertainers (like *kwangdae*), prostitutes, chair-carriers, butchers, night-soil collectors, even shamans. And last of all came the slaves. Korea had the highest percentage of slaves of any country in East Asia: a census register surviving from 1663 so defined a massive three-quarters of the population of Seoul, over half its households. (Don Clark has pointed out to me that the percentage outside Seoul, where the figure was inflated by government slaves, was more likely around 30.) Known as *nobi*, they or their ancestors had usually fallen into this status either as captives in war or through felony, or even voluntarily because they had seen financial advantages in it. They had, naturally, lost their freedom, and were hereditarily consigned either to be distributed by the king as bounty for loyal service or to be bought and sold as chattels. There were public slaves and private slaves, fulfilling a wide variety of jobs in offices, post-stations, schools, *yangban* households and farms. No wonder Chŏngjo's aim of abolishing slave status, implemented in the case of government slaves in 1801, had ruffled the feathers of the Dogmatists. Yet liable as they were to suffer ill-treatment, slaves did sometimes manage to find opportunities for self-advancement. Some had slaves of their own; some even owned land. It was sometimes hard to spot the difference between slaves and *sangmin*, and by the time the Kabo reforms officially liberated them in 1895 the enslaved residents of Seoul had fallen to around 5 per cent of its inhabitants.

Neo-Confucian prejudice reinforced discrimination against women. As in other pre-modern civilizations, the birth of a girl was often, though not invariably, a cause of disappointment. The proper place for a woman in any respectable Korean home was out of sight, in the inner quarters (*anch'ae*). This is where she was consigned at the age of ten or twelve, perhaps with some basic education, and prior to being married off by arrangement. When this happened she left her natal home and went to live with her new husband in his. She had learned that she must be submissive to her father, her husband and her in-laws, and only when she herself attained the status of a matriarch could she look forward with any assurance to being treated with honour. Cases did occur of women being loved and respected for what they were and even making names for themselves; but it is notable that among the renowned writers, artists and musicians of the Chosŏn dynasty very few were women. A man's principal wife (*ch'ŏ*) might take some satisfaction from supervising the family finances and domestic arrangements, managing children's basic upbringing and servants' behaviour, and carrying out rituals to the household spirits; secondary wives (*ch'ŏp*) could expect no such responsibilities. The world beyond the

17 Detail from a nectar ritual painting

Detail from a wall-painting, 1865, Yŏngam-sa, Seoul.

Ceremonies assisting the rebirth into the Western Paradise of souls otherwise fated through bad karma or sudden and unfortunate death to become wandering spirits were the Buddhist equivalent of Neo-Confucian ancestor worship: there could be no greater proof of filial piety than to aid the migration of a relative's soul into Paradise. Large crowds specially enjoyed the music, dancing and substantial banquets sponsored by the rich that accompanied these 'nectar rituals' (*namjangsa*). Early Chosŏn kings might have driven Buddhism from court and capital, and *yangban* might further their family interests by observing Neo-Confucian etiquette, but outside Seoul Buddhism still crossed social barriers, providing services for commoners and nobility alike. Yŏngam Temple, lying just outside the West Gate of Seoul, was patronized by local people and city residents.

Inside the main prayer hall of a temple, usually on its right wall in the form of a large painted mural or hanging banner, might be seen a 'sweet dew painting' (*kamno-jŏng*). It was, says Kang Woobang, 'the most characteristically Korean and perhaps the most widely produced type of religious painting' in the eighteenth century, and examples continued to be produced throughout the nineteenth century and into the twentieth. They show, at the top, the deities watching over the life of the temple; in the centre, a hungry ghost or ghosts observing the performance of the rite; and at the bottom, scenes related to the life and death of people deserving this particular form of salvation. They are full of detail about social activities: a religious procession winds its way towards the temple gate, conch shells tooting; stall-keepers haggle over prices in the marketplace, voices raised; children watch acrobats tightrope walking; adults shout encouragement to a *p'ansori* singer; a shaman dances herself into a trance; a magistrate supervises the beating of a criminal; soldiers fight battles; a traveller is attacked by a tiger; a woman gives birth; *kisaeng* entertain customers; a farmer ploughs a field. Whatever the artistic quality of these Buddhist genre pictures, their value to the social historian is never in doubt. Figures in Korean dress, rather than the Chinese styles usually seen in literati painting, indicate a growing awareness of Korea's own cultural integrity.

The detail seen opposite comes from the lower section of a 'sweet dew picture', and is painted in bold, primary colours with a kind of *naif* exuberance. Monks are chanting from sutra books; nuns dance to the clash of cymbals and banging of drums; a line of men and women crosses from left to right in the foreground, carrying baskets of what may be food offerings for the temple; waving aloft at the very bottom of the picture are the feet of an acrobat crossing a tightrope on his hands, apparently unnoticed on the other side of a hedge by three men sitting deep in conversation and a group of farmers wearing straw hats.

home, that of work and socializing, was male territory, and even in rural areas, where the nature of the village economy meant that women played a fuller part in communal life, they had to acknowledge many no-go areas. For instance, they were unable to play in the farmers' bands that accompanied so many religious and social events in the annual calendar.

Clothing was a matter of pride to people whatever their class. Respectable women wore a long, high-waisted dress, a short tight jacket with left side crossed over the right and tied with a tape below the shoulder, thin under-trousers and soft shoes with turned-up toes. The effect was colourful and elegant, and modern women in both the ROK and DPRK still like to dress up for special occasions in a version of this *hanbok* costume. Girls were spared the cruel Chinese custom of foot-binding, but opportunities for them to leave the home and encounter the outside world were nonetheless few. *Yangban* women with occasion to travel did so within a closely curtained box chair. *Sangmin* wives who had to move around to follow their trade covered themselves with a *changot*, a long coat worn over the head that concealed their features. For his everyday wear, a scholar put on loose trousers tied at the ankles, a long collar-less white coat with wide sleeves, and soft cloth boots; for formal duties and court appearances there was a range of heavier, coloured gowns bearing symbols of rank. Korean officials followed the Chinese practice of wearing 'Mandarin squares' (*hyungbae*), embroidered panels on the chest and back that indicated their status in the civil or military hierarchy. What happened above the neck was almost as important as what was worn below it. The capping of a teenage boy as an adult was a vital rite of passage. After the ceremony his hair remained uncut and piled up on his head in a topknot (*sangtu*), of which he was extremely proud. It was kept in place by a tight headband of lacquered horsehair, surmounted by a tall hat of black-lacquered horsehair or split bamboo (and eventually, or so he might hope, an official's winged cap).

For both women and men the style and decoration of headdress constituted a social marker and there were numerous varieties, but for *ch'ŏnmin* women in two ancient and largely hereditary professions dress and headwear were particularly important. These were the *kisaeng* and shamans, and they exercised a power far beyond their status. The prime considerations for a *kisaeng* were sophistication and elegance. She was a courtesan, trained to serve gentlemen at banquets and to entertain them with the arts of conversation, poetry, music and dance, and outdoors with horsemanship and archery skills. She might provide sexual favours, but a *kisaeng* could not be hired like a prostitute. She became a highly valued personal companion, sometimes even a secondary wife in a *yangban* household. Like her superiors she dressed well and wore her long hair bound up in a complicated coiffeur.

The lowly status of the shaman was less ambiguous, yet she could exploit her powers to just as good effect as the *kisaeng*. Strictly speaking, the shaman should have been excluded from the Neo-Confucian environment of the Chosŏn court, but queens and other palace women made recurrent use of her, and her white cowl and rounded black felt or tall red hat decorated with feathers were a familiar enough sight within the palace walls. Like Buddhism, shamanism was patronized by the upper classes and indispensable to the lower. The poor performed their own worship of the household spirits, including those of the kitchen, the privy, the roof and the courtyard, but they looked to the shaman for assistance when their lives were plunged into crisis, as they not infrequently were, by drought, disease and death. She lifted them, too, out of their humdrum routine during the New Year and harvest (*ch'usŏk*) celebrations, events in which the court and *yangban* joined with equal enthusiasm. These and the whole raft of rituals connected with folk religion around which much rural life revolved had changed little since the Three Kingdoms period, and were an essential part of the vibrant, colourful social tapestry. The pair of wooden posts (*changsŭng*) that often stood on either side of the path at the entrance to a village was symbolic of popular beliefs. Crudely carved and painted with faces, they were its tutelary gods, one male, one female, companions in a manner of speaking of the spirits who might inhabit an ancient tree, a dangerous hillside pass or other sacred spots. *Changsŭng* can still occasionally be seen, and a pair of Bronze Age standing stones found at Hwangsŏngni suggests that their origins lie far back in time. The most ubiquitous and prominent folk deity was the *sansin* ('mountain spirit'). Every mountain had one, who was prayed to by travellers, women in childbirth, in fact anyone in need. He was often pictured as a tiger or Daoist-style Immortal, and popular opinion sometimes associated him loosely with the Tan'gun myth.

And if lives were lived in the shadow of shrines dedicated to local gods, they were also in thrall to the lunar and solar calendars. Observance of the New Year came to an end on *taeborum-nal* (1m/15d). It was the end of a fortnight's kite flying, and men – boys, too – made a final show of outdoor energy by staging blazing torch fights. Walking across a bridge on this night was said to give protection against foot diseases in the coming year (though women had to wait until the following night). Lanterns were strung up to celebrate Buddha's birthday on 4m/8d. On *tano* (5m/5d), people would wash their hair, put on summer clothes and follow a centuries-old tradition of giving presents of fans in anticipation of the coming heat. (Earlier in the dynasty large numbers of fans, no doubt beautifully crafted and hand-painted, had been included in official gifts sent from the Korean court to the Ryūkyū kingdom.) Men and boys had dangerous running stone fights against those of neighbouring villages, supposedly to decide which of them would enjoy the better harvest that year. (The Japanese colonial government later put a stop to this custom.) On 7m/7d books and clothes were aired in the sun to counteract summer dampness, while the double ninth (9m/9d) was the time to arrange outdoor parties for old people in the pleasant autumn sun or to go viewing chrysanthemums. Farming activities were planned according to climatic expectations for 24 fortnightly periods (*chŏlgi*) through the year. So, the fifteen days around 4 February were *ipch'un* ('beginning of spring'); those around 21 May were entitled *soman* ('fattening grain'); on 8 October *hallo* ('cold dew') could be expected; and doors should be firmly fastened against a fortnight of *taesŏl* ('great snow') by 7 December. On my first visit to South Korea in 1972 I was told that I couldn't go swimming at the end of August because we were now past *ch'osŏ* ('the end of heat'). Since it had been a long hot summer and the temperature outside was still over 30 °C, I got an idea of how compartmentalized life must have been in traditional times.

Festivals were a chance for relaxation and entertainment. Marketplaces resounded to laughter at the familiar butts of satirical humour mocked in masked dance dramas; quieter audiences listened attentively to a performance by the *p'ansori* singer. The origins of this oral tradition, the nearest Korean equivalent to opera, are shrouded in mystery, but written mention of it began to appear once members of the literate classes showed an interest in it, perhaps under *sirhak* influence. One of the earliest references comes in a text by Yu Chinhan (1711–1791), *Kasa Ch'unhyangga ibaekku* ('The Song of Ch'unhyang's Two Hundred Words', 1754). Titles of twelve *p'ansori* stories are known, and of the five still extant and performed today *Ch'unhyang* remains the most popular. The daughter of a *kisaeng*, Ch'unhyang secretly marries the son of a nobleman before he is transferred to Seoul. Despite all manner of improper propositions from the local magistrate she remains faithful to her true love. He subsequently returns as a government inspector, punishes the magistrate and rescues his wife. Ch'unhyang's honour and fidelity were, and still are, qualities much admired in Confucian society. She is one of the nation's greatest lovers and its favourite fictional heroine. A shrine stands to her today in Namwŏn, South Chŏlla, where she was supposedly born in 1675, and the town holds a Ch'unhyang festival. The *p'ansori* singer, who may be either male or female, uses a fan and a handkerchief as props and employs a mixture of narrative and sung passages; the accompanist plays either a *puk* or a *changgo* drum. For both of them a performance is a considerable physical feat. The complete telling of a single story might take as long as eight hours, though shortened versions are permissible for modern audiences. The sung parts are performed in an unnaturally strong voice that requires years of arduous training. The great female singer Kim Sohee (1917–1994) developed her technique by practising for hours on end in front of a roaring waterfall. *P'ansori* was on the *kwangdae* programme of popular entertainments, but as the nineteenth century wore on it successfully crossed the class divide and private performances were sponsored by *yangban* and rich merchant families, until in the twentieth century it also took its place on the indoor, Westernized stage.

Children, and adults too, would wander away from a seemingly never-ending *p'ansori* performance in search of fun and games (*nori*). Games, of course, are no respecters of local or national boundaries, and Korean variants of worldwide favourites such as chess, backgammon, dominoes and fives were played long before the early nineteenth century. The popular East Asian board game of strategy known as *go* in Japan is called *paduk* in Korea and was known in Silla times. The game of pitch pot (*t'uho*), in which competitors aimed to throw arrows or sticks into three bottles from an agreed distance, had been played back in the Three Kingdoms period, and a set of equipment was among the gifts sent to King Yejong by the Chinese court in 1116. It continued to be enjoyed both in and out of court, and was incorporated – in highly stylized fashion – into a court dance performed to the present day. Both children and adults could play *yut*, a board game in which the movement of the counters is determined according to how four sticks or beans fall when thrown in the air. Children had fun spinning tops and jumping on seesaws. For those who still needed to give vent to their energy, tug-of-war contests (*chultarigi*), using enormously thick ropes, were popular; strong men wrestled (Picture Essay 18); and for more personal excitement a session on a Korean swing (*kunettwigi*), traditionally up to 7 metres high, should have been enough to satisfy the most daring. Tests of strength such as these may have had ancient military connections.

Playtime over, people would go home. China, Korea and Japan have been called 'three families under the same roof'. Citizens of all three would find plenty to object to in that description nowadays, but as far as architecture was concerned it was certainly true that they all

18 Kim Hongdo, *Wrestling* (*ssirŭm*)

Kim Hongdo, *Wrestling*, ink and light colours on paper, 27 × 22.7 cm;
Treasure no. 527.

This is one of a series of 25 delightful studies of ordinary men, women
and children at work and at play. We see them tiling a roof, drawing
water from a well, weaving, shoeing a horse, ploughing, threshing,
fishing, horse-riding, suckling a baby, making music and dancing, and
discussing a picture. We find them in a smithy, a village inn, on heavily
laden ferry boats, on country paths, at a village school, and taking an
archery lesson. We sense their concentration and evident satisfaction
(even devious enjoyment in the case of the gentleman spying from
behind his fan on four washerwomen working in a stream, their thin
under-trousers rolled up high above their knees). These little scenes

demonstrate Tanwŏn's empathy for the strength of social gathering and mutual assistance, his mastery of composition and his ability to suit style to subject. He chooses brushwork of fine but firm outlines infilled with thin ink wash, sometimes executed with precision but more often giving the impression, like Western newspaper cartoons, of being dashed off. The Ming artist Wu Wei (1459–1508) had used a similar technique for his amusing *Scenes in the Life of the People* (British Museum), but there is no evidence that Tanwŏn was aware of this work.

Wrestling was an ancient sport, one of a range of martial arts practised during the Chosŏn period. Comparison of Tanwŏn's album leaf with a Koguryŏ tomb mural at Kungnaesŏng, showing two men grappling in combat, suggests that the objective and style of Korean wrestling had changed little over the centuries. The contestants balanced their weight on their forward leg, thrust their chin into their opponent's right shoulder, locked arms into his thigh strap and strove to topple him into touching the ground. It was a slow business, encompassed by ritual and calculated to build up atmosphere. Disagreement about the outcome of a bout was common. Tanwŏn's picture is designed like a wheel, the wrestlers at its hub, the excited spectators round the rim. At the heart there is tension, on the periphery relaxation. The wrestlers have taken off their shoes to give them more grip; some of the spectators have taken off their hats to get more air, thereby revealing their topknots. Cleverly, however, Tanwŏn desists from making the wrestlers the only object of the viewer's attention. Instead, he also draws it to the rice-sweetmeat (*yŏt*) seller standing patiently on the edge of the ring, ignored by the audience while the action goes on but confident of more sales when it is over.

lived under similar roofs, of curved and decorated tiles mounted on complicated wooden bracket support systems. Moreover, from the Tang period onwards China influenced the style, layout and internal decoration of Korean and Japanese buildings. The epitome of the Korean craftsman's admiration for the Chinese model was to be seen in the palaces of Seoul and their furnishings. The early nineteenth-century court used three of the four that survive today, Changdŏk, Unhyŏng and Tŏksu, along with another, Kyŏnghŭi, which was demolished by the Japanese in 1910. (The palace most commonly associated these days with the Chosŏn monarchy, Kyŏngbok, had been King T'aejo's residence and seat of government back in the fourteenth century, but its post-Imjin rebuilding did not begin until 1865.) What modern tourists see as they wander round the sandy courtyards, stare into the lofty audience halls, shadowy ceiling spaces and more intimate residential apartments, and admire the stone platforms, great wooden columns and intricately patterned windows, may bring back memories of what they have already seen in Beijing. When, however, they admire the sets of clay figurines (*chapsang*) lined up along the corner ridges of the roofs, guarding the buildings against fire and evil spirits, and the five-coloured paint system (*tanch'ŏng*) that protects and brightens so much of the woodwork here and in other important buildings, they see ancient crafts that Korean artisans had made their own. Xu Jing had been impressed by *tanch'ŏng* in Kaesŏng back in the twelfth century.

Like the palaces, domestic houses were built on platforms raising them above ground level. They were of timber-frame construction with outer walls that often had to be buttressed with strong poles to prevent collapse under the weight of heavy roofs, and non-load-bearing walls infilled with wattle and plaster. Floors were either wooden, which were cooler in summer, or of cement covered in tough waxed paper, hiding the flues of the *ondol* heating system that Koreans had enjoyed for more than 1,000 years. It gave them a warm surface on which they sat, worked, ate and lay down to sleep between embroidered quilts, as they still do in many a rural community. For the elite, living conditions reflected a more genteel quality of life. They were the ones whose houses boasted tiled roofs, sliding doors and lattice windows. Male accommodation was generally on the south side of the compound, kept separate from the women on the north by servants' quarters. Privacy was counted so essential that every family, rich or poor, preferred to live behind a wall or fence, and later in the century the American missionary Homer Hulbert said that large households had so many compounds that they were 'a veritable labyrinth of numberless gates and alleys'. Today's tourists can wander round a house inside the Changdŏk Palace in Seoul. It was built for King Sunjo in 1827, when, sick and unhappy at widespread discontent among the *sangmin*, he attempted to hand over the reins of government to his son, Prince Ikchong. And in the folk village near Suwŏn they can look inside a reconstructed Chosŏn scholar's study typically furnished in Chinese style. Maxims drawn from the Confucian Classics hang from the walls, extolling virtues such as sincerity, loyalty, altruism and persistence; screens keep draughts and casual observers at bay (Picture Essay 19); books written in Chinese characters are laid on low tables; the writing desk stands ready with brush, inkstone, water dropper and a floral arrangement. Koreans of all classes loved flowers. Not only did they provide colour and scent and attract butterflies and insects to the garden, but they were symbols, too, of hope and virtue, the peony representing prosperity, the chrysanthemum dignity, the orchid frugality, and so on. And while the plants and trees growing in the thinking man's garden stimulated his mind, vegetables grew in the kitchen garden to satisfy his palate. Strict Neo-Confucian households ate in silence, the men in their rooms, the women in theirs. Meals usually consisted of a large bowl of rice, with numerous side dishes of meat, fish and vegetables, and a bowl of soup. A varied diet was eaten, and by the mid-nineteenth century potatoes, sweet potatoes, chilli peppers and tomatoes had been introduced from abroad.

Royalty and the aristocracy liked fine porcelain on their tables and their writing desks. Early in the Chosŏn dynasty even Chinese emperors had collected the beautiful pure white vessels that came from the kilns at Kwangju, outside Seoul, and for Korean *yangban* white symbolized their pride in the dynasty they served and the Neo-Confucian philosophy that underpinned it. (Green, the colour of celadon, had been associated with Buddhism and the unlamented Koryŏ era.) As the centuries passed the taste for monochromes persisted and shades of whiteness varied, but no attempt was made to match the spectacular colours of China's mid-Qing monochromes. The Korean upper classes preferred simplicity. When decoration was applied, subjects were drawn from nature and the human world and might be painted on with underglaze cobalt or iron oxide, producing blue and red designs against a white background. The use of inlay continued. But the emphasis was on restraint and balance rather than the complex polychrome patterns being turned out by so many Chinese and Japanese kilns. Where tableware was concerned, commoners, too, liked muted tones. Vessels were made of coarser clay; patterns were all-over and made by stamping rather than the slow and laborious craft of inlaying; and an overall white slip was incised. This kind of pottery, known as *punch'ŏng*, had a rustic aesthetic of its own, one that

19 An eight-panel screen

Literary and artistic appreciation were hallmarks of the scholar, and respect for Chinese form and style influenced the standards and content of much of his own output. But when it came to painting the screens that furnished homes across the land – both upper and lower class – literati and folk artists alike drew on themes from Korean *minhwa* (folk art) as well as Chinese tradition. Among these were historical events (Yi Sunsin's naval victories being especially popular), hunting scenes, *paekchado* ('hundred-boys pictures') and longevity symbols. One of the most distinctive of these cultural bridges across the class barrier was that known as *ch'aekkori* ('books, etc.'). In Neo-Confucian vein, it depicted the books and furniture in a scholar's study, together with his writing implements and indications of his cultured interests, such as musical instruments, pieces of porcelain and selected antiques. His hat and his pipe might also put in an appearance, and gradually the range of items widened to include other domestic items. Dishes of fruit and vegetables, vases of flowers, goldfish bowls and incense burners, for example, provided opportunities to incorporate ever-popular symbolic meanings. Allusion and decorativeness actually took precedence over realism in this form of art, for one of its intriguing, perhaps even charming, characteristics is its skewed sense of perspective and proportion. This, it has been suggested, may have stemmed from Chinese artists' first attempts to copy Western ideas of perspective introduced by Jesuit painters to the Qing court in the eighteenth century. *Ch'aekkori* was one of King Chŏngjo's favourite types of painting.

An eight-panel screen with *ch'aekkori* decoration, 19th century, ink and colours on paper, 50 × 140 cm.

Japanese and Westerners such as Yanagi Soetsu and Bernard Leach found attractive in the twentieth century and that enables it still to command high prices in international auction houses.

Commoners frequently had to put up with conditions that were, by comparison with *yangban* homes, uncomfortable, cramped, dirty and unhealthy. Under the thatched roofs of *sangmin* houses – breeding grounds for lice – were perhaps only one or two rooms, standing on floors of earth and stone. The American Horace Allen described them as little better than 'a collection of haystacks that have wintered out'. His compatriot Lillias Underwood complained that 'houses [were] fearfully unsanitary, and many of them filthy and full of vermin. All sewage flows out into unspeakable ditches on either side of the street.' (None of which, of course, means that the slums of Seoul in the early nineteenth century were any worse than those of Philadelphia or Paris, or that the smoke-laden atmosphere resulting from countless wood-burning stoves was necessarily dirtier than that polluted by the coal fires and furnaces of Manchester or Moscow. As Mrs Underwood pointed out later in the century, 'Compared with the most destitute of London or New York, there are few who go hungry in Seoul.') Squalor bred disease. Across East Asia much research had traditionally gone into medicine. Herbalism and acupuncture could cope with a great deal, and *insam* (ginseng) was taken to increase resistance, but when epidemics of measles, smallpox, malaria, tuberculosis, typhoid and cholera (a newcomer in 1812 that caused consternation and immense loss of life) periodically swept the land, people of all classes died. Both poverty and disease were to blame as census figures showed the population falling from 7.4 million in 1799 to 6.4 million in 1850.

Paintings brightened a place up, and folk artists copied the subjects admired by the gentry. They used the same symbols and conveyed the same messages: the Diamond Mountains as a haven of peace and beauty, the lotus as a metaphor for purity, mandarin ducks as a celebration of wedded bliss, carp on the bedroom wall as a fertility charm, the pine tree as a reminder of respect due to the elderly. But in folk art cheerfulness mattered more than exactitude, and panache was prized above refinement and brightness over subtlety. Portraits too: sometimes even commoners liked to keep pictures of their immediate ancestors, carrying them when they fled home in time of war. Because much Chosŏn painting is unsigned, the dividing line between literati and folk art is sometimes blurred, and the great treasurer of rural life and customs Zo Zayong (1926–2000) preferred to divide painting into 'pure' and 'utilitarian'. So, series of linked pictures such as *p'yŏngsaeng-do* that adorned screens and kept out draughts were utilitarian, whether painted for a palace or a cottage. Even some paintings from the Tohwa-sŏ earned this description, instead of the usual and flattering 'literati art'.

Like painting, music and dance also crossed the social divide. A song composed in 1844 refers to the rich variety of instrumental and vocal forms that entertained people in the capital. 'When the opening music is over', it says, 'a young *kisaeng* with beautiful eyebrows, correcting her hairpin, is ready to sing traditional songs.' She performs a long programme including the difficult lyric songs *kagok*, *kasa* and *sijo*, 'all good to hear', and when she has finished, other *kisaeng* introduce a sequence of slow and fast dances. It is a courtly scene, but there is every reason to assume that those who heard and enjoyed it would have been just as familiar with tunes played and sung outside the palace walls. A wealth of folk songs (*minyo*) – some local, others putting a local interpretation on tunes that somehow crossed regional boundaries of river and mountain – lightened the peasant's work load and accompanied his relaxation, and could be spotted hidden away in the shaman's chanting. By the early nineteenth century they had been incorporated into the sung tales of *p'ansori* and the free-wheeling form of instrumental ensemble, *sinawi*, and before long would appear again in the solo instrumental suite *sanjo*, a complicated sonata-like form that gave the *kayagŭm* performer ample chance to show off his virtuoso skills. Court music was an extension of the power of government, so its melodic lines had to be followed exactly. In contrast, *sinawi*, *p'ansori* and *sanjo* encouraged the display of individual improvisational techniques, and *yangban* with *sirhak*-inspired pride in their native culture took to them, either playing themselves or sponsoring performances.

SOCIETY AND GOVERNMENT

In 1801 Chŏng Yagyong (brush-name Tasan) might have felt relieved. As a young man he had shown interest in the Catholic faith and perhaps even received baptism, but as Chŏngjo's favourite he had recanted, and now, when others died in the persecutions, his sentence was only to seventeen years in exile. His eldest brother, Yakchŏn, was also banished, to the island of Hŭksan off the north-east coast. But Yakchong, the middle one of the three, refused to apostatize and was executed, as his two nephews would be in 1839, and Tasan's personal relief was compromised by a lasting sense of shame and guilt. To a *yangban*, moreover, concerned about public opinion and the effect of disgrace on his family and his descendants, exile was not seen as a soft touch. At its lightest it might mean exclusion from his native town or the capital; in serious cases a miscreant was sent to a remote area or confined on a distant island such as Cheju, where as a last resort he could be condemned to live imprisoned behind a thorn hedge. Some exiles famously made the best of a bad job: Tasan accumulated a large library and wrote copiously on the Chinese classics. In the productive writing period of his later years he combined *sirhak* conviction with the critical qualities he had absorbed from Chinese historical scholarship, and his *chip* ('collectaneous works') cover such diverse topics as principles of government, civil engineering, farming techniques, horticulture, sericulture, medicine and proverbs. He refers to his early Catholic beliefs, but is tantalizingly vague about whether or not he returned to the fold before his death, as Bishop Dallet claims in his *Histoire de l'église de Corée* (1874). And while this prolific writer served out his punishment in the obscure south-western district of Kangjin (where a bronze statue to him now stands), brother Yakchŏn was compiling an extensive scientific study of marine life on Hŭksan.

Another famous exile was the great artist, calligrapher and *sirhak* historian Kim Chŏnghŭi (Ch'usa, 1786–1856) (Picture Essay 20). Kim's exceptional artistic talent was spotted as a boy by the Pukhak official and calligrapher Pak Chega, who took him as a student. A visit to Beijing in 1809 introduced him to the self-expression of literati art, the pleasures of epigraphy and the rigour of careful historical research, giving him the experience and intellectual independence that would make him a leading figure among fellow Pukhak artists on his return. Although not renouncing Neo-Confucianism, he was critical of its narrow and introspective aspects, and found deep satisfaction in Sŏn Buddhism. Working with contemporary calligraphers in China also made him dissatisfied with his former brushwork, and after intensive study of earlier Chinese masters he evolved a unique style that has earned him the epithet 'Korea's most eminent calligrapher'. It is bold, unorthodox and intensely expressionistic, perfectly complementing the quasi-naive simplicity of some of his painting. So much did contemporaries appreciate the realism of his landscape and Four Gentlemen (prunus, orchid, bamboo, chrysanthemum) paintings that he has been blamed for a decline in genre painting. The picture for which he is best known today is of a single orchid bloom with a few bent and broken leaves, a mixture of dark and light strokes applied with a dry brush, surrounded by colophons in matching calligraphic style. Neither Ch'usa's connection by marriage with the royal family nor a distinguished government career was enough to save him when his family sided with the P'ungyang Chos in their bitter rivalry with the Andong Kims. He was banished to Cheju island. Nearing the age of 60 he might justifiably have given way to depres-

20 Yi Hanch'ŏl, *Portrait of Kim Chŏnghŭi*

Figure painting occurred less frequently in Korea than in China. Genre scenes enlivened the walls of Koguryŏ tombs, but we do not encounter them again until the nectar ritual paintings of the eighteenth century. (Mural decorations in a Parhae tomb, however – that of Princess Chŏnghyo, the daughter of King Mun [r. AD 737–93] – do depict portraits of her retainers in contemporary Tang style.) Buddhist figures shine forth from illuminated manuscripts and hanging scrolls of the Koryŏ period, and no doubt adorned temple walls and altars as well, but by their very nature these were inclined to didacticism and stylization rather than realism. Portraits of Buddhist monks were also respected. It was against such a patchy background that the painting of human beings, either as individuals or in social situations, at last gained a measure of popularity during the Chosŏn period. Then, it was Neo-Confucianism that provided the spur, and in formal portraiture we see it reach its artistic apogee. King T'aejo made quite a habit of having himself painted. King Yŏngjo, too, had his picture redone every ten years. Early in the dynasty some officials revived the ancient Koguryŏ practice of being painted with their wives, but this fashion died out again, and thereafter the subjects were mostly individual royal and *yang-ban* males. Monks now made unfashionable – though not altogether unknown – subjects, and the question of painting non-royal women scarcely arose.

Albums recording meetings of the Kirosŏ and Kiyonghoe might depict the distinguished members honoured there, and portraits of ancestors gazed down on their descendants as they carried out their devotional rites. Such serious matters were normally translated into a sombre, though not necessarily stern, expression. Unlike Chinese subjects, who always looked straight ahead, most Korean sitters turned their heads slightly to the right, revealing one ear instead of two. (In contrast, the famous modern portraitist Chae Yŏng-shin [1850–1941] almost always had his subjects adopt a full-frontal pose.) Formality of approach and style did not mean standardization and impersonality, especially when shading techniques developed in the eighteenth century and introduced more three-dimensional effects. Artists attempted to convey both appearance and character with accuracy, and devoted most attention to the face. Bone structure and skin texture were carefully observed. Hands were generally concealed, but the hairs of a man's beard, the warts on his face, the weave of his hat and the embroidery of his official square of rank were picked out with precision. Several portraits of Kim Ch'ŏnghŭi survive. In this one his beard has already turned white; another, remarkably similar, by Hŏ Yu shows him with

Yi Hanch'ŏl,
Portrait of Kim Chŏnghŭi,
19th century.

bushier eyebrows and heavier cheeks. Both depict him as a considerate, patient and even-tempered man, giving no hint of the trials of his later years. Yi Hanch'ŏl was a professional painter, a member of the Tohwasŏ, who painted the last kings of the Chŏson dynasty. Born in either 1808 or 1812, he enjoyed a long life and died some time in the first decade of the twentieth century.

Self-portraiture was uncommon before the twentieth century. The poet-calligrapher Kim Sisŭp (1435–1493) did one; so did Yun Dusŏ (1668–1715), who played no small part in the eighteenth-century move to depict character; and a third was the 'true-view' artist Kang Sehwang. But when Ko Hŭidong (1886–1965) studied in Japan and painted the first portrait in oils – his own – he was severely criticized for rejecting Neo-Confucian ideas of what portraiture should be.

sion at being imprisoned in a single room 'no bigger than a rice measuring bowl', damaging his health. Instead, he found plenty to keep himself busy and happy, reading, painting, answering correspondence and teaching local children. Only in the bare trees of *Winter Scene*, painted after the death of his wife, do we sense the grief afflicting his soul. Even when King Hŏnjong pardoned him and he prepared to return to Seoul after nine years away, his ordeal was still not over. Hŏnjong's unexpected death gave the Andong Kims the chance to regain some of the power they had seen ebbing away, and they accused Ch'usa of engineering opposition to the choice of Ch'ŏlchong as his successor. He was exiled again, this time to the chilly northwestern province of Hamgyŏng, where he served another year before finally being released. Stories like these, of the Chŏng brothers and of Kim Chŏnghŭi, demonstrate the fate of *sirhak* modernization in the first half of the nineteenth century. Whereas individuals or groups of like-minded scholars had for centuries published detailed and often critical research studies, those who now saw the value to their country of broadening their terms of reference and pursuing more innovative lines of enquiry came up against entrenched Neo-Confucian suspicion of anything that threatened to re-shape the traditional social order. There was as yet no concept of national development that separated economic and social progress from either ancient political philosophy or vested clan interest.

Arguments about the succession to the throne had caused trouble throughout the Chosŏn dynasty, but if Yŏngjo and Chŏngjo had overcome the worst manifestations of factional division, the pernicious influence of clan rivalry at court had not been destroyed. Ancestry and descent had been important in the acquisition of political power ever since the Three Kingdoms period. The Koryŏ nobility perpetuated itself through both patrilineal and matrilineal descent groups, and inheritance might even skip a generation, but Chosŏn rules were stricter. The state orthodoxy of Neo-Confucianism required the nobility to practise ancestor worship by laws and much high-level discussion took place about the related principles of succession and inheritance. A son was essential for continuation of the rituals honouring the ancestors, and if none was forthcoming adoption was resorted to. In a country where history and record-keeping had so long been respected, the compilation of genealogies must have begun at an early stage. By the fifteenth century they were appearing in print, and by the seventeenth factionalism had highlighted their value. As *yangban* families exploited them to the full, political supremacy became inseparable from lineage considerations and machinations. Much of the tension at court stemmed from the ambitions of families that provided the king's female consorts and that expected to benefit as a result. *Sedo-jŏngch'i* ('government by the way of power'), implying the emasculation of royal authority by a king's affined families, was first linked with the name of Hong Kugyŏng, a relative of Lady Hyegyŏng and tutor to the young Chŏngjo. But with Chŏngjo's death the Hongs were finished and the P'ungyang Chos, Dogmatists, managed to reassert a hard political line. The three kings of the period 1800–64 were all nominated by dowager queens, who according to an ancient privilege known as *suryŏm ch'ŏngjŏng* ('lowering curtain, hearing government') were allowed to exercise regency on behalf of a minor by listening to state business from behind a screen. They used the privilege to advance the power of their own clans. Sunjo was only ten in 1800, when he was chosen by Yŏngjo's widow, Dowager Queen Chŏngsun. As a supporter of the Dogmatists, she now enabled them to mount the comprehensive anti-Catholic persecution they had striven for under Chŏngjo's more benign rule. But she died in 1802, and it was Sunjo's widow, Dowager Queen Sunwŏn, who nominated both Hŏnjong and Ch'ŏlchong, the former at the age of seven and the latter at eighteen. Sunwŏn came from the Andong Kims, a traditionally powerful lineage that under Ch'ŏlchong wrested authority back from the Chos.

Of course, lineage and family meant more than gaining political advantage, settling an inheritance or even honouring ancestors. Filial piety was concerned with serving the living as well as the dead, and sons and daughters-in-law were legally obliged to pander to the wishes of their older relatives. In return, grandfathers and fathers often had strings that they could pull on behalf of their offspring. In East Asia a feeling of shared responsibility has long been acknowledged, especially for the elderly within a family and for poorer or stricken families within a wider lineage, occupational or residential grouping. In traditional China government took advantage of this by organizing families into groups of ten for purposes of control and tax collection, and in modern China the Communist Party manipulated the tight-knit groups in cooperatives and communes throughout the 1950s to have people spy on and denounce their neighbours. In Korea, Cho Kwangjo (1482–1519), a staunch but somewhat idealistic scholar, introduced village charters (*hyangyak*) to try and instil Neo-Confucian principles into the pattern of peasants' lives, nominating an ideologue and other prominent members of the community to work alongside the local magistrate in encouraging a sense of corporate responsibility and, rather heavy-handedly, relaying politically approved instructions. But a more spontaneous type of voluntary mutual-aid organization for peasants or members of occupational groups appeared in the early sixteenth century. This was known as *kye*. Members contributed to a communal fund, saving for an agreed purpose such as the purchase of an animal or piece of equipment, or borrowing from it at a known rate. On occasion a disgruntled *yangban* might try and whip up political feeling within a *kye*: the Tongin politician Chŏng Yŏrip (d. 1589), for example, incited opposition to the Sŏin among *kye* in Chŏlla, and committed suicide when his plot was discovered. In modern times, after war had devastated agriculture in the DPRK, Kim Il Sung introduced mutual-aid teams. *Sogyŏri* ('cow exchange') teams of three to five families shared one animal and their labour, and labour teams (*p'umasi*) of up to ten families marched off to work together. After a disastrous harvest in 1955 the drive towards advanced cooperatives was stepped up, until by 1958 the entire countryside, over a million households, had been 'socialized'. The interest of the group, as defined by the prevailing orthodoxy of the ruling Communist Party, was paramount and triumphed over the freedom of the individual.

In December 1811 Hong Kyŏngnae took advantage of *kye* cooperatives in gathering support for the first peasant uprising of the new century, the rebellion he launched in North P'yŏngan province. The causes of discontent were various and familiar: poor local government, onerous taxation, natural disasters, resentment against the politics of the Andong Kims. To these we must add Hong's personal unhappiness as a minor *yangban* figure unable to gain the official status he thought he deserved. Modern historians have devoted a lot of attention to this rising, some recognizing frustration at the non-realization of hopes raised by Chŏngjo's plans for social and economic reform, and some seeing it as the anticipation of late twentieth-century *minjung* (populist) ambitions. Whether or not it is really accurate to call the rising a peasant movement has been questioned, given the involvement of *yangban*, rich farmers, merchants, even discontented military units. Anders Karlsson sees it principally as a conflict between local society and central power, with the rebel leadership taking advantage of the mutual assistance and fund-raising functions of *kye* groups and the organizational skills of the more formal association, the *hyangyak*. Both, in his view, were capable of drawing together people of different social standing. One of those who joined the protest was a local administrator, Kim Iksun, but his capture and execution ruined his family, and his grandson Pyŏngnyŏn, now deprived of his inheritance, turned itinerant poet. In time he became known as 'Reed-hat Kim' – Kim Sakkat (1807–63) – after the mourner's hat (*satkat*) he took to wearing. Verse is the form of literature primarily associated with the early nineteenth century, especially the tightly regulated Chinese styles favoured by the literati. Kim Sakkat's poems, first collected and written down in the 1930s, were quite different. They shared the terseness, satire and love of nature of the *sijo*, but in character they were quite different, conveying folksy and often earthy material. He summed up his life of suffering with these lines:

> As my hair grew longer,
> My fortunes travelled a rough road:
> The family line in ruins,
> The blue sea a mulberry grove.

The rebels briefly controlled a wide area north of the Ch'ŏngch'ŏn river and held out against government counter-attack in the Chŏngju fortress, but Hong Kyŏngnae was killed and the rising collapsed after just four months. To say that it lit a fuse that would eventually culminate in the great Tonghak Rebellion of 1894–5 might imply a causal relationship involving the many other local risings that took place throughout the century and even a defined nation-wide objective. Neither was true, though outbreaks of violence continued through the reigns of Hŏnjong and Ch'ŏlchong. Most serious were those in 1862, when the three southern provinces (*samnam*) of Ch'unch'ŏng, Chŏlla and Kyŏngsang, including Cheju island, all resounded to the sound of battle against the land tax, the cloth tax and the rice-loan system (*hwan'gok*). At the end of them, in 1864, a fuse of a kind *was* lit, by the execution of Ch'oe Cheu (1824–1864). Ch'oe, like Hong Xiuquan, the leader of the great Taiping Rebellion that swept China from 1850 to 1864, felt that social discrimination denied him the kind of job he deserved, and had a vision encouraging him to begin a new religious movement. Named *Tonghak* ('Eastern Teaching') and preaching Ch'oe's idea of *Ch'ŏndo* ('Heaven's Way') it was an amalgam of Confucian, Buddhist, shamanistic and – ironically, considering its anti-Western leaning – Catholic ideas. It also denounced bureaucratic corruption and spoke up for the impoverished and oppressed peasantry, and what really tipped the scales against Ch'oe was his prediction that 1864 would bring it some new but unspecified success. The authorities, well aware of the devastation brought to China by the Taipings, tried to pre-empt anything of the sort in Korea by arresting him. And they seemed to have succeeded, as Tonghak support faded away. But just as Hong Xiuquan's rebellion resulted in Western soldiery arriving to prop up the government, so too would Ch'oe's teachings reap a similar and devastating harvest in the last decade of the century. The year 1864, in fact, was loaded with foreboding for Korea. It may have seemed to the rulers of the 'Hermit Kingdom', as foreigners later began to call it, that their efforts to outstare the novel ideas of the Realists and Catholics were working, and that traditional beliefs, practices and standards were safe. But Ch'oe Cheu's death was not the only one that year that would have unforeseeable results. On 16 January, King Ch'ŏlch'ŏng also went to join his ancestors.

CHAPTER SIX

Incursion, Modernization and Reform, 1864–1905: Tradition at Bay

The first half of the nineteenth century had brought Korea a few alarms, but nothing to shake its underlying confidence in the ideas and lifestyle described in previous chapters. The 41 years covered in this chapter, however – corresponding roughly to the reign of just one king – comprised a period as confusing as it was unprecedented, as determinative as it was alarming. Suddenly, as the distant world – dismissed and despised as barbarian – embroiled eastern Asia in a bitter struggle for empire, Koreans found that earlier assumptions and debate about matter and principle, the nature of kingly rule, even the hierarchy of states, took on a different twist or were rendered outmoded; and social habits that had contented the ancestors for centuries were called into question. Ch'ŏlchong's death was a turning point.

REFORM AND DEVELOPMENT

Women helped to shape the political fortunes of three countries engaged in the East–West confrontation at the end of the nineteenth century, which, given the patriarchal nature of British, Chinese and Korean society, made their simultaneous appearance on the political stage a curious irony. If Queen Victoria (1819–1901) alone occupied a throne as of right, China's Empress Dowager Ci Xi (1835–1908) and Korea's Queen Min (1851–1895) shared no less responsibility than she in the moves and counter-moves to create a new world order. While Victoria's appreciation of Korea and its civilization may have been limited, Queen Min was said to be 'possessed of a very intelligent idea of the great nations of the world and their governments', and had a fair idea of what the nations ruled by her fellow matriarchs could do to or for her own. This was another, more particular, irony, for political consciousness, still less participation, was no part of the future that had been planned for her.

When King Ch'ŏlchong died early, only one of his eleven children was still living and she was a girl. The designation of his heir lay in the hands of another woman, King Hŏnjong's mother, the Dowager Queen Cho, and Prince Yi Haŭng (1820–1898), a great-grandson of Prince Sado, persuaded her to nominate his son. In 1864, therefore, the eleven-year-old became the new King Kojong, and effective power of regency fell to his father, better known today by his princely title, the Taewŏn'gun. Two years later he married Kojong to a niece of his wife, a teenage girl from the Yŏhŭng Min clan with no sign of political awareness or personal ambition. He counted on maintaining his personal power for a long time to come, and in fact did so for almost a decade. By the end of this time he had made rivals – outright enemies even – of both his son and his daughter-in-law, Queen Min, and Korean politics and the nation's fortunes had entered a turbulent period.

The Taewŏn'gun cannot be faulted for his determination to clear up the political mess that had long stifled efficient government and reduced the country to poverty. As to how to achieve this, well, he was scarcely a radical, or even a *sirhak* sympathizer, and his later reputation as one of the dynasty's greatest orchid painters suggests a solid appreciation for tradition. If anything he was ultra-conservative, trying to give the throne his son would inherit more authority than it had ever had in Korea. But neither were the measures he introduced as reactionary as the manner in which he had assumed power. He balanced and neutralized the influence of the Andong Kim and P'ungyang Cho clans by appointing men of genuine ability to top government posts, though the *sedo* acquired by the Yŏhŭng Min by marrying into the royal family would feature prominently in politics for the rest of the century: the head of that clan, Min Sŭngho, quickly managed to get posts for a considerable number of its members. The Taewŏn'gun sacked corrupt officials and punished extortionate landlords. He replaced the military cloth tax with a household tax, and imposed it on the *yangban* as well as other classes. He closed down most of the *sŏwŏn* private academies, confiscated their lands and some of those belonging to royal affine families, and tightened up on the tax liability of what land remained in private hands. By restoring supreme civilian authority to the State Council (Ŭijŏngbu), shutting down the Frontier Defence Office (Pibyŏn-sa) – the sixteenth-century military command bureau that had grown into the most important government organ – and re-creating the old Three Armies Office (Samgunbu) to run all military affairs, he separated civilian and military command in the biggest shake-up the military system had undergone since the sixteenth century. Such was his strength of character that he was ready to take on the most powerful vested-interest groups, thereby earning himself considerable popularity across the country at large.

It all sounds reasonable and effective, but the Taewŏn'gun's retirement at the end of 1873 represented a victory for his enemies. A junior minister, Ch'oe Ikhyŏn, had impeached him on behalf of those who had lost out as a result of his new measures. Somewhat disingenuously, the critics cited as unfair the sale of government offices, the setting of new taxes on salt, fishing and the movement of goods, and the minting of devalued coinage. For much of the growing financial hardship they blamed one undertaking, the reconstruction of the Kyŏngbŏk Palace. This was the Taewŏn'gun's pet project and it was, it is true, ruinously expensive. But King T'aejo had built 'Shining Blessings' as his residence and the first seat of Chosŏn government in the 1390s and to the Taewŏn'gun, if not to every taxpayer, the restoration of this languishing symbol of early dynastic grandeur was worthy of sacrifice. (President Kim Young Sam felt the same when he too announced a grand restoration of the palace in 1997, some ninety years after the Japanese had once again ruined most of its splendid halls, pavilions and gates.) Perhaps the Taewŏn'gun would have got away with it had not his credibility been damaged by his apparent inability to deal with the foreign threat, a fateful story told in the next section. As it was, Queen Min – already showing that she was no pushover – pressurized the State Council to put the 20-year-old king in charge. The Taewŏn'gun withdrew in dudgeon to his country estate and his supporters lost their jobs, but, in the manner of tit-for-tat revenge with which we are familiar today, a parcel bomb sent to Min Sŭngho's home killed him and his son. The Taewŏn'gun was assumed to be behind the outrage.

King Kojong, it turned out, lacked the acumen and forcefulness to handle the conflicting forces within his own political establishment, let alone those of rivalrous foreign powers. In particular, arguments about the need for modernization eddied around him and he was washed back and forth, not averse to change but incapable of understanding or managing its implications. During the 1870s he gradually fell under the spell of a group of scholar-officials, including Kim Okkyun (1851–1894), Pak Yŏnghyo (1861–1939) and Sŏ Chaep'il (1866–1951), who formed the Kaehwadang ('Progressive Party'). Looked at in retrospect the innovations they managed to implement were modest: they included the setting up of a government Information Office, the opening of a Post Office and the creation of a modern army unit (quickly rescinded by the Min clan). Where should a Korean government bent on modernization – even though this one fell far short of such a description – look for guidance? America's long-term intentions were as yet unknown but might provide examples that Korea could turn to advantage. America's recent converts in Meiji Japan were viewed with greater suspicion, although the Kaehwadang saw Japan as a possible model for gradual reform in Korea and sent students to study there. Queen Min, meanwhile, took her chances to influence policy, and sided with the conservative Sadaedang ('Serve the Great Party'), rivals of the Kaehwadang. Although not hostile to all thought of reform, when it came to international allegiance they supported the Chinese stance rather than the Japanese. Sino-Japanese rivalry was laid bare in July 1882, the Imo year, when army units in Seoul mutinied over lack of pay. With Japanese support the Taewŏn'gun took advantage of the turmoil to stage a coup against his daughter-in-law. Many of her supporters in the palace were killed and she herself escaped from Seoul in disguise. Kojong asked his father to take charge, but the Chinese government also moved fast. Stung by the inroads of Western imperialism into the Middle Kingdom, it now embarked on a face-saving attempt to rescue a little traditional influence of its own by reasserting its supposed *droits de seigneur* in Korea. Three thousand of its soldiers arrived. The Taewŏn'gun was taken prisoner and hauled off to China. Queen Min returned to the palace, and in September Kojong, with a public apology for the upheaval, promised the country a fresh start.

But the cycle of tumult and counter-attack was far from over. On 4 December 1884 (the Kapsin year), Hong Yŏngsik, director of the new Post Office, was hosting a dinner to celebrate its opening. As the distinguished guests were enjoying their meal a fire broke out, and amid the confusion men rushed in with swords, killed Hong and badly injured Min Yŏngik (1860–1914), the head of the Min clan and the queen's nephew. He escaped, but uproar engulfed the capital. King Kojong found himself in the Japanese legation, which had advance warning of the plot and approved the move against the pro-Chinese leadership. Some say he fled there, others that Japanese guards took him there. Whichever, it was the very next day he announced a new, reform-orientated government. Straight away Chinese troops intervened to ensure that it was virtually still-born. As they returned Kojong to his palace, where their own commander Yuan Shikai and the Min clan could keep an eye on him, Kim Okkyun, Sŏ Chaep'il and other leaders of the Kapsin plot fled to Japan. Korean optimism rose in April 1885 as Li Hongzhang and Itō Hirobumi signed a treaty in Tianjin pledging to remove their armies from the peninsula except in the event of trouble. Nine years later, that reservation would prove to be crucial. For the time being it was agreed that the Taewŏn'gun should be returned to Korea, where both sides hoped he would persuade Kojong and Queen

Min to stop the growth of Russian influence. The ex-regent, once so dedicated to Korean isolationism, then linked with pro-Japanese atrocity in the sorry story of the Imo Incident, returned from exile something of a convert to the Beijing cause (even to its clothing as well: he is credited with introducing Korean men to the Manchu style of loose-fitting, collarless jacket, *magoja*, that became a popular form of casual wear); and as Kojong now deferred to his father, the Qing court could feel fairly reassured that the correct diplomatic hierarchy was being restored across East Asia. True, its plan that Yuan Shikai, boasting the new title Resident General it awarded him, should depose Kojong and put the Taewŏn'gun on the throne came to naught, but China's influence in Seoul was nevertheless paramount. The US chargé d'affaires George Foulk called Yuan 'the most important man in Korea'. Just how powerful, in fact, he was quickly to discover: Yuan had him recalled to America after less than three years in Seoul for urging the government to buy US-built steamers. The Korean capital was turning into a nest of international suspicion, accusation, intrigue and rivalry. Their fortune-tellers could have told its leaders they were heading for two major wars, neither of their own making.

Suspicion of Western religion had been a factor in the appearance of Ch'oe Cheu's Tonghak movement in the early 1860s. The age-old theme of reaction to peasant hardship joined with new, but still limited, expressions of anti-foreignism, and also drew on a rising nativist belief in a single supreme deity, Hanŭnim, as a counter to the Christian God. Ch'oe's execution in 1864 failed to eradicate the organization, which expanded under his successor Ch'oe Sihyŏng (1829–1898), and when over-taxation and oppressive local officialdom combined to exacerbate intolerable rural conditions in the Chŏlla and Ch'ungch'ŏng provinces, dissidents took up arms on 19 March 1894. A nationalist element among them, fearful of what modernization would mean to traditional livelihoods, targeted the Japanese, whose growing communities of merchants, craftsmen and fishermen provided unequal and often underhand competition. Government forces failed to suppress the rebels, and when Chŏnju fell on 31 May, Seoul called a truce and appealed to Beijing for assistance. Li Hongzhang, following advice from Yuan Shikai, dispatched 1,500 Chinese troops, and in accordance with the Tianjin Treaty informed Tokyo that he was doing so 'to restore peace to our tributary state'. It is also possible that he had succumbed to Japanese persuasion, perhaps even fallen into a trap, for Itō Hirobumi's government now lost no time in ordering 7,000 of its own soldiers to Korea. In fact, any intervention proved to be uncalled for. The Tonghak rebels quickly dispersed, issuing a list of demands that included the abolition of slavery, punishment of corrupt officials and appointment of future officials on merit. Hilary Conroy calls theirs 'a rising against the government for reactionary rather than progressive reasons'. Their aspirations were, it is true, utopian rather than modernizing, as peasant rebellions generally were, and Kojong and his government probably anticipated the restoration of the status quo with some satisfaction. They could scarcely have been more mistaken.

The Japanese minister Ōtori Keisuke and Yuan Shikai agreed to withdraw their troops, but suspicions were aroused as more and more Japanese poured ashore at Chemulp'o. On 28 March 1894 Japan had been shocked by the assassination of Kim Okkyun by two of his compatriots. He had lived there for ten years after the Kapsin debacle and the Japanese press proclaimed him a martyr to the cause of modernization. Sensing a chance to get its feet under the mainland table, Tokyo took up the Korean reformist cause with a vengeance. On 27 June the cabinet approved its own list of proposals that would begin the process of transforming the Seoul government, updating its financial, military, law-enforcement and educational systems, and putting Japan's position in Korea on an equal footing with China's. Ōtori presented them to the Korean government, which rejected them. On 16 July 8,000 Chinese reinforcements arrived. A week later Japanese soldiers entered the Kyŏngbok Palace, and as the king ordered its Chinese guards to end their brave but unequal resistance, quickly occupied the remainder of the capital. Ōtori, counting on the Taewŏn'gun for collaboration because of his antipathy for Queen Min and her clan, had him brought in to give advice. (The Western residents' new periodical, *The Korean Repository*, called the ex-regent 'a kind of storm petrel, making his appearance and getting to the front only when there has been trouble and disorder in the country'.) The old man showed little hesitation in relieving his son of the reins of government, but less readiness to go along with a reform agenda. His reported association with the Tonghak might have suggested that this time, unlike 1882, he would not necessarily see things Japan's way, even though its foreign minister Mutsu repeatedly stressed the Korean right to independence.

On 25 July, as three British steamers ferried more Chinese soldiers from Weihaiwei towards Chemulp'o, one of them was sunk by the Japanese navy and 905 men lost. Itō's cabinet had evidently approved hostilities with China a fortnight earlier, and on 1 August the two countries mutually declared war. The Chinese Northern fleet was twice as large as the Japanese, but on 17 September twelve of its newest warships were humiliatingly defeated by a similar number of Japanese vessels off the mouth of the Yalu river. On land, the Japanese captured

P'yŏngyang and forced Chinese armies back into Manchuria. The following month they took Dalian and Lushun (Port Arthur), and in February 1895 they captured Weihaiwei, where they destroyed the remainder of the Chinese fleet. The Chinese had no option but to seek an armistice, and by the Treaty of Shimonoseki, which ended hostilities on 17 April 1895, they surrendered the Liaodong peninsula, Taiwan and the Pescador islands. Furthermore, by conceding recognition of the independence of Korea, China closed its age-old claim to suzerainty over the peninsula. Japan was now free to concentrate on extending its influence and authority there. It did not immediately, however, have everything its own way. International pressure condemned the fruits of its victory as ill-gotten gains, and the so-called Triple Intervention of Russia, France and Germany forced it to return Liaodong to China.

Japan had also hypocritically asserted Korean independence when it signed an agreement with the Advisory Council set up in Seoul under Kim Hongjip (1842–1896) and Yu Kilchun (1856–1914) in July 1894, the Kabo year. Over the next three months the Council passed 210 acts, the first phase of the Kabo reforms. One of them formally abolished slavery (though it would take years to eradicate completely such a deep-rooted institution); another ended discrimination against *sŏŏl*. The second phase, from December 1894 to 6 July 1895, coincided with the service of Count Inoue Kaoru as Japanese minister in Seoul. Inoue, who arrived to replace Ōtori on 20 November, knew Korean politics well. One of his first moves was to sideline the Taewŏn'gun, and his hand was clearly to be seen behind the oath that Kojong made at the royal ancestral temple on 7 January 1895. Having reported to his ancestors that 'a neighbouring Power and the unanimous judgement of all our officers unite in affirming that only as an independent ruler can We make our country strong', the king went on to enumerate fourteen new laws, the third of which emphasized his personal responsibility for deciding matters of state and affirmed that 'the Queen and members of the Royal Family shall not be allowed to interfere'. Far from really confirming Korea's independence, the measures opened the gate for further Japanese manipulation. A new cabinet (*naegak*) under Kim Hongjip and Pak Yŏnghyo replaced the old State Council, and in March it approved 20 Articles of Reform presented by Inoue that put quasi-constitutional limitations on the formerly absolutist monarchy. The first spelled out in plain language that neither the Taewŏn'gun nor Queen Min was entitled to appoint or demote government officers; others recognized that the army must be reorganized and better trained and the law code updated, 'introducing such foreign laws as are adapted to the national needs'. Foreign advisers were introduced to every government department except the foreign ministry. On 19 April the Taewŏn'gun's 23-year-old grandson Prince Yi Chunyong was arrested for allegedly conspiring to murder the king and sent into exile on Kyodong island, off Kanghwa. (A single-roomed house was specially built for him and he served only a small part of his ten-year sentence. The brains behind the plot may have been the Taewŏn'gun himself.) In June the Taewŏn'gun was intercepted on his way to visit the prince and escorted by the police to his summer villa, where he now stayed in permanent retirement. Meanwhile Inoue, suffering from rheumatism, returned to Tokyo on leave, to be replaced by Miura Gorō.

The third phase of the reforms began with disaster and ended with drama. In the early hours of 8 October 1895 a band of Japanese and Korean cut-throats infiltrated Queen Min's private quarters in the Kyŏngbok Palace and killed her and her ladies-in-waiting. Shock and undisguised grief poured out, and sincere tributes to Her Majesty came from home and abroad. Even the *Japan Daily Advertiser* called her 'a woman of remarkable character . . . a personality even more noteworthy than her neighbor [the Empress Dowager] of Peking'. She possessed, it said, such 'powers of mind and will as would have rendered her a striking figure in any station and in any age', and both her life and the nature of her death turned her into a lasting nationalist icon. (In 2002–3 she toured the world as the subject of Korea's first Western-style musical extravaganza, *The Last Empress*.) Ultimate responsibility for her murder probably belonged to Miura, acting on pre-planned instructions from Tokyo and possibly with the Taewŏn'gun's connivance. Korean fury was not assuaged when he was recalled, tried and acquitted. Piling insult upon assault, another pro-Japanese cabinet was now nominated and in December introduced still more reforms. One of the most ill-considered of these was the order that men should cut off their topknots. Turmoil ensued, for Korean males treasured this 'glory of their manhood' above all else. Rioters murdered the prime minister, Kim Hongjip, and the home minister, Yu Kilchun, escaped to Japan. In the confusion Kojong fled with his son from the Kyŏngbok Palace on 11 February 1896 and sought sanctuary in the Russian embassy. Another new cabinet was sworn in. This one was sympathetic to Russian interests, and for the new foreign minister, Yi Wanyong (1858–1926), it marked an important step up what would prove to be a significant career ladder.

Most of the Kabo reforms, though welcomed by the foreign community, were either rescinded or quickly lapsed. Rumours implicated the Japanese in the plot to install Yi Chunyong as king, and guerrilla bands turned on Japanese army detachments, reviving the name *ŭibyŏng* and memories of successes against the odds in the 1590s. The current of public and international opinion in 1895–6 suggested that Japan might have done its reputation serious harm. Positive expressions of Korean nationalism, not all of which stemmed from negative sentiment towards Japan, or took reactionary form, included the formation of a new club in July 1896 dedicated to social and political reform. Its founders included Sŏ Chaep'il, Yun Ch'iho (1865–1945) and Yi Sŭngman (Syngman Rhee, 1875–1965). Yi Wanyong took the chair. Although primarily a *yangban* venture, the Independence Club (Tongnip hyŏphoe), as it was called, was openly supported by the Ch'angyang women's organization and counted democratization among its goals. Its dedication to self-strengthening was recognition that it accepted the need for foreign advice on modernization, although it was equally determined to remove what is nowadays termed foreign imperialism from its shores. It built a hall (Tongnipgwan) for the weekly meetings of the Paejae Debating Society, which discussed topics ranging from education to industry; collected funds for the erection of the Independence Gate (Picture Essay 21); promoted the use of the national flag and national anthem; and published a *han'gŭl* newspaper, the *Tongnip Sinmun* ('Independent News'). The king was a supporter, and in turn the Club approved in October 1897 when, having reluctantly left the Russian embassy on 21 February and moved into the newly renovated Tŏksu Palace nearby, he put himself on a par with the rulers of China and Japan by proclaiming himself emperor (*hwangje*). At the same time he upgraded his country's official title to that of Great Han Empire (Taehan-cheguk) (Picture Essay 22). The ceremonies took place at the Altar of Heaven, on the site of today's Seoul Westin Chosun hotel, where one pavilion from the former complex still stands.

'The general opinion among both Koreans and foreigners', the editor of *The Korean Repository* had written in 1895, 'is that the King is one of the most urbane and gracious sovereigns that ever sat on the throne of Chosŏn.' True, His Majesty had taken unprecedented steps to meet and learn from foreign advisers, and he got on well with them. They felt flattered. Whatever his personal qualities, however, some saw through him as a ruler. Isabella Bird Bishop, who liked him and was even allowed to take a photograph of him for Queen Victoria, felt that he had 'not the capacity for getting a general grip of affairs'. 'His weakness of character is fatal', she wrote, accusing him of '[making] havoc of reigning' once he had found safety in the Russian embassy. No one, apart from the Russians, was happy while he was there. The Japanese, of course, were particularly alarmed, especially since Russian troops were training the Korean army, and in May 1896 they pressured

21 Independence Gate

The Independence Gate was the brainchild of Sŏ Chaep'il and was built to his design. Just outside the West Gate (Sodae-mun) of Seoul stood the Yŏng'ŭn-mun ('Welcoming Favours Gate'), a complex where arriving Chinese envoys were given a ritual greeting. It had been erected by King Sejong in 1429 and extended about 110 years later. Effectively condemned by Kojong's declaration of independence in 1895, it began to be dismantled the following year. On 21 November 1896 foreign diplomats were among the large crowd that watched as the foundation stone of its replacement was laid. The ceremony included demonstrations of drill by boys of the Royal English School and songs sung by those from Paejae School. The new gate now celebrated the liberation from Chinese vassaldom gained at Shimonoseki, and might be interpreted as a thank-offering to Japan. That, at least, was how it managed to escape damage through the colonial period, and even came to be repaired by the Government-General when, in contrast, the nearby

Independence Gate (*Tongnim-mun*), height 12.8 m.

Independence Hall was destroyed. On one side it bore an inscription in Chinese characters (the script in which literate people still communicated) and on the other the same text in *han'gŭl* and the national flag, *taegukki*, which the Independence Club was anxious to promote.

Modelled on the Arc de Triomphe in Paris, this is one of the few examples of novel, Western-style architecture from the late Chosŏn still to be seen in Seoul. (Others include the spire rising over the red brick neo-Gothic of Myŏngdong Cathedral [1892], and the white stone neo-Renaissance building in the corner of the Tŏksu Palace [1909], designed by J. R. Harding and now used as a branch of the National Museum for Contemporary Art.) A contemporary called the gate 'probably the finest piece of masonry in Korea'. In 1979 a road-building scheme caused it to be moved to a new location in the Sodaemun Independence Park.

22 A *Ŭigwe* screen

The Chosŏn court was ruled by study, protocol and ritual. Hours were spent every day in analysis of the Confucian Classics, histories of China and Korea, and the analysis of books on philosophy and politics that would assist current rulers in their search for moralistic programmes of government. Scholars lectured princes and princes lectured bureaucrats on the lessons to be learnt from past experience. Still more time was passed in the punctilious preparation for, and conduct of, rites and ceremonies intended to please Heaven, deities and ancestors. Precedent was everything. Filial piety dictated that what was good enough for the founders of the dynasty must be perpetuated. So rubrics (*ŭigwe*) for today's liturgy and protocol had to be written down in detailed compendia for the guidance of future generations, information provided about the participants, their implements, instruments and costumes, and illustrations added to aid comprehension. *Akhak kweibŏm* was an early Chosŏn example of this. Among the most detailed and best known are the nine-volume set of instructions for the construction of Hwasŏng, with an accompanying eight-panel painted screen and a long handscroll depicting Chŏngjo's excursion there in 1795, the occasion of his mother's 60th birthday. Among the artists who worked on the latter was the famous

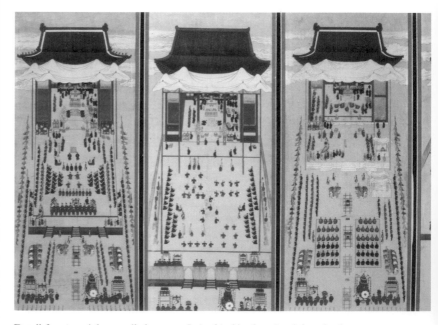

Detail from an eight-panelled screen, *Imin chinch'ando pyŏng*, ink and colour on paper, 1902.

genre painter Kim Tŭksin (Kungjae, 1754–1822). The importance of accuracy meant that responsibility for artwork was given to the Tohwa-sŏ, which came under the Ministry of Rites. Fifteen books of *ŭigwe* survive, covering the period from 1719 to 1902.

Rites fell into five categories, those of worship and sacrifice, celebration and congratulation, greeting, military affairs and mourning. All but the last were accompanied by music and dance, and were arranged by the Court Music Office (Changagwŏn). The ceremonies themselves, and the feasting and entertainment that followed, involved considerable amounts of drink and spanned several days and nights. Military musicians in yellow robes played for processions, and those who accompanied ritual and entertainment wore red. Banquets for the king and his officials were 'outer', those for the dowager queen, the queen consort and other royal women 'inner'. Dancers were of both sexes, though it was only King Chŏngjo who first allowed men to perform at inner banquets. Many of the musicians were blind, though not all, as the hereditary status of court musician before the twentieth century demonstrates.

Aak and *tangak* dances alike were slow and stately. (This was not, of course, a characteristic of Korean dances alone, or one denying the possibility of genuine enjoyment: consider Thomas Morley's description of the pavane as 'a kind of staid music ordained for grave dancing' [1597], and those elegant dances so seriously and so pleasurably performed in the ballrooms of eighteenth-century European houses.) The regular recurrence of the boat dance, fan dance, sword dance, ball-throwing dance and four fairies' dance, not to mention the ever-popular Ch'ŏyong dance, *Ch'ŏyongmu*, points to the underlying conservatism of both rites and entertainment. But change within tradition was not impossible: Crown Prince Ikchong substantially revised the choreography in the late 1820s, dispensing with singers, and the screen depicted here shows some of the modifications to instrumentation that had followed the declaration of independence in 1895. Despite modernization, perfect rites had to be maintained. Nineteenth-century orchestras were rather larger than their predecessors in the eighteenth century: the two orchestras playing in 1902 numbered 104 men. Wind players (of *p'iri* and *taegŭm*) were in the majority, with *kŏmun'go* and *kayagŭm* predominant among the strings and the grand sets of bells and chimes first witnessed in 1114 still evident. The huge double-headed *kŏn'go* drum, 1.5 metres long and surmounted by an ornate wooden pagoda, can be seen in the foreground of the three panels opposite and imposed its authority on the performance.

The screen belongs to the National Center for Korean Traditional Performing Arts.

Moscow into signing a Protocol that, despite reiterating Korean independence, also acknowledged each country's right to station equal numbers of troops and to further its interests in the kingdom. The Independence Club's concern at this was widely shared.

Isabella Bird Bishop left Korea in 1897 'with great regret . . . with Russia and Japan facing each other across her destinies'. Russia had been extending its power in Manchuria during the 1890s, hence its concern when the Treaty of Shimonoseki ceded the Liaodong peninsula to Japan. In 1896 the Russo-Chinese Bank won approval to build the Chinese Eastern Railway (CER) across Manchuria as part of the Trans-Siberian Railway. It also began to build the South Manchurian Railway (SMR), linking the CER with ice-free Dalian (Port Arthur) and, via a branch line, the Korean border town of Sinŭiju. As the imperialist powers carved up China into spheres of influence, Russia seized on Manchuria as a base for industrial expansion, and in March 1898 acquired a 25-year lease on Dalian and territory at the end of the Liaodong peninsula. Although Japan's equivalent region of paramountcy was far away in south-east China, facing Taiwan, Tokyo, which had its own eye on the rich natural resources of Manchuria, could not fail to view growing Russian influence on both sides of the Korean threshold with concern. The Protocol was not enough, and on 25 April 1898 the foreign minister, Nichi Tokujirō, signed an agreement with the Russian minister to Japan undertaking that neither country would provide Korea with financial or military aid, and that Russia would not interfere with Japanese business or industrialization projects in Korea. A victory for Japan, then, and in October it was followed by another. Kojong and the Independence Club, which had more than 2,000 members as the Taehan Empire was inaugurated, pressed their luck too far by trying to introduce 25 of them into the king's Privy Council. Fighting broke out on the streets of Seoul; the king lost his nerve and closed the Club down; its members were tortured and imprisoned (thus disproving one of Mrs Bishop's assertions, that 'brutal punishments and torture are done away with'). It was another instance of Kojong's besetting sin, his habit of backtracking instead of sticking up for his convictions.

In 1900 the Boxer Rising brought Russian troops into Manchuria to protect their interests. The following year Russia obtained a concession to develop timber resources at Andong, on the Manchurian-Korean border, and by now it was not only Japan that was troubled by the bear's growing power across the region. In April 1902 Great Britain signed an alliance with Japan in which each country acknowledged the other's special treaty rights in China and Korea respectively, and promised assistance if they were threatened by conflict. A year later Russia reneged on a deal with China to withdraw its troops from Manchuria, and tried on the contrary to acquire and build on land at Yŏngamp'o, at the mouth of the Yalu. When negotiations between Tokyo and St Petersburg failed to resolve their differences in late 1903, the countdown to war had really begun, and the Japanese extracted permission from Kojong to disperse their troops across Korea for its supposed protection. In January 1904 Kojong proclaimed Korea's neutrality in the dispute. On 9 February Japanese ships attacked Russian warships in Dalian and Chemulp'o (Inch'ŏn) without warning; next day its soldiers marched into Seoul; Tokyo's declaration of war followed. The land campaign was fierce: Japanese casualties – 81,455 dead and 381,313 wounded – were far greater than in the Sino-Japanese war. It was, however, inconclusive and mercifully brief: by March the two armies had fought themselves to a standstill around Shenyang. Two months later 35 ships of the Russian Baltic fleet arrived in Korean waters, ending a long journey that proved to be not only fruitless but disastrous. To the utter amazement of the Western world, all but three of the vessels were destroyed as the Japanese fleet attacked them off Tsushima.

If the war was virtually over, Tokyo was already planning the next, diplomatic, stage of its offensive to redraw the map of north-east Asia. In April 1905 it concluded a fresh treaty with Great Britain, which again recognized Japan's privileged status on the peninsula and this time failed to refer to Korean independence. A memorandum following a meeting on 27 July between the US secretary of state, William Taft, and the Japanese prime minister, Katsura Tarō, showed that Taft saw a Japanese protectorate as holding out the best chance of peace in the region. In August the Korean government accepted a demand for Japanese-nominated foreign advisers to take up posts in ministries concerned with finance and foreign affairs, and very soon they were introduced into the defence, education, police and even royal household ministries too. So by the time that the Treaty of Portsmouth, New Hampshire, was signed in September 1905, the Japanese could be sure that world opinion was running their way. It gave them the former Russian concessions in Lushun and Dalian, development rights in Manchuria and possession of the SMR. Two months later armed Japanese soldiers shut up Emperor Kojong in the Tŏksu Palace and forced the foreign minister Pak Chesun to sign a treaty with the Japanese minister Hayashi Gonsuke on 17 November. As heinous crimes go it may not have ranked with their assassination of Queen Min ten years before, but its implications were immense. The Protectorate established by the treaty afforded Japan almost unlimited powers over the Korean people.

Another triple intervention, that of the imperialist nations into Korea's understanding of sovereignty, reform and modernization, had helped explain the country's hastening collapse through the late nineteenth and early twentieth centuries. Put another way, Korea had long been accustomed to enjoying de facto independence in return for observing Chinese and Japanese customs of ritual diplomacy and trade. It did not appreciate the sudden revival of either Chinese claims to suzerainty or Japanese assumptions of tutelage rights. Left to themselves, Koreans might have embraced change in time (think, for example, of Yŏngjo's dreams of ending slavery). But the *sirhak* persuasion, though well intentioned, was too gradualist and unfocused when compared with the determined Meiji transformation of Japan and Japanese modernizers' vision of what they could do, given the chance, with a reorganized Korean economy. In that contrast the heart of the issue is laid bare: committed leadership was vital in the handling of modernization, and modernization was the burning issue in the understanding and manipulation of nationalism. Korea's leaders could not agree on the best way forward. In both court and government advocates of self-strengthening were to be found. Late in the century, some began to accept the need for political reform. But consensus was impossible, not least because the strongest supporters of change were pro-Japanese, or at least associated with foreigners who themselves seemed to accept Japanese ideas on Korean development.

MOVES TOWARDS MODERNIZATION

Korea knew of old how it stood – or according to its own perspective expected to stand – in relation to its regional neighbours. In diplomatic terms, that meant China first, Korea second, Japan third, and the Ryūkyūs fourth; in non-tributary, commercial terms, the playing field was more level. It even had a fair idea of what to expect of imperial Russia, given past experience of its predecessors in Manchuria. The *Imjin Waeran* and Manchu conquests had given Korea's world a severe shaking, but it had quickly recovered its familiar, and fairly comfortable, size and shape. *Sirhak* and Catholicism had scratched its surface a little in the first half of the nineteenth century, but nothing had forewarned the inhabitants of the Hermit Kingdom of its impending total fracture in the second half of the nineteenth century. How did such a cataclysm come about and who was to blame: was it failure on the part of Korea's own leaders, or did the impact of Western imperialism on China and Japan make it inevitable?

Europeans had set foot on Korean soil well before the mid-nineteenth century. The first was Gregorio de Cespedes, a Spanish missionary from Omura who landed on 27 December 1593 to minister to Konishi Yukinaga's Catholic troops. A Dutch pirate, Jan Weltevree, was next, abandoned by his Chinese ship near Kyŏngju in 1627 and making his home there. And in 1653 thirty-six Dutchmen, including Hendrik Hamel, were shipwrecked on Cheju island. On their return to Holland in 1669 Hamel published the story of their adventures, which included a period of service as musketeers in the royal guard at Seoul. It was the first account of Korea in any Western language, and was translated into French and English. In 1797 a British sloop, HMS *Providence*, landed Captain William Broughton and a party of men near Pusan. In 1832 the Prussian Protestant missionary Karl Gützlaff sailed along the west coast of Korea on an East India Company vessel, *Lord Amherst*, and spent a month there, meeting officials and villagers. He gained some idea of the flexibility permitted within the country's tributary relationship with China, and formed a favourable impression of the prospects for commerce. But before it could take advantage the Honourable Company lost its monopoly in the East, and with the advent of free trade the Western nations became deeply embroiled in competition for commercial, diplomatic and missionary influence in China and Japan. Korea did not really impinge on their notice until 1866, when ominous events occurred.

As regent, the Taewŏn'gun endeavoured to protect Korea's international isolation. It is easy to understand why he would hesitate to upset the status quo: pre-Meiji Japan seemed content with the existing pattern for exchanging diplomatic and cultural missions, and since the late 1830s China's attention had been distracted by problems around its coasts. Word would certainly have reached him about the dire consequences of the 'Opium Wars' and the Anglo-French destruction of Beijing's wonderful Summer Palace in 1860, and if Western bees were beginning to swarm round the honeypot of northern China, they should be discouraged from buzzing around Korea too. After a number of inconsequential foreign efforts to trade during the 1830s, '40s and '50s, an American merchant ship, the *General Sherman*, sailed from China in August 1866 and entered the Taedong river, heading towards P'yŏngyang. It ran aground and local people killed all on board, not without some degree of provocation. And as they died, a wider tragedy was engulfing Catholics across the kingdom. Since 1845 three French bishops, Ferréol (d. 1853), Berneux and Daveluy, had worked quietly and unopposed in and around Seoul. The Taewŏn'gun's wife was a convert, but more important to the Great Prince was the fact that he owed a favour to the anti-Christian family of Dowager Queen Cho, and a misunderstanding over a meeting he called with Berneux was the innocent signal for the start of the worst anti-Christian persecution in Korean history. Nine French missionary priests, including the two surviving bishops, were executed in 1866, and over the next two years perhaps 8,000 out of an estimated total of 23,000 Catholics were martyred. The French Asiatic Fleet in northern China was ordered to take revenge, and in October of that fateful year seven of Admiral Roze's ships inflicted heavy damage on Kanghwa island, though they made little progress towards their main target of Seoul. Almost five years later, in 1871, the American authorities in China, having failed to get compensation for the loss of the *General Sherman*, dispatched a punitive expedition of their own under Admiral John Rodgers. Once more poor Kanghwa suffered badly, despite better protection by cannonry in the aftermath of the French expedition. When the five American ships sailed up the Han river towards Seoul, the intensity of the resistance forced them back. Isolationism was standing firm, just.

The new Meiji government of Japan, however, instituted in 1868, was determined to put an end to it, and in September 1875 the warship *Unyō* provoked incidents on and around Kanghwa and Tongnae to give the Japanese an excuse. A strong naval force carried General Kuroda Kiyotaka to Kanghwa to open negotiations, and there in February 1876 Korea signed its first international treaty of modern times. It gave the Japanese diplomatic representation, extraterritoriality, entry to Korean ports, the right to use their own currency there and exemption from import taxes. Kojong saw advantages in opening up his country to foreign influence, and later that year dispatched Kim Kisu on an investigative mission to Japan, the first of several that would study examples of Meiji modernization at first hand. Kim's report was lukewarm, but in 1880 a group led by Kim Hongjip returned with a strongly worded memorandum from a Chinese counsellor in Tokyo, Huang Zunxian, arguing that for its survival and progress Korea must align itself with China, Japan and the United States and copy the Meiji model. In January 1881 Kojong authorized the creation of a foreign ministry, the T'ongni-gimu Amun, with twelve departments handling not only diplomatic relations but also such things as foreign trade, foreign-language teaching and shipbuilding. The following month twelve senior officials led a 62-man delegation to Japan to investigate industry, commerce, law, military affairs, education and medicine. Five years on from the Treaty of Kanghwa *sirhak* sympathizers were entitled to feel encouraged, but strict Confucian defenders of tradition were by no means beaten, and the battle for influence over the king intensified. This was the background against which the Kaehwadang and the Sadaedang adopted their respective positions, and into which the Taewŏn'gun again intruded, plotting against his son and Queen Min.

A flurry of treaties now followed. In May 1882 Commodore Robert Shufeldt signed a Treaty of Amity and Commerce giving Americans diplomatic and commercial opportunities in Korea and inflaming anti-foreign feeling. It contributed to the Imo Incident in July and was not appeased by the consequent Chemulp'o Treaty with Japan, settled on 30 August. Korea agreed, *inter alia*, to pay 50,000 yen compensation for twelve Japanese soldiers killed, 500,000 yen for damage to Japanese property and the cost of military expenses, and to accept the stationing of Japanese soldiers at the Seoul legation. (In November 1884, shortly before the Kapsin coup, Japan wrote off nearly 80 per cent of this debt, but a similar rate of compensation was demanded in respect of Japanese killed during the Tonghak rebellion, a claim strongly denounced by *The Independent News* in May 1896.) Kaehwadang members Pak Yŏnghyo, Kim Okkyun and Sŏ Kwangbŏm (1859–1897) were sent to Tokyo with an apology, but Japanese satisfaction was dampened the same month by a trade agreement signed with China. Li Hongzhang posted Ma Jianzhong and Paul-Georg von Möllendorff to the Korean court as counsellors. The Prussian, the first Westerner to be accredited to the Korean court, was 'stared at by a crowd of thousands' as he arrived on 13 December 1882. He was quick to assist Kojong with the signing of treaties with Great Britain and Germany in 1883 and Italy and Russia in 1884.

Min Yŏngik spent nearly five months of 1883 in the United States, presenting a request from Kojong for American advisers and returning to Korea via European capitals. What the king had in mind was principally military advice. What he got was no more than the posting of a single naval attaché, George Foulk, from Yokohama. Foulk, however, was a man of wide interests and many accomplishments. He helped with agricultural and mining developments, promoted new furniture design and even found to his surprise that he liked Korean music. Meanwhile the course set by the would-be modernizers was leading into choppy waters. The Kapsin coup attempt reflected their impatience for Japanese-style reforms, but its aftermath only whipped the storm up further. The Treaty of Seoul (Hansŏng) obligated Seoul to pay further compensation of 150,000 yen for damage to property and Japanese victims, and the Li-Itō agreement in April 1885 left Chinese claims to suzerainty over Korea unimpaired. When, nevertheless, Seoul appointed a minister of its own to Japan in 1887 without informing Beijing, Korea sailed into the thick of Sino-Japanese rivalry as well as its own political maelstrom.

To make matters worse, Anglo-Russian rivalry now also appeared on the Korean horizon. London was worried that von Möllendorff might persuade King Kojong to favour Russia as a counter to Japan. Russia was already threatening British interests in Afghanistan, and might also compete with British commercial interests in north-east China and Korea, modest though the latter still were. In 1885, therefore, three British naval craft landed sailors on the small group of Kŏmun-do islands off Korea's south-west coast, which London believed would deter any similar Russian moves off the north-east coast. In fact, despite the presence of an able minister, Karl Waeber, in Seoul, Russian plans were not yet as advanced as the British feared, and by February 1887 the futile occupation was over. Von Möllendorff may (or may not) have been misjudged. He served Kojong well over the Western treaties, set up the T'ongni-gimu Amun's English Interpreters' School, and advised on the creation of a Maritime Customs Service (1883). Li Hongzhang thought that he was over-encouraging Korean dreams of independence, while George Foulk, as acting US envoy, shared Britain's concern over Russia and was instrumental in having the Prussian recalled to China in 1885. The antipathy between Foulk and von Möllendorff was not the only personality clash to disturb the foreign community. Men, and occasionally women, who represented their governments, mission boards or merchant companies in this newly opening land, or who blazed their own trails to get there, were frequently forceful characters, and amid novel, difficult and sometimes dangerous circumstances animosities were bound to occur. Foulk also distrusted Yuan Shikai's personal ambition, but when Yuan complained about Foulk's anti-Chineseness, the State Department withdrew him in 1887: Washington was more sensitive to its relations with China and Japan than with Korea, which in terms of international priorities was not of front-rank importance. King Kojong, even so, regarded the United States as an essential guide to modernizing his country, and sent young men to study there in 1889.

Japan's view of itself as the entitled regional leader remained unshaken. The Tonghak Rebellion and Sino-Japanese war enhanced its position in Korea and its continental ambitions. It could scarcely have predicted the sudden propulsion of Russia into a lead part in the international drama as an aftermath of the Kabo reforms and Queen Min's murder, but within ten years it managed to turn even this to its advantage. It is easy for today's historians to pick Japan's motives through the period 1864 to 1905 to pieces, and to see its policies in Korea as imitation of Western imperialism in China. But we should not forget that the West had little idea at the time of Japan's strength and was shocked by the ease of its success over much larger neighbours. It acknowledged Tokyo's order that Westerners in Korea were not to be victimized, and largely accepted Japan's claim to be acting in the interest of Korean independence. China, of course, was under no illusions about the threat it posed in Korea, that is to say the threat to China's own interests – it was not in the least bothered about the Koreans and their fate. But without the benefit of hindsight, Westerners in Korea, especially those with the country's modernization and improvement at heart, did not subscribe to today's critical view of imperialism in action. They harboured no long-term suspicions and generally got on well with their neighbours from the Land of the Rising Sun, despite Count Inoue's later admission that his compatriots were arrogant, uncooperative and violent towards Koreans. (The foreign diplomatic community appreciated his urbane and courteous manner, and when he left in October 1895 King Kojong apologized for not being able to confer a decoration on him.) *The Korean Repository* for May 1895 declared: 'Korea is independent. But she is ignorant of the duties and responsibilities of this independence. She must have a teacher, a guide, a reformer. Japan has taken her hand. She did not wait to be invited. The country must follow. *The country will follow.*'

Even Koreans with later reputations as strong nationalists were not yet sure which way to turn. Yun Ch'iho and Sŏ Chaep'il had both been fired with enthusiasm for ideas of modernization and reform after visiting Japan as young men. Both fled there in 1885, and went on to gain university educations in America before returning to Korea in the 1890s. Yun had also spent time in China, where he was baptized a Methodist. Though profoundly ashamed of his own country's backwardness and traditional dependence on China and impressed by Japan's progressiveness, he wrote during the Sino–Japanese war: 'For the good of the East, may Japan succeed.' He was under no illusions about its self-interest, however, and as one of the founders of the Independence Club, opted for the West and Christian civilization as a preferable model for Korea's modernization and emancipation. Sŏ also took the social Darwinist view that Western civilization was essential to the survival of a backward Korea, and that Japan would be the Asian filter through which Korea would receive and understand it best. Korea's future, he believed, might have to be tied for some time to Japanese tutelage, even if a cautious eye would have to be kept on its political goals. He envisaged the economic revival of north-east Asia based on Korea as a supplier of raw materials to Japan as a manufacturer. Japan had, after all, cornered the market for such diverse and popular items as silk handkerchiefs, toothbrushes and safety matches. And at least Japan was an Asian neighbour, unlike Russia, whose motives he also began to suspect. Soon, even Emperor Kojong himself wearied of these opinions, and six months before the Independence Club's violent closure in November 1898 Sŏ returned under pressure to the United States, handing over editorship of the *Tongnip Sinmun* to Yun Ch'iho until it ceased publication on 4 December 1899. Other Korean-language papers arose to take up its theme of nationalism, while the drive for modernization continued and the Japanese increased their power commensurately. They acquired a lucrative ginseng monopoly, started a steamship line, and after buying Korea's first railway (the 28-mile line from Seoul to Chemulp'o; the journey took two-and-a-half hours) from the American company that built it, then tried to take up parts of Seoul's new electric tramway system where it crossed the track. According to Kojong's American adviser William Sands, 'Japan had a definite policy and . . . nothing should stand in the way of it. If it was a concession or a company or any other business entity it must be acquired or controlled by Japanese capital.' Some Koreans, of course, found opportunities to benefit, for some were less than scrupulous about working with or for the Japanese, and as official corruption increased, the peasantry felt the predictable burden of excessive taxation. The Tonghak leader Son Pyŏnghŭi (1861–1922) supported an uprising in 1901 and was exiled to Japan, where he changed the organization's title to Ch'ŏndo-gyo ('Heavenly Way Teaching'), the name under which it continues to the present day. He at least saw the link between Japanese policy and the suffering of Korea's lower classes. For others, disillusionment with Japan's motives still lay in the future. Early in 1905 even such ardent later nationalists as Yi Sŭngman and An Chunggŭn welcomed Japan's victory over Russia.

CHANGES IN CONTEMPORARY CULTURE

Lucius Foote arrived in Seoul in May 1883 to set up the American legation, the first for a Western nation, and on 22 September 1884 the 26-year-old Horace Allen joined him as its physician. Coming from Shanghai, Allen was unimpressed by his first sight of the capital city. The great city gates, the extensive royal palaces and the Japanese legation opened after the Kanghwa Treaty were all impressive in their way, but virtually everything else was single-storeyed and most of the constructions were thatched. Trees and flowering shrubs brightened Allen's first September impressions, but wood-burning stoves soon draped a pall of smoke over winter streets; the stink and sound of open drains and disease pervaded narrow alleys; and the tolling of the curfew bell shut people up through the hours of darkness. Little did Allen, the first Western doctor and first Protestant missionary in Korea, imagine how he would grow to love this country and its people; what recognition he would receive from King Kojong; or how much he would contribute to its modernization and changing cultural outlook. On 4 December, summoned to the scene of carnage at the Post Office, he must have wondered just what he had come to. He could do nothing for Hŏng Yŏngsik, but it was his skill that saved Min Yŏngik's life, and Kojong was quick to show his gratitude. He awarded foreigners land for the establishment of their own quarter, and authorized the founding of a Western-style teaching hospital, the Kwanghye-wŏn. It was the breakthrough the foreigners needed to launch their work. Their quarter, Chong-dong, was situated close to the Tŏksu Palace. At first they bought or rented Korean property. Then, as time passed, they built their own churches and chapels, their legations, shops, houses and social meeting places. There the Methodist missionary Mary Scranton bought 'nineteen straw huts and unsightly strips of unoccupied land' in 1886 for the first girls' school in Korea, forerunner of today's Ewha University. Protestant missionaries formed the biggest occupational group among the Westerners, but the most conspicuous sign of the Christian presence in Seoul, the red-brick, Gothic-style Catholic cathedral soaring high over the city, was not in Chong-dong but on a hilltop in Myŏng-dong. Also outside the Chong-dong community, near the South Gate, lay the Japanese enclave. The Japanese minister 'lived in his citadel as in a feudal castle', wrote Sands, protected by a 'miniature army' of artillery, cavalry and infantry. There were 2,366 Japanese in Seoul in 1901, fewer than the Chinese who spread across the whole city, but considerably more than the 200 or so Westerners, of whom the British were the largest contingent.

Foreigners worked for the court and government in a range of capacities. The king appointed Horace Allen as his physician; Queen Min did the same for Annie Ellers Bunker and Lillias Underwood (though she did not dispense with the services of her favourite shaman, Chillyŏng-gun). The Irishman John MacLeavey Brown joined the Maritime Customs Service in 1893. As chief financial adviser to the government after 1896 he had the main streets of Seoul (Picture Essay 23) widened and cleaned up. The Englishman William Hutchinson was appointed to run the Royal English School when Kojong reformed it in 1894, struggling to gain *yangban* acceptance of Western learning as a training for future officials instead of traditional Chinese classicism. American William Dye, one of those involved in spiriting Kojong from his palace to the Russian embassy in 1895, trained soldiers at the newly

23 Map of Seoul

The Korean branch of the Royal Asiatic Society was formed in 1900 by a group of Westerners, among whom were the missionaries James Scarth Gale and Homer Hulbert and the international diplomat J. MacLeavey Brown. It announced its presence by publishing its *Transactions*. (Produced regularly to the present day except for the years 1904–11, 1941–7 and 1951–6, this series remains a major source of information on Korean culture.) Among its first activities was the preparation of a map of Seoul, drawn in the manner of Korean maps of the capital dating back to the late eighteenth century. In keeping with Korean custom it adopted – though not consistently – an itinerant perspective, sometimes presenting the viewer with buildings and text on their side and upside down. Place and street names were shown in characters and *han'gŭl*, but not in any romanized form. The letters and numbers of a grid appeared round the edges, though grid lines were not drawn across the face of the map and the copy of the *Transactions* that printed the map contained no descriptive article that would have rendered grid references useful.

Cartography had a long history in Korea. Old maps, like their Chinese counterparts, emphasized the situation of mountains and rivers, as much for their *p'ungsu* (Ch. *fengshui*) importance as for navigational assistance. Maps were also valued for administrative and military purposes, and under the Chosŏn government their compilation was the responsibility of the Tohwa-sŏ. *Sirhak* scholars were aware of the advances in cartography introduced to China by Jesuit missionaries, and their efforts to improve their accuracy and content culminated in the work of the greatest of all Korean mapmakers, Kim Chŏngho (d. 1864). From 1885 foreigners used a version of his 1861 map of Seoul, and this was the basis of the RAS map, which added much more information about roads, buildings and names.

There were eight gates in the walls of Seoul, plus a water gate. Their official names, appearing on maps and in formal documents, were ornate, but commonly they were known simply as the Great East Gate, Great South Gate, Little West Gate, etc. Attempts have been made in modern times to reintroduce the official names for the two that survive in today's metropolis, the East and South gates. The North Gate, Sukch'ong-mun, was located south-east of Pugak-san, the mountain that looked down protectively on the Kyŏngbok Palace. Because of *p'ungsu* problems it was rarely used, and after 1413 it remained permanently shut. The South Gate, the main entrance to the old city, was actually in the south-west corner, to one side of the 'southern mountain', Namsan. Today its only function, as it stands lonely and surrounded by skyscrapers, is as a traffic island. Just inside the West Gate (seen near the bottom left of this pic-

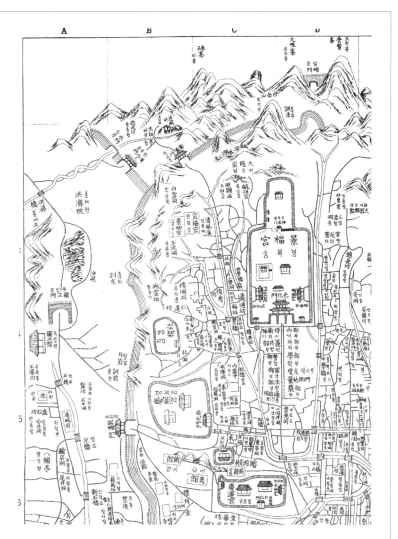

RAS Map of Seoul (detail), 1902.

ture) lay the Kyŏnghŭi Palace, built as a detached palace in 1616 and pulled down during the Japanese colonial period. Foreigners called it the Mulberry Palace, after the trees planted there by one of their number in 1884 as part of a sericulture experiment. Outside it, and a little to the north, the Independence Gate can be seen straddling the road. Below, on its side, stands the Independence Club's debating hall.

established Military Academy until the Japanese had him dismissed. By the beginning of the twentieth century Seoul had electric lighting, tramcars, a railway, a telegraph, running water, modern hospitals and schools, orphanages, a YMCA, and Korean- and English-language journals. It had been introduced to concepts of democracy and Protestant interpretations of the Christian message. (Koreans failed to understand the relationship between Catholicism and Protestantism, regarding them as separate religions. Catholics concentrated on doctrinal teaching rather than the good works of modernization and social welfare, and many Koreans still associated them with the controversy over Neo-Confucian rites.) But even in the cities change came slowly and in the countryside it was scarcely noticeable. In Seoul, for example, traditional medicine, with centuries of empirical expertise in herbalism and acupuncture, was not simply going to roll over in the face of novel and expensive Western medical prescriptions. Western medicine was an offshoot of Protestant Christianity, and public opinion was wary of missionaries' motives. That said, their sacrificial work on behalf of the needy, especially at times of epidemic and natural disaster, and their contributions to modern education gradually made the public tolerant of their presence and eccentric ways. Baptizing converts mattered to them, naturally, but was not immediately their primary target, and a degree of vagueness surrounds the figures given by different sources for their success. Horace Allen baptized only about forty in his first four years. Lillias Underwood wrote of a hundred Methodists and Presbyterians in 1889, but according to the *Korea Review* the number of baptized converts had risen to nearly 20,000 by 1905.

The coming of the West was not in itself the panacea that transformed Korea. Certainly, Westerners were the agents of a great deal of change. But much of Korea's progress was the result of its own people's positive outlook. They looked with grudging admiration at Japan's leap forward, and while eschewing the totality of the Meiji conversion, they knew how greatly it contrasted with China's dithering response to Western offers of help. Like the Chinese, they reacted with a debate about modernization and reform and with a Self-Strengthening Movement (*chagang undong*), and, softened up perhaps by earlier *sirhak* arguments, they were prepared to relax the narrow introspection of Chinese classicism to reap the consequent benefits. Of course, the scale of mobilizing change was vastly different in Korea than in China, and in the face of events from 1894 onwards it was easier to concentrate the creative energy of nationalism in a more focused way, an anti-Japanese way. It was not so much that the West was liked, rather that it offered the same advantages as Japan but in a less aggressive manner.

When it came to art, it was too soon for Western styles to make much impact on Korean culture in the nineteenth century. At least the Japanese had the advantage of being part of the shared orientalist tradition, and it would – ironically – be they who were the catalysts for the most sweeping changes in Korean cultural habits, by introducing Korean painters to the new waves sweeping through European and American art. That would not take place until the twentieth century. Meanwhile, Kim Chunggun (Kisan) achieved some renown among Westerners in the last years of the century by selling them simple pictures of Korean occupations and amusements, an unlikely interpretation of genre painting that has earned him a valued place in several European and American museums (Picture Essay 24). Westerners introduced novel concepts in the form of oil painting, newspapers and hymn singing – the last especially via Ewha and Paejae schools. But the overwhelming preference among Korean artists swung in favour of traditional Chinese subjects and styles. Top-quality genre painting and *t'aenghwa* (Buddhist painting) were in decline; landscapes, flowers, birds, animals and bamboo ruled. Painters even deserted the True View to return to the expressionism of the Chinese Southern style. The porcelain industry, on the other hand, had never chosen to follow the mid-Qing path by developing its range of colours, decorative patterns or technical innovations such as overglaze enamels. The *yangban* still preferred the monochromes, plain lines and simple textures that had so distinguished early Chosŏn porcelain and *punch'ŏng*. Potters had introduced variety in the form of blue and white ware and through the greater use of decorative inlay, but the refinement that had accompanied early Chosŏn products was no longer startling in its originality or perfection. Ceramics suffered the characteristic heaviness of *fin-de-siècle* art. Nor had Korean metalworkers found the highly coloured cloisonné enamels so admired in China to their taste, or that of their customers. The single most important cultural development of the late Chosŏn era was musical, the growth of instrumental *sanjo*. Even that, really, belonged to the realm of folk rather than high art, though its evolution and popularization were undoubtedly assisted by the fact that the *yangban* enjoyed it.

The pages of *The Korean Repository* show that Western residents in Seoul were aware of and took an interest in the great arts of the past. But on the market stalls they fell for the bright folk paintings, wood carvings, embroidered textiles, intricate knots and tassels, stitched wrapping cloths, shining brasswork, coloured fans and bamboo items such as pipes, brushpots and woven mats. To be sure, the late nineteenth century was not a great period for high art, and if Western writers today tend to pass

24 Kisan, *Chess Players*

Kisan, *Chess Players*, ink and colour on paper, late 19th century.

On my early visits to Seoul in the 1970s I quickly noted that in middle-class, Westernized company it was impolite to smoke in the presence of elders and social superiors. And when I was asked if I smoked and answered in the negative, I was somewhat nonplussed to get the reply, 'Oh, so you're a Christian then?' Both reasons for my surprise – the conventions associated with the habit and the apparent link between the habit and a matter of personal faith – have historical explanations, though an element of uncertainty hangs over both. Tobacco is said to have arrived in Korea in 1618 from Japan, where European merchants had introduced it. Five years later the king, Kwanghae, had himself become an addict and issued an embargo on a habit that was presumably cloaking and choking with smoke those who felt their dignity compromised by it. The habit of smoking, however, quickly became widespread among men and women, and by the early eighteenth century tobacco was grown as a valuable cash crop. Smoking was a popular social activity, especially among the *yangban*. Seniority and superiority were underlined by the length and quality of the pipe (see Picture Essay 29), and a scholar might expect to have his servant light his pipe for him. He might also use his pipe as a conversational aid to emphasize a point in his argument. Many of Kisan's late nineteenth-century genre paintings show gentlemen playing board games, watching musical performances and entertaining *kisaeng*, pipe in hand or laid on the ground beside them. But working men also smoked long pipes, and other pictures show them, the end of their pipe supported by a loop of cord or leather hung from the ceiling, with both hands free to get on with their job. To many of the early Protestant missionaries, smoking tobacco came into the same category as taking opium, drinking alcohol, gambling and taking concubines, and they had considerable success in commanding their converts to give up the habit. Some were already concerned at the economic effects of smoking on the individual and the country as a whole; others, we must suspect, simply added it to their list of activities banned as a means of 'improving' a backward race.

Korean chess commemorates the battles between Liu Bang and Xiang Yu that resulted in the founding of China's Han dynasty. The board is marked with ten horizontal and nine vertical lines, and the 32 pieces stand on their intersections. They are flat, and inscribed with the names 'general', 'aide', 'horseman', 'elephant', 'chariot' and 'catapult'. Players move them along the lines, trying to checkmate their opponent's general within his base camp.

Chess (Kor. *changgi*) must not be confused with the pebble game *paduk* (Jap. *go*). This is also about capturing territory, but the *paduk* board has nineteen lines in each direction and the pieces are flat black and white stones, 181 against 180. It is a more intellectual struggle, and its aficionados tend to think themselves superior to chess players.

rather quickly over its output in the literati tradition, those with a feeling for the spirit and passion of its folk artists, like those early expatriates, find plenty to enthuse over. Nor, to be honest, was this an exceptional period for folk art, either in quality or variety, but it *was* the age to which many museum collections around the world now turn to illustrate what cultural identity meant to the majority of Koreans, for the artefacts they display frequently come from collections made by foreigners who saw it at first hand, and who bought up the evidence for it. They took photographs, too. The first to do so was an enterprising Venetian, Felice Beato, who sailed with Admiral Rodgers in 1871 and returned with dramatic pictures of the fierce fighting on 10–11 June. Mrs Bishop, too, was an inveterate photographer as well as an incisive observer of politics and society. She, and missionaries such as the Presbyterian Horace Underwood, laid the foundations of photographic archives that are widely used today.

III

A Century of
Suffering

CHAPTER SEVEN

Culture under Threat, 1905–45: The Colonial Era

This chapter looks at the only period when the whole of Korea has been under foreign occupation. It was a time of intense suffering and one that still prompts feelings of shame and anger among Koreans. Yet Japanese modernization brought benefits, and the resistance movement also spawned elements of progress, especially in cultural spheres.

THE POLITICAL FRAMEWORK

From Protectorate to Annexation, 1905–10

Five years after the Protectorate Treaty in 1905, the Treaty of Annexation turned Korea into a fully fledged Japanese colony. Twenty-one years after that, in 1931, Japan would take over Manchuria too, with such unwarranted ease that deconstructionist historians like to see therein the origins of World War Two. In the example set by the League of Nations' failure to act against militarism they certainly have a point. But the international community had already given implicit encouragement to Japanese expansionism. Where was the condemnation of the annexation in 1910, and who, other than Christian missionaries, showed solidarity with Koreans in their suffering under the oppressive colonial rule that followed? Why would the Hague Peace Conference in 1907 not denounce the Japanese imposition of the Protectorate, as Emperor Kojong begged it to do, thereby saving him from enforced abdication? Was it that Western nations were too stunned by Japan's recent defeat of imperial Russia? Had the Japanese prime minister Katsura Tarō really laid to rest all doubts about Japanese ambitions at his meeting with Secretary of State Taft on 27 July 1905? If we like to imagine that today's response to a Japanese seizure of Korea would be different, we have to remember that, in those far-off times, when imperialism and colonialism were widely accepted as semi-philanthropic in their intent, President Roosevelt was probably quite sincere in viewing regional progress under Japanese direction as the best bet for peace in the Pacific. And neither he nor the Japanese were impressed by the image of backwardness and division that Korea had created for itself in the late nineteenth century.

The Protectorate Treaty was the brainchild of the great Meiji states-man Itō Hirobumi. The *Hwangsŏng Sinmun* ('Capital News') had wel-comed him on a visit to Seoul in March 1904, proclaiming that 'Korea and Japan must from this day onward unite their hearts and combine their strength'. On 9 November 1905 he was back, and Homer Hulbert's *Korea Review* greeted his appointment as the first Japanese resident-gen-eral (Tōkan) in December 1905 by writing: 'His early return will not only be pleasing to the Korean emperor, but very many of the common peo-ple will expect much better treatment from officials and citizen represen-tatives of Japan than they would otherwise hope to have.' However, *Hwangsŏng Sinmun* quickly changed its tune: 'This treaty . . . destroys our nation', it lamented, and by November 1906 the *Korea Review* also was complaining: 'Korea is being treated as conquered territory. In spite of rights that are centuries old Koreans are being treated precisely as the Ainus or Formosans would be if they were here.' Prince Yonghwan, nephew of Queen Min and a passionately nationalistic former prime minister, who had done his best to resist the treaty, committed suicide on 30 November 1905. An immense crowd watched his funeral procession and shops stayed closed for days. In a farewell note to the Korean people he wrote: 'It pains me to think that my twenty million compatriots shall perish in the coming struggle for existence.' He was spared the ignominy of witnessing Itō take up his new post in February 1906.

Itō's responsibility, according to the treaty, was to direct Korea's diplomatic and commercial affairs, and nominally he was answerable to its emperor. The resident-general has been described as a sort of 'super-ambassador'. The Japanese government sent an American citizen, Durham Stevens, to advise the Koreans on foreign affairs, but he worked secretly for Itō, and in 1908 two Korean Christians assassinated him in San Francisco as he tried to argue the case for Japanese policy in Korea. By that time the tentacles of Japanese interest were reaching into all areas of Korean life, and even the ability to control domestic affairs was spi-ralling beyond Korean reach. The pretence that Japan was defending Korea's independence quickly disappeared, and when Kojong sent envoys to The Hague Peace Conference and Washington in June 1907 vainly appealing against the Protectorate, the cabinet in Tokyo made its next fateful move. On 22 June Kojong was forced to abdicate, and no sooner was Crown Prince Yi Ch'ŏk enthroned as the puppet emperor Sunjong than his younger brother, ten-year-old Yi Ŭn was hauled off hostage-wise to Japan for his education. Koreans with long memories might have recalled that back in the Unified Silla period this had been a common feature of 'serving the great', though the 'great' had at least then been the respected China, not the hated Japan. On 24 July the prime minister, Yi Wanyong, signed a new treaty legalizing the resident-general's authority over virtually all matters of government.

Japanese officials now took effective control of the country. The Korean army of almost 9,000 soldiers was disbanded and Japanese military police (Kempeitai) harshly enforced the law, supported by Japanese courts. Many former soldiers joined *ŭibyŏng*, partisan guerrilla forces in Korea and Manchuria, whose mainly peasant members welcomed the new recruits. Their name, 'righteous armies', was an inspirational reminder of the irregular forces that had so harassed the Japanese back in the 1590s. But the authorities could count on support from the growing number of Japanese immigrants, who by 1908 totalled 127,000, and from compliant Koreans. Among numerous groups spawned by the Self-Strengthening Movement there were those that believed that Koreans must make political and economic progress by their own efforts, but others, despairing of 'backwardness' and 'incompetence', felt that advantage should be taken of Japanese assistance. These roughly equated with the Sinminhoe ('New People's Association'), established in 1907 by An Ch'angho, and the Ilchinhoe ('United Progress Society'). Later Koreans over-simplistically lauded or condemned their members as nationalists and collaborators respectively. Sinminhoe was instrumental in launching Korea's first joint stock company, the P'yŏngyang Porcelain Company, in 1908. With its encouragement, patriotic Koreans reacted against Japanese control of education and the press by opening new schools, printing new papers and pro-Korean books, and forming patriotic societies that functioned until the authorities closed them down. Ilchinhoe faced no such risk. Founded on the eve of the Protectorate in 1904, it went so far as to call for unification with Japan in 1909, and on Annexation its 140,000 or so members made it the largest political party. The Japanese undertook a much-needed modernization programme. They encouraged industrial development and the building of roads and railways. They directed the running of financial and postal services. Telegraph and telephone systems were extended and harbour facilities improved. Exploitation of natural resources – gold, copper, coal and iron – was made a priority. The Oriental Development Company, a bond-issuing stock company backed by the Japanese government, opened in Seoul on 28 January 1909 with the aim of modernizing agriculture and opening up new lands for use by Japanese and Korean farmers. New water-supply works were installed in Pusan, P'yŏngyang and Inch'ŏn. Particular emphasis was put on sanitation and programmes to combat endemic diseases, including cholera and smallpox.

If their governments saw no reason to distrust developments in Korea, few of the Westerners who lived and worked there did so either. By 1908 the largest national cohorts were the 464 Americans and 153 British. They rarely thought of Korea as their permanent home, even though they knew that the hazards of travel, disease, lawlessness and privation reduced their chances of seeing their homelands again. Generally, the largest occupational group, the missionaries, saw Japanese ideas of efficiency and modernization as cause for optimism, though some were wary of the sudden revival in folk religion. The operators of two American and one French gold mine at Unsan and Taeyudong were relieved to be allowed to continue their operations, and would go on ill-treating their workers appallingly for the next thirty-plus years. Durham Stevens was posthumously awarded the Japanese Medal of the Order of the Rising Sun with Grand Seal, and has been excoriated by Koreans ever since. But two foreigners whose reputations remain untarnished to the present day among patriots are Homer Hulbert and Ernest Bethell. Hulbert, a Methodist missionary, had been in Korea since 1886. He was not blind to its needs, but after 1905 his initial support for Japanese influence changed to strong condemnation, and he pleaded the cause of Korean independence in The Hague and Washington so outspokenly that he was unable to return to the suffering land. The English journalist Ernest Bethell stayed on in Korea after covering the Russo-Japanese War. The two newspapers he founded, one in English and one in *han'gŭl*, were critical of Japanese intentions, and twice the authorities had him tried. When he died in May 1909 his collaborator Yang Kit'ak (1871–1938) continued the *Taehan Maeil Sinbo* ('Korean Daily News') until the new Government-General bought it in 1910 and published it as *Maeil Sinbo*.

Annexation: Japan sets course, 1910–19

In the third week of August 1910, Japanese soldiers once more surrounded the Korean emperor in his palace. Again they forced imperial acquiescence to a treaty surrendering his country's independence. He did not, however, have to sign it himself, for his own prime minister, Yi Wanyong, had already done so. The Treaty of Annexation renamed Korea Chōsen, Seoul Keijō and P'yŏngyang Heijō. At the head of the Government-General (Sōtokufu) was to be a governor-general, appointed by the Japanese prime minister and answerable to the cabinet and emperor in Tokyo. He would govern with a central advisory committee that included a small number of cooperative Koreans. General Terauchi Masatake, a former Japanese war minister, was the first appointee, and held the post until returning to Tokyo as prime minister in 1916. Government bureaux, originally six in number, were increased to ten in 1912, and the country was divided into thirteen provinces. After 1910 all senior administrative posts, including those in banking, law, industry, business and land management, were held by Japanese, most of whom knew no Korean language. The Japanese military police, operating as a virtual army of occupation, turned the whole country into what a London *Daily Mail* reporter called 'a military camp', and initiated what the historian Andrew Nahm has referred to as 'a reign of terror' (Picture Essay 25).

According to the *Annual Report* for 1910, the number of Japanese residents in Korea was 171,543, or just over 1 per cent of the population. Even through the 1930s the ratio remained below 3 per cent, but despite their relatively modest overall total, Japanese command of the Korean economy was disproportionately great. Between 1910 and 1918 the Government-General conducted a comprehensive land survey intended to make Japanese acquisition and management of land easier. Any property not registered with the authorities was confiscated, along with lands formerly owned by the government and royal household, and Japanese ownership of arable land rose from under 4 per cent in 1910 to around one third in 1930. Productivity rose, though Koreans scarcely felt the benefit of it. In 1918 rice shortages in Japan led to rioting, and Korea was seen as the answer to the need. In 1910, 4.7 per cent, and in 1919, 22 per cent of the rice crop was exported to Japan. In 1928 the figure was a massive 51.9 per cent. The Japanese controlled finance and dominated the industrial scene. To benefit domestic Japanese manufacturers the Government-General concentrated on improving communications, docks and rice production. It limited corporate development: in accordance with the Company Law of 1910, new ventures must obtain a licence and investments were mainly channelled into existing *zaibatsu*, but pressure from Japanese producers increased after World War One until the Company Law was repealed in 1920 and more expansion was permitted. Urbanization grew, beginning the transformation of traditional Korean community life and simultaneously creating conditions in which the seeds of radical nationalism could germinate.

Japan's colonialism needs to be understood not only as a step towards the fulfilment of an age-old dream of continental domination, but also against the background of Western colonial imperialism in East Asia, from which Meiji leaders had learned. Neither colonialism nor

25 The former Japanese Government-General Building, Seoul

Japanese policy was to eradicate nostalgia for recent history in Korea, and to get rid of the old-fashioned, the inefficient and the superstitious. Hundreds of buildings in the Kyŏngbok Palace were destroyed in a symbolic washing away of the Chosŏn heritage, and the great Kwanghwa Gate that had stood in front of it was removed. The new neo-Renaissance Government-General Building was commissioned from a German architect, George de Lalande, and built provocatively in front of the old throne hall, Kŭnjŏng-jŏn. It not only hid this from view but also interrupted the flow of *p'ungsu* energy from Pukhan mountain down the north–south arterial road, Kokamon-dori (today's Sejongro), towards Namsan. Begun in 1915 and completed in 1926, the Government-General Building was a splendid edifice. (So were other demonstrations of what the Japanese would do architecturally for their new province, among them Seoul railway station, City Hall and the Central Post Office. Most Koreans, however, felt emotionally attached to their traditional single-storeyed and thatched styles and remained unappreciative.) The white-marble grand hall made a huge and spectacular entrance. Its curved ceiling was supported on Corinthian columns and its walls decorated with murals by the Western-trained artist Sanzo

Wada (1883–1968). Long corridors were adorned with tiles and mould-ed reliefs; a wide staircase led up to the second floor, and surmounting the building was a dome of stained glass. In the basement was the inter-rogation and torture centre used by the police.

Following Liberation in 1945 and the division of the country, the building was first commandeered by the American Military Government, which gave it the unofficial title of Capitol, and in 1962 it became the seat of government for the Republic of Korea. Rising nationalism found this inappropriate in view of its Japanese origins, and in 1986 it was converted, none too happily, into new headquarters for the National Museum. In time that too was deemed to require a purpose-built home, and one of the most impressive modern buildings in Korea was condemned to demolition.

imperialism was yet tainted by the vitriol heaped on them later in the century, and their advocates no doubt believed sincerely in the benefits bestowed by spreading their own way of life. Liberal colonialism offered the recipient potential growth benefits: to reject them invited charges of reactionary nationalism. In September 1910 the Manila-based *Far Eastern Review* blamed Korean 'suspicion and misgiving' for the slow rate of progress over the previous five years and looked ahead to 'a remarkable era of development under the new regime'. Its editorial went on:

> It is generally realized that Korea, in its decadent state, was a menace to Japan. It offered temptation for international intrigue. It is now an added safeguard to the integrity of the Japanese Empire . . . [Japanese writers] claim that Japan's control of Korea will give it the same authority there to carry out its policy as that enjoyed by America in its [Philippine] island possessions, and, while it is the present pronounced policy of the administration at Washington to give the islands independence at some indefinite date, it is the generally accepted belief that the advantages of American sovereignty over the islands will become in time so apparent to the Filipinos that they will refuse to countenance agitation favoring withdrawal.

So Korea took its place alongside Taiwan as the second of Japan's outer provinces (*gaiji*) and was expected to be grateful. In December 1910, speaking to the Colonial Academic Society, Governor-General Terauchi promised that Japan would lead Korea to civilization. The Japanese were well aware that a great many of the 14 million Koreans (or the 20 million of Prince Yonghwan's dying hyperbole) were not yet grateful enough. In particular, the new colonialists perceived a link between Christianity, especially Protestantism, and Korean nationalism, and unearthed what they claimed to be a plot to assassinate General Terauchi at a meeting scheduled with the American Presbyterian missionary George McCune in North P'yŏngan province on 28 December 1910. The police made many hundreds of arrests, including the Sinminhoe leaders Kim Ku and Yun Ch'iho and the journalist Yang Kit'ak. On 28 June 1912 the trial began of 123 defendants, mostly Christians, accused of treason. It was known later as the Korean Conspiracy Trial. Falsified evidence and torture got 105 convicted, and although most were released on appeal in 1913 after worldwide publicity, Yun served four years and Kim Ku three. In the words of Donald Clark, the case 'proved that the freedoms guaranteed by the Meiji Constitution were not to be extended to the Koreans, and perhaps least of all to Korean Christians under the influence of foreigners'. Missionary schools were to be found all over the country. Besides the basics of Christianity, which the Japanese insisted should gradually be phased out, they also made a point of teaching *han'gŭl*, and Korean patriots were increasingly recognizing the value of the native script. Some of the private Korean schools that had sprung up under the Protectorate and survived into the colonial period also taught it. Patriotic periodicals such as Ch'oe Namsŏn's *Sonyŏn* ('Young People', appearing 1908–11), and *Ch'ŏngch'un* ('Youth', 1914–18) used *han'gŭl*. So, more surprisingly, did the government mouthpiece, *Maeil Sinbo*.

Faced with the takeover and suffering of their country, what could Koreans do? Many former *yangban*, who traditionally eschewed radicalism anyway, saw sufficient opportunities to adapt to new circumstances without losing their familiar privileges. But the majority of the population who struggled against rising odds to earn a precarious living were predictably drawn from the lower classes. Many of these were driven from their villages, forced out by Japanese victimization or economic circumstance. Some left home to join partisan armies. Considerable numbers went abroad, swelling the Korean communities in Japan itself, and in Manchuria, the Soviet Far East and China (by 1944 more than 10 per cent of all Koreans lived abroad). Others sought solace through religious affiliation, whether Ch'ŏndogyo, Buddhist, Christian or shamanistic. After the way they had been treated over the last half-century or so, Koreans might just have rolled over and succumbed to a kind of universal depression. Instead, Donald Clark has pointed out (in a personal communication) that whereas in 1910 'most Koreans accepted annexation without protest, [it was] only nine years later [when] they rose up against the Japanese in nationalist fervor', the famous *Samil* (March First) movement.

Ironically, the first shot was fired in Tokyo. Young Koreans could discuss radical political ideas more freely abroad, and, stirred by emotion – and for some, suspicion – at the death of ex-Emperor Kojong on 21 January 1919 and hopeful of the impact of Versailles peace negotiations after Woodrow Wilson's defence of national self-determination, they heard a Declaration of Independence by Yi Kwangsu (1892–1950), student founder of the Korea Youth Independence Association in Tokyo, read out on 8 February 1919. News of this enthused patriots at home, and on the morning of 1 March sixteen Protestants, fifteen members of Ch'ŏndo-gyo (among them Son Pyŏnghŭi) and two Buddhists signed an affirmation of Korea's right to independence in a Seoul restaurant. The document was composed by Ch'oe Namsŏn, and they bravely read it aloud. At 2 p.m. the same day, in Pagoda Park, a teacher read it again to a large crowd waving the Korean flag and singing the national anthem,

Aegukka. Then, as they took to the streets shouting *Manse!* ('Long Live [Korea]!'), the mood turned nasty. The 33 signatories were arrested, their plea for non-violence went unheeded, and the police response as they struggled to contain the uprising was brutal. Contemporary reports, smacking of hyperbole as such things inevitably do, told of suspects rounded up and imprisoned; schools, church buildings and other property destroyed; schoolgirls raped; entire villages massacred. Order was restored by May, but students went on fanning the flames into a wider resistance movement, and over the next twelve months estimates of casualties rose to 7,645 dead and 45,562 wounded.

Some of those who escaped abroad ended up in Shanghai, where they formed a Korean Provisional Government (KPG). They elected Syngman Rhee (Yi Sŭngman, 1875–1965), then in America, as their president *in absentia*. The KPG had no authority over any Koreans and struggled to achieve any kind of international recognition; it was not recognized even by many of the anti-Japanese activists continuing the fight across the peninsula itself; but it helped to keep the notion of sovereignty alive. This was the make-or-break time for Korean independence, for as Shin and Robinson put it, 'The notion of the nation was not [yet] an immutable given . . . It was contested, negotiated, reformulated and reconstructed during the colonial period.'

Nationalism, culture and politics, 1919–31

Admiral Saitō Makoto, brought in with the unenviable job of handling the aftermath of March First, arrived in September 1919 to the same sort of welcome that had greeted Terauchi, a botched assassination attempt. The appointment of a more cultured man than the two generals who preceded him as governor-general was a sign that Tokyo at least recognized the failure of hard-line militarism. Saitō was not, however, a soft touch, as he soon showed by ordering a military expedition against Korean *ŭibyŏng* attacking the Japanese in the rugged Manchurian border region of Jiandao (Kor. Kando). This became infamous as the 'Jiandao Incident', and a Canadian missionary there reported that 'Koreans are daily being shot and whole villages burned'. Both sides made exaggerated casualty claims, with missionary sources estimating more than 3,000 Korean deaths and nearly 2,500 homes burned in October–November 1920.

Taken aback by the Samil Movement's ferocity and the growing resistance, the admiral eased open a safety valve. He was not about to make any concessions to Koreans over the right to run their own country, but he did aim to produce more cooperation from his citizens, and the terms *kyōson* ('coexistence') and *kyōdo no fukuri* ('mutual welfare') were increasingly heard. An embargo on Korean publishing was lifted in 1920 and two newspapers were immediately launched, *Tonga Ilbo* ('East Asia Daily') by the industrialist and cultural entrepreneur Kim Sŏngsu and *Chosŏn Ilbo* ('Korea Daily') by Sin Sŏgu. A dispensation to organize societies led to the sprouting of well over 5,500 new ones, including the influential Han'gŭl Research Society in December 1921. More than one-third had religious affiliations. Not unnaturally, the Government-General also made use of the trend. Pro-Japanese Koreans were recruited into its Kungmin Hyŏphoe ('People's Society'), and in 1922 it set up the Korean History Compilation Committee. Responding to powerful denunciations of the annexation by the exiled journalist Pak Ŭnsik (1859–1926), the Committee saw its prime task as proving Korea's ancient links with and dependence on Japan. Schools were already using Sōtokufu-approved textbooks asserting the colonial power's claims to dominion. Nationalists like Ch'oe Namsŏn countered by reviving interest in Tan'gun as an independent progenitor of the Korean people.

Korean radio broadcasting did not begin until 1927, and three years previously foreigners had been forbidden to use short-wave sets. Newspapers and magazines were therefore vital to people who cared about their country and could read. *Tonga Ilbo* and *Chosŏn Ilbo* immediately provided a forum for debate on the nation's ills and ways of alleviating them. Both promoted the use of *han'gŭl* and spoke out in favour of social reform. In the February 1922 issue of the Ch'ŏndogyo-backed intellectual journal *Kaebyŏk* ('Dawning'), Yi Kwangsu denounced the sterile, ritualistic political and social systems of the past, the kind of thing the Government-General might have been glad to hear had it not been for the author's avowedly nationalistic tone. As political opinion polarized, censorship increased, and the police – whose numbers grew from 6,000 in 1920 to around 20,000 in 1930 – were given harsher powers of search and confiscation. *Kaebyŏk* was closed down in 1926, and journalists moderated their tone and followed a more accommodating path.

New decade; fresh opportunities; greater outspokenness. Nationalist critics were quick to condemn the country's economic ills. Yi Kwangsu launched a Native Production Society in December 1922 and Ch'oe Namsŏn a Korean Products Promotion Society the following February, both aimed at stimulating Korean manufacturing and sales. *Kaebyŏk* supported both. But the Government-General itself, albeit out of self-interest, was already talking about the promotion of co-prosperity (*kyōei*) and taking steps to bring Korean capitalists on board. It abolished the

Company Law and selected Korean businessmen to join a new industrial commission. As tariff revision made cheap Japanese imports more accessible to poorer Korean consumers, the two societies lost their impetus, and were further undermined when the Government-General began offering subsidies to Korean companies that would cooperate with the authorities and employ Japanese-speaking staff. One of those that accepted was Kim Sŏngsu's Kyŏngsŏng Spinning and Weaving Company (Kyŏngbang). As it widened its manufacturing operations and diversified into railways and financial services it became the first *chaebŏl*, the Korean equivalent of the Japanese *zaibatsu*. On the plus side it provided employment for Korean workers, but against that must be set the fact that conditions in its factories were horrible, and remained unimproved despite strikes in 1925 and 1931.

In the 1910s the Government-General had put agriculture first. Although the 1920s began with a drive to open up new lands, increase the use of chemical fertilizers and improve irrigation, it was industry and commerce that benefited most as the decade unrolled. Landowners were persuaded to invest in financial services such as the Korean Life Insurance Corporation. Joint ventures were permitted and the country opened up by an expanded rail network. Noguchi Jun's development of the Hŭngnam industrial complex in South Hamgyŏng represented the first step in the industrialization of north Korea. It began with a fertilizer plant and eventually expanded into electro-chemical sections, important to the Japanese even though ordinary Koreans derived little benefit from them. The suffering of the peasantry deepened. They were growing ever more rice but eating less and less of it themselves, a pattern that would persist and multiply. Seventy-five per cent of them were in debt by 1930.

Thanks to moderate nationalists' efforts to stir up a sense of patriotism among businessmen, the number of Korean small entrepreneurs rose. But many thought no further than profit-making for their immediate families and associates, and Yi Kwangsu denounced the general attitude towards growth as too blinkered. Implying, as he did in *Tonga Ilbo* in January 1924, that Koreans must build up a better educational and economic base in the hunt for eventual independence opened him up to accusations of accommodationism, and his plea met with no widespread response. One company that did briefly show that his vision was not incompatible with demonstrative nationalism was An Hŭije's Paeksan, a Pusan-based import-export company founded in 1914 that set up schools, financed Korean students in Japan and channelled funds into the independence movement across Korea and Manchuria. The police closed it down in 1927.

The Government-General remodelled the education system, entitling Koreans to secondary education in 1922 and enabling more teenagers to go to colleges in Japan. (Ch'oe Namsŏn, Kim Sŏngsu and Yi Kwangsu were all alumni of Waseda.) But since it still failed to make even primary education compulsory and racial discrimination was undisguised, it was Japanese children who benefited from the best educational opportunities. At the tertiary level, moderate nationalists launched a Society to Establish a National University (Minnip Taehak Kisŏng Chunbihoe) in November 1922. The Government-General upstaged them and opened its own Keijō Imperial University (today's Seoul National University) in 1926. But most of its teachers and (male-only) students were Japanese, and even the Society's own plans were no more inclined to break the heritage of traditional elitism. In the end, it diverted what funds it accumulated into a library at Posŏng College, founded in 1905 by Yi Yongik and later to become Koryŏ University.

Radical nationalist thinking aimed beyond the limited advantages that Koreans derived from Japanese measures. What Yi Kwangsu called for in his newspaper articles of 1924 was an extension of practical education in rural areas and training in basic administrative skills. Real education must be progressive. Students took part in a campaign against mass illiteracy. Women, too, became involved in nationalist politics. They demonstrated actively in the course of the March First Movement, and formed the Patriotic Women's Society of Korea (Taehan Min'guk Aeguk Puinhoe) and the Korean Women's League, or Friends of the Hibiscus (Kŭn'uhoe). The vice-chairman of the former, Yi Hyegyŏng, endured three years' imprisonment with hard labour.

Moderate nationalists formed no single representative organization, but at the opposite end of the political spectrum the Korean Communist Party was launched in April 1925. Its survival was straight away put in jeopardy in November when secret messages from one of its founders, Pak Hŏnyŏng, in Seoul to Yŏ Unhyŏng in Shanghai were intercepted at Sinŭiju, and many of its members arrested. More were jailed in 1926, as mass demonstrations followed the funeral on 10 June of the last emperor, Sunjong. But in 1927, in a classic attempt to spread its appeal from within a more broadly based organization, it participated in the establishment of the Sin'ganhoe ('New Shoot Society'), a common front of radicals and moderates. Sin'ganhoe created a nationwide network of branches and quickly acquired some 35,000 members. Not only did it steady communist fortunes, it also helped to keep anti-Japanese feeling simmering until the next boiling-over point was reached. This came late in October 1929. Localized fighting erupted after Japanese youths insulted three Korean schoolgirls at Kwangju railway station, and

Korean students across the country, already resentful of the better facilities enjoyed by their Japanese peers and the inadequate teaching of Korean language and history, took up the fight. The police invaded school campuses; students were expelled and suspended; many were imprisoned. It was the greatest nationalist demonstration to occur in Korea for ten years. Forty-four of Sin'ganhoe's left-wing leaders were arrested in January 1930, and when surviving moderates tried to take control of the society the communists – unhappy at its loss of revolutionary impetus – closed it down in May 1931.

The June 10th Incident of 1926 and the Kwangju Incident of 1929 showed that Saitō's velvet-glove approach had failed to meet with universal success. Ethnic integration was not progressing as planned, and Koreans wanted still more political freedom. But they also indicated the failure of the moderate nationalists' gradualist approach to defuse racial tension and satisfy aspirations for short-term victories. Moderate leaders were the intellectual inheritors of the elitist *yangban* tradition; but now they identified long-term salvation with middle-class intellectual leadership and its eventual re-education of the labouring masses, whom they seemed prepared to neglect in the interim. Colonial status, they conceded, had to be accepted and its rules kept for the time being. Michael Robinson writes: 'In retrospect, cultural nationalism could be interpreted as a program that would allow Korean intellectuals to maintain their own status as a social and cultural elite by monopolizing a truncated version of nationalism that tolerated national cultural autonomy within the confines of Japanese sovereignty.' It was, he suggests, *sadae* in new guise, putting their own Westernized values in place of traditional *yangban* admiration for Chinese inspiration. If ever the situation of a country called for the closing of ranks in resistance to a common foe, this was it. Past experience had shown, however, that where political decisions were concerned Koreans did not come by unanimity easily, and the multiplicity of small parties and groups that sprang up in the 1920s posed no serious threat to the colonial power.

What of the religious organizations? Ch'ŏndo-gyo continued to help the peasantry, forming a Korean Farmers' Association in 1925 to try and improve living and working conditions in the countryside; but its involvement in the June 10th Incident led to the arrest of many members and deepened Japanese suspicions of its motives. The Buddhist community had greater experience in dealing with governments, centuries of it in fact. It was used to welcoming their support and tolerating their periodic interference in its affairs. Now, Buddhists felt they were regaining a measure of respect denied them by Chosŏn Neo-Confucians. Soon after Annexation the Government-General had reorganized and taken effective control of the Korean community, and Buddhists were encouraged to go to Japan for study. One of the leading Buddhist scholars, Yi Nŭnghwa (1869–1943), later sat on the Korean History Compilation Committee, where as an expert on shamanism he also acknowledged the vital role that folk religion had played in traditional Korean society. This did not mean that all Buddhists were collaborationist. The Wŏn sect, or Society for Dharma Research (Pulbŏp yŏn'guhoe), founded in Chŏlla Namdo by Pak Chungbin in the late 1920s, may have appeared to the occupiers to be accommodating, but actually advocated material and spiritual strengthening for its own sake.

Christian missionaries, meanwhile, did their best to maintain the ethos of social concern introduced by their nineteenth-century predecessors, especially through medicine and education, though the mission bodies were far from agreed about how best to counter pressures from either official policy or individual Japanese persecutors. Dedication to the saving of souls in East Asia provided men and women of widely varied Western upbringing with no automatic, God-given empathy for their flock. It was not easy to disregard their own cultural heritage and to adjust to Asian priorities and sensitivities. Some of them were just as liable as the Japanese to write off traditional Korean ways as backward and in need of foreign-determined change. Despite the Government-General's restoration of the right to teach religion in 1925, Korean Christians and their foreign pastors experienced discrimination and persecution, and some gave way to apostasy and accommodationism. Nevertheless, many instances of selfless devotion to Korean needs and sensitivities and dedication to the cause of social reform helped Christianity to make strong progress. So committed did P'yŏngyang become as a centre for Protestantism and Catholicism that it has subsequently been dubbed – albeit on doubtful grounds – the 'most Christian city in Asia': by the mid-1930s, 30 churches were serving its 200,000 inhabitants. Ominous for Christians, however, was the Government-General's decision in 1925 to build a national Shintō shrine, Chōsen Jingu, at a site on Seoul's Namsan.

Cultural cleansing and the advent of war, 1931–45

Approximately 527,000 Japanese were living in Korea in 1930. Rather more Koreans (sources estimate 600,000–800,000) lived in Manchuria, where they farmed mainly rice and opium poppies. Their relations with local Chinese were not always peaceful, yet as far back as the Jiandao Incident in 1920 the Japanese had suspected the regional warlord Zhang Zuolin of siding with them, and poor social and economic circumstances made the Koreans a fertile recruiting ground for the Chinese Communist Party. A Japanese–Manchurian agreement in 1925 promised a reward for every Korean 'communist' arrested by local officials and led to numerous outrages. When Kwantung army officers instigated the small explosion that gave General Hayashi Senjurō a pretext for sending an invasion force across the Yalu river on 21 September 1931, the prospects looked bleak for Chinese and Koreans alike. As Korean guerrillas linked up with Chinese in the struggle against the conquerors, an army regiment sent into Jiandao from Korea in April 1932 killed 1,200 suspected communists of both races. To the Japanese, the newly inaugurated puppet state of Manzhouguo (Manchuria) acted as a cushion between its Korean colony and the unattractive axis of Guomindang China and the USSR. The Government-General encouraged entire communities to shift from northern Korea to Manchuria to assist in the urgent drive for industrial output, and 270,000 Japanese migrants, mostly peasants, poured in at the rate of about 20,000 per annum between 1932 and 1945. The new *gaiji* would take time to yield its undoubted benefits, but in the mean time the basis for industrial development had already been laid in northern Korea, where the production of raw materials and the growth of manufacturing, especially in the munitions industry, became the top priority under Governor-General Ugaki Kazushige (1931–6). With the formation of the Chōsen Petroleum Company in 1935, Western companies in the oil and mining industries, including Caltex, the Royal Dutch Shell subsidiary Rising Sun and the Oriental Consolidated Mining Company, began to suffer. Japanese *zaibatsu* such as Noguchi, Mitsubishi and Matsui, on the other hand, received substantial funding, and as pressure on land increased in the south, starving peasants headed north in search of factory jobs, poorly paid though these were. Thousands more crossed the sea to Japan.

Moderate nationalists came under pressure to collaborate. The industry of publishing newspapers, magazines and books was allowed to expand. Michael Robinson, analysing popular culture, found that '1930s Korea was relatively densely saturated with printed materials', and that 'the Korean middle class was also reading Japanese publications'. In line with the *Naisen Ittai* (Kor. *naesŏn ilche*, 'Korea Japan One Body') assimilation policy, attempts were made to convince Koreans that the fate of the two nations bound them together; and as Korean culture was reinterpreted as a relative of Japanese culture, appeals were made to the Korean sense of sacrifice for the communal good and hierarchical obedience to those in authority. Some Koreans may have been convinced by the argument that assimilation into the *Yamato minjuku*

('Great Japanese Race') would help achieve the supremacy of oriental over Western races. The editors of *Tonga Ilbo* were not, and provocatively demonstrated it on 26 August 1936 by publishing a picture of the marathon winner Son Kijŏng receiving a gold medal at the Berlin Olympic Games, but replacing the rising sun on his vest with the Korean *t'aegŭk* roundel. It was the very day the new governor-general, General Minami Jirō, arrived in Seoul, and the paper was immediately suspended.

To modernize Korea without simultaneously encouraging Koreans' nostalgia for past traditions or aspirations of future independence was a delicate line for the Japanese to tread. The Government-General accepted that an educated workforce was essential to sustain industrial expansion and economic development. More schools were opened in manufacturing centres, and enrolment in elementary schools rose from 25.5 per cent in 1931 to 55 per cent in 1939, with boys in the majority. But in 1939 only 12.6 per cent of Korean applicants to Keijō Imperial University were admitted. Nearly 4,000 Koreans gained their tertiary education in Japan, most at private rather than the imperial universities, but nonetheless of better quality than anything available in Korea.

Naisen Ittai was trumpeted the more loudly as the war effort mounted. But when the Japanese began to force all Koreans to visit Shintō shrines in late 1935 and make obeisance, tension was heightened. Presbyterian leaders in P'yŏngyang urged their members to refuse, and although Catholics and Methodists saw no objection to what they termed a secular ritual, a conflict reminiscent of the fateful Rites Controversy in eighteenth-century China loomed. General Minami's credentials gave no reassurance. An ex-commander of the Japanese army in Korea and former ambassador to Manzhouguo, he came to gear Korea up for war. He was also determined to get the Western missionaries out of his country. The police used extensive powers to intimidate and arrest Koreans and foreigners alike. In 1938 alone they threatened and detained 126,626 people. From March 1938 use of Japanese language was made compulsory by all those younger Koreans who already spoke it, and efforts to teach it to the older generations were stepped up; November 1939 saw the compulsory, ignominious adoption of Japanese names for use by all Koreans. Korean newspapers were closed down: strict censorship was imposed, and news was hard to come by. In 1940 the traditional East Asian mutual-responsibility system was revived as local communities were organized into ten-family neighbourhood units for the enforcement of rules and regulations. Spying and denunciation were encouraged, especially against those – such as Christians – who were suspected of harbouring sympathies with foreigners. By the end of the year, though, most Westerners had left Korea.

Conscription into Korean mines and factories was introduced in 1942, and thousands of men left for war work in Japanese factories. About 17,500 volunteered to enlist in the Japanese army between February 1938 and 1943. Those who became officers, like those who joined the Japanese police, later came in for the strongest condemnation as collaborators. Some were accused of coercing others into service as student volunteers and 'comfort women' (*ŭianbu*). Ten times as many were compulsorily conscripted in 1944–5, and a further 150,000 drafted into manual war work. In wartime everyone expects to tighten belts, and as the US inflicted growing losses on the imperial forces after the Battle of Midway in June 1942 the Japanese people endured great hardships. But as they did so, ill-treatment of their Korean 'compatriots' increased commensurately. Korea was spared Allied bombing but suffered dreadfully nonetheless. Materials were commandeered for the Japanese war effort; rice output, which had risen in the early 1930s thanks to better irrigation and more use of fertilizers, fell to about 3 million tonnes in the years 1942–4, and as exports to Japan rose, Koreans were reduced to eating more barley and millet; heating fuels were in short supply. The ordeals of comfort women (a euphemism for young girls forced into prostitution and quite wrongly regarded by some Japanese as the successors to the *kisaeng* whom they had got to know well) were so appalling that shame forced them to conceal the truth about their abuse for almost fifty years, until the end of the century. Koreans, wrote the US missionary Ethel Underwood in 1942,

> revile and hate their rulers and despise them. Thousands of Korean leaders from schools and churches, from newspapers and farms [who have been] thrown into jails these last few years report that the only conversation of the police is of drink, and of the lustful delights of girls from inns and cafés, and from the registered brothels. Brutal by day and bestial by night, the policeman is both hated and despised.

SURVIVAL AND THE ARTS

Reinterpreting history to demonstrate consanguinity; enforcing the use of the Japanese language, Japanese names and Japanese state religion; educating the most promising Korean youth at Japanese universities; banning a wide range of publications: in today's terminology, *Naisen*

Ittai amounted to cultural cleansing. Yet where Korean ancient history was concerned, at least, the trouble taken by Japanese anthropologists and archaeologists early in the twentieth century constituted a form of flattery. They published beautiful photographic studies of memorials, stelae and ancient buildings, and their reports would inspire and serve researchers long after Liberation. Sekino Tadashi made the first survey of Korean antiquities in 1902, and later he, Yanagi Soetsu, the Asakawa brothers and Imanishi Ryū all published extensive data on the Lelang period. Yanagi's empathy for Korean art and sympathy for the sufferings of the Korean people fired his passion for Chosŏn porcelain and helped to inspire the Japanese *mingei* (folk crafts) movement. The Research Division of the South Manchurian Railway, the Mantetsu Chōsabu, contributed to important discoveries across north-east Asia. The formation of the Committee for Archaeological Investigation (Chōsen Kōseki Chōsa Iinkai) in 1916 led to the publication of many volumes of detailed and careful reports on sites and monuments over the next twenty years. On the face of it, the Japanese were simply doing in Korea what Western archaeologists were concurrently doing in China. There was, however, a difference in underlying motivation: as well as filling cases in European museums, the British, Swedes and French enthusiastically digging across China had a more detached interest in unearthing the story of early life in the Orient; the Japanese, on the other hand, were out to find proof of shared ethnicity, and hence to legitimize their claim to govern Korea. Archaeological discoveries were sent back to Japanese museums until the Government-General established the Chōsen Sōtokufu Museum (later to become the National Museum) in 1916. Among its first notable acquisitions were finds made in the Dunhuang region by the Japanese monk-explorer Count Kozui Otani a dozen years before, including wooden masks and a straw basket. (The discovery by Chinese archaeologists in December 2002 of similar masks and a basket confirmed a Tang/Silla-period dating for the Otani objects.)

Individual Japanese also began acquiring Korean artefacts, setting an example to wealthy Koreans who had traditionally lagged behind both the Chinese and Japanese in the collecting habit. The landowner Chŏn Hyŏngp'il (1906–1962), an antiquarian bibliophile, was guided in his purchases by one of the Ch'ŏndo'gyo signatories of the Declaration of Independence, the master calligrapher O Sech'ang (1864–1953). Chŏn built a private gallery for his treasures that later became the Kansŏng Museum (1938). The interest of the Kyŏngbang owner Kim Sŏngsu lay in folk materials rather than fine arts, and when he took over the struggling Posŏng College in 1932 his own collection was displayed there as a token of determination to preserve national consciousness. The college received a substantial bequest from a female landowner, An Hamp'yŏng, which Kim devoted to building up an archive on women's lifestyles, and when Posŏng became Koryŏ University in 1945, the basis had been laid for one of Korea's finest university museums.

Korea's supposed dependence on Japan was emphasized in a 37-volume *History of Korea* (*Chōsen-shi*) completed in 1938 by the Korean History Compilation Society. But if the Japanese viewed culture as a means of binding Korea into their empire, Koreans under occupation had different ideas. For some, the arts offered a diversion from the depression of the world around them. Critics who were unable to appreciate art for art's sake accused them of escapism, though by preserving and building upon traditional styles and patterns made so familiar through the long years of the Chosŏn dynasty it could be said that they were, in their way, doing their bit for their country. Others, as they became aware of the great Western traditions, were anxious to develop their own aesthetic taste and expand the parameters of Korean art by experimentation with new forms, including abstract art. Radical nationalists, meanwhile, found that painting, music and writing all offered opportunities to protest, either overtly or more subtly, at the pillaging of their land.

Painting

The Sŏhwa Misulwŏn ('Calligraphy and Painting Fine Art School'), founded by a group of leading artists in 1911 in succession to the Tŏhwa, lasted only until the Japanese closed it down in 1919. One of its alumni was Kim Ŭnho (1892–1979), the last artist to paint the portrait of a Korean monarch. In 1925 he headed for Japan, where he studied with Yūki Somei. On returning to Korea he opened his Nakchŏnghŭn ('Linking with the Young Pavilion') in 1930. No specialist art colleges existed in colonial Korea, and it was only through privately run groups such as this that young painters could learn their craft. Kim Kichang (1913–2001) was one of Nakchŏnghŭn's protégés; so was Chŏn Hyongp'il; a third was Chang Woosung (b. 1912), renowned nowadays for his reinterpretation of Northern Song literati-style painting. Groups of artists also gained encouragement by joining associations such as the Tongyŏnsa ('Society for the Like-minded'), set up by Yi Sangbŏm (1897–1972) in 1923 for artists to study old and modern art together. Traditional landscape and figure painting underwent transformation, with the appearance of female nudes provoking predictably hostile criticism from Confucian moralists. Some joined the politically motivated Korean Proletarian Artists' Federation, formed in 1925, and produced cartoons and prints in Socialist Realist style reminiscent of the Chinese woodblock artists' movement. Among Japanese teachers who introduced students in Korea to Western methods, such as the use of oils, and fostered an interest in modern art was the abstract pioneer Yamaguchi Takeo (1902–1983). In Japan, Koreans could study either Eastern- or Western-style art. There, Japanese painters were swept along through the 1930s on a patriotic tide of subjects inspired by the expansionist political mood. Nationalist Koreans joined the symbolically named Paek U Hoe ('White Bull Society'), which managed to hold several exhibitions before the authorities disbanded it. The Japanese felt less inclination than the Koreans for individual experimentation, though even a Korean and admirer of Western modernism such as Kim Whanki (Suhwa, 1913–1974) could still begin to make a name for himself in Japan, and was one of those selected to exhibit by the progressive art group Jiyū Bijutsuka Kyōkai ('Free Artists' Exhibition').

While the Japanese art establishment was happy to absorb non-controversial Korean artists into its own evolving world, the colonial authorities were anxious to nip in the bud any development that might be viewed by Koreans as a means of affirming independence through reform. So when the Sŏhwa Hyŏphoe ('Calligraphy and Painting Association'), founded in 1918 by Ko Hŭidong to promote modern artistic concepts, introduced an annual art exhibition (the Hyŏpchŏn) in 1921, the Government-General immediately countered with its own annual series, the Senten (Kor. *Sŏnjŏn*). Known later as Korean National Art Exhibitions (Chosŏn Misul Chŏllamhoe, or simply Mijŏn), these lasted from 1922 until 1944, eight years after Minami Jirō's arrival marked the end of the Hyŏpchŏn. By the 1930s the Japanese could congratulate themselves that both in terms of size and quality the Mijŏn outdid the Hyŏpchŏn, even if most of their exhibitors, and all the judges, were Japanese. Artists were by no means averse to expressing their opposition to colonial rule through their work, but their nationalist conviction was generally of the moderate rather than the radical kind (Picture Essay 26). Among those who showed in the Eastern-style section of the Mijŏn but tried to create an updated Korean style were the figure painter Kim Ŭ nho and the landscapist Yi Sangbŏm. Yi was a member of the Sŏhwa Hyŏphoe, showing his work for the first time at its exhibition of 1921, but the next year he entered the Eastern-style section of the Mijŏn, where he won the top prize every year from 1924 until 1934. Among his innovations was the introduction of fixed-point perspective.

26 Yi Insŏng, *One Autumn Day*

In the 1930s the number of Korean painters submitting work to the Sŏnjŏn, and being accepted by the Japanese judges, rose. Were they collaborating or awakening to an opportunity to express nationalist sentiment? Some used the palette favoured in Japanese art colleges, brighter and more varied than that of traditional Chosŏn artists, while others, recalling Chŏng Sŏn's True View style, responded by working in colours they saw and associated with the Korean landscape and the physiognomy and clothing of the Korean people. Some later critics have seen the preference for 'local colours' as an antidote to Westernization in art. Others argue that it was an alternative contribution to a Japanese-favoured 'Pan-Asianism'. Although the subjects and styles it favoured were perhaps anachronistic, it was part of a rising debate over the definition of Korean art that would roll on throughout the rest of the century. And if, as Kim Youngna claims, 'a desolate or pastoral landscape lacking any sign of modernisation was the prevailing image of Korea among most Japanese', this should not be seen as an admission of neglect on the part of the colonizers, rather as a statement of the modern superiority of the centre (*naiji*) over the backward provinces.

Easily the most successful artist of his time, in Kim Youngna's view, was Yi Insŏng (1912–1950). To Japanese viewers, the bare-breasted peasant woman seen in *One Autumn Day* (1934) may have confirmed their image of Korea as a land of forbidden fruits. Koreans, on the other hand, might have recognized a defiant note in her face and noted the unusual fertility of the typically reddish soil of the field in which she and the smaller girl stand, gestures of optimism.

Yi Insŏng, *One Autumn Day*, 1934, oil, 97 × 162 cm.

Music

Korean traditional music is itself commonly known as national music (*kugak*), but under the influence of the late Chosŏn modernization movement the concept of a Western-style national anthem was also introduced. Kojong ordered the writing of an anthem in 1902, and a tune was composed by his German bandmaster, Franz Eckert, who had worked in the music department of the Japanese imperial household since 1888. (Ironically, he had also written the tune for the Japanese national anthem *Kimigayo*.) From 1904 all schools began the day by singing the song, but the sentiment expressed by the opening words, 'High Lord of Heaven assist our Emperor', failed to endear them to the Japanese, and the practice ceased in 1905. The words of today's ROK anthem, *Aegukka* ('Love Country Song'), are said to have been written by Yun Ch'iho in the 1890s, and are sung to a tune written in 1936 by An Ikt'ae and incorporated into his *Symphonic Fantasia, Korea* of 1938. The first verse speaks stirringly of the land flourishing 'till the Eastern Sea and Paektu-san [Mount Paektu] dry out and wear away', and the refrain begins with a reference to the national flower, the hibiscus, 'Thirty thousand leagues of mountains, streams and deathless flowers'.

After 1910, as Koreans went to study music in Japan and Germany, *kugak* was generally considered to be outdated. According to the musicologist Han Manyoung, Japanese research into its history was inadequate and 'attempted to show Korea merely as a bridge between the high cultures of China and Japan'. *Kugak* was, nevertheless, to be heard on Kyŏngsŏng Broadcasting programmes, along with folk music, during the 1930s. The establishment of a wholly Korean-language service in 1933 further promoted traditional cultural performances, including *p'ansori*. The Japanese also began to popularize Western music, anticipating perhaps, as in the case of modern painting, that in time it would wipe nostalgia for past native traditions out of mind. Players took up Western instruments and a few went abroad to study, in European, American and Japanese conservatories. Prominent among composers who began to write in modern idioms was Yun Isang (1917–1995), whose music – though some Koreans dispute it – has subsequently been described as embodying an instinctive Korean spirit. At a more popular level new Korean songs, *ch'angga*, derived partly from late nineteenth-century hymn settings, borrowed Western and Japanese tunes, and 'trot' music introduced from Japan was even adapted to reflect nationalistic sentiment.

And did all this mean the demise of court music, one of the glories of traditional Korean culture? Fortunately not, for it was kept alive in the Yi Royal Court Music Office (Yi Wangjik Aakpu), saved from extinction perhaps because of the respect the Japanese held for their own surviving imperial court music, *gagaku*. The director and *kŏmun'-go*-player Ham Hwajin (1884–1949) made a significant contribution to Korean musicology and published four works on the basis of his research. Although most of the court rites were abolished, *aak* was still performed at the Confucian and Royal Ancestral Shrines. The Royal Conservatory, as the Aakpu is commonly known, was drastically reduced in size; the principle of hereditary membership was officially abolished; and students were recruited on only six occasions between the years 1922 and 1945, when it comprised just 30 musicians. Standards at the Conservatory fell, but with American technical collaboration, Japanese companies such as Shinsegi issued records of traditional Korean music. The Royal Conservatory made a disc entitled 'Essence of *Aak*' in 1928; *p'ansori* was recorded by the great Yi Tongbaek (1877–1950); and a photograph taken after the recording of the 'Song of Ch'unhyang' in 1937 shows a formal group of six traditionally attired musicians, including Chŏng Chŏngnyŏl in a tall horsehair hat and a 20-year-old Kim Sohee. Between them these two bridged a generational divide: Chŏng had been one of the male singers who performed at Korea's first Western-style theatre, the Wŏn'gak-sa, during the Protectorate period, and Kim Sohee lived on to become one of the ROK's best-loved and outstanding singers of *p'ansori* and folk-songs.

The Koreans are a musical people, and they were neither the first nor the last to understand that in time of warfare and occupation music offers solace and stiffens resistance. Not *aak*: however highly valued that may have been by the former nobility for its royalist traditions, to most people it was too class-bound and esoteric. Even adaptations of native folk tunes as instrumental suites (*sanjo*) were beyond popular appreciation. Folk-songs, however, were a different matter. Numerous local styles enlivened the daily labour and social life of peasants and workers, and however much the Japanese may have tried to discourage them and their patriotic connections, it was beyond the powers of non-Korean-speaking officials to eliminate them. The popularity of singing and songs with regional connections led to the formation of a Korean Song Research Society in 1930, followed by a Korean Song and Dance Research Society the following year. Yun Isang brought out a volume of folk-song settings in 1935. The Japanese even went so far as to honour one of the greatest exponents of traditional folk dance, Han Sŏngjŭn (d. 1938).

Today's best known of all Korean songs, *Arirang*, dates from some time in the Chosŏn period. By the 1930s it had already spawned many variations. It tells of lovers parted by a hill, or in the late Chosŏn dynasty of workers carried away from their homes to help rebuild the Kyŏngbok Palace. Besides the sorrow of the separated, it came to bear the lament of Koreans mourning the loss of their homeland, whether to the Japanese or through the division of their country after 1953. What particularly helped transform it from a pleasant-enough, lilting melody with commonly encountered sentiments into an icon for Korean nationalism was its choice as the title for a silent film by Na Un'gyu in 1926. It was just seven years since the appearance of the first Korean film ever and only four since the first feature film, *Kuggyŏng* ('National Border'), had been completed, but banned by the Japanese from public release. But Na Un'gyu's silent film excited the prospect of a national film industry, and profit-seeking Japanese business helped finance what Michael Robinson calls 'a golden age of [Korean] silent films', with up to 160 being issued between 1926 and 1935. The hero of Na Un'gyu's *Arirang* is Yong Jin (played by Na himself), a student leader of the March First protest arrested and driven insane by torture in police custody. On returning home he kills his bullying landlord, a Japanese informer, and is rearrested. The film's success was guaranteed by its political message alone, but its artistic quality went further and ensured it a place in cinematograph history.

Literature

In China the end of the imperial era in 1911 prompted radical heart-searching about the exclusivity of literati culture and the classical language in which it was ineluctably embedded. As part of the New Culture Movement originating around 1915, the scholar-diplomat Hu Shi launched a campaign for the use of 'plain speech' (*baihua*), citing the progressiveness of Western countries where people wrote in the vernacular language. However inevitable the eventual success of the *baihua* movement, the power of the scholar class meant that it made comparatively slow progress, undermining as it did Confucianism's canonical foundations. In Korea, as we have seen, scholars were also brought up on the classics and were accustomed to using Chinese characters. But though many scholars clung to them with genuine emotional attachment, the existence of an efficient native alphabet, and the fact that even character-based Korean literary styles had evolved away from the strict syntax of classical Chinese, meant that the forces of reaction were less deeply entrenched. So when Korean nationalists launched their own New Culture Movement it met with some, but less convincing, opposition. Given the pride with which Koreans today exalt the merits of *han'gŭl*, the only surprise is that the colonial power should have tolerated its use as long as it did. The first of nine editions of *Ch'angjo* ('Creation') was produced by Korean students in Japan in February 1919, and in the culturally relaxed era of the early 1920s literary magazines in Korea were able to promote the use of *han'gŭl*. Their outspoken nationalism risked Japanese censure, and to avoid government action the three issues of *Paekcho* ('White Tide') were published under the name of a Methodist missionary.

The literary revolution had begun some years earlier. When Ch'oe Namsŏn returned to Korea from Waseda University in 1907 he immediately founded the first of his innovative journals, *Sonyŏn* ('Youth'), in which he introduced Koreans to a new style of poetry (*sinch'e-si*). Echoing the four-square pattern and rousing content of the Christian hymn-like *ch'angga* songs, its form was novel; so was its style, appealing to the modernizing, patriotic instincts of the younger generation. Poets such as Kim Sowŏl (1903–1934), with *Chindallae kko* ('Azaleas'), and a Buddhist monk who had signed the Declaration of Independence in 1919, Han Yong'un (1879–1944), with his collection of poetry *Nim ŭi ch'immuk* ('Silence of Love'), responded and expressed the popular sense of loss somewhat wistfully. A poem by Yi Sanghwa (1900–1943) in the June 1926 edition of *Kaebyŏk* was more blatantly daring, beginning with the lines: 'The land is no longer our own / Does spring come just the same / to the stolen fields?'

Other writers were not slow to follow the poets' lead. Yi Injik (1862–1916) and Yi Haejo (1869–1927) rewrote old stories and composed new novels in language that ordinary people might understand, staging some of them between 1908 and 1910 in Seoul's Wŏn'gak-sa theatre. But as the repression of the colonial era deepened, writers sharpened their wits along with their powers of criticism, turning them against the decadence of their own nation as much as the oppression of the Japanese and discovering new scope for nationalism in both present-day realism and historical fiction. The prolific Yi Kwangsu's varied works included *Yŏjaŭi ilsaeng* ('A Women's Life') and *Tanjong aesa* ('The Tragic History of Tanjong'). Hong Myŏnghŭi (1888–1968), following the tradition of the epic Chinese novel *Shuihuzhuan*, broke away from upper-class subjects with his innovative tales of the low-class *ŭibyŏng* hero *Im Kkŏk-chŏng*, appearing in *Chosŏn Ilbo* from 1928 to 1938. And Yŏm Sangsŏp (1897–1963) was surely lucky to escape censure for his novel *Samdae* ('Three Generations'), serialized by the same paper in 1921, which offered a forthright exposé of pressure experienced by ordinary people in Seoul under Japanese rule.

Some authors naturally wanted to avoid confrontation and to write simply for the sake of it. One of these was the tragic poet Yi Sang

(1910–1937), whose disgust at the nature of the times led him into out-
rageously decadent behaviour. He composed the semi-autobiographical
story *Nalgae* ('Wings'), in which he described the life of a man living off
his wife's earnings as a prostitute, and was one of those who formed the
Club of Nine Men (Kuin-hoe, 1933–7), a short-lived group of writers
with no strong ideological persuasion. Radicals who saw literature as a
means of advancing class struggle formed the Korean Proletarian
Artists' Federation. At the peak of its ten-year existence, before the
Japanese disbanded it in 1935, it claimed around 200 members, some of
whom – such as Han Sŏrya (b. 1900) – would later become active in
post-war North Korean cultural life. Wartime conditions inevitably
brought forth more expressions of grief and resentment, and the poets
Yi Yuksa (1904–1944) and Yun Tongju (1917–1945) died in prison, victims of putting unrepentant nationalism into symbolic word form.

KOREANS UNDER PRESSURE: HEROES AND VILLAINS

Spirit and intellect thrive in adversity and artistry responds to repression with originality. Through Admiral Saitō's partially opened doorway of opportunity cultural nationalists glimpsed a passage leading to a
brighter Korean future, and before Ugaki and Minami slammed the
door shut they had risked a few steps along it. They espied a world free
from Japanese domination, free too from the restricting priorities of
yangban culture, a world still happily unconscious of the conundrum –
acknowledged later in the painting of Hwang Yŏngyŏp (b. 1931) – of
how an Asian culture might extract the benefits of Western civilization
without becoming subservient to it. For all that, the roots of *yangban*
culture spread wide and deep through traditional Korean society and
were not going to be dug out in a hurry. Among them, the Confucian
predilection for holding up 'praise and blame' figures was – and still is
– deeply embedded in the national psyche. With the death of ex-
Emperor Sunjong on 25 April 1926, Koreans found themselves for the
first time in their history with neither royal nor military leaders. Barring
them, to whom should people look for inspiration and guidance?

Heroes and villains are not going to be in short supply during a
period of foreign occupation. But besides contemporary or recent
champions, the most ancient founders of Korea also found themselves
being resurrected rather surprisingly to counter Japanese assertions
of ethnic and political relationships between the two countries. In
response to claims that Kija had instigated the spread of civilization
from China onto the peninsula and that the Kwanggaet'o stele proved

Japan's early rule over parts of it, Sin Ch'aeho and Ch'oe Namsŏn talked up the historicity of Tan'gun as the first dynastic founder, and the importance of Wiman Chosŏn Manchuria, rather than China, in the formation of the early state. Today, both men are identified with the origins of the nationalist concept of a Korean *minjŏk* ('ethnic nation'). Not for them the *yangban* mentality of Confucian culturalism with its acceptance of hierarchical inferiority: according to Sin the social Darwinist, this had emasculated native Korean initiative and values and must be done away with. Ŭlchi Mundŏk had been a great hero, but Silla's dependence on Chinese help had encouraged the Sinocentric rot. Nationalism, moreover, should be vested in populism. When he wrote his *Declaration of Korean Revolution* in 1923, Sin the anarchist may, indeed, have been the first to use the term *minjung* in its subsequently recognized political sense. During the colonial period *minjŏk* was a source of anti-Japanese inspiration, and whatever we may think of its erstwhile irredentist claims to Manchurian territory or fanciful stories of creation by divine intervention, it remains fundamental to modern desires for reunification.

But a people must have heroes and villains to guide them, and immediately after Liberation in 1945, even as crowds welcomed Syngman Rhee back to Korea to lead them into what they expected to be their sovereign future, attacks began on recent collaborators. The debate about whether, in the flush of emotionalism, they got their definitions right straight away goes on to the present day. Sometimes the dividing line between goodies and baddies was blurred, and even with the benefit of hindsight the interpretation of an individual's motives and behaviour might be unsure.

One of the earliest martyrs honoured with a plaque at the National War Memorial is An Chunggŭn, the man who assassinated Itō Hirobumi on 26 October 1909 and inspired his brother, An Myŏnggŭn, to repeat the gesture, but with less success, on General Terauchi. Other political nationalists made their protest less dramatically. The *curriculum vitae* of Yi Tonghŭi (1873–1935) was unimpeachable in its anti-Japanese credentials. A member of the Sinminhoe and head of the military garrison on Kanghwa island until 1907, he was twice imprisoned before seeking sanctuary in Jiandao and assisting the *ŭibyŏng*. In 1918 he founded the Korean People's Socialist Party in Khabarovsk and sent anti-Japanese agents into Korea. After moving to Shanghai, where he served for a spell as prime minister of the KPG, he established the Koryŏ Communist Party. It was his partisans who were behind the anti-Japanese rising in Jiandao in 1920, and Yi himself soon moved back to the north-east, where he lived out the rest of his life in Vladivostok. The career of An Ch'angho

(1878–1938) was not unlike that of Yi Tonghŭi. A founder member of Sinminhoe, he travelled the world for two years rallying overseas Koreans against the Annexation. In 1919 he too joined the KPG in Shanghai, but quickly tired of its squabbling and returned to Seoul. He was back in the USA in 1925, fighting alongside *ŭibyŏng* guerrillas in Manchuria the next year, and was arrested by the Japanese in Shanghai in 1928. From there he was taken back to Korea to spend most of his remaining years in prison. In the rivalrous post-Liberation years, political activists risked gangland-style killings rather than Japanese execution squads. Two undoubted patriots who met violent ends were Yŏ Unhyŏng (1885–1947) and Kim Ku (1876–1949). Both, like Yi Tonghŭi and An Ch'angho, had been early members of the KPG. Yo was a moderate left-winger who spent three years in prison after returning from China and edited the *Chungang Ilbo* ('Central Daily') after his release. Despite his post-war efforts to achieve consensus across the political spectrum, he was murdered in July 1947, probably on the orders of Kim Ku. Kim had been a tireless worker for independence ever since his youthful Tonghak days. He had even been sentenced to death for killing a Japanese officer in vengeance for the murder of Queen Min. He had been implicated in Itō Hirobumi's murder; imprisoned among the 105 in 1912; made leader of the KPG in 1926 and instigated an anti-Japanese terror campaign in Shanghai; founded his own Korean Nationalist Party; moved the KPG to Chongqing in 1940 and assumed its chairmanship in 1944; and returned to Seoul in 1945 as a proven champion of the centre right. But therein lay the seeds of his undoing. After making unavailing efforts in 1948 to unite north and south, he was passed over for office in the government formed by his rival Syngman Rhee, and it was Rhee's agent, An Tuhŭi, who gunned him down in his home. It was, perhaps, poetic justice for one whose life had been spent in the shadow of violence. By contrast, a hero whose reputation was not associated with violence of any kind was the gold medal-winning marathon runner Son Kijŏng. Born in 1912, he graduated from Meiji University in Tokyo. Although forced to compete in the Berlin Olympic Games under his Japanese name, Son Kitei, he used his own name to sign documents while he was there, and drew a map of Korea composed of his signature. After Liberation his picture was used as an emblem of Korean patriotism, and he carried the Olympic torch into the stadium for the opening ceremony of the Seoul Olympics in 1988.

Yi, An, Yo and Kim may be celebrated for their resistance, but what should we think of the majority of those who emigrated and went to Manchuria, China, the Soviet Far East, North America or even Japan? By 1944 some 3.5 million Koreans lived abroad. Critics condemned them for fleeing their homeland and compatriots. Were they really to be disparaged for un-Korean behaviour, or could they serve their country better from there? Syngman Rhee himself could boast of being a founder member of the old Independence Club and of a brief period of imprisonment in post-Annexation Korea, even of being elected president *in absentia* of the Shanghai KPG, yet he spent most of his life in the United States. There his strong right-wing nationalist views were well known on Capitol Hill, and in spite of reservations the Americans saw him as the obvious choice to help them run their sector of Korea in 1945. Thereafter, he was transformed from hero to villain in far less than the fifteen years it took to oust him from leadership, and to the present day he remains a largely discredited figure. (When it comes to the predictability of political reputation, however, one never quite knows. Hatred for Park Chung Hee as president from 1963 to 1979 stemmed from the ruthless suppression of his political opponents and from his pro-Japanese activities during the war years. Any thought of rehabilitation seemed impossible in the aftermath of the military dictatorships and rise of democracy from 1988 onwards. Yet nobody ever accused him of personal gain from corruption, and as ROK politics slid into a mire of financial scandal in 2004 voices were heard praising the success of his economic policies and calling for acknowledgement of his patriotism, and his daughter Pak Kǔnhye was chosen as chair-woman of the Grand National Party.)

From revisionist views of history it is but a short step to deconstruc-tionist efforts to evaluate and re-evaluate the actions and motives of the so-called villains in modern Korean history, pro-Japanese collaborators. Many former *yangban* fared comfortably under colonial rule, whether or not through deliberate acts of cooperation, and articles in the autumn 2002 issue of *Korea Journal* (entitled 'The Issue of Settling the Past in Modern Korean History') showed that arguments were in fact far from being settled. In August 2004 President Roh Moo-hyun announced the setting up of a national commission to look into colonial collaboration, and also into human-rights abuses committed by ROK governments before 1987. To use a chilling phrase from the vocabulary of China's Cultural Revolution, decisions about former reputations may still be reversed. Goodies cannot rest on their laurels; baddies may yet hope for understanding. Yun Ch'iho died after taking poison at the age of 81, public opinion having long since rejected his earlier nationalist creden-tials and cast him as a turncoat. He rejected the stultifying influence of China and Confucianism, was impressed by what he saw of Japanese modernity and determination, and associated the progressiveness of Western civilization with Christianity, in which he was a strong believer.

Hating and ashamed of the backwardness of his own country, he developed a love–hate relationship with the United States, where he studied and had many friends. He endured four years' imprisonment after the Korean Conspiracy Trial, but as time went by and Japanese pressure increased, especially under the *Naisen Ittai* policy, he became what Koen de Ceuster calls 'a consenting colonial subject', and wrote of the need for mutual Korean-Japanese tolerance if 'the concept of assimilation [is] to be successful'. He was a moderate nationalist, an imprecise description liable to misunderstanding. Those who are now so labelled ought not *ipso facto* to incur any slight to their nationalism: the fact is simply that in contrast to radical nationalists they took a longer-term view of how Korean independence might be restored. Accepting that the Japanese had too firm a grip on their country to be dislodged quickly, they aimed for survival and gradual change. And that meant accepting the Japanese presence, and, in unavoidable situations, working with the Japanese for the betterment of Korea. To radicals, and to those quick to rush to judgement after 1945, that was anathema, and some of Korea's most significant cultural figures, men like Yi Kwangsu and Ch'oe Namsŏn, suffered adverse criticism, which in some cases has taken decades to correct. Rather than vilification as collaborationists, the two deserve at the very least recognition for their determination to introduce modern vernacular literature to Korea as a self-strengthening agent. (Ch'oe it was, too, who developed the old poetic form *sijo* as a modern style and concept, exalting it as an expression of Korean-ness in the face of Japanese efforts to destroy national consciousness.) Other cultural figures who saw their reputation marred by political prejudice were Chŏng Chiyong (1903–?1950), described by Richard Rutt as 'the finest modern Korean poet', whose work was banned in the ROK from 1950 to 1988, and the composer Yun Isang, tortured by the Japanese police, captured by North Koreans during the Korean War, and tried as a collaborator. Outstanding artists like Kim Ŭnho and Yi Sangbŏm were denounced for having exhibited in the Mijŏn. And among the accused landlords and business tycoons who did, it is true, stand to profit more than most Koreans by collaborating with the enemy, were Chŏn Hyŏngp'il and Kim Sŏngsu. Chŏn's 'incorrect attitude' can be overlooked by most of today's visitors to the Kansŏng Museum, grateful that he saved so many important works of art from export to the Japanese fatherland. As for Kim Sŏngsu, the views daringly published in his outspoken nationalist newspaper *Tonga Ilbo*, and the formation of the museum and library at Posŏng College, speak for themselves.

Seemingly beyond the pale and incapable of restitution was the group known as the Seven Traitors, the senior officials who accepted the

Protectorate Treaty in 1905. They comprised the prime minister, Han Kyusŏl, and the ministers of finance, war, home affairs, education, agriculture and industry, and justice. Irrevocably attached to the name of the education minister, Yi Wanyong, is the epithet 'quisling', for he also accepted the Protocol Treaty of 1907, served as prime minister from then until 1910, and then signed the Annexation Treaty. He later became vice-president of the Government-General's Central Council, and by the 1920s was one of the richest men in Korea. His recent biographer Yun Dokhan calls him 'the very picture of the spiritless, feeble-minded intellectuals and opportunists who accepted the status quo in return for personal gain'. Was Yi Wanyong a traitor or, as he himself claimed, a *sadae*-style nationalist? He had, after all, once served as foreign minister in the anti-Japanese cabinet of 1896 and as chairman of the Independence Club. Perhaps Mencius might have accepted the rationale of his self-defence, even if few others have. Yet throughout Korean history there have been those who continued to argue or to imply empirically that 'serving the great' – whether the great be identified as China, Japan or the West – is not incompatible with promoting long-term national interest. Can a distinction be made between Silla's admiration for China, and readiness to imitate it from a position of self-confidence and relative independence, and what is sometimes described in later eras as political expediency? What did 'serving the great' mean to *sirhak* advocates? Were the policies of Kojong and Kaehwadang ministers a modernized version of the same thing? Was collaboration with the Japanese colonialists defensible as a modern interpretation of defending Korea while recognizing some of the admirable features of Japanese culture? Indeed, was the entire colonial process around the world a case of the weak surviving to learn and grow by paying unavoidable lip service to the strong? If assassins take the law into their own hands, it is sometimes because governments seem to bow lower to political advantage than to the defence of principle. In September 1948 Syngman Rhee's government acted in haste to pass a law leading to the arrest of pro-Japanese collaborators, and then showed how touchy an issue the proof of treachery was by rescinding it almost immediately. So few Japanese were brought to trial as war criminals because the United States, in the person of General Douglas MacArthur, needed to revive that country quickly as a bulwark against the threat of Soviet expansion into the Pacific. But, like the Israeli Nazi-hunters of the Simon Wiesenthal Center, there are some Koreans who will not give up, and early in the twenty-first century the Korea Parliamentary League on National Spirit issued a preliminary list of 708 collaborators of the colonial period. It appears there are still scores to be settled.

CHAPTER EIGHT

Partition and War, 1945–53: Return to Disunity

The lack of an Allied strategy for post-Liberation Korea and the failure of the United Nations to understand or handle its problems created a country divided along the lines of the Cold War world. In 1950 a bitter conflict broke out that shattered Korea and brought the world to the brink of a nuclear catastrophe.

THE MIRAGE OF LIBERATION

Sometimes the coming of peace and longed-for liberation turns into anti-climax. Parisians danced in the streets to see the Nazi occupiers go in August 1944, only to begin quarrelling over everything from scarce rations to cases of impugned honour. Londoners, released from the tyranny of night-time bombing in 1945, found that they missed the comradeship it stimulated. That same summer, Koreans were about to find the experience even worse, far worse in fact. After 40 years of occupation, oppression and struggle for survival they were unprepared for the sudden Japanese collapse on 14 August, and confusion and social divisions quickly threatened to turn into chaos. The hasty dedication of a shrine to Yi Sunsin at his birthplace in Asan, Ch'ungch'ŏng Pukdo, was not enough to dispel a deepening mood of despondency as a reputed million deportees from Japan descended on a denuded country with little to offer. Euphoria quickly turned into what the artist Park Seobo called 'a period of despair and misery, a time of absolute hopelessness', and harsh retribution against suspected collaborators broke out. Politically, the lack of a ready-made plan also proved disastrous. The capitulation came so suddenly that in order to prevent the rapid deployment of Soviet troops into northern Korea turning into nationwide occupation, the Americans had to come up with a dividing line to delineate Russian and American spheres of responsibility. As a temporary expedient, hastily conceived in Washington during the night of 14 August and based on nothing more than a *National Geographic* map, they chose the 38th parallel. The Yalta Agreement in February had stipulated that no foreign troops would be stationed permanently on Korean soil, but swift action was called for and there was no time to

Principal Events: February 1945–May 1950

1945

3–11 February	Yalta Conference, attended by Churchill, Roosevelt and Stalin
16 July–2 August	Potsdam Conference, attended by Churchill, Truman and Stalin
8 August	The USSR enters the war against Japan
14 August	Japan announces unconditional surrender
6 September	Proclamation of the Korean People's Republic
27 December	Agreement concluding the Moscow Conference of Foreign Ministers

1946

23 September	General strike begins in South Korea
1 October	Beginning of the Autumn Harvest uprising

1947

12 March	Pronouncement of the Truman Doctrine signals the beginning of the Cold War in Europe
5 November	UN approves the creation of a Temporary Commission on Korea (UNTCOK)

1948

3 April	Beginning of the Cheju Rising
10 May	Elections in South Korea create the ROK
25 August	Elections in North Korea create the DPRK
18 October	Beginning of the Yŏsu-Sunch'ŏn Rising
12 December	UN recognizes the Republic of Korea
26 December	National Security Law passed; UNTCOK ceases to be 'Temporary' (becomes UNCOK); withdrawal of Soviet troops

1949

26 February	Withdrawal of US troops
5 March	Kim Il Sung visits Moscow

1949–50

December–February	Mao Zedong in Moscow; signs the Sino-Soviet Treaty of Friendship, Alliance and Mutual Assistance

1950

12 January	Announcement of the US Defense Perimeter by Secretary of State Dean Acheson
March	Kim Il Sung makes secret trip to Moscow
May	Kim Il Sung visits Beijing
30 May	South Korean legislative elections

weigh the long-term consequences. Lieutenant-General John R. Hodge and the XXIV Army Corps arrived off Inch'ŏn from Okinawa on 8 September, and instead of the freedom they dreamed of, P'yŏngyangers and Seoulites awoke once more to the sound of foreign boots marching through their streets. This time they were Soviet and American.

Hodge, infamous for his reputed observation that 'Koreans and Japanese are all the same breed of cats', was quickly cast as de facto ruler of southern Korea, a role for which he had no political training, no local knowledge and no desire. His first step was to establish an American Military Government (AMG) to await the implementation of trusteeship. This had been agreed at the Tehran Conference in 1943 and was part of the late President Roosevelt's vision of a post-war world in which US influence dominated the Pacific basin. It was based on the assumption that ex-colonial states would not be ready to assume full independence immediately after liberation, but would require an indeterminate period of tutelage to prepare for it. The Koreans themselves had different plans. A hastily formed Preparatory Committee for Building the Country was headed by the leader of the Korean Workers' Party, Yŏ Unhyŏng, and though Hodge envisaged a Democratic Advisory Council working alongside the AMG he was unable to persuade Yŏ to join it. Yŏ's Committee had already proclaimed a Korean People's Republic (KPR) with Hŏ Hŏn as its temporary prime minister. The KPR delegated its authority to People's Committees to keep order in local areas and to oversee the redistribution of former Japanese-owned land to Korean peasants. Despite the KPR's professed intention of creating a united front, Hodge distrusted leftist moves of this kind. In October Syngman Rhee returned to Korea on a plane arranged by General MacArthur. Though a former head of the Korean Provisional Government in China, Rhee had not gone unchallenged (he had been impeached and ousted in 1925), and Washington itself had already seen plenty of him and was tiring of his extreme right-wing nationalism. Having dreamed of heading a unified Korea for so long, he perceived this as his best, perhaps his last, chance. American administrators regarded him as determined and devious, and were anxious to restrain his headstrong tendencies, but *faute de mieux* they had to work with him.

The Russians approved Yŏ's and Hŏ's leftist inclinations and accepted the KPR in the North, where the Christian nationalist Cho Mansik (1882–1950) was made head of the People's Committee for North Korea. The artificial dividing line and the assumption of power by left- and right-wing leaders to north and south of it respectively did not reflect any pattern across the population at large. There were more communists in the South than the North, twice as many Christians in

the North as in the South, and cultural figures were randomly distributed. But adjustments were soon being made. As persecution of
Christians increased in the North, many of them were to be found
among the 650,000 refugees heading south. Even the popular Cho
Mansik, a leading Presbyterian layman, was arrested. P'yŏngyang, in
turn, attracted socialist activists from the South. Pak Hŏnyŏng (d.
1955), who had reorganized the Korean Communist Party in Seoul in
September, fled to P'yŏngyang in December, the same month as Kim Il
Sung (1912–1994) assumed the leadership of the Party's northern
branch. Kim had emerged from the Manchurian shadows with an envi-
able name as an anti-Japanese resistance leader. Bruce Cumings calls
him 'one of the few Koreans who joined forces both with Chinese and
Soviet communism yet still seemed to keep a patriotic image and the
loyalty of Korean comrades'. In July 1946 he and Pak Hŏnyŏng went to
Moscow, where Stalin endorsed Kim as leader, with Pak as his second-
in-command. Later, however, as Kim pressed his case for invading the
South, an aging and ailing Stalin would discover that his left-wing
nationalism made him just as difficult to manage as the Americans
found Rhee.

It was hard to see just what was cooking inside the bubbling political cauldron. In Seoul, the KPR aimed to work with the KPG returning
from Chongqing. Rhee was to be its president, Yŏ Unhyŏng its vice-
president. But when Rhee arrived, followed in November by Kim Ku
and Kim Kyusik (1881–1950), Hŏ Hŏn failed to gain their cooperation.
The Americans, anxious to avoid the risk of communist control over
the whole peninsula, were inclined to support the recently formed,
more right-wing Korean Democratic Party, one of whose founders in
September was Kim Sŏngsu, but when Hodge had difficulty finding
any figures of national significance other than Kim Kyusik who would
work with him, the AMG brought the old independence fighter Sŏ
Chaep'il back from the United States to advise it. It would not recognize the People's Committees, and instead reappointed Japanese
bureaucrats to help in maintaining essential services and even Japanese
policemen as the core of a new paramilitary Korean gendarmerie. It
had to contend with trouble instigated by both left- and right-wing
organizations, and overreacted by imprisoning many independence
activists. Internecine Korean rivalries brought about the assassination
of Yŏ Unhyŏng – on Kim Ku's orders – on 18 July 1947 and of Kim
Ku – probably on Syngman Rhee's – on 26 August 1949.

The Moscow Resolution of December 1945 established a Joint US-
Soviet Commission to consult with Korean political parties and social
organizations until a provisional Korean government for the whole land

could be set up, and to organize trusteeship under the supervision of the USA, the Soviet Union, Great Britain and China. Announcement of this caused outrage in Korea, and the Commission turned out to be ineffectual. So much in disagreement were the two sides that they held only two rounds of talks, in January 1946 and May 1947, and when the latter proved fruitless the Americans turned for help to the United Nations, which established a (Temporary) Commission on Korea (UNTCOK) to oversee elections. Its team of advisers, drawn from nine nations, arrived in Seoul on 14 January 1948, but the Soviet Union refused it entry to the North. Overriding objections from UNTCOK itself and from many Koreans, US proposals for elections in the South were put to an Interim Committee of the United Nations General Assembly and approved. Thus, on 10 May 1948, the first independent election ever held in Korea took place. Against a background of 323 deaths, the arrest of thousands of leftists and disenfranchisement of many more, and a boycott by Rhee's political opponents, independents won 83 of the 198 seats and Rhee's Independence Party 54; 100 seats were left vacant for the North. The United Nations nevertheless recognized the new Assembly as the legitimate government, and Rhee was elected as its president: the Republic of Korea (ROK) was officially born, its name (Taehan min'guk) seeking legitimation by recalling the Taehan Empire created in 1897. Not to be outdone, the communist authorities held their own elections, filling 572 seats of a Supreme People's Assembly for constituencies across both North and South Korea, and enabling the Democratic People's Republic of Korea (DPRK) to be inaugurated on 9 September 1948 amid claims of its own legitimacy derived from proximity to the Manchurian heartlands of Tan'gun and Koguryŏ, and of anti-Japanese colonial resistance. The United Nations route to unified self-government was looking like a dead end, and those who professed their nationalism too forcefully found that they were criticized as counter-revolutionaries in the North and as communists in the South.

In signs of what returning normality should be able to offer, the Chōsen Sōtokufu Museum was re-designated the National Museum of Korea and opened to the public in the former Capitol Building in September 1945, while P'yŏngyang established a Central Historical Museum. Any such show of optimism was to be welcomed, but in truth the examples were few enough. Through the winter of 1945–6 an influx of refugees from the North and returnees from Japan exacerbated food shortages and unemployment in the South. Simmering discontent, fuelled as well by corruption, landlordism and oppressive policing, erupted in the autumn into a general strike and widespread peasant rebellion, which the AMG denounced as communist-inspired and Soviet-assisted.

Many died as US troops and the hated Korean National Police ruthlessly suppressed the dissidence, and People's Committees were among the victims as right-wing authority was reinforced. One of the police officers involved in the violence, the son of a poor farmer, had been a prize-winning cadet at Japanese military academies in Xinjing (Changchun), Manchuria and Tokyo in the early 1940s. His name was Park Chung Hee.

The suppression of what has become known as the Autumn Harvest Uprising failed to douse the smouldering embers of communism, and they burst into flame again on Cheju island in April 1948. Rebellion raged for a year. More than 160 villages were destroyed and 30,000 peasants, one third of the island's population, may have died as the ROK army followed American directions to suppress it. Soldiers of Rhee's Fourteenth Regiment mutinied against their orders and instigated an uprising of their own around Yŏsu and Sunch'ŏn in Chŏlla Namdo. Thousands more died before it was put down by the Fourth Army, sent from Kwangju, and in the aftermath thousands of political dissidents were arrested and sent to re-education camps. Among the detainees this time was Park Chung Hee, who turned state's evidence and betrayed fellow rebels to the Fourth Army. Paradoxical as it might seem, given both his earlier and later career, stories that he was once a Communist Party member have refused to go away. Some amateur psychologists like to think that his extreme anti-communism as president was intended to cover his earlier tracks. There is no proof of either suspicion.

Nearly five years on from Liberation the political situation was a shambles; food was in short supply; inflation was rampant; and border fights multiplied as rivals on both sides of the 38th parallel became jittery. Who or what might offer deliverance? The poet Sŏ Chŏngju (b. 1915) cloaked the feelings of many of his compatriots when he wrote:

> The red and green pattern mottling the shell
> is the sea's hope, the sea's,
> that has seethed alone for thousands of years.
>
> The flowers that unfold till the branches crack
> are the wind's hope, the wind's,
> that comes and whispers here day after day.
>
> Ah! The revolution now spreading like a flood
> Across our land with its crimson servitude
> Is truly heaven's own long-kept hope.

Hope was what kept many Koreans going. But events in the second half of 1950 destroyed even hope. At 4 a.m. on the morning of 25 June, North Korean artillery opened up a heavy barrage across the 38th parallel, taking the unprepared South Korean army by surprise. Hours later, several columns of armour thrust their way south over the border, two down the east and west coasts, two in the centre and two headed directly for Seoul.

THE KOREAN WAR AND ITS VICTIMS

The course of the war and its implications

The War Memorial of Korea is more than its name suggests. Situated near the former Yongsan base of the US Eighth Army in Seoul, it is actually a fine museum covering the history of warfare on the peninsula from prehistoric times to the twentieth century. At its main gate stands a 6.25-metre-high replica of a Bronze Age notched dagger, and near the east gate a copy of the Kwanggaet'o monument of AD 414. Much of the Memorial is devoted to the Korean War. On 27 June 1950 the UN Security Council voted in favour of a US resolution condemning the North Korean invasion: and inside a replica bunker near the west gate are the flags of the member countries that came to South Korea's aid. Over the next three years sixteen sent troops, from the USA (sources go as high as 2.4 million men involved throughout the whole war, though perhaps never more than 325,000 were involved at one time) and the UK (87,000 men) to Belgium and Luxembourg (one infantry battalion), Ethiopia (one infantry battalion), the Philippines (one infantry battalion and tanks), South Africa (one fighter squadron) and Cuba (one infantry company). Five more – Denmark, Italy, India, Norway and Sweden – contributed medical teams. In the grounds of the War Memorial stand lines of aircraft, tanks and guns from the combatant nations on both sides, mute reminders of the constant cacophony that Korea endured for three years; inside the building is a numbing collection of *matériel*, film and documents that graphically describe the progress of the war and the horrors it inflicted on the entire population of the peninsula, fighting men and innocent victims alike.

The results of what happened over three years in Korea were of unforeseeable scope and complexity, and did more to change the world order than any other similar period in the twentieth century. Foreign intervention on a devastating scale turned a civil war of unimaginable brutality into a surrogate for World War Three. Both Stalin and Truman were anxious to avoid a third world war, even though the arms race started by Truman's approval of increased defence spending on 25 April 1950 would heighten fears of it for years to come. Yet Dean Acheson's speech to the National Press Club on 12 January 1950 had indicated that America felt no automatic commitment to defend Korea for its own sake. Korea must help itself. What Truman was intent on doing was containing Soviet communism, opposing its march wherever in the world it threatened. The fall of Korea would endanger Japan and thence the US, but a democratic Japan ready to accept US military bases should help to render costly intervention in Korea unnecessary. A Japanese peace treaty concluded on terms favourable to the US was therefore central to Truman's vision of Pacific security. It was, of course, entirely contrary to Stalin's concept of the same thing, as was the thought of Siberia bordered by a Korea unified under Syngman Rhee.

Ironically, communist China did not worry Truman in the way the Soviet Union did, and in anticipation of improved Sino-American relations the president was even ready to tolerate the prospect of Taiwan's final fall. Chiang Kai-shek had, after all, proved a severe disappointment through so many years of expensive support. At the same time, Mao Zedong's visit to Moscow gave Stalin an opportunity to reassess his view of him now that the People's Republic of China had become a reality. Fraternal allies or no, it was vital that Stalin's own command of the world communist movement should not be challenged, and crucial that Beijing should *not* get on well with America. But having refused Kim Il Sung's request in September 1949 for permission to invade the South, Stalin later saw how this might open a window of opportunity for him. The withdrawal of Soviet and US troops from Korea in 1949 had not diminished the reliance of North or South on their political mentors. It had, however, removed the hedges against precipitate action from either side of the 38th parallel, and Stalin now worried that Syngman Rhee, who would have loved to be able to mount a reunifying campaign of his own, might try and go it alone with an attack on the North. His forces were vastly inferior in number to those of the North, and even with the weaponry left behind by the Americans they were inadequately equipped. But Rhee was obsessive enough to be unpredictable, and Stalin decided that a pre-emptive strike against him might be easier to handle than a defensive campaign. Moreover, the completion of the USSR's own A-bomb and the formation of NATO in January 1950 both implied that the time was right to issue a warning to the West. So he gave Kim the go-ahead, subject to Chinese approval. Mao was not enthusiastic. China's own revolution had not yet been carried through to its logical end in Taiwan and Tibet, and was still meeting resistance even in parts of China proper. But like

Stalin, Mao was concerned about the threat of a Korea under Rhee, and he was won round. Kim Il Sung's visit to Moscow in March 1950 was rewarded with the delivery of aircraft, tanks, armoured vehicles and guns to North Korea in June, and the die was cast.

Once the war had begun, the stakes were raised for Stalin, Mao and Truman, and Kim Il Sung and Syngman Rhee were reduced to little more than supporting cast. On the communist side Mao took major command decisions, though Stalin retained ultimate authority. Although no Russian troops were committed to fight, all weaponry came from the USSR – all, that is, except *matériel* captured from UN armies. For its part, the ROK leadership had no alternative but to accept UN/US direction. Whether Korea had been implicitly included within the US Defense Perimeter or not, the Truman Doctrine of support for peoples 'resisting attempted subjugation by armed minorities or outside pressures' now clearly applied, and if Stalin's henchmen were allowed to get away with their invasion the prospects for West Germany and Europe looked ominous. The Americans, therefore, immediately intervened. Strategic and field command was given first to General Douglas MacArthur. He had been an outstanding leader in the Pacific War, and as head of the post-war US administration in Japan enjoyed a dominant political position in rebuilding Japan's economy and steering it towards US-style democracy. His natural vanity was flattered by the power he had exercised in protecting Emperor Hirohito from war-crimes charges and redefining the Japanese monarchical system, and now, returning to his familiar role as military commander-in-chief, he was little inclined to listen to or obey orders from what he perceived as a weak president, or even his own joint chiefs of staff. But the 'viceroy of Japan' himself rarely visited Korea from his Tokyo headquarters, and historians have not been kind to him in assessing these, the declining stages of his career. Adjectives such as egotistical, pompous, arrogant, dangerous, misguided, eccentric (even lunatic), paranoid (almost as much in his despising of Europe as his hatred of communism) and megalomaniac abound, and had it not been for his magnificent past record, Truman would certainly have dismissed him sooner than he did in April 1951.

Compared with the political complexity of the years that preceded it, the confusion and intensity that characterized the fighting and the breadth of its worldwide effects, the pattern of the war was fairly simple. With the advantage of surprise and superior forces, North Korea quickly swept the ROK and American defenders southwards. Within only three months the Allies were forced to establish a last-ditch enclave around Pusan, and only then did the arrival of reinforcements

The Korean War: Principal Events

1950

April	South Korean guerrilla leaders go to P'yŏngyang for planning
12 June	North Korea moves combat troops towards the 38th parallel
25 June	North Korea's invasion of South begins at 4 a.m.
27 June	The US announces its intervention; UN Security Council passes a resolution authorizing assistance to ROK
29 June	North Korea captures Seoul
1 July	First US troops of the Eighth Army arrive
3 July	Kim Il Sung asks for greater Soviet aid in view of serious US bombing
5 July	The first US troops are involved in fighting, retreating from north of Osan
14 July	UN takes over operational command authority
1 August	UN troops blow the last bridges over the Nakdong river and isolate the 'Pusan perimeter'
10 August	Molotov concludes talks with Mao in Beijing, agreeing that if UN troops re-cross the 38th parallel, Soviet-equipped Chinese soldiers will enter Korea
28 August	2,000 UK troops arrive in Pusan from Hong Kong, the first non-US UN brigade to reach Korea
15 September	The Inch'ŏn landing; North Korea mistakenly believes that Japan has entered the war
20–28 September	Seoul is re-taken
30 September	Kim Il Sung sends a plea to Stalin for Chinese or other outside aid; Moscow pressurizes Mao to intervene
1 October	ROK troops cross the 38th parallel; Mao unwillingly joins the war
14 October	Chinese troops secretly cross the Yalu river
19 October	The US Eighth Army takes P'yŏngyang
25 October	Chinese People's Volunteers enter the war
1 November	First battle between US and Chinese troops
1 December	US general retreat begins

1951

4 January	Communists re-take Seoul; the UN line is held 40 miles to the south
15 January	US counter-attack begins
15 March	Seoul is recaptured
3 April	UN troops cross the 38th parallel

11 April	MacArthur is relieved of his command
22 April	Communist spring offensive begins
25 April	Battle of the Imjin river begins
18 May	Acheson informs Moscow that the US will negotiate
12 June	Kim Il Sung and Gao Gang go to Moscow, where Stalin agrees to armistice talks
10 July	Talks begin in Kaesŏng: Mao wants to settle along ceasefire line, Stalin insists that fighting should continue
30 July	UN/US bomb P'yŏngyang
22 August	US breaks off talks after attack on the Kaesŏng talks area
8 September	Japanese peace treaty signed; US occupation of Japan officially ends
25 October	Talks are resumed, at P'anmunjŏm
1952	
23 June	US planes bomb electricity-generating plant on the Yalu river
11 July	UN planes bomb P'yŏngyang
29 August	UN planes again bomb P'yŏngyang
8 October	Peace talks are halted *sine die*
4 November	Dwight D. Eisenhower is elected president of the United States
1953	
5 March	Stalin dies; two weeks later Soviet Council of Ministers orders Mao and Kim to seek peace
26 April	Peace talks resume at P'anmunjŏm
27 July	Armistice signed
5 August	Repatriation of POWs begins

from other UN countries stiffen resistance and begin to tilt the scales. The real retaliation, however, devised by General MacArthur, proved to be as dramatic and decisive as the initial communist advance had been. A daring seaborne landing at Inch'ŏn in September led to the recovery of Seoul, and ROK troops, with US support, swept northwards into the DPRK. Their advance towards the Yalu was the trigger for the entry of Chinese 'volunteers', and with it the transformation of the scale and nature of the war. The communists drove the United Nations back and recaptured Seoul before a defensive line held 40 miles to its south. By now it was January 1951, and the war was still little more than six months old. When the UN counter-attack came and the capital was retaken on 15 March, it had changed hands four times in fewer than nine months, and was a city in ruins, inhabited by starving vagrants. Once more the US/UN crossed the 38th parallel, their aim this time being to establish a defensible line above it rather than to carry the war to the Yalu and beyond. The latter was MacArthur's preference, but the president's patience with his insubordinate commander was running out.

Throughout the war, rivers and frontiers were of critical significance: the Han helped to hold up the first communist advance and was defended with valiant if doomed courage by the Student Volunteer Corps; the Nakdong helped form the Pusan perimeter round the last ROK/UN bulwark. Above all, the two political dividing lines, the 38th parallel and the Yalu river, dominated strategic-planning issues on both sides. Should US troops be allowed to respond to the initial invasion by bombing the North? After Inch'ŏn, should UN troops cross the demarcation line? How close to the Yalu should they advance, and should communist bases in China be attacked? (On 24 October MacArthur countermanded orders from his own chiefs of staff and instructed US troops to make for the border regions.) Should the communists, after their second advance, be allowed to hold the line at the 38th parallel? MacArthur certainly thought not, and exceeded his powers on 24 March 1951 by threatening Beijing with humiliation if China did not withdraw from Korea and permit unification by the ROK. He and John Foster Dulles were prepared to extend the war into China if necessary; Truman, however, feared that this would make World War Three inevitable. When it came, the second crossing of the 38th parallel by UN forces prompted a massive communist counter-offensive. Losses were heavy on both sides. In fierce fighting along the Imjin river between 22 and 30 April the Gloucestershire Regiment won lasting fame for its brave resistance, and the Chinese were left exhausted and demoralized by their failure to capitalize on their numerical superiority.

Both sides were now ready for peace. Armistice talks began in July 1951, only Syngman Rhee refusing to take part in them. They dragged on, first in Kaesŏng and then in P'anmunjŏm, for almost two years, during which time 12,300 more American soldiers were killed. The main sticking point was argument over the repatriation of prisoners of war. The UN held approximately 132,400 prisoners, comprising 95,500 North Koreans, 20,700 Chinese and 16,200 communist South Koreans, against the communists' declared total of only 11,500. The US refused to accept the automatic exchange of such imbalanced numbers, fearing that it would strengthen their enemies for a renewed fight: instead, it proposed voluntary repatriation, offering Koreans the chance to return to their homes and the Chinese the choice of going either to the mainland or to Taiwan. The final agreement, reached in May 1953, gave each government 90 days in which to try and convince their own soldiers to go home. Two crises threatened it. President Rhee, unhappy at the dwindling prospect of a reunited Korea, tried to sabotage the peace process by releasing around 25,000 North Korean POWs on 17–18 June, before the screening process began. And the communists suffered a propaganda blow when only about 70,000 chose to go home: more than 14,000 of the Chinese, among them former Guomindang soldiers and sympathizers, opted to be sent to Taiwan. The main parties, however, were by now too war-weary to take up the fight again: in August the communists began freeing 13,000 captives. Most were South Koreans; 3,500 were Americans, including 21 who made headline news by choosing to be released in the PRC. Most of the North Koreans went home, but the 5,640 Chinese who returned to the People's Republic found themselves treated as pariahs for supposedly having surrendered rather than fight to the death. They suffered badly, especially during the Anti-Rightist Campaign of 1957 and the Cultural Revolution.

The victims

Early in the war the numbers of combatant and support troops had escalated rapidly. The initial confrontation set 135,000 North Korean against 98,000 South Korean soldiers, and estimates suggest that the communists, already reduced by casualty to 65,000, were reinforced in late November 1950 by up to 340,000 Chinese. Confronting them stood 440,000 combined ROK and UN troops. In December the US Joint Chiefs of Staff, concerned at MacArthur's lack of judgement as the situation on the ground settled into an evenly balanced stalemate, refused his request for 75,000 more US/UN troops and 50,000–60,000 Nationalist Chinese from Taiwan. But the numbers ranged against the South went on rising, and by April 1951 communist strength was estimated at around 700,000. By late 1952, against the background of ineffectual armistice talks, the respective figures were almost one million against 768,000, each side having some 300,000 men at or near the front. Korean nationalist sources claim there were a further 20,000 in guerrilla armies hostile to both Kim Il Sung and Syngman Rhee.

Figures can create such a false impression. Numbers like these of fighting men raise images of professionalism, ruthlessness, unanimity of purpose. One hopes that in time of war, such an impression of one's own side does not mislead. Yet the truth is invariably more fractured. In June 1950 the North Korean soldiers were Soviet-trained, determined and fired up with self-confidence. Many were veterans of the Chinese civil war. After just one week's fighting against them, 'Syngman

Rhee's army could account for only 54,000 of its men. The remaining 44,000 had merely disappeared, many of them never to be seen again' (Hastings). But sweeping through the South, the North Koreans replaced their mounting casualties with men and boys forcibly conscripted from 'liberated' areas. Their morale was low and their training inadequate. Today, we are shocked when we see TV pictures from such places as Afghanistan, Sierra Leone and Haiti of boy soldiers armed with machine guns. But we forget perhaps that the involvement and exploitation of children in warfare has a long history. Fourteen-year-olds falsified their age and signed up to fight in World War One, and when the US Eighth Army found itself capturing, and, worse still, shooting, equally young boys in 1950 it was not really such an unprecedented thing. If most of these children must have been desperately unhappy, they were not the only ones. The Chinese soldiers, when they came to Korea, were called volunteers. They were no such thing, but even as professionals fighting – so they believed – to defend their own country against US imperialism they were none too happy about laying down their lives in foreign territory. Proud though many undoubtedly were to wave the flag of the newly proclaimed People's Republic, they were exhausted by years of their own civil war, and fighting abroad in Korea was not the same as mopping up the last remaining areas of resistance to the revolution in China. They were anxious about conditions back home, and what most of them wanted was a quiet life. The same went for the Americans. The Eighth Army, so recently decimated by the Pacific War, was under-funded and poorly equipped, its ranks filled with drafted youths whose experience as occupying forces in Japan had given them no inkling or preparation for the horrors of continuous fighting to come. When I paid my first visit to the United Nations' cemetery in Pusan I was struck by the low average age of the enlisted men against the relatively high age of the senior officers, veterans of the anti-Japanese war who had already passed regular call-up age when Pearl Harbor first jerked them out of retirement. American morale was often little better than Korean, a contributory factor to the Americans' high death rate as POWs. Survival rates among the better disciplined Turkish and British contingents in captivity were more favourable.

Both sides committed atrocities against soldiers, POWs and civilians. Rhee's government ordered mass killings of suspected communists across the country in July and August 1950: up to 7,000 victims died near Taejŏn in a mass execution that was later compared with the rape of Nanjing. A massacre of villagers by ROK troops at Koch'ang in February 1951 later became the subject of Kim Wŏnil's novel *Winter*

Valley. Monica Felton, a British member of a fact-finding mission that visited North Korea in 1952 for the Women's International Democratic Federation, wrote: 'The total picture is one of horror on a scale that can be compared only with the behaviour of the Nazis in occupied Europe.' Stories of Americans abusing South Koreans, when attested after the end of the war, contributed to long-simmering anti-American feeling, but US soldiers found it hard to distinguish between Korean friend and foe, and sometimes had neither the time nor the inclination to try: their massacre of 300–400 civilian refugees, mostly women and children, at Nogŭn-ni, South Chungch'ŏng, in July 1950 has become notorious. Conditions in prison camps on both sides were harsh, especially during the first year of the war, and prompted many suicides. Food and medical supplies were scant and ill health abounded. Political and national divisions among the prisoners added to natural tension and strains, and the use of psychological and physical torture by the Chinese was widely condemned around the world. But in UN / ROK prison camps Chinese prisoners also had much to endure. Pro-Taiwan inmates, among them veteran Guomindang fighters from the Chinese civil war, were rewarded with posts of responsibility, and they victimized the communists. Particularly cruel was the practice, adopted in mid-1951, of tattooing prisoners with anti-communist slogans, driving some to self-mutilation and even suicide. One of the main UN prison camps was on the island of Kŏje, off the south-east coast. There, communist prisoners began rioting in February 1952, and on 7 May took the American commandant hostage. Deaths and injuries occurred as US troops were sent in to restore order.

In winter the cold was so severe that, according to one British officer, 'the only way to dig was to put some petrol on the ground, light it, and when it had stopped burning, dig the bit that had softened and start again'. Across the peninsula the homeless were beset by starvation, illness and bad weather. Families were divided. Forced to take up arms by whichever army happened to pass by and pick them up, some found themselves fighting against relatives: a sculpture at the War Memorial recalls the actual meeting of two brothers on opposite sides of the battlefield. The psychological effects on a people to whom kinship and social relationships meant so much were shattering. On one hand, people could not but have sympathy for friends and relatives suffering and dying on the opposite side. On the other, passionate hatred for the enemy and its ideology turned friends and relations against each other and led to mutual suspicion and betrayal. Amid so much confusion and panic, it comes as no surprise that the instinct for self-protection led to instances of opportunistic side-changing.

American aircraft dropped more high explosive on Korea than they used throughout World War Two, more napalm even than they would use in Vietnam, and before his dismissal General MacArthur was ready to release atom bombs along the Chinese border. Between them both sides destroyed historic and cultural treasures on a scale unprecedented in Korea since the 1590s. The South Korean authorities did what they could to protect the country's heritage. The Royal Conservatory had been re-formed as the Music Office of the Former Royal Palace (Ku Wanggung Aakpu) in 1945, and was officially reinstituted at Pusan in January 1950 as the National Classical Music Institute (Kungnip Kukakwŏn). Performances began in April 1951. The National Theater was established in Seoul in April 1950. The Cultural Preservation Act of 1952 boasted of resurrecting national culture by improving the status of artists and guaranteeing freedom of artistic expression. Painters, however, remained sceptical. The government's annual Kukchŏn art exhibition, inaugurated in 1949, perpetuated the bland conservatism of the old Sŏnjŏn series and was shunned by avant-garde artists like Park Seobo. Painters had had little chance to learn how to express their feelings through their work. The only way that Park Seugun and Hwang Yŏngyŏp, subsequently renowned for their stylistic originality, managed to subsist in the immediate aftermath of Liberation was by painting portraits of US servicemen. The abstract movement appealed, but painters needed time and experience to participate in it effectively, and the war came as an impediment. Members of the left-wing Artists' Federation who gravitated to the North after 1947 soon found conditions there less conducive to self-expression than in the South, where artists did manage to unleash their pent-up anguish in *art informel* after 1953. Even so, it would be years before painters, among them *minjung* artists in the 1980s, confronted detailed treatment of war subjects.

Literary organizations sprang up after Liberation displaying the ideological factionalism associated with earlier social politics. Unsurprisingly, technique was subordinated to message, and a tendency towards self-criticism was apparent. The war called forth expressions of bitterness, resentment and mental turmoil. Suh Ji-moon's analysis of patriotism in conflict with brotherhood in Korean war poems includes the following by Mo Yun-suk (1910–1990):

> I gladly forego a grave for my body
> Or even a small coffin to shield me from wind and rain.
> Soon rough winds will whip my body
> And worms will feast on my flesh.
> But I will gladly be their companion.

My ardent wish is to become a handful of earth
In this valley of my fatherland
Waiting for better times for my country.

If poets reacted quicker than artists in recording this latest encounter with their people's pain and suffering, *han*, novelists would also take time to confront their anguished tales of the war. When their own reckoning came, Pak Wansŏ's *The Naked Tree* (1970) interpreted the war as the end of the social solidarity that Korea had known under Japanese occupation; Hong Songwŏn's *North and South* (1987) marked it as the turning point away from Confucian social values based on trust, respect and decorum and towards materialism and short-term gain; and Yi Munyŏl blamed Koreans' subservience to foreign ideology for the collapse of the family unit and its values, which meant so much to him and to Yi Chungsŏp (Picture Essay 27). In *The Age of Heroes* (1984) he analysed the career and philosophy of his father, a Confucian turned socialist revolutionary who brought deprivation to his wife and children by defecting to the North. Yi spoke for the psychological suffering of all divided families.

THE AFTERMATH OF WAR

Once again foreign powers had taken advantage of Korea's political inexperience and divisions and used it for their own ends. But this time the stakes were higher, the confusion more intense and the suffering of the Korean people far greater than in 1904 or 1894. Despite its brevity, the eight-year period from 1945 to 1953 is one of the most complicated in Korean history. Its interpretation is mired in ideological claims and theories, chief among them being the question of whether it was Korean domestic issues that led to conflict – in other words, whether it was really civil war that erupted in June 1950 – or whether festering Soviet–American hostility was to blame. Even the war years themselves are clouded by rival interpretations of both sides' political and military aims. One certainty, though, is that all Koreans are ever conscious of the legacies and unfinished business of a war that has still not officially ended.

The world has become familiar with, and appalled by, the sufferings involved in the recovery from colonialism – think of Cambodia, the Balkans, Rwanda and many others. All too often, political confusion and psychological trauma have been compounded by ethnic violence and retribution against those suspected of benefiting from occupation. Korea's liberation was among the first of such kind in modern times, and though it was spared the horrors of ethnic rivalry,

27 Yi Chungsŏp, *Family*

Yi Chungsŏp's personal relationship with Japan was an equivocal one. As a teenager he shared his people's resentment at the attempted suppression of Korean identity, but on going to the Department of Western Painting in the Tokyo Cultural Academy (Bunka Gakuin) in 1937 he enjoyed the company of other artistically open-minded Korean students such as Kim Whanki, met the Japanese girl who was to become his wife, and experienced the first thrill of professional recognition and acclaim. He came under the exciting influence of works by avant-garde painters such as Gauguin, Matisse and Picasso, and after experimenting with Cubism he eventually settled into his own style, a typically Korean form of expressionism characterized by bold and swift curving linear movement, which has been likened to the strong simplicity of Koguryŏ wall paintings and the dynamic descriptiveness of Van Gogh. Yi returned to Korea in 1943 and married in 1945, but ironically the country's liberation from Japan marked the tragic disintegration of his personal life. During the Korean War Yi and his family wandered in the vicinity of Pusan, but starvation forced him to send his beloved wife and two children away to Japan, from where they would never return. He continued to paint prolifically with passion and not a little eroticism, whether expressing his fury at foreign interference in Korea with forceful cock or bull fights, or his agonized love for his own and all children, in whose nakedness he proclaimed unconcerned vitality but vulnerable innocence. One of his best-known pictures is entitled *Bull* (1954). To many Koreans, the ox, the unremitting tiller of the soil, suggests the idea of self-sacrifice, and in a series of vigorous studies Yi used its relative the bull as a symbol of national fortitude amid the hardships of occupation and war. An exhibition of his work was held in 1955, but despite his growing reputation many of his pictures were banned on grounds of immorality, adding to his sense of anguish and rejection. Schizophrenia developed, and he died in poverty at the age of 40. He has been called an indisputable genius, a nationalist whose influence helped to free other artists from the restraints of tradition to pour out their emotions at being Korean in the twentieth century.

Yi Chungsŏp, *Family*, 1950, oil on paper, 27 × 37 cm.

its agony was exploited by the ideological *naïveté* of a Cold War world prepared to battle in defence, it believed, of right against wrong. Then, after three years of concentrated destruction, that world quickly forgot Korea and switched its attention to Vietnam. No such amnesiac relief could be granted to Korea itself, where the torment would continue across both halves of the shattered country. First must come recovery from the physical damage and the rebuilding of economies: with support from outside, notably the USSR, China and the USA, both states could take encouragement from their progress by the 1960s. In contrast, the mental trauma would take decades of gradual rehabilitation.

The final toll of the human tragedy was immeasurable. The War Memorial claims 1,520,295 North and South Korean combatants and civilians killed, more than 535,274 wounded and 421,103 left missing. If those figures look unacceptably precise, they do roughly tally with the more rounded figures quoted by Western historians of the war: nearly three million, about 10 per cent of the population, killed, wounded or lost. Five million fled their homes. Hundreds of thousands of families were divided, and many refugees ended up in the 'wrong' end of their country. (Claims that 4,000,000 Northerners crossed to the South are surely exaggerated, but much of the human traffic was undoubtedly in this direction.) More than 40 per cent of the ROK soldiers, over 40,000 men, may have become casualties in the first week. According to the War Memorial, 1,455,797 Chinese were killed or wounded, and Western authorities agree that not fewer than half a million must have died. 54,246 Americans lost their lives either on the battlefield, in prison camps, or from injury or exposure; 105,785 were wounded and 5,866 unaccounted for. Of other United Nations soldiers, 3,194 died, 11,297 were wounded and 2,769 taken prisoner or lost.

The statistics are appalling. We are shocked by them – briefly – and then forget them as we come across the totals from some other crisis. It is not so much facts and figures that stay in the mind as images. Who does not recall the little girl running naked and crying down the middle of a road in the midst of a Vietnamese battle zone? Or remember the unarmed man heroically confronting a tank outside Tiananmen in 1989? So too in Korea, pictures tell the horrors of the war better than words, pictures of mud, snow, shattered buildings, mangled bridges, streams of hopeless refugees, bayoneted corpses, napalmed civilians, demoralized soldiers, ill-clad POWs and overloaded, panic-filled boats carrying people and their scanty possessions across swollen rivers (Picture Essay 28): people who literally did not know which way to turn because they were liable to abuse and attack from both sides.

28 Taedong river, December 1950

Refugees struggling to escape P'yŏngyang across a bombed-out bridge over the Taedong river, December 1950. Pulitzer Prize-winning photograph by Max Desfor.

Without doubt, the entire Korean people were the losers. The pre-war division of power remained unaltered; the frontier between the two equally misnamed 'republics', frozen by the Armistice into the 1.86-mile (3 km) wide, 150-mile-long demilitarized zone, was little different from the arbitrary dividing line along the 38th parallel; and the political polarization between left- and right-wing leaderships in the North and South respectively was more entrenched than ever. Death removed Stalin's baleful domination on 5 March 1953, leaving Kim Il Sung free to develop his own interpretation of communism, socialist revolution and utopianism into the all-embracing concept of *juche*. The Central Committee Plenum, meeting in August 1953, hailed him as a 'national hero'. North Korean citizens, however, soon found their lives in thrall to class struggle, land collectivization and the chasing of unattainable economic targets. Syngman Rhee, too, grew increasingly out of touch with his people's hopes and needs as the First Republic's military, economic and political reliance on the US deepened. He revised and strengthened the National Security Law of 1948, and extended it in December 1958 to cover a range of loosely defined activities, including publishing attacks on the president and spreading 'false information'.

Both Kim and Rhee, with equal lack of justification, claimed victory in the war; none of the foreign participants, however, could claim to have achieved anything. The United States, it is true, had 'contained communism', but despite terrible losses it had failed to achieve Roosevelt's vision of a pro-American democracy in a unified Korea, and McCarthyism now hung like a lead weight round the neck of the American people. Stalin's hope of making his backyard in the east secure while he concentrated on expanding his powers over Europe was left unfulfilled. And the newly established Chinese government, even if its armies had earned grudging respect for their bravery, was now faced with unforeseen resistance across the Taiwan Straits and the unexpected prolongation of its domestic revolution. Perhaps the only country to experience short-term relief as a result of the Korean War was Japan, a non-combatant. There, the war gave added impetus to the settlement of a peace treaty and international rehabilitation, and thanks in no small measure to MacArthur's personal scheming, the issue of Emperor Hirohito's war guilt was relegated to a matter of secondary concern, something for which the Japanese people were generally grateful. The absence of victors, however, does not lessen the huge significance of the war in defining the future direction of American, Soviet and Chinese policy and shaping the new world order. Stalin may have been deterred from considering European expansionism and even World War Three, but now, not only Korea was condemned to continued bifurcation, but Germany and China too. Germany had played a large part in the thinking of both Soviet and American leaders in the run-up to June 1950. When war broke out, the Western powers believed it might be a trial run for a Soviet-backed attack on West Germany. Walter Ulbricht openly exalted North Korea's aggression as an example of how Germany could be reunified. (Chancellor Adenauer, however, was prepared for an attack: he had 200 pistols ready in his office.) Soon after the war, in October 1954, West Germany was admitted to

NATO, and the European mould hardened. In East Asia, the war further damaged the Chinese economy after years of crippling corruption and anti-Japanese and civil war. The new communist authorities, who had been looking towards the US as a potential partner, found themselves excluded from the United Nations and world trade opportunities, and condemned to unprofitable alliances with P'yŏngyang and East European states. The Sino-Soviet rift deepened, and amid the break-up of the monolithic world communist order Kim Il Sung's Pavlovian adherence to Moscow weakened. Truman's reversal of his earlier refusal to endorse Chiang Kai-shek's rule in Taiwan created a major new international alignment that divided the world's 'Eastern' (communist) and 'Western' (non-communist) blocs until the 1970s. The Americans found themselves being drawn willy-nilly into Asian politics, though Vietnam would soon show that they had learned no lessons from the war they were widely perceived as having lost.

CHAPTER NINE

Post-War Korea:
Tradition and Change

In 1953 Korea confronted a new and unwelcome phase of its
modern history, the prospect of a peninsula divided once more
between rival states. Of course, everybody hoped, and still does,
that 'post-Armistice' Korea really would mean 'post-war'. But
earlier plans for unification and national elections had clearly
foundered; talks at P'anmunjŏm dragged on and became mean-
ingless; and North and South failed to sign a peace treaty.
Tension between them periodically rose and fell, and Korea
remained one of the world's flashpoints where devastating conflict
could break out at any moment. Yet though the paths followed by
the two halves of one country since 1945, still more since 1953,
have led them to utterly different destinations, the people on both
sides of the DMZ have a strong sense of ethnic and cultural unity,
and neither side is willing to abandon the prospect of eventual
reunification.

THE POLITICAL OUTLINE

The Republic of Korea (South Korea)

The South Korean transition from dictatorship to democracy was hard
work. Syngman Rhee's autocratic and corrupt government, somewhat
ironically called the First Republic, ended in 1960 with a student-led
revolt on 19 April against his rigged re-election. Troops killed around
115 of them, but university professors joined the call for Rhee to go,
and pressure from the US Ambassador, Walter P. McConaughy, and the
military commander, General Magruder, finally forced him into exile.
A brief and unsuccessful flirtation with democratic plans known as
the Second Republic ended prematurely in May 1961 when right-wing
officers, fearful that elections would mean communist successes, staged
a coup against the prime minister, Chang Myŏn, and brought Park
Chung Hee, now General Park, to power. Most influential in the mili-

264

tary caucus was Kim Chŏngp'il, founder of the Korean Central Intelligence Agency (KCIA) and a collaborator with Park in setting up the Democratic Republican Party. Park claimed to believe in 'Koreanized democracy', yet within a year thousands of politicians, bureaucrats and military officers had been purged or banned from public life, communists outlawed, newspapers closed down, rural markets banned and tough limitations imposed on people's freedom. Nevertheless, he narrowly won a presidential election in October 1963 and, having silenced or intimidated his opponents, was re-elected with a greater majority in 1967. This was the Third Republic, following a new constitution drafted by a KCIA committee under the guidance of a Harvard University political scientist, Rupert Emerson. The education system expanded rapidly, with schools still favouring the military-style uniforms and discipline reminiscent of the Japanese colonial period; compulsory military service helped the enforcement of government authority; and the rapidly growing *chaebŏl*, nominally independent but having strong links with government and receiving substantial financial aid from it, implemented tight control over labour. The reward for restricted social freedom was at least a decade of economic progress. Through the 1950s superior mineral resources and Soviet aid had help-ed industrial output in the North to outstrip that in the South, but Park made steel, chemicals and machine tools top priorities and embarked on an industrialization programme to rival that of the DPRK. Against strong criticism in 1965 he sent troops to fight in Vietnam, where their distinguished service earned not only praise from their allies but also trading deals. Exports rose, and a measure of stability and wealth was appreciated by a country unaccustomed to such things. Not yet having any strong commitment to concepts of democratic rights, it gave Park the benefit of the doubt. Nationalist sentiment, however, was another matter, and his drive to improve relations with Japan stirred more passion, especially among students. A treaty of Basic Relations signed in June 1965 brought welcome cash and loans for industry, but failed to make adequate apology or reparation for all Japan's past offences against Koreans. On the face of it, Park's haste to build bridges with Tokyo looks surprising. But it was important to the US administration, anxious to build a strong East Asian buffer against advancing communism. And to an obsessed militarist like Park there was plenty to admire in recent Japanese history. He could appreciate, too, the efficiency of its economic development of Manchuria during the 1930s.

If the North were blessed with better mineral reserves, South Korea had the advantage in land and manpower. After all it had suffered, however, the countryside remained depressed in outlook and conservative in method until Park Chung Hee aimed at reviving and modernizing it with the New Community Movement (Saemaŭl Undong), launched in 1971. At last wealth and health began to spread into provincial towns and mountain villages. Banking, sanitation and medical services improved; new schools were built; and garishly coloured red, blue or green metal roofs replaced the attractive but highly flammable and insect-ridden thatched roofs of traditional rural houses. In Park's view, economic progress was an essential precursor of democratic change. Now, as he addressed the gulf that separated town and country, he was personally involved in the Movement and responded fiercely to charges of aloofness and authoritarianism.

Park was shocked when he almost lost the presidential election of 1971 to Kim Daejung. On 17 October 1972 he suspended the existing constitution, replaced it with a new one entitled (like that of Japan's Meiji constitution of 1889) Yusin, 'Revitalization', and imposed martial law. The old constitution would have barred him from a further period of office, but now he had the right to unlimited six-year terms. As the Fourth Republic took shape, popular resentment increased against his now dictatorial rule. And while heavy industry and the *chaebŏl* forged ahead, critics complained that too much of the profit from the country's rapid economic growth was going into the coffers of the government-*chaebŏl* alliance. A curfew was imposed; criticism of the constitution became a punishable offence; and party-political opposition – never really effective under the old constitution – was emasculated as the KCIA jailed and tortured the president's opponents. Three things led Park further and further from the path of 'Koreanized democracy': the continuing threat from the North as America, in the wake of détente with China and defeat in Vietnam, reduced its troops in the ROK from 62,000 to 42,000; the president's anxiety for tighter government controls over financial and labour aspects of industry; and the psychological effect of the assassination of the First Lady in 1974 in a bungled attempt on his own life. In summer 1979 rioting broke out when Park expelled the opposition leader Kim Young Sam from the National Assembly, and within weeks the president himself was dead, killed on 26 October by the gun of his own KCIA director, Kim Chaegyu.

Chun Doo Hwan, head of the Defence Security Command, quickly took charge of the KCIA, suspended the constitution, closed universities, banned political gatherings, and arrested political leaders, including Kim Daejung and Kim Young Sam. Violent counter-demonstrations followed and came to a head in May 1980, when special army forces killed more than 1,000 demonstrators and bystanders in Kwangju, Chŏlla Namdo. It was as infamous an event in Korean history as the Tiananmen Square massacre in Chinese nine years later, and it lit a slow-burning fuse that would take seven years to reach the powder keg. Those who were students through this radicalized era later became known as the 386 Generation: born in the 1960s, activists in the 1980s, and 30-something years old as momentous events unfolded in the 1990s. Hostile to their own dictators' interpretation of us-inspired democracy, they took to studying Marxism. (To the present day they claim that their conversation in those days was always about politics and social change, even Maoism, rather than normal student concerns such as sex and pop music.) In August 1980 the acting president, Ch'oe Kyuha, resigned. Chun temporarily took the reins, but his confirmation as president in February 1981 brought no prospect of an end to military rule. His presidency was a period of frequently unhappy news, of riots, strikes and political repression. The United States was condemned for not reining him in, and anti-Americanism began to link it with the massacre of the Kwangju victims. Attempts to negotiate with the DPRK got nowhere, and in 1983 a North Korean bomb killed several ROK ministers in Rangoon, though Chun himself escaped. Ironically, despite his globe-trotting efforts to raise South Korea's international image and his success in getting an aid and loan agreement with Japan (1983), the two most positive aspects of his presidency were appreciated only when it was over. They were the election of his successor and the Seoul Olympic Games, for which his administration had successfully bid and begun to prepare.

Up to then, no president had been chosen in open competition, and Chun intended to hand the presidential baton on to another former general, Roh Tae Woo. Roh had played a major part in bringing Chun to power and held important posts under his Fifth Republic. However, public outrage at the proposal and continuing fury at police repression led to two weeks of nationwide demonstrations that began on 10 June 1987. The so-called June Uprising persuaded Roh to insist on an election in December. He won it with 36.6 per cent of the vote. Had the two Kims (and a third, the veteran Kim Chŏngp'il, who also stood and polled around 8 per cent) done a deal to field just one candidate, as once seemed likely, Roh would have lost, for the opposition vote was split fairly evenly between Kim Young Sam and Kim Daejung. It was another example of Chosŏn-style political factionalism, but it was also a valuable lesson in the ROK's democratic learning curve. Under the Sixth Republic, Roh introduced a more liberal approach to party politics and press freedom. Yet even though his term of office, from 1988 until 1993, has been praised in retrospect as marking the birth of democracy, mass arrests continued under the National Security Law and workers still went on strike over anti- labour discrimination. Nor was the president himself untainted by scandal, and in 1996 his successor, Kim Young Sam, brought both him and Chun to trial for bribery, corruption, mutiny and treason. Chun's venality was such that he is believed to have taken bribes worth more than one billion pounds sterling. Initially sentenced to death and 22 years' imprisonment respectively, the pair were released from jail late in 1997 by special dispensation of the president and president-elect Kim Daejung. Chun returned to the Buddhist monastery where he and his wife had sought sanctuary before his trial.

Kim Young Sam was Korea's first elected president with no military background. The 386 Generation, now leaders of the new social and political environment, embraced the growing mood of democratization and cosmopolitanism, and backed measures aimed at putting the ROK at the forefront of the drive towards globalization. In 1997 it was admitted to the OECD in recognition of the part it was already playing in global trade. Progress indeed, yet Kim would not complete his term with his name untarnished. The fear of rough justice was still not removed: between 1993 and 1998, 3,438 arrests were made under the National Security Law and a further 13,357 under the Assembly and Demonstration Act. The dangerous liaison between government and *chaebŏl* was highlighted in autumn 1997 by the economic crisis that followed the bankruptcy of the Hanbo Business Group and Kia Motors. Financial scandal engulfed Kim's family. And he was accused of illegal attempts to hamper Kim Daejung's election as his successor by spreading slanderous accusations.

Kim Daejung was aged 74 when he entered the Blue House, the presidential residence, in 1998. He had been an opponent of every one of its previous occupants. He had been kidnapped, imprisoned, sentenced to death and exiled, and had survived two assassination attempts. His very election was mould-breaking (among other things, he was the first president to come from the south-western Chŏlla provinces), and the story of his presidency continued to show his determination to look forward. He appointed his old rival Kim Chŏngp'il, now turned running mate, as prime minister. An Honour Restoration Act (2000) compensated democratic campaigners who had suffered under previous regimes, a majority of whom were students and teachers, and a National Human Rights Commission was set up in 2001. A Ministry of Gender Equality was created, and discussion initiated on the abolition of patriarchalism in Korean society. Confronted at the very outset by economic crisis, Kim accepted the IMF terms for a rescue package (he could do no other) and agreed to break the anti-competitive power of the banks and the *chaebŏl*. He was passionate about détente with the North, visited P'yŏngyang for an unprecedented summit meeting with Kim Jong Il in 2000, and that same year was awarded the Nobel Peace Prize for his 'sunshine policy'. The Korean tiger had regained its self-confidence. And yet. The Honour Restoration Act, and a measure to investigate the Truth on Suspicious Deaths (2000), had been conceded only after a long campaign by associations representing bereaved families. By the time Kim retired in 2003, the monetary and manufac-turing systems were still in need of radical reform; relations with the North were still marked by distrust rather than cooperation; two of his sons were under arrest for accepting bribes; and questions about finan-cial irregularities hung over his own reputation. True, almost every home might be wired up for broadband reception and almost every passenger in a subway carriage might carry a mobile phone, but real, fundamental change would take longer to achieve. In March 2004 Professor Song Duyŏl, after speaking out openly in favour of North Korea, was sentenced to seven years' imprisonment under the National Security Law for 'spying'. President Roh Moo-hyun (elected 2002) spoke for many of the electorate when he proclaimed his personal wish to repeal the Law, but fierce resistance continued to come from his political opponents.

Against all the charges laid against them of political non-account-ability and repressive behaviour, these presidents could plead the need for stern authority in the face of imminent trouble from the DPRK, the support of successive US administrations and the empirical fact of remarkable economic progress. Between them, despite what according to modern Western (and increasingly, modern South Korean) concepts constituted so many infringements of human rights, they had brought their country a long way since 1953. Like the bad fairy excluded from the party, however, the DPRK leadership was determined to spoil any feeling of triumphalism in Seoul.

The Democratic People's Republic of Korea (North Korea)

The history of North Korea after the Armistice was at best a severe disappointment to Korean nationalists who hoped for reunification, at worst a political and humanitarian disaster for those concerned about the rights and welfare of its people. Kim Il Sung had been Stalin's choice as Korean leader, and his regime held the whip hand over Syngman Rhee's in terms of natural resources and popular support.

Through the 1960s aid from the Soviet bloc and the PRC helped North Korea to chase Japan as Asia's most industrialized country. But all this was marred by the extension of party and personal command. The People's Committees of the 1940s were not translated into any effective means of representing ordinary people's views in the quasi-imperial dictatorship of the Kim 'dynasty'. Despite the façade of a Supreme People's Assembly, democratic centralism – operated through the Central People's Committee, the Administration Council and the National Defence Commission – maintained a tight grip on political activity. Decision-taking and control rested in the hands of the Korean Workers' Party (KWP; secretary-general, Kim Il Sung), the Korean People's Army (KPA; commander-in-chief, KIS), and the secret services (under KIS). The KWP Central Committee, whose National Congress met only irregularly, controlled mass organizations to which the majority of the population belonged. These included the Democratic Women's League, the Young Pioneer Corps and occupational bodies for scientists, factory and farm workers, artists and writers, and others. In the countryside, the formation of rural co-operatives in 1954 imitated Chinese land reforms but stopped short of replicating the People's Communes in 1958. Collectives probably brought communal advantages to poor peasants, even if they were of no appreciable benefit to richer ones, and gave the Party another command tool.

The personality cult raised the 'Great Leader' onto a lofty plinth where his policies, deeds and sayings received the kind of adulation enjoyed by Mao Zedong in China. Perhaps the most popular communist in Korea, North and South, had been Kim Il Sung's deputy and foreign minister, Pak Hŏnyŏng, and Kim executed him in 1955 as a warning to other would-be rivals. Though no heads appeared over the parapet, further purges occurred. One of those who disappeared with the election of the third Supreme People's Assembly in 1962 was Han Sŏrya (b. 1900), the veteran communist writer who was minister of education and held the chairmanship of the Federation of Literature and Arts from 1948 to 1962. His fall was accompanied by that of other cultural figures, including the prominent stage performers Sim Yŏng and Ch'oe Sŭnghŭi. In 1972 Kim Il Sung became president under the new Socialist Constitution. He still retained his KWP post, and in the fashion of a Chinese emperor chose his son as his heir. After the rupture of Sino-Soviet relations in 1960 he managed delicately to balance his allegiance to his two great mentors, simultaneously promoting his own political philosophy of self-reliance (*juche*) into an all-encompassing mantra. He had first underlined its importance in December 1955, and over the next half-century it would be cited as the source of inspiration behind everything from steel production to music-making, shaping people's attitudes, driving them to strive constantly to improve standards, and subordinating the individual to the group.

Juche was the antithesis of *sadaechuǔi*, the old-fashioned concept of 'serving the great' now condemned as 'flunkeyism'. As P'yǒngyang continued to pour out propaganda about the Great Leader's achievements and the US (with ROK support) sullied its reputation in Vietnam, the Third World was increasingly attentive, and by 1975 the DPRK and ROK had roughly equal numbers of supporters in the UN General Assembly when it came to votes on matters concerning the divided peninsula. At enormous cost, the DPRK maintained embassies all over Africa, funding aid projects from Guinea to Zimbabwe that ranged from the self-evidently valuable (construction, agriculture) to the distinctly questionable (military training, statue-building). But then, just as world diplomacy began to acknowledge that economics mattered more than ideology, a succession of unsuccessful Five- and Six-Year Plans sent the DPRK economy spiralling downwards, and foreign trade fell from 29.4 per cent of GNP in 1975 to 10 per cent in 1994. The country grew increasingly isolated from the outside world, especially after the collapse of communism elsewhere in 1989. From a position of economic strength, *juche* could have denoted self-confidence; from one of growing weakness, it hinted at desperation and encouraged deceptiveness on the part of the leadership. To try and achieve its ends the regime turned to subversion, intimidation and criminal activity. North Korean undercover agents had little trouble in fomenting resentment and rioting against the ROK president's autocratic rule, especially among students. In October 1983 DPRK agents assassinated many of the ROK cabinet on a reviewing stand in Rangoon, and on 29 November 1987 a bomb planted by terrorists brought down a KAL airliner en route from Iraq to Seoul. Evidence accumulated that North Korean diplomats around the world were engaging in drug dealing to help finance their poverty-stricken government's imbalanced spending. High on its list of priorities was its nuclear programme, using an experimental reactor at Yǒngbyǒn. Few would have imagined, when the Soviet Union installed it in 1962, that more than forty years later this plant would still pose one of the greatest threats to world peace.

To the surprise of many foreign commentators, Kim Jong Il (b. 1942) proved that he was up to the challenge when his father died in 1994. He avoided taking the presidency. His supreme title, now the highest office of state, was Chairman of the National Defence Commission. Not only did the widely predicted military coup against him fail to materialize, but the 'Dear Leader' soon showed himself to be a wily manipulator of foreign relations. Although the DPRK signed the Nuclear Non-proliferation Treaty in 1985, the IAEA suspected by 1992 that the DPRK had developed the facility for making nuclear weapons. In 1994 P'yŏngyang exploited international fears to extract concessions from the USA and the United Nations: two light water reactors and the promise of economic aid in exchange for a halt to work on nuclear weapons. On 31 August 1998 it tightened the screws by test-firing a three-stage missile over Japan, quickly followed by a statement giving heavy industry economic priority. Yet as emphasis on agriculture was downgraded, worldwide concern mounted at the suffering of ordinary North Koreans from famine. On 17 May 1999 P'yŏngyang admitted that 220,000 people had died from famine in the last four years (compared with 600,000 estimated by Bruce Cumings and even four million by one over-emotional commentator), and WHO and UNICEF officials set up offices for the first time in the DPRK capital. In the aftermath of 11 September 2001 P'yŏngyang denounced the use of terror, and its ambassador to the UN, Ri Hyŏngchŏl, signed two international conventions against terrorism. Despite this, President George W. Bush took a much harder line than his predecessor Bill Clinton over the regime's nuclear record, and P'yŏngyang retaliated by reactivating its uranium enrichment plant.

IMPLICATIONS: LOOKING FORWARD, LOOKING BACK?

In the kaleidoscope of Korean history since the Armistice we can see the recurrence of four patterns already encountered in our journey through the politics of earlier ages. These show an impulse for unification; limitations on popular expressions of political opinion; periods of foreign backing, interspersed with displays of political independence; and the use of culture to underpin authority.

Frustration at disunity

Around midday on 29 August 1972 the streets of Seoul were deserted. It was not one of the regular air-raid practices that had driven people, resigned as usual, into the shelters, but the fact that the International Red Cross had been allowed for the first time to send a team to North Korea and to broadcast live television pictures, and Seoulites were as desperate to get their first glimpse of P'yŏngyang since the war as Westerners were to see the first pictures transmitted from the moon on 20 July 1969. Whether in the time of Kwanggaet'o, Kim Yusin, Myoch'ŏng or Yi Sŏnggye, the inhabitants of the Korean peninsula have always felt that it should be one. Gina Barnes may be right in saying that 'the peninsula has never been one integrated unit of the type envisioned by its modern inhabitants', but a sense of guilt over the split personality of modern Korea is apparent, at least in the South, and the Red Cross visit was seen as the harbinger of progress towards reunification. But as the Armistice talks dragged on year after year at P'anmunjŏm, and not even a postal link followed the Red Cross visit, hopes dwindled again. In 1980 the North proposed a Federal Republic of Koryŏ, a transitional bipartite state in which different ideologies would be tolerated in either half. As a preliminary step the proposal demanded the abolition of the South's anti-communist laws and the removal of US troops, and in the context of the ROK's current political difficulties it was obviously a non-starter. Thereafter the South grew richer and the North grew poorer, and the economic and social problems that followed the sudden end to the bifurcation of Germany at the end of the decade sounded a cautionary note to South Koreans. When the DPRK finally agreed in 1991 to the ROK's regular proposal for dual membership of the United Nations, the two-Koreas mould seemed more unbreakable than ever. Nevertheless, nobody gave up, and in 1992 an agreement was signed on Reconciliation, Non-aggression, Exchanges and Cooperation. Nothing had resulted from it when Kim Il Sung died in 1994, and even south of the DMZ a chill filled the summer air as President Kim Young Sam refused to express any form of condolence to the Northern leadership.

Kim Daejung's determination to achieve at least a thaw in relations won him emotional support in the election of 1997. The response from the North was more suspicious, and although it was DPRK initiative that brought about talks in Beijing in April 1998, P'yŏngyang rejected Seoul's request for a permanent meeting place for divided families. At the same time, however, a press release from Kim Jong Il issued through the United Nations stressed the need to improve North–South relations, and behind the scenes more moves were afoot. The founder of the Hyundai Group and native of the North, Chung Juyŏng, visited P'yŏngyang with Kim Daejung's personal encouragement, and financial inducements persuaded Kim Jong Il to grant Hyundai permission to establish a tourist link with the North. It was also awarded business contracts as Southern companies were allowed to invest in small-scale manufacturing enterprises across the DMZ. Work started on rebuilding a rail link from one end of the Korean peninsula to the other. South Korea became the largest contributor of humanitarian aid to its famine-stricken neighbour. Now, optimists looked forward to the opening of bilateral relations between the two countries rather than their rapid reunification, and to more chances to reunite long-separated family members.

The expression of political opinion

Recovery from a bitter and destructive civil war is never quick or easy. When, as in the case of Korea after 1953, both sides claim to have won yet peace is unattained and the outcome inconclusive, rehabilitation may be a long way off. Neither, so soon after the Japanese colonial period and its messy aftermath, could rehabilitation in Korea mean the restoration of a status quo. Korea had no experience of self-government in modern times. Fewer than ten years before, Koreans were not even allowed to use their own language or their own personal names. Now, the South was expected to learn new political skills under the tutelage of a Great Power that was itself undergoing radical reassessment of traditional attitudes and practices, struggling through the Cold War and the nuclear age, the McCarthy era, and the problems of racial and sexual emancipation. The North, beholden first to the Soviet Union and then to the People's Republic of China, had still less chance to learn the techniques of self-government. Both North and South sought sanctuary in patterns that were already familiar to them, to wit those associated with authoritarian control based on traditional notions of legitimization, and the Neo-Confucian appeal to respect for hierarchy and superiority.

In China, where Confucianism had been denounced by the May Fourth Movement in 1919 yet had to be re-confronted in the Thought Reform movement of the early 1950s, the Cultural Revolution of 1966–76 and the Anti-Confucian Campaign of 1973, it was associated with strong feelings of kinship loyalty, relationship (*guanxi*) responsibilities and respect for seniority and precedent. In twentieth-century Japan, the Confucian tradition lived on in the rigid hierarchy, sense of duty and self-sacrificing spirit of the military heritage, and in the all-embracing care of the great *zaibatsu* for their workers. In South and North Korea it was recognizable in society and economics, through 'exhortatory' campaigns such as Park Chung Hee's Saemaŭl Movement and Kim Il Sung's Three Revolutionary Teams Movement of 1974 (which dispatched teams of young activists into factories and other workplaces to stimulate revolutionary fervour via songs and study of Kim Jong Il's writings); through mass participation in highly choreographed global-scale undertakings, like those associated with the 1988 Olympics and the 2002 World Cup; and in the role of the exemplar and adulation of heroes both ancient and modern. Bruce Cumings sees the Kim Il Sung personality cult in North Korea as Neo-Confucian rather than Stalinist.

A further adjunct of imperial Chinese-style government in Korea, however antithetical to the principles of Confucianism, was the use of the military and undercover agencies to aid law enforcement. In the ROK, the Honour Restoration and Compensation Act subsequently acknowledged 10,807 victims of government oppression. The deaths of 507 people during the military period, including many suicides, may have been the result of improper official pressures. And 80 cases were accepted for investigation under the Suspicious Deaths Act. Cases of victimization by the Party and military in the DPRK are impossible to compute.

In the pattern of government organization the DPRK perpetuated the monolithic pyramid structure of the dynastic era. In local areas, KWP authority was backed up by the KPA, and soldiers worked alongside peasants in the fields as they did in Maoist China. In both countries it was a case of 'the Party commands the gun', and a continuation of the imperial tradition that in the tripartite command system of administration, censorate and military, Confucian officialdom was *primus inter pares*. It contrasted with the Tokugawa interpretation of Confucianism, which translated respect for discipline into superior military power through the shogunate, and paved the way for the military–civilian cabinet crisis in the 1930s. In all three countries the traditional recognition that a non-elected oligarchy would take decisions following state or particular interests led to a non-accountability that sat uncomfortably with the Confucian theory of imperial responsibility for Heaven's people. It also encouraged an ad hoc attitude to keeping agreements and treaties rather than one of principled respect. Neither in the PRC nor in the DPRK were the national CCP or KWP congresses given a real say in policy-making, and the DPRK Politburo earned a reputation for untrustworthiness in international affairs. Critics would cite as examples its disregard for the IAEA agreement of 1992, and its rejection in December 1973 of the Northern Limit Line, the de facto maritime border between North and South Korea observed since the Armistice of 1953. Armed clashes occurred across the North's redefined Line in June 1999 and July 2002. In fairness, no country has a monopoly of virtue or of fault when it comes to adherence to treaties, and none can really afford to adopt a 'holier than thou' stance when accusing others of breaking them. We must bear in mind that much of the denunciation of DPRK's foreign policies stems from its enemies; that time has helped to allay some of the unmitigated blame for the Korean War long attributed to North Korea and the PRC; and that even Seoul took the view that President Bush had gone too far in denouncing the DPRK as part of his 'axis of evil'.

In the ROK, reliant on US support yet anxious too to maintain some sort of independence, the transition to democratic institutions was slow and not consistently convincing. The first three presidents all ended their terms of office in unhappy style, and even the next two, the most popularly elected and democratically inclined, saw their reputations marred by scandal. The political parties of the First to Sixth Republics had to struggle against unfair and illegal opposition waged by the presidency, and they formed and re-formed themselves and their principles in a manner reminiscent of Chosŏn factionalism. Democracy was not an established East Asian tradition. In Japan, the post-war leaders worked skilfully to create a system 'respecting "the imperial will" instead of the will of the people' (Herbert Blix). In the ROK, Park Chung Hee's 'Koreanized democracy' relied like Kim Il Sung's on military thuggery, and to this day the National Security Law justifies the presence of intimidating riot police on the streets.

Crowd control and crowd manipulation have been brought to a fine art in both Koreas. What the Seoul authorities would like the world to remember are the pictures of the intricately choreographed displays that opened and closed the Olympics of 1988 or the huge, happy multitude filling City Hall (Square) when South Korea did so well in the World Cup of 2002. What they would prefer it to forget is the sight of Chun Doo Hwan's armed police firing tear gas into massed ranks of protesting students on 10 June 1987. Crowds periodically celebrate and demonstrate in North Korean cities too. Western observers may be inclined to write off all mass gatherings there as politically ordered, although the grief of thousands of mourners weeping publicly at the death of their Great Leader on 8 July 1994 was undoubtedly sincere. Displays of public emotion have long been familiar in Korea. The crowds who lined the streets to witness Queen Min's bier pass by on 21 November 1897 cloaked their feelings in silence, in striking contrast to those who marched on 1 March 1919 or 19 April 1960. Of course, modern as well as past authorities are bound to try and prevent the expression of improperly motivated feeling. But as Mencius conceded, in the last resort the people have the right to express complaints with force. If suffering, over and beyond simple hardship, really becomes insupportable, Heaven might back their demands for a change in policy, even of ruler. In the DPRK, the Kim 'dynasty' seems to have crushed its citizens' bodies and spirits beyond even the possibility of righteous rebellion. In the ROK, however, the *minjung* movement, involving what Kenneth Wells calls a 'struggle over legitimacy', became an expression of populist nationalism heedless of establishment policy. Enthusiasm for Park Chung Hee's Saemaŭl Movement waned after 1976 as government direction increased and corruption spread, and country people were learning to use their voice. The countdown to Kwangju, where peaceful crowd control was lost with awful results, gathered pace.

The reliance on foreign support

Any reader who has stuck with me thus far won't be surprised to be told yet again how important foreign relations were, this time to the two republics desperately trying to recover dignity and international standing in the second half of the twentieth century. After the Armistice both the ROK and the DPRK remained dependent on Great Powers, the former on the USA and Japan, the latter on the USSR and China. Recognition of inevitability nevertheless failed to dispel embarrassing implications of 'serving the great', made all the worse by resentment at recent ill-treatment by all four. Self-strengthening (*zijiang*) had been a target of nineteenth-century Chinese politicians. Nearly a century later, Koreans were more realistic than to deny their need of foreign aid. But speedy self-reliance, otherwise known as the right to political independence, was something both Koreas aspired to and might be pursued with their own agendas for modernization. It had served the Japanese well in the Meiji era. Now both Kim Il Sung and Park Chung Hee used *juche* to motivate their people; Kim Il Sung went further and turned it into a weapon of thought control.

The United States and the Soviet Union polarized the Cold War world, including post-Armistice Korea. The two Koreas, sucked into the ideological rivalry, aligned themselves with Washington and Moscow without any sense of deep-rooted enthusiasm. For all the benefits the Western powers had brought in the late Chosŏn, their own political antipathies were even then an added irritation to the peninsula, already embroiled in the traditional Sino-Japanese struggle. Now, ironically, Western hegemonism and East Asia's instinctive aversion to it revived the status of the traditional team leaders of the Eastern 'bloc', the Chinese.

Immediately after the Armistice, China wrote off the DPRK's war debts and offered economic assistance to its ally, a gesture with particular significance since the USSR refused to waive repayment of its own loans to China. In the context of their growing rivalry, the two communist giants competed for influence by helping to rebuild North Korea's heavy industrial base. Kim Il Sung took advantage of both and carefully avoided committing himself to either, though historical, cultural and ethnic linkages gave China the edge, and as Soviet influence dwindled it was Beijing that remained as the DPRK's principal supporter in international affairs. Cold War and Korean War alignments had thrown the ROK willy-nilly into partnership with the Republic of China (Taiwan), two repressive regimes that struggled to create a favourable image abroad. Eventually, the success of the Seoul Olympics persuaded the world that South Korea's economic 'miracle' could not be ignored, and the ROK began to shake itself free of diplomatic reliance on Japan, the US and Taiwan. Relations improved with Russia, and even more with communist China. Roh Tae Woo refused to join in international sanctions against China after Tiananmen (1989), and following further contacts made during the Asian Games of 1990, the China Chamber of International Commerce and the Korea Trade Promotion Corporation opened permanent trade offices in Seoul and Beijing. In Chinese university dormitories South Korean students, who could afford to pay the fees, replaced North Koreans, who couldn't. And in 1992 Seoul switched diplomatic recognition from Taipei to Beijing. Not surprisingly, China's self-interested show of even-handedness towards the two Koreas led to strains with the North. P'yŏngyang was especially incensed when the high-level defector Hwang Jangyŏp, the brains behind Kim Il Sung's *juche* ideology, escaped to South Korea via Beijing and the Philippines in 1997. On the other hand, it may have been secretly relieved in late 2003 that Beijing took the lead in trying to act as broker to defuse tension with the United States.

Park's efforts to restore relations with Japan brought economic benefit to the South, but won little popular support and failed to heal rifts. Putting up memorials to Yi Sunsin and Queen Min could not mitigate public concern that the Japanese apology for its past ill-treatment of Korea contained in the Treaty of Basic Relations of 1965 was inadequate. Rights of residence and education guaranteed to Koreans in Japan failed to solve anti-Korean discrimination. And the agreed 12-mile fishing limits were so vague in respect of the disputed Tokto islands that arguments over sovereignty remained unresolved and broke out again in 1997 and 2001. Further apologies for past wrongs made in 1998 and 2001 by the prime ministers Keizō Obuchi and Junichirō Koizumi were still deemed insufficient. Despite an olive branch held out by President Roh Tae Woo in 1990, reminding both sides that good relations had been quickly restored and long enjoyed after the *Imjin Waeran*, the story of Korean–Japanese relations continued to be a roller-coaster. A summit between Kim Young Sam and Prime Minister Ryūtarō Hashimoto in 1996 pledged to use sporting and cultural links to strengthen regional peace. But in 2001 Seoul objected to accounts of World War Two in Japanese school textbooks and to Koizumi's visit to the Yasukuni Shrine in central Tokyo, a focus of nationalism where Japan's war dead are honoured. Contrary to many expectations, the sharing of the World Cup in 2002 was managed without rancour. But in 2003 the Ministry of Foreign Affairs and Trade published a pamphlet insisting that the Sea of Japan be co-termed the East Sea (a more ancient name) in international usage, saying that 'it is inappropriate to name the sea area surrounded by many countries after one particular country'. And a fortnight after Koizumi had again outraged Korean and Chinese sensitivities by feeling 'refreshed' when offering the New Year's Day prayers of 2004 at the Yasukuni Shrine, South Korea ruffled the waters once more by announcing a series of postage stamps featuring the Tokto islands, prompting both countries to reiterate their claim to these rocky outcrops.

Like China, Japan tried to keep diplomatic and commercial doors open to the North as well as profiting from economic commitment to South Korea, and the United States found Tokyo a useful intermediary for communicating with P'yŏngyang. The large Korean communities in Japan included many northerners favourable to the communist regime, which came to depend on the money they sent to their relatives back home. But the firing of the Taep'o-dong 1 missile over Japan in August 1998 severely strained Japan's own efforts at detachment from the internecine Korean dispute. In September 2002 an unprecedented visit to P'yŏngyang by Prime Minister Junichirō Koizumi gained a promise from Kim Jong Il of an indefinite moratorium on missile testing.

THE CULTURAL INFILLING

Government and the arts

Both the DPRK and the ROK politicized arts and culture, using them to promote nationhood and cement their own legitimacy, but whereas the effect in the North was to constrain artists almost unremittingly, the situation of their counterparts in the South developed and progressed throughout the military dictatorships and into the democratic era. In 1959 an annual folk festival was introduced in every province, though it soon became apparent that authenticity was not the main criterion for winning performances: sanitized versions of masked dance drama, for instance, endeavoured to deflect social criticism by cutting out scenes satirizing the ruling class. Park Chung Hee regarded cultural development as an essential part of economic reconstruction, and as he tried to swing ordinary people behind him, a succession of measures created an impression of his personal concern for Korean culture. They also gave him a means of directing the nation's thinking about social groups, traditional activities and their economic potential. In 1962 the Cultural Properties Protection Law was introduced. With this, the regime laid claim to the protection of national cultural treasures, which it classified under the headings of Tangible Cultural

Assets, Intangible Cultural Assets, Folk Cultural Properties, and Monuments (Picture Essay 29). Inspiration for the system followed pioneering research and lobbying by the journalist Ye Yŏnghae and others. (The Japanese Diet had introduced a similar measure in 1950, so here was another example of Park's admiration for Japanese models.) Four years later the Japanese government was persuaded to return cultural assets removed from Korea by the colonial government. A Ministry of Culture and Information was created in 1968, and the Culture and Arts Promotion Law of 1972 was accompanied by a five-year plan for cultural development, the first statement of long-term strategy and part of a greater economic plan. It included the inauguration of the Korea Culture and Arts Foundation in 1973, the introduction of the Culture and Arts Promotion Fund, and the formation of the Korea Motion Picture Promotion (Commission). The translation of traditional Korean literature from Chinese characters into han'gŭl was speeded up, and in 1979 the Academy of Korean Studies was opened. All these were positive measures. Perversely, however, they stiffened the pride of patriots involved in the *minjung* movement, and emboldened their criticism of official censorship of the arts.

In both DPRK and ROK, cultural sites and assets were safeguarded, and new monuments and shrines sprang up. Those with potential for political advantage, such as the Tan'gun shrine and the birthplaces of Admiral Yi Sunsin and Kim Il Sung, were singled out for particular refurbishment. In the DPRK, archaeological research was encouraged and a new building constructed for the Central Historical Museum (1977). In the ROK, universities were encouraged to pursue archaeology, and many formed museums to display their finds. A new home for the National Museum of Korea, surmounted by a traditional-style pagoda, went up in the grounds of the Kyŏngbŏk Palace in 1972, and from 1975 onwards replacements were constructed for its six provincial branches dating from the First Republic. This time, instead of being identical products of image-driven cultural policy, they boasted individual and imaginative designs reflecting their regional and historical character. In Seoul itself, the Museum courted controversy. It outgrew its purpose-built home, which was handed over to the National Folk Art Museum in 1986, and moved into the nearby colonial-era Capitol Building. This, though spacious and handsome, was not ideally suited for the requirements of a great museum. Nevertheless, when Kim Young Sam's government demolished it in a demonstrative fit of nationalism in 1997 many defenders spoke up for it, especially from abroad. A Korean architectural firm won the competition to design a successor, which would place it among the world's top museums.

29 Making long-stem bamboo pipes

The Cultural Properties Protection Law (1962) revived and encouraged folk crafts incorporating traditional skills. Some of these represented nationwide customs, others aspects of regional culture. All were threatened by the imperatives of mass production and global taste and the use of modern tools and manufacturing techniques. Nowadays it is rare to see anyone smoke a long pipe, but they continue to be made for sale as collector's pieces and tourist souvenirs.

In Chosŏn Korea three lengths of pipe were smoked, the longest (perhaps up to 80 cm) by the oldest and the shortest by the youngest members of society. A pipe was tucked into the belt at the waist, where a tobacco pouch also carried a flint and a bundle of dry herbs as lighting equipment. The quality of a man's pipe was a mark of his wealth and standing. The stem was of polished bamboo, into which were fixed a mouthpiece at one end and a bowl at the other. The metals of which these were made and the intricacy of their decoration were marks of the owner's opulence. Most prized were black copper and white bronze, with inlay of gold, silver, porcelain, jade or cloisonné. On cheaper pipes, mouthpiece and bowl might be made of soapstone instead of precious metal, and carving, painting or burning used to provide a degree of decoration.

(Opened in October 2005, the new National Museum is claimed to be the sixth largest in the world.)

Both regimes, viewing culture as a legitimate means of social control, imposed restrictions on artistic freedom and were guilty of persecuting individuals who overstepped the mark. In the DPRK, heavy emphasis was laid on Socialist Realism in art, and scenes of smiling steel workers, self-sacrificing soldiers and peasants greeting their Great Leader replicated the sort of thing being produced by artists in the PRC. In the ROK, when *Chosŏn Ilbo* inaugurated the Modern Artists' Invitational Exhibitions in 1957, the government was concerned by the number of pictures that displayed people's sufferings and launched its own National Art Exhibition series in 1961, a vain continuation of the Government-General's policy of promoting anodyne subjects and styles to try to restrain artists from expressing their personal feelings. By now the Korean avant-garde movement was in full swing, forcefully expressing anger at twentieth-century experiences. Hwang Yŏngyŏp's 'Human Being' series, for example, symbolized the shackles of colonialism and war, and also of modern technology (Picture Essay 30). Hwang escaped retribution, but others were not so lucky. The composers Kim Sunnam (1917–1986) and Yun Isang had gone to North Korea and Paris in 1948 and 1955 respectively. Neither would ever return to the ROK. (Actually Yun did, in a manner of speaking. He was kidnapped from Berlin in 1967 by the KCIA and taken to Seoul, where he was tried for sedition and imprisoned. He was freed following international protests, went back to Germany and became a naturalized citizen. He declined to accept a later invitation to visit Seoul.) The work of the outstanding poet Chŏng Chiyong (b. 1903), believed to have died in the Korean War, was proscribed from 1950 until 1988. His crime was to have belonged to the communist Korean Proletarian Artists' Federation during the colonial period.

The Fifth Republic (1981–8) saw a broadening in the official definition of culture to embrace modern and contemporary arts. No fewer than eleven pieces of statutory legislation were enacted, covering subjects as far apart as broadcasting and the preservation of traditional temples, and including the Cultural Properties Protection Act of 1982. The same year saw the announcement of a five-year plan for enhancing local culture. It was progress. But in promoting what it called 'sound' culture and condemning 'harmful', 'pornographic' or 'low' culture, the nanny state was still motivated more by political correctness than by ethical considerations: in 1988 riot police closed down a play entitled *Maech'un* ('Prostitution'), part of the popular *madanggŭk* drama movement by students aiming to break free of conventional theatrical traditions. Not until Roh Tae Woo's presidency, at the start of the Sixth Republic, did state control of the arts visibly begin to relax. The first ever minister of culture, Lee Oyoung, was nominated in 1990. A well-known writer on many subjects ranging from philosophy to fiction, Lee was concerned to try and strengthen the position of traditional arts amid the changing values of the international world. In October of that year he permitted a group of musicians to attend a Pan-Korea Reunification Festival in P'yŏngyang – the only one of its kind ever to be held – and in December North Korean musicians paid a return visit to Seoul.

Kim Young Sam emphasized the social and economic value of national and regional culture, and his government's five-year cultural plan (1993) gave regional authorities and amateur organizations more autonomy over cultural policy, removed earlier restrictions on arts bodies and encouraged international cultural exchange. Under his regime, the criterion for official support became the excellence of the product as determined by the consumer rather than by government agencies. Emphasis was placed on youth culture and lifelong learning, and a Korean National University for the Arts was established. In 1994 the university entrance-examination system was revised, placing more value for the first time on interpretation than rote learning, and encouraging the younger generation to express its own opinions. The Cultural Welfare Implementation Plan of 1996 allocated more government funding for cultural (including sports) facilities to counter 'negative problems resulting from society's rapid economic development'.

Kim Daejung's inaugural address on 25 February 1998 defined four themes in relation to cultural policy: the development of national culture and arts, the globalization of national culture, the nurture of the cultural industry and cultural exchange with the DPRK. Like Park Chung Hee, Kim saw the link between culture and the economy, and in reaffirming Kim Young Sam's optimistic view of the arts in all forms, he particularly stressed their role in getting Korea on its feet again after the financial collapse of 1997. And, his sense of nationalism and every Korean's goal of eventual reunification lurking not far behind, he saw the part it could play in his hoped-for détente with the North (the so-called 'sunshine policy'). He set up the Korea Culture and Content Agency (2001), a think-tank of cultural policy administrators, to advise the Ministry of Culture and Tourism and to promote the development of film, animation, cartoon, IT games and pop music within the entertainment industry. He authorized the importing of Japanese films for the first time, but moved more cautiously in response to US free-trade complaints about Park Chung Hee's law of

30 Hwang Yŏngyŏp, *Human Being*

Hwang Yŏngyŏp,
Human Being, 1974, oil on
paper, 90.5 × 72.5 cm.

Hwang Yŏngyŏp was born in P'yŏngyang on 18 December 1931, and
was enrolled in the Fine Art College there when the Korean War broke
out in 1950. His formative years were marked successively by colonialism, communism and military brutality, and his work continually
reflects the scars that these etched on his psyche. In 1957 he graduated
from Hŏngik University in Seoul, where he had studied under Kim
Whanki. The formative influence of Picasso on Whanki's work is plain
to see in Hwang's abstract expressionist painting. So too is his admiration for Park Seugun, in whose pictures the figures of country folk are
recognizably but crudely drawn and permanently struggle to free themselves from enveloping textures of muted colour. Like Park, Hwang has
been described as a 'lonely artist', though he did belong to a small group
of six, the Engagement Group, which sought to escape from convention
in the 1960s.

In keeping with Korean tradition, Hwang's style is notable for its use
of line, monochrome and subsequently colour. In his early pictures the
symbolic shapes of his figures, like those of Park Seugun, lay semi-con-
cealed beneath rather oppressive blankets of colour, and by the time
they escaped into greater visibility in the monochromes of the early
1970s they were already enmeshed in the geometrical shapes and web-
like lines that would define, for Hwang, the ensnared, struggling nature
of human existence through the rest of the century. By this time Hwang

was confronting and denouncing Park Chung Hee's repressive regime and expressing sympathy for fellow artists in the North. Art, he said, must criticize reality, even at the risk of the artist's isolation.

Hwang defines his professional mission as the affirmation of human dignity in the face of constant adversity. Shaman-like, he seeks to cast out the despair and bondage of the past through his art. His 'Human Being' series, on which he has worked continually for more than 30 years, exemplifies man's struggle to break the shackles that bind him, be they political, military, economic or technological. It is a theme not much suited to traditional Korean ink or watercolour, and Hwang has worked principally in oils. The subjects of the series are generic, and portray neither individuality nor personal characteristics. He has not sought to create a peculiarly Korean art genre, though his later pictures, with themes such as *My Village* and *Shaman*, do reflect the strength of Korean nationalism. He opposes narrow fundamentalism, even going so far as to liken *minjung* populism to the restrictive outlook of North Korean *juche*, yet in both style and subject matter his work is imbued with Korean-ness.

1966, under which cinemas were still obliged to show Korean films on 146 days of the year.

What we see from the brief survey above is that every president from Park onwards has recognized the value of his nation's culture to its – and his own – fortunes, and has responded accordingly. From a cultural to overall annual budget ratio of less than 0.2 per cent in the 1970s, government expenditure rose to 0.38 per cent in 1986, 0.5 per cent in 1994 and 1.01 per cent in 2000. Of course, money for the arts did not necessarily mean either respect for artists or concern for their public. Park Chung Hee built the huge National Theater on Seoul's Namsan, which opened on 17 October 1973, and Chun Doo Hwan began the Seoul Arts Center (SAC) in 1984 (Picture Essay 31). They patted themselves on the back at the creation of such symbols of national pride: ordinary people, who had not been consulted, were less sure. Namsan was not well served by public transport, and as for the location of the SAC in Kangnam, it lay well south of usual theatre-going haunts and few Seoulites were even sure how to get there. Meanwhile, money was lavished on the same kind of bureaucratic ostentation in the DPRK. P'yŏngyang opened the grand Mansudae Arts Theatre in 1977, housing the eponymous Arts Ensemble, which performed Chinese-style revolutionary operas. Generally speaking, however, the complex was used more often for political meetings than for popular cultural events.

The military dictatorships in both South and North invested a high percentage of their cultural expenditure in grandiose building schemes and spectacular displays of music, dance and drama. Only under the influence of the ROK's democratization process in the 1990s, however, did it really become possible to speak of a vibrant national culture. Then, the sense of artistic liberation was welcomed, even if it was not hard to find critics in a society with a wide generation gap who feared that the term 'minjung culture' had taken on a new meaning – that of young people's pop culture – and that the older, more refined arts of the literati were increasingly being sidelined; or that in the new, increasingly affluent society, everybody was now middle class, and the old-style minjung culture of the rural peasantry – folk-songs as sung in the fields, popular entertainments as enjoyed in the village square, shamanistic rites as performed in answer to a community's heartfelt needs – had been transformed into concert-hall versions.

Because Korean governments on both sides of the DMZ emphasized the political role of culture, there were few opportunities for extra-governmental arts sponsorship. In the ROK, however, an important exception existed in its National Commission for UNESCO (KNCU). Founded in 1954, KNCU may be termed one of the oldest of arts organizations in modern Korea, and as an international grant agency it enjoyed a unique status and independence. Its non-political career officers developed an expertise that politicians could not match, and they were not afraid to express differences of opinion with government even during its most authoritarian periods. Generally content with the governments' own efforts in the fields of education and science, KNCU did nevertheless offer financial vouchers redeemable against its own resources to cash-strapped schools and hospitals. Its main efforts, however, went into the preservation and encouragement of traditional culture. The development of cultural agencies in Korea after 1988 was in keeping with a worldwide appeal from UNESCO, and in 1995 three Korean treasures were added to its World Heritage list for the first time: the Royal Ancestral Shrine in Seoul, Pulguk-sa and the Sokkuram Grotto in Kyŏngju, and the set of Tripitaka printing blocks preserved at Haein-sa.

Among corporate sponsors of the arts the great *chaebŏl* led the way in the Sixth Republic. Some pulled in their horns after the economic collapse of 1997, and cultural organizations claim that it has never been easy to attract money from them, though Kim Daejung's government took measures to stimulate their renewed support. Most active were Samsung, Hyundai and Daewoo. In 1982 Samsung opened the Hoam Museum at Yong'in to show off its priceless art treasures, based on its founder Lee Byung-chull's collection. Ten years later it established a gallery in central Seoul and a Korean gallery at the Victoria and Albert Museum in London, and in 1993 it initiated prizes for literature and traditional music. In 2004 Hoam was superseded by the Leeum Museum complex in the Yongsan district of Seoul, built to the innovative design of three foreign architects. Hyundai's Asan Foundation and the Daewoo Corporation demonstrated a more offbeat concern for cultural values by creating an annual Filial Piety Award (1991) and funding the intellectual journal *Tradition and Modernity*. Nor have 'green' issues been neglected. Like many countries, South Korea now encourages private enterprise to join with government in preserving important aspects of its environment, whether the natural habitat of migrating birds or buildings of historical importance. The first project undertaken by the Korean National Trust, launched in 1999, was the restoration of the traditional roof-tile house of the late Choi Sun-u, a former director of the National Museum.

31 The Seoul Arts Center; The Whanki Museum

Pride in cultural characteristics and technological prowess shines out in modern Korean architecture. On the campus of the Seoul Arts Center (below), for example, the fine concert hall built for Chun Doo Hwan and completed in 1988 is shaped like a fan, and the even bigger opera house behind it, commissioned by Roh Tae Woo and finished in 1993, like a traditional conical hat. By contrast, Mario Botta's Kyobo Tower (2003) dominates the Kangnam skyline by virtue of its very height (118 m.). But size is not everything. In the modest Whanki Museum (1992, opposite), the Korean-American architect Kyu Sung Woo combined the spirit of tradition and modernity, the feeling for *p'ungsu* with the forms favoured by Korea's leading abstract artist Kim Whanki. It is an innovative and sensitive construction, a building that fits into its background on Pugak Mountain as country homesteads once nestled into folds in the hills, simultaneously complementing and enhancing the famous works of art it contains; a combination of yin and yang, the natural and the artificial, the rounded and the straight, the abstract and the physical.

Two rounded tops to an end wall evoke the shoulders of the *meibyŏng* vase (see Picture Essay 12), the epitome to Kim of his country's cultural heritage and a shape that was central to the art of his early period. Beneath the eaves a line of small windows, and below them a design of light and dark tiles, anticipate the patterns he created in the early 1970s as he explored the possibilities of dots and squares. Inside is a cool combination of light, space and proportion. Staircases, galleries and showrooms rise around a central atrium, making skilful use of natural light shining through effectively placed openings. Space has been carefully

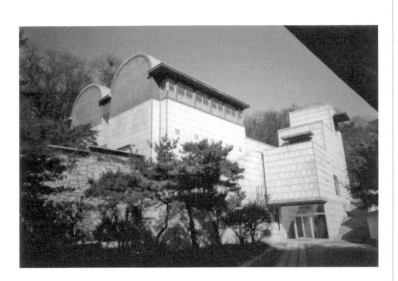

planned, walls appropriate for large and small works, and floors for free-standing showcases displaying papier-mâché creations from the late 1960s and early 1970s.

Kim Whanki's fascination with the avant-garde and the use of colour began during his education in Japan, and when he returned to Korea in 1937 he helped to form the Freedom Group of abstract artists. Through the 1950s his work was semi- representational, drawing on human, natural and still-life subjects. Between 1956 and 1959 he studied in Paris, and after his return to Seoul he concentrated on symbols traditionally loved by Koreans: the moon, cranes, clouds, mountains and the ceramic vase that reminded him of his first appreciation of beauty. In 1963 Kim moved to New York, where he remained until his death. Here his work became more experimental and more abstract. He painted in gouache, in oil on newspaper and, later on, fabric. The preoccupation with blue that marked his middle period gave way to a wider range of colour. And gradually he surrendered himself to the tiny dots, encased in squares, out of which so many of his later paintings were constructed. Each one was painted with thoughtful care, and though they could not, in Kim's view, compare with the stars in the night sky, each encapsulated the ancient oriental symbol of the universe, the round earth on the background of the square heavens. Richness of colour and depth of texture distinguish Kim Whanki's work, and are shown off to perfection against the plainness of the museum's layout and decoration.

Government and religion

A theme throughout this book has been the role of religion and ideology in the shaping of the nation – Buddhism, shamanism, Neo-Confucianism, Christianity, Marxism. Successive states have patronized them and their associated institutions for their perceived protective and strengthening powers, even though they have not been averse to challenging or resisting official policy. The reader may reasonably wonder where they feature in the story of modern and contemporary Korea.

Although both Buddhist and Christian organizations were nominally tolerated in the DPRK after 1953, persecution of their followers occurred and drove believers underground. Christians were blamed for compromising the success of the North's war efforts. The atheistic state philosophy of *juche* was supposed to cater for everybody's spiritual as well as material needs. The only rightful recipients of worship were Kim Il Sung and his son. In the ROK, President Park's attempts to invoke virtues such as loyalty, filial piety and self-sacrifice in the service of the state were reminiscent of Chiang Kai Shek's ill-fated attempt to revive Confucianism in China's New Life Movement of 1934. The churches spoke out bravely against corruption and oppression and enjoyed rapid growth as they took up human-rights issues and publicity was given to '*minjung* theology'. Catholics received a boost to their morale when Pope John Paul II visited Korea in 1984 and canonized 103 late Chosŏn martyrs. The event was particularly significant given that Cardinal Kim Souhwan (b. 1922) was unflinching in his defence of democracy against the prevailing dictatorship. Apologists claim that Protestant Christianity scaled the peak of its fortunes around 1992 with 12 million church members, or roughly a quarter of the population. Dispassionate observers put the figure at 8 to 9 million. Many of these were associated with the new religious sects that proliferated especially in poorer regions. As the need for political criticism declined through the 1990s, more orthodox churches turned to championing ecological and humanitarian causes. The Korean Roman Catholic Church, with an ROK membership of around 4.5 million, helped to found a hospital in North Korea, opened in 2005 at Rason, North Hamgyŏng province. In December 2005 it launched a campaign against the death penalty in the ROK.

South Korean leaders, searching for a preferably native ideology that might counter the force of the DPRK's *juche*, were obliged to adopt an even-handed approach to Christianity and Buddhism, which had roughly equal numbers of adherents and powerful international backers. Shamanism was a possible candidate: it had ancient Korean roots and still enjoyed popular support in towns as well as rural areas. Banned in the North, practising shamans were still numerous in the South (estimated at 100,000 in 1966), and although they were officially condemned as perpetuating old-fashioned superstition, an attempt was made to update shamanism into a new universal cosmic philosophy of Korean origin. To many Koreans, however, the new Pentecostal churches seemed to offer the same kind of services in a more up-to-date format. In the mid-1990s they attracted international attention, even if mainstream Christian churches did regard them with caution. Meanwhile, intellectual debate among Koreans was focused on a revival of interest in Confucianism and its applications in increasingly liberal times. The ingrained traditions associated with filial piety, the work ethic, sense of duty, and corporate and social responsibility were all trotted out as explanations for the success of Korean capitalism, and at a time when neither China nor Japan seemed to subscribe officially to any strong moral or spiritual system, and when North Korea's philosophy of self-reliance had patently failed, it seemed as if South Korea was bidding for leadership of East Asia in regard to ethical politics. Then came the financial crisis of the autumn of 1997, the strict terms of the IMF rescue package, revelations of institutional corruption and the shaming of the *chaebŏl* system. The fickle praise of the wider world temporarily turned to scorn. Ironically, however, it was the very Confucian virtues of self-sacrifice and determination that set the country on the swift path to recovery, and the denunciation of corruption in high places that rose to a crescendo in 2002 was deeply rooted in the Confucian ethos.

THE EVOLUTION AND APPLICATIONS OF CULTURE

Painting

In South Korea, it was as if artists emerged from a box in 1953, looked around at their devastated environment and the brighter lights shining abroad, and used their brushes to vent decades of pent-up emotion. Hwang Yŏngyŏp found that oils and abstract art, besides being 'modern', provided the most suitable medium for expressing the suffering of recent decades. Despite his intense nationalism, he would stick with oils all his life, even after the 1970s when he turned to more graphic depictions of traditional Korean subjects. Like others, his teacher Kim Whanki, who had trained in Japan, left for Paris after the Korean War and later moved on to the USA. Whanki's early abstract work had expressed his admiration for the Western avant-garde, but during a return stay in Seoul (1959–63) he concentrated on expressing his strong love of oriental culture. In the work of Kim Kichang, the source of determination and anger was more personal, namely resentment at the fact that he was virtually deaf and dumb. As the Park government affirmed its commitment to Korean traditional culture, painters like Kim with a strong feeling for Korean history experienced a returning sense of relief, and enjoyed the luxury denied to them by the Japanese of exploring their native traditions. In the 1970s some found minimalist styles appropriate for plumbing their depths and expressing their love of Korean paper, brush and ink. But if the quasi-Daoist quest for unification of the world of man and nature, and if Lee Ufan's (b. 1936) and Park Seobo's (b. 1931) study of the properties of the calligraphic line, and Song Sunam's (b. 1938) and Suh Seok's (b. 1929) experiments with oriental ink, were typical of a fairly introspective, scholarly mood, that was to change amid the turmoil that followed the killing of Park Chung Hee and the Kwangju massacre. While ink painting (*sumukhwa*) continued to transport aficionados to a more spiritual plane, and the properties of traditional Korean paper (*hanji*) inspired Park Seobo and others, another avenue was being opened up. The stirring of *minjung* priorities during the 1980s produced 'art with a message' (*minjung misul*), the contemporary interpretation of traditional subject matter with popular rather than literati appeal. It took a lead from the great genre paintings of the past and found the rediscovery of colour refreshing, especially the brightness of the five-colour *tanch'ŏng* system. If the colours of the family figures by Park Seugun (1914–1965) were muted and almost self-conscious, those of shamans by Park Sangkwang (1904–1985) were positively exuberant. The dominance of monochrome ink painting was being superseded.

The 1990s were characterized by widespread artistic experimentation, even anarchy, as the young 'Orange Tribe' generation used Western styles of satirical, pop and action art to express criticism of a rapidly changing social and cultural environment. In the hands of serious artists, fascination with *hanji* now developed into elaborate collage and papier-mâché compositions. Installation and video art, some of it highly inventive, was led by Paik Nam-june (1932–2006). Paik had moved to the United States after studying in Japan and Germany, and, having first been trained as a musician and gained his PhD in aesthetics, made his name in the 1960s as a media and performance artist. In contrast to Hwang Yŏngyŏp, Paik was intent on exploring means of humanizing technology and the electronic medium. In his *TV Bra for Living Sculpture* (1969), an assemblage of video-tubes, televisions, Plexiglas, boxes, vinyl straps, rheostat, foot switches, cables, copper wire and a cello, the musician Charlotte Moorman gained wide attention by playing the instrument with miniature TV sets on her breasts. In later years Paik's attention turned to financial themes: his *My Faust - Economics* (1992) comprised a neo-Gothic temple made of paper money, encasing 24 television screens on which international currency symbols continually changed, with a scattering of coins on the ground in front of it. His obituarist in the London *Times* called him 'one of the very few artists who single-handedly changed the course and tone of art in the 20th century'. Another reflection of changing times was Kim Min's and Choi Moon's *Tourist Project* (2003), an imaginative and amusing moving montage employing slides of well-known world tourist sites, a screen made of white feathers, an electric fan and a tape of *The Flight of the Bumble Bee*. Yet amidst the cultural confusion, even young Korean artists living and working abroad continued to display the power of their traditional ethnic roots. Tom Lee (b. 1969) moved to New York when he was ten. In *Reverberating Bell* he interpreted the sound escaping through the acoustic tube characteristic of the Korean bell, and to calm his traumatized mental state after the attacks on the World Trade Center in New York on 11 September 2001 he turned to a similar theme in 'Arcanum Series', a set of explorations painted on linen and based on an abstract realization of Sokkuram and a Korean bell.

The first Korean artist to exhibit on the post-war world stage was Park Seobo, at the second Paris Biennale of 1961, and in 1969 the foundation of the National Museum for Contemporary Art (NMCA) provided Korean art with an international forum of its own, one that would play a leading part in sending it abroad and hosting outstanding exhibitions from abroad. Korea made its first appearance at the Venice Biennale in 1995, when *T'ou – Spirit of the Korean People* by Jheon Seecheon (b. 1947) provided a reminder of the terracotta figurines of the Samguk period as well as of Anthony Gormley's *Field* (1991). The same year saw the introduction of the Kwangju Biennale, and among the multitude of festivals encouraged by the government's devolution of cultural organization the Kŏchang International Theatre Festival (established 1989) acquired a regional reputation and the Pusan International Film Festival (established 1996) quickly became one of the world's most prestigious cinematic events. In 2004 it showed films from North Korea.

Pride in past characteristics and achievements is one thing; knowing how to assess the new evidence of cultural awareness that pours out month by month from Korean artists working at home and abroad is quite another. 'Korean artists', according to the critic Lee Doo-shik, 'are struggling to respond to trends towards globalization while at the

32 Song Shiyŏp, *The Sound of Creation*

In keeping with the principles adopted in Communist China (and before that the Soviet Union), where Mao Zedong's talks at the Yenan Forum on Literature and Art in 1942 achieved scriptural status, North Korean art had to serve the masses by reflecting scenes and activities familiar to them and their masters by bringing home political messages that people could not fail to understand and obey. From gigantic statues down to humble paper-cuts, subjects extolled the virtues of self-sacrifice, unremitting effort, and cheerfulness and optimism in confronting obstacles. Ordinary workers took their place alongside Stalin, Mao and Kim Il Sung in the artistic pantheon. The West knew the style as Socialist Realism and deemed it dull, repetitive and probably counter-productive. It seemed to be confined in scope, and predictable and naive in message. Chinese and Koreans were less critical and found more to admire in it. Top-class artists, whether on the operatic stage or in the potter's studio, were able to show that they had not suddenly lost their skills, even if individualism did have to give way for the time being to conformism; in traditional times oriental painters had not drawn upon such a wide range of natural or social subjects as those in the West; and after the humiliations suffered by their countries in the early twentieth century some of them were glad to sacrifice the self-expressionism they had been introduced to by the West and Japan in return for the respect

Song Shiyŏp, *The Sound of Creation*, c. 1998.

now paid to them, nominally at least, by their leaders. Nationalism, too, was only thinly disguised in the supposedly universal socialist philosophy. In what was called the '*juche* realism' of North Korean art, traditional ink continued to be preferred to oils, silk and mulberry paper to canvas. Women appeared not only in blue dungarees but also in Korean *hanbok* dress. Landscapes placed enormous construction sites alongside locations of national historic importance and views of the Diamond Mountains. Jane Portal finds a parallel here with the 'true view' aims of Chŏng Sŏn and fellow artists in the eighteenth century.

Song Shiyŏp (b. 1934) came from Hamgyŏng province and was trained at the P'yŏngyang Fine Art University. Appointed a Merit Artist in 1980, his subjects included the newly built Tan'gun Mausoleum (1999) and Kim Jong Il's claimed birthplace on Mount Paektu (2001). *The Sound of Creation* was acquired in P'yŏngyang for the British Museum in 2002.

same time maintaining a sense of their own regional tradition.' In his view Korea's contemporary art movement has been overly dependent on Western ideas and too uniform in approach. Kim Young-uk would not go quite as far, but admits that 'we must consider what it means to be Korean. That is, we must identify what is contemporary Korean art.' So what *does* make Korean art Korean? Pak Yong-suk tries to hijack the most famous principle of traditional Chinese painting, identified by Xie He in the sixth century AD as *qiyun shengdong* (Kor. *kiun saengdong*, 'spirit resonance'), claiming that it first appeared on Koguryŏ tomb murals. Korean brush aesthetics, she says, are divided into the ink tradition that associated the literati with the transcendent force of nature, and the colour tradition that depicted the human world and its routine activities. The generation of energy that gives painting its vitality is like taming a horse, something Koguryeans knew all about.

Others see Korean-ness in art as an awareness of human beings and nature working together. It takes form in Chang Woosung's modernist approach to traditional landscape or flower-and-bird painting. It is shaped by an approach to minimalist art that explores materials and their qualities beyond what man does with them. The semi-abstract ink paintings of Suh Seok also refer back to Korean tradition and are imbued with a distinctive calligraphic quality. In the *Line* and *From Point* series of Lee Ufan, and Park Seobo's *Ecriture* series, the quest ends in complete abstraction. Nature is not only physical, but spatial and temporal as well. Its depiction is not to be confused with reproducing the so-called realism of a visually perceived scene, but with the examination of the interaction of yin and yang in both space and time. According to Park Seobo, 'Koreans intrinsically possess a minimalist tendency'. They see monochrome work as more natural and intuitive. The principal medium of Korean painting is ink, and artists unite with it in striving for spirituality: 'The Korean concept of beauty is less objective than subjective, less rational than ethnic in character' (Yu June-sang).

Artists in South Korea confess to having little idea of the work of their colleagues in the North, and although the NMCA acquired some paintings by DPRK artists around 1990 they were not put on show. Rather more is known abroad. Western and Japanese collectors have been able to make purchases in P'yŏngyang (Picture Essay 32), and exhibitions have been held in Tokyo, New York and London. Professional artists in the North belong to national and regional organizations that monitor and assess their work, and make recommendations for acquisition by the National Art Gallery (Chosŏn Misul Pangmulgwan). Most important of these is the Korean Artists' Federation, formed in 1961, with sections for painters, writers and composers, whose role as educators in socialist society was quickly recognized after Liberation. Artistic prowess became associated with political awards, the most important being the title People's Artist (*Inmin yesulga*), which also conferred social status. As in Maoist China, much art in the 1960s and '70s was characterized by monumentalism, whether the enormous bronze statues of Kim Il Sung or huge paintings of revolutionary events used to decorate public buildings. Artists who found themselves north of the 38th parallel in 1953 had been trained in Japan, P'yŏngyang and Seoul. They had shown in the Sŏnjŏn National Art Exhibitions, and favoured the same subjects and styles as their erstwhile colleagues south of it. Among them were Chŏng Onnyŏ (b. 1920), North Korea's leading female artist; Kim Kiman (b. 1929), brother of Kim Kichang; Kim Chugyŏng (1902–1981), a prolific oil painter who was the first director of P'yŏngyang Art College in 1946; and the renowned printmaker Pae Unsŏng (1900–1978). Despite the emphasis on Socialist Realism and the importance of glorifying the state, Kim Il Sung and Kim Jong Il, and the *juche* philosophy, not all paintings are political in nature. Landscapes of the Diamond Mountains, Mount Paektu and the Kaesŏng region, flower-and-bird subjects, and portraits of women and children in traditional Korean dress are all popular. Standards are high, but the tight imposition of state control means that in contrast to the dramatic changes taking place in the South, little stylistic evolution has been possible. *Juche* and individual creativity do not mix.

Music

The fortunes of traditional Korean music after 1953 followed altogether a different kind of upward curve in the ROK from that enjoyed by painting. The music for the annual rites at the Chongmyo Royal Ancestral Shrine was the first Intangible Cultural Asset to be designated in 1964, along with *p'ansori*, four masked dance dramas and a female song-and-dance genre. In the 1970s scholars and artistes at the National Classical Music Institute (situated today at the Seoul Arts Center and renamed the National Center for Korean Traditional Performing Arts) brought performances of court music and dance to a high standard of perfection and played it before visiting state dignitaries. Individual musicians like the *kayagŭm* player Hwang Byungki (b. 1936), *taegŭm* player Lee Sangkyu (b. 1944) and folk singer Kim Sohee enjoyed strong reputations, and the government sponsored performance trips abroad. Musicians attending the Durham Oriental Music Festival series between

1976 and 1982 were asked by the organizers not to make any concessions to supposed foreign taste. Audiences whose expectations were based solely on the fan dances performed by the Little Angels of Korea, already well known in the West, were surprised – though not unpleasantly so – by what they heard, and in due course Korean music was introduced to the BBC Promenade Concerts and the Edinburgh Festival. Korean classical music is quite unlike that of China, Japan or any other country. Played by an ensemble of plucked and bowed strings, flutes, reeds and percussion, it has complexities of sonority, tempo and mode that give it a unique textural richness and colour. When played by a solo instrument it has a minimalism akin to that of monochrome ink painting. In particular, the plucked strings of the *kŏmun'go* make positive use of dying notes and the silence that binds them in the way that the calligrapher uses the failing ink at the end of his brush strokes and the blank space on the paper that links them in a dynamic tension. The player isolates himself from his surroundings and seeks the Dao. It is not, and never was intended to be, music for the masses. That is why, as I found during my early visits to Korea, classical music was not widely appreciated, in contrast to the raucous, intoxicating cacophony of *nong'ak* associated with the still unspoilt farming routines in the countryside. The *minjung* movement was always more likely to popularize farmers' music, masked dramas and the marketplace theatre of *p'ansori* than scholars' classical music. *Nong'ak* became associated with the nationalist appeal of the percussion group SamulNori, formed in 1978, and tapped into a rhythmic violence that was recognized worldwide and witnessed again from the Korean drummers Tokaebi Storm at the Edinburgh Festival of 2002.

But Hwang Byungki showed that there was scope for modernizing high-art music. Using memories of his own youth and stories of Korea's past glory as inspiration, he broke with precedent during the 1960s and began to compose new pieces in traditional style. While rooting his music firmly in the Korean soil, he later collaborated with the Western composer John Cage and performer Evelyn Glennie, and in his hands and those of like-minded composers, 'modern traditional' Korean music began to flourish. In the 1950s, Hwang recalls, no more than 20 *kayagŭm*s were built each year: fifty years later, between 3,000 and 4,000 were being turned out. In the early 1970s there were two traditional orchestras in South Korea: thirty years on there were upward of twenty. The number of university colleges teaching traditional music increased correspondingly, and freshmen now entered with higher standards than ever before. In 1981 a group of composers including Yi Kŏnyong (b. 1947) drew on folk melodies to write music, they said, for Koreans rather than Westerners. Calling themselves the 'Third Generation', they aimed to make traditional music accessible to ordinary Koreans in updated form. Still more transformation occurred during what Hwang describes as the decade of broad diversity, the 1990s. This eclectic age also brought crossover music – Korean music played on Western instruments and vice versa – a 22-hour radio station devoted to traditional music, and traditional tunes harmonized and adapted for Western tuning methods. The latter came through North Korean influence. Refugee musicians arriving in the South from the DPRK earned good money in Seoul, where students found their playing styles easier to master, and by the end of the decade even the previous ban on playing North Korean tunes had been lifted.

In North Korea, says Keith Howard, 'no musical production [is] possible in public or at any professional level outside state institutions'. Every aspect of musical creativity, from subject matter to composition and performance style, conforms to *juche* rules. If these stifle personality they nevertheless encourage high standards, and audiences particularly enjoy 'revolutionary' and 'people's operas'. The story lines, like the themes of popular songs, may be repetitively concerned with the qualities and achievements of the two Kims, but the collective groups responsible for writing them incorporate references to well-known folk songs and traditional tunes.

Literature

Among the delicate and sometimes provocative themes explored by modern South Korean authors have been emancipation from the traditions of the Chosŏn period, such as the subordination of women; experiences under occupation and the anguish and possibilities accompanying liberation; the social and mental effects of the North–South polarization; the strains accompanying rapid economic growth; and the struggle for political freedom and recognition of human rights. With the curtailment of freedom after the 19 April Uprising (see p. 264) and the banning of overt political activity through the 1960s and '70s, writing became a substitute forum for expressing concerns. Issues of sovereignty, both national and personal, became something of an obsession, and because so much writing was concerned with Korean issues, translation into English was slow to happen and Korean literature remained of scant interest to the outside world.

Poets experimented with modernism as well as preserving traditional forms. Kevin O'Rourke, a long-time Irish resident of Korea and professor of literature at Kyunghee University, has accused them of being too abstract, moral and intellectual, and wished that they would rediscover the passion and physical focus of Yi Kyubo. But the dissident poet Kim Chiha (b. 1941) seemed to have his feet on the ground. His father was tortured as a communist, and he himself spent six years in jail for writing poems such as 'Five Thieves' (1970), a satire on the rapaciousness of the ruling classes. Abroad, he was nominated for the Nobel Prize. Another who surely wrote from the depths of personal experience was Ch'ŏn Sang Pyŏng (1930–1993). Tortured and made impotent by the KCIA in 1967, he suffered a mental breakdown that left him with 'the heart of a child, and a child's fragility' (Brother Anthony). His wife, Mok Sun Ok, supported him from the proceeds of a small café in Insadong named Kwi-ch'ŏn ('Back to Heaven'), while constant drinking ate away at his liver. Even when medical opinion wrote him off in 1988 he lived for a further five years. Perhaps directness, rather than O'Rourke's wished-for emotion, sums up the style of Ch'ŏn's poetry, yet passionate he certainly was, in his love of nature, his preference for simplicity and his gratitude for life.

> I'll go back to heaven again.
> Hand in hand with the dew
> That melts at a touch of the dawning day,
>
> I'll go back to heaven again.
> With the dusk, together, just we two,
> At a sign from a cloud after playing on the slopes
>
> I'll go back to heaven again.
> At the end of my outing to this beautiful world
> I'll go back and say: It was beautiful . . .

Literature also expressed renewed pride in Korea's past and the best of its own traditions, and writers 'struggle[d] to cultivate the spirit and determination of the Korean people' (Kim Byong-ik). Outstanding novelists included Pak Kyung-ree (b. 1926), whose epic historical tale *The Earth* (1994) took 25 years to write; Lee Oyoung (b. 1934), professor of literature at Ewha University, whose novella *The General's Beard* (1967) displayed his interest in the interaction of different cultures, and who later achieved international acclaim for his skill at uniting them visually in the thrilling cultural performance of the opening and closing ceremonies of the 1988 Olympic Games; Cho Chŏngnae (b. 1943), who tackled issues of ideological and personal rivalry in South Chŏlla between 1945 and the Korean War in his ten-volume *The T'aebaek Mountains* (1986); Yi Munyŏl, whose fictionalized account of the nineteenth-century poet Kim Sakkat (*The Poet*, 1992) raised profound questions linked to Korean tradition and modernization; and Yi Inhwa (b. 1966), whose novel *Who Can Say What I Am?* won the first Writers' World Literature Award in 1992. By the end of the decade young writers, openly professing that to them the sufferings of the past were ancient history, turned to more universal topics such as feminism, sex, ecological issues and popular culture. Theirs was 'literature of the new generation'.

For all the struggle demanded of South Korean writers, the task confronting their colleagues in the North could scarcely have been greater. There, writing was no longer for entertainment, for *juche* demanded and ensured that art serve ideology. According to one of Kim Il Sung's famous dicta, authors were to be 'engineers of the human soul', not mirrors to its infinite variety and capacity for individuality. What they were to create was a people faithful to the Great Leader and dedicated to his view of social revolution. Luckily for him, Hong Myŏnghŭi, described by Kang Young-Zu as 'Korea's finest historical novelist', had passed the age of having creative ambition, and found his political loyalty rewarded in September 1948 by his appointment as a vice-premier. One who failed the test was Kim's biographer, Han Sŏrya (b. 1900). After his purge in 1962 there was no let-up in the outpouring of writing eulogizing Kim and his son, but it was now attributed to anonymous Creative Groups that also depicted them in visual art and films. Drawing, inevitably, on the same range of subject matter as writers in the South, the authors of short stories, novels, plays and operas in the DPRK dwelt on the sufferings of the twentieth century, but gave every story a positive twist with examples of heroism, self-sacrifice and patriotism. Readers and audiences, whether or not they were aware of the constraints under which they were written, undoubtedly found satisfaction and enjoyment in them. Stephen Epstein concludes that 'perhaps the most salient feature of North Korean literature in contrast to its southern counterpart is its eternal optimism', a finding shared by Keith Howard with regard to popular songs. Both disagree with the frequent view of critics that the mandatory depiction of triumph over hardship through self-reliance defies characterization and means a complete masking of reality, and see in the short stories and popular songs of the 1990s an underlying tendency to reveal the strains of the decade, in the face of which literature and music provide psychological comfort.

Cinema

In January 1978 Ch'oe Ŭnhŭi was kidnapped by North Korean agents in Hong Kong. (Nothing very surprising in that: kidnapping features large in modern Korean history. Victims of hit squads from both North and South range from the opposition politician Kim Daejung, seized in Japan in July 1973, to the avant-garde painter Yi Ŭngno, the composer Yun Isang, and hundreds of anonymous suspected dissidents on both sides of the DMZ. A teenage girl made the headlines in 2002, when Kim Jong Il admitted that agents had kidnapped ordinary Japanese citizens in the 1970s and '80s and taken them back to North Korea to teach Japanese language and culture to its trainee spies. Most of them, including thirteen-year-old Megumi Yokata, had since died.) Ch'oe Ŭnhŭi was a glamorous actress, the ex-wife of South Korea's leading film director Shin Sang'ok (1926–2006), who already had some 50 titles to his credit. She was taken to P'yŏngyang to satisfy the 'collector' instinct of the Great Leader's film-loving son Kim Jong Il and to act as bait for her former husband. In June he too was seized, and both of them were eventually set to work in the Korean Film Studio. Perhaps Kim was trying to practise what he already preached. Five years earlier, he had published *Yŏnghwa yesul ron* ('The Theory of Cinematic Art'), a book that came to enjoy the same degree of scriptural veneration in North Korea as did Mao Zedong's famous *Talks at the Yenan Forum on Literature and Art* (1942) in China. In the book, Kim urged workers in the film industry to interpret working-class experience and to take the principle of self-reliance to heart. In this case, self-reliance meant acquiring a leading director and actress ready-made. Over the course of the next eight years Shin made seven films in the Socialist Realist mould and won awards in Moscow and Prague. The couple became trusted favourites of the Kims, father and son. They were showered with expensive gifts, and permitted to travel to Eastern Europe on business. Then, on 13 March 1986, they slipped their minders in Vienna and escaped to the US Embassy.

The plots of Korean films had never yet lived up to the real-life drama of Ch'oe Ŭnhŭi's story. Both the ROK and the DPRK recognized the propaganda value of cinema, and after 1953 the nationalistic and social value of film-making took precedence over artistic or economic considerations. Stories centred on resistance to the Japanese invaders, the horrors of the Korean War, the continuing suffering of the people under either communist or American-oppressed rule, and the inevitability of reunification under the appropriately proper regime. Those from the North emphasized the role of women in the revolutionary struggle, and in both North and South class hierarchy was treated as right and proper. But film-makers demonstrated their courage in conveying dissident political messages as well as the words of their sponsors. In 1955 the ROK director Yi Kyuhwan made a version of *Ch'unhyang-jŏn*. Depending on one's point of view, the heroine Ch'unhyang may be seen as a paragon of filial piety and loyalty, but also – in a *minjung* context – as a symbol of class and female oppression. Shin Sang'ok filmed the same story in both South and North Korea, and in the latter version he daringly managed to draw out the power of the Confucian virtues. In *Hong Kiltong* (1967), too, the first full-length colour film made in South Korea, audiences could recognize the popular novel's underlying theme of political and social injustice. And in the North, Cho Kyŏngsun's *Bellflower* (1987) defended the regime's system of social stratification while cleverly exposing its limitations and abuses.

By the 1990s high-quality South Korean films were winning international recognition, even if the universal themes they addressed continued to be set in the particular context of recent Korean suffering, such as the Korean War (*Spring in My Hometown* and *Taebaek Mountains*), comfort women (*The Murmuring*) and North Korean subversion (*Swiri*). The classic 1926 version of Na Un'gyu's strongly nationalistic *Arirang* was revived more than once, and a new version of the story was shown to audiences in both Seoul and P'yŏngyang in 2003. Cinema was a principal component of the so-called Korean wave (*Hallyu*), a taste for Korean popular culture that swept over East and South-East Asia from the late 1990s onwards and had hit the USA by 2004. This remarkable phenomenon also incorporated films for the small screen – ROK soap operas – as well as popular music, comic books, electronic games and dress items.

CONCLUSION: THE QUEST FOR KOREAN IDENTITY

Few people can have debated their origins, identity, and characteristics as long or as publicly as the Koreans have done since 1905. A combination of ethnic and national pride, intensified since 1953 by the P'yŏngyang and Seoul regimes' need to legitimize their right to the whole peninsula, has nurtured something of a national obsession. Pride in perceived virtues, such as the group solidarity exhibited in *kye* rural organizations, or the dutifulness of the wife popularized in the Ch'unhyang story, has been matched by fervent denial of negative practices in earlier society, like ritual suicide and honour killings. One of the chief areas explored, exploited and strengthened in the hunt for a definition has been Korean culture, both traditional and modern. For example, KNCU's *Main Currents of Korean Thought* (1983) was 'dedicated to seeking [the] real character of Korean culture'; and the spring 2003 issue of *Korea Journal* was devoted to 'How Korean is Korean Culture? The Quest for National Identity'. Having read the answer from Korea, Chinese, Western and African perspectives, readers might still have been left with a feeling of uncertainty. The trouble is, of course, that culture is too vague and too enormous a concept to reduce to easy definition. This book alone has ranged across a spectrum of often controversial topics, from inexplicable burial practices in neolithic times to political control over modern music and dance. It has looked at single creations by individual craftsmen and movements by groups of artists reflecting broad social upheavals. And yet it has barely scratched the surface. Where, their admirers might say, is its recognition of fine wooden furniture, or decorative knots, or Buddhist dance, or the Korean love of mountain climbing or gastronomy?

Modern Koreans are inclined to speak of their special shaping as a people by the psychological and physical suffering their nation has endured. They call it their *han*, an untranslatable and perhaps indefinable word. They also boast of their peculiar ability to recognize and respond to beauty, a power they call *mŏt*. Kevin O'Rourke would evidently prefer them to stop analysing and express themselves more spontaneously. '*Mŏt* is universal. What distinguishes Korean *mŏt* from *mŏt* elsewhere in the world is the Korean attitude to beauty. The Korean artist . . . looks to moral rather than physical beauty; his concern is with the universal rather than the particular. The approach is conceptual, the emphasis is moral.' It is an attribute of their Confucian heritage. Ch'ŏn Sang Pyŏng's life was the very personification of *han*, yet his delight in the natural world defies rationalization except as a manifestation of *mŏt*.

Park Chung Hee's first five-year cultural plan spoke unashamedly, even perhaps with pride after the cultural cleansing of the colonial period, of 'creating a new national culture and a cultural identity by establishing a nationalistic perception on Korean history'. Both he and Kim Il Sung, understanding Korea's past role as a lynchpin of East Asian civilization, spoke of self-reliance, and if *juche* was never going to set the region alight, vestiges of Confucian thinking persisted in the DPRK and seemed to be on the verge of reinvigoration in the ROK. In 1991 Kim Kwangŏk noted that 'Confucian activities are becoming more and more widespread among the younger generations'. And in 1996 the Seoul newspaper *Tonga Ilbo* and the Beijing *Renmin Ribao* organized a conference on the theme of Confucianism and political development within what they perceived as an evolving regional framework. In particular, the South Korean *chaebŏl* conglomerate corporations were hailed as modern incarnations of traditional Confucian capitalist structures. But as the morning clear-up begins from the night before's frenzied youth spending spree under the neon lights of Seoul's Myŏngdong shopping centre; as the Hyundai Group chairman Chung Monghun, hounded by corporate scandal, commits suicide in August 2003; and as riot police come under Molotov-cocktail fire three months later from trade unionists in Seoul protesting against restrictive labour laws, the cold dawn of the twenty-first century sheds a rather different, more speculative light. Even so, Lee Jaehyuck could still write in the summer of 2003 that 'the spirit of Confucianism, if not its explicit pedagogic content, is still alive all over contemporary Korean society'.

Park Chung Hee's promotion of *han'gŭl* and the move towards universal education in the ROK after 1953 meant the retreat of elitist *yangban* culture, and the message went out that true national culture was to be found in popular traditional arts such as masked dance, farmers' music and *p'ansori*. But in a political context culture functioned better as a means of criticism than of indoctrination, even if it was not until the 1990s that Koreans really experienced the freedom to discover worldwide cultures for themselves and to experiment radically with their own. In the DPRK, meanwhile, education meant unremitting ideological pressure, and exploited the arts powerfully for this purpose. Painting was imbued with Socialist Realism. Dramatic productions, like that of *Celebration* (*Kyŏngch'uk Daehoe*, 1988), proclaimed revolutionary themes. The message of Kim Jong Il's *Theory of Cinematic Art* was that 'writers and performers must have a firm understanding of the role of class in the characterization of our enemies in order to depict clearly their reactionary nature and their inherent vulnerability.

Our enemies must be portrayed accurately.' The final nails were being hammered into the coffin of 'art for art's sake'.

Those who look for indicators of Korean identity and its strength, whether at individual or national level, might think to find them in the remarkable emotion poured out over the reuniting of relatives 'lost' across the DMZ, or the persistence of the ROK government in trying to get mapmakers to use the term 'East Sea' rather than 'Sea of Japan'. But a more subtle suggestion comes from Kang Woobang (U-bang): 'Few Korean art works are as perfectly finished as the art works in China or Japan. However, I find them even more satisfying because, instead of perfection, I can detect a sense of humor, freedom and beguiling innocence.' Here he echoes Yanagi Soetsu's discovery of the 'beauty of loneliness' in Korean ceramics, what he later re-evaluated as the 'beauty of naturalness'. Kim Byong-ryol notes the 'beauty of "improvisation" [as] an underlying characteristic of Korean traditional arts', and likens flexibility in architectural styles to deliberate asymmetry in music and literati painting. And Godfrey Gompertz also appreciates the deliberate lack of exactitude in the lion on the lid of a Koryŏ celadon incense-burner:

> A self-respecting Chinese lion would surely have been seated squarely in the centre, but here we are dealing with a wayward Korean beast, who refuses to do exactly as he is told: when viewed from above, he is seen to be sitting well over to one side of the lid, a position which was doubtless as comfortable as it was unorthodox!

Perhaps, then, the definition and strength of Korean-ness is related to a distrust of being cast in either a Chinese or a Japanese mould, or of being either pretentious or predictable. Perhaps, on the other hand, it is something only a Korean can understand, and an empathetic foreigner who tries to analyse Korean society and its culture is liable to appear patronizing if and when he fails to get the whole picture. If so, then Lee Hye-ku (p. 15) was leading me up the garden path back in 1972, and that would certainly not have been in his nature. We have got to make the attempt, provided we keep our wits about us as we do so. After all, how successful were Yi Yinhwa or Yi Munyŏl in their attempts to conjure up the atmosphere of eighteenth- and nineteenth-century Korea? Was Korea ever a country as Isabella Bishop or Lillias Underwood saw it through the eyes of Victorian lady and Presbyterian missionary? Were the early peninsular peoples ever as Japanese anthropologists thought them to be in their efforts to shape modern Korea in their own image? We simply don't know. We can't really tell whether Mira Stout has got the Korea of living memory right in *A Thousand Chestnut Trees*: when it was published in 1997 Koreans and so-called Korean experts around the world argued hard over the accuracy of the book's circumstantial detail. Some things, of course, are certain. The portrayal of North Korea in the James Bond movie *Die Another Day* (2002) is plainly fictitious, even if that country does have a leadership capable of starving its own people and threatening the world's most powerful nation with nuclear blackmail. We know that *M*A*S*H* is fictitious, even though the South Korean riot police did fire tear gas to dispel student crowds protesting against the continued American presence on their soil. We know that the brilliantly choreographed shows that opened and closed the World Cup of 2002, and the serried ranks of smiling girls and boys singing in adulation to their Dear Leader in P'yŏngyang, bear as much relation to authentic popular culture as the Reverend Moon's massed weddings did to traditional Buddhist or Christian rites, even though spectacle, colour, music and dance really are an essential component of the Korean world-view, past and present.

What it all amounts to is that whoever or whatever we are, historian, novelist, poet or politician, trying to encapsulate in words the spirit of a proud nation with a long and varied history is like fishing for the image of the moon reflected in a pond, for as the *Dao De Jing* puts it: 'The Way that can be told is not the true Way.'

Sources and Further Reading

GENERAL

Covell, Jon, *Japan's Hidden History: Korean Impact on Japanese Culture* (Seoul, 1984)
Goepper, Roger, and Roderick Whitfield, *Treasures from Korea* (London, 1984)
Han Woo-keun, *The History of Korea* (Seoul, 1970)
Kim Donguk, *History of Korean Literature* (Tokyo, 1980)
Lee Ki-Baik (Yi Kibaek), *A New History of Korea*, trans. Edward Wagner (Seoul, 1984)
Lee, Peter H., *Anthology of Korean Literature* (Honolulu, HI, 1981)
——, ed., *Sourcebook of Korean Civilization*, 2 vols (New York, 1993–6)
——, and Theodore de Bary, eds, *Sources of Korean Tradition*, vol. I: *From Early Times through the Sixteenth Century* (New York, 1997)
McKillop, Beth, *Korean Art and Design* (London, 1992)
Nahm, Andrew, *Korea: Tradition and Transformation* (Seoul, 1988)
Portal, Jane, *Korea: Art and Archaeology* (London, 2000)
Pratt, Keith, *Korean Music: Its History and Its Interpretation* (London, 1987)
——, and Richard Rutt, *Korea: A Historical and Cultural Dictionary* (Richmond, Surrey, 1999)
Rutt, Richard, *Korean Works and Days* (Seoul, 1964)
——, *The Bamboo Grove: An Introduction to Sijo* (Berkeley, CA, 1971)
Sohn Pow-key, Kim Chol-choon and Hong Yi-sup, *The History of Korea* (Seoul, 1970)
Song Bang-song, *Source Readings in Korean Music* (Seoul, 1980)
Tennant, Roger, *A History of Korea* (London, 1993)
Twitchett, D., and J. K. Fairbank, eds, *The Cambridge History of China* (Cambridge, 1978–)
Uden, Martin, *Times Past in Korea* (London, 2003)
Various authors, 'Korea', in *The Dictionary of Art*, ed. Jane Turner (London and New York, 1996), vol. XVIII, pp. 245–385

INTRODUCTION

Hong, Wontack, *Paekche of Korea and the Origin of Yamato Japan* (Seoul, 1994)
Pai, Hyung Il, and T. Tangherlini, eds, *Nationalism and the Construction of Korean Identity* (Berkeley, CA, 1998)
Palais, James, 'Nationalism, Good or Bad?', in *Nationalism and the Construction of Korean Identity*, ed. Hyung Il Pai and T. Tangherlini (Berkeley, CA, 1998), pp. 214–28
Robinson, Michael, *Cultural Nationalism in Colonial Korea, 1920–1925* (Seattle, WA, and London, 1996)
Wells, Kenneth, *New God, New Nation: Protestants and Self-Reconstruction Nationalism in Korea, 1896–1937* (Sydney, 1990)
——, ed., *South Korea's Minjung Movement: The Culture and Politics of Dissidence* (Honolulu, HI, 1995)

CHAPTER ONE: FROM EARLIEST TIMES TO AD 668

Bailey, Lisa, 'Bronze Metalwork', in *The Dictionary of Art*, ed. Jane Turner (London and
    New York, 1996), vol. XVIII, pp. 344–7
Barnes, Gina L., *The Rise of Civilization in East Asia* (London, 1993)
——, *State Formation in Korea* (Richmond, Surrey, 2002)
Holcombe, Charles, *The Genesis of East Asia, 221 BC–AD 907* (Honolulu, HI, 2001)
Kim Won-yong, *Art and Archaeology of Ancient Korea* (Seoul, 1986)
Nelson, Sarah, *The Archaeology of Korea* (Cambridge, 1993)
Pai Hyungil, *Constructing 'Korean' Origins: A Critical Review of Archaeology, Historiography,
    and Racial Myth in Korean State-Formation Theories* (Cambridge, MA, 2000)

CHAPTER TWO: UNIFIED SILLA, AD 668–936

Anon., *La Montagne de dix milles Bouddhas* (Paris, 2002)
Picken, Lawrence, *Music from the Tang Court* (Oxford, 1985)
Steinhardt, Nancy, 'The Monastery Hōryūji: Architectural Forms of Early Buddhism in
    Japan', in Washizuka Hiromitsu, Park Youngbok and Kang Woo-bang, *Transmitting the
    Forms of Divinity: Early Buddhist Art from Korea and Japan* (New York, 2003), pp. 154–67
Washizuka Hiromitsu, Park Youngbok and Kang Woo-bang, *Transmitting the Forms of
    Divinity: Early Buddhist Art from Korea and Japan* (New York, 2003)
Yang Han-sung and Jan Yun-hua, *The Hye Ch'o Diary: Memoir of the Pilgrimage to the Five
    Regions of India* (Seoul, n. d.)

CHAPTER THREE: KORYŎ, 918–1392

Condit, Jonathan, *Music of the Korean Renaissance* (Cambridge, 1983)
Duncan, John, *The Origins of the Chosŏn Dynasty* (Seattle, 2000)
Gompertz, Godfrey, 'Hsu Ching's Visit to Korea in 1123', *Transactions of the Oriental Ceramic
    Society*, XXXIII (1960–2) [London, 1963], n. p.
Kim Kumja Paik et al., *Goryeo Dynasty: Korea's Age of Enlightenment* (San Francisco, 2003)
Kim Won-yong, *Art and Archaeology of Ancient Korea* (Seoul, 1986)
Rogers, Michael, 'National Consciousness in Medieval Korea', in *China Among Equals: The
    Middle Kingdom and Its Neighbors, 10th–14th Centuries*, ed. Morris Rossabi (Berkeley,
    CA, 1983), pp. 151–72
Shultz, Edward, *Scholars and Generals: Military Rule in Medieval Korea* (Honolulu, HI, 2000)

CHAPTER FOUR: EARLY TO MID-CHOSŎN, 1392–1800

Ch'oe Wan-su, Youngsook Pak and Roderick Whitfield, *Korean True-View Landscape:
    Paintings by Chŏng Sŏn (1676–1759)* (London, 2005)
Choi Byonghyon, trans., *The Book of Corrections: Reflections on the National Crisis during the
    Japanese Invasion of Korea, 1592–1598* (Berkeley, CA, 2002)
Chun Hae-jong, 'Sino-Korean Tributary Relations in the Ch'ing Period', in *The Chinese
    World Order*, ed. J. K. Fairbank (Cambridge, MA, 1968), pp. 90–111
Clark, Donald, 'Sino-Korean Tributary Relations under the Ming', in *The Cambridge
    History of China*, vol. VIII, pt 2 (Cambridge, 1988), pp. 272–300
de Bary, W. T., and JaHyun Kim Haboush, eds, *The Rise of Neo-Confucianism in Korea*
    (New York, 1985)
Ha Taehung, *Nanjung Ilgi: War Diary of Admiral Yi Sun-sin* (Seoul, 1977)
Jungmann, Berlind, *Painters as Envoys: Korean Inspiration in 18th Century Japanese Nanga*

(Princeton, NJ, 2004)

Kalton, Michael, *The Four–Seven Debate: An Annotated Translation of the Most Famous Controversy in Korean Neo-Confucian Thought* (New York, 1994)

Kim Haboush, JaHyun, *The Confucian Kingship in Korea* (New York, 1988)

——, *The Memoirs of Lady Hyegyŏng* (Berkeley, CA, 1996)

Kim Hongnam, ed., *Korean Arts of the Eighteenth Century: Splendour and Simplicity* (New York, 1994)

Kim-Renaud, Young-Key, ed., *King Sejong the Great: The Light of Fifteenth-Century Korea* (Washington, DC, 1997)

Ledyard, Gari, *The Korean Language Reform of 1446* (Seoul, 1998)

Lewis, James B., *Frontier Contact between Chosŏn Korea and Tokugawa Japan* (London, 2003)

Provine, Robert, *Essays on Sino-Korean Musicology: Early Sources for Korean Ritual Music* (Seoul, 1988)

Sohn Pokee, *Social History of the Early Chosŏn Dynasty* (Seoul, 2000)

Turnbull, Stephen, *Samurai Invasion: Japan's Korean War, 1592–1598* (London, 2002)

Wagner, Edward, *The Literati Purges: Political Conflict in Early Yi Korea* (Cambridge, MA, 1974)

——, 'Social Stratification in Seventeenth-Century Korea: Some Observations from a 1663 Seoul Census Register', *Occasional Papers on Korea* (Cambridge, MA, April 1974)

Yi In-hwa, *Everlasting Empire*, trans. Yu Young-nan (New York, 2002)

CHAPTER FIVE: THE HERMIT KINGDOM, 1800–64

Various authors, 'Portraits in the Joseon Dynasty: Style and Function', *Korea Journal*, XLV/2 (Seoul, 2005), pp. 107–215

Deuchler, Martina, *The Confucian Transformation of Korea: A Study of Society and Ideology* (Cambridge, MA, 1992)

Janelli, Roger, and Dawnhee Janelli, *Ancestor Worship and Korean Society* (Stanford, CA, 1982)

Kang Woobang, *The World of Nectar Ritual Painting* (Seoul, 1995)

Karlsson, Anders, *The Hong Ky'ŏngnae Rebellion, 1811–1812: Conflict between Central Power and Local Society in 19th Century Korea* (Stockholm, 2000)

Kim Haboush, JaHyun, and Martina Deuchler, eds, *Culture and the State in Late Chosŏn Korea* (Cambridge, MA, 1999)

Robinson, Michael, 'Perceptions of Confucianism in Twentieth-Century Korea', in *The East Asian Region: Confucian Heritage and its Modern Adaptation*, ed. Gilbert Rozman (Princeton, NJ, 1991), pp. 204–26

Setton, Mark, *Chong Yag Yong: Korea's Challenge to Orthodox Neo-Confucianism* (New York, 1997)

Underwood, Lillias, *Fifteen Years Among the Topknots* (New York, 1904)

Yi Mun-yŏl, *The Poet*, trans. Chong-hwa Chung and Brother Anthony (London 1995)

Zo Za-yong', 'Symbolism in Korean Folk Paintings', in *Traditional Korean Painting*, ed. Korean National Commission for UNESCO (Seoul, 1983), pp. 96–120

CHAPTER SIX: INCURSION, MODERNIZATION AND REFORM, 1864–1905

Baker, Donald, 'Sirhak Medicine: Measles, Smallpox and Chŏng Tasan', *Korean Studies*, XIV (Honolulu, HI, 1990), pp. 135–66

Bishop, Isabella Bird, *Korea and her Neighbours* (London, 1897, reprinted 1985)

Chandra, Vipam, *Imperialism, Resistance and Reform in Late Nineteenth-Century Korea: Enlightenment and the Independence Club* (Berkeley, CA, 1988)

Choe, Ching Young, *The Rule of the Taewŏn'gun, 1864–1873* (Cambridge, MA, 1972)

Conroy, Hilary, *The Japanese Seizure of Korea, 1868–1910* (Philadelphia, 1960)

Harrington, F. H., *God Mammon and the Japanese* (Madison, WI, 1944, reprinted 1966)

Kim, K.-H., *The Last Phase of the East Asian World Order: Korea, Japan and the Chinese Empire, 1860–1882* (Berkeley and Los Angeles, 1980)

Kim, C. I. Eugene, and K.-H. Kim, *Korea and the Politics of Imperialism, 1876–1910* (Berkeley and Los Angeles, 1967)

Korea Branch Royal Asiatic Society, reprint, *The Korean Repository* (1892–8) (Seoul, 1975)

Ledyard, Gari, 'Cartography in Korea', in *The History of Cartography: Vol. 2, Book 2: Cartography in the Traditional East Asian and Southeast Asian Societies*, ed. J. B. Harley and David Woodword (Chicago, 1994)

Palais, James B., *Politics and Policy in Traditional Korea* (Cambridge, MA, 1975)

Pratt, Keith, *Old Seoul* (Hong Kong, 2002)

Sands, William, *At the Court of Korea: Undiplomatic Memories* (reprinted London, 1987)

Schmid, André, *Korea Between Empires, 1895–1919* (New York, 2002)

Underwood, Peter, Samuel Moffett and Norman Sibley, eds, *First Encounters: Korea, 1888–1910* (Seoul, 1982) [a collection of early photographs]

CHAPTER SEVEN: CULTURE UNDER THREAT, 1905–45

Ahn, Choong-sik, *The Story of Western Music in Korea: A Social History, 1885–1950* (eBookstand Books, 2005)

Clark, Donald, *Living Dangerously in Korea: The Western Experience, 1900–1950* (Norwalk, CT, 2003)

de Ceuster, Koen, 'Colonized Mind and Historical Consciousness in the Case of Yun Ch'iho', *Bochumer Jahrbuch zür Ostasienforschung*, XXVII (2003), pp. 107–32

Gragert, Edwin, *Land Ownership under Colonial Rule: Korea's Japanese Experience, 1900–1935* (Honolulu, HI, 1994)

Han, Manyoung, *Kugak: Studies in Korean Traditional Music* (Seoul, 1990)

Hicks, George, *The Comfort Women: Sex Slaves of the Japanese Imperial Forces* (St Leonards, NSW, 1995)

Howard, Keith, ed., *True Stories of the Korean Comfort Women* (London, 1995)

Kim, Youngna, 'Artistic Trends in Korean Painting during the 1930s', in *War, Occupation and Creativity: Japan and East Asia, 1920–1960*, ed. M. J. Mayo and J. T. Rimer (Honolulu, HI, 2001), pp. 121–46

——, *20th Century Korean Art* (London, 2005)

Robinson, Michael, 'Mass Media and Popular Control in 1930s Korea: Cultural Control, Identity and Colonial Hegemony', in Suh Daesook, *Korean Studies: New Pacific Currents* (Honolulu, HI, 1994), pp. 59–82

Shin, G. W., and Michael Robinson, *Colonial Modernity in Korea* (Cambridge, MA, 1999)

Yŏm Sangsŏp, *Three Generations*, trans. Yu Young-nan (New York, 2005)

CHAPTER EIGHT: PARTITION AND WAR, 1945–53

Anthony of Taizé, Brother, *Midang: The Early Lyrics of So Chong Ju* (London, 1993)

Cumings, Bruce, *The Origins of the Korean War: Liberation and the Emergence of Separate Regimes, 1945–1947* (Princeton, NJ, 1981)

——, *The Origins of the Korean War: The Roaring of the Cataract, 1947–1950* (Princeton, NJ, 1990)

Goncharov, S. N., J. W. Lewis and Xue Litai, *Uncertain Partners: Stalin, Mao and the Korean War* (Stanford, CA, 1993)

Hastings, Max, *The Korean War* (London, 1987)

Stueck, William, *Rethinking the Korean War: A New Diplomatic and Strategic History* (Princeton, NJ, 2002)

West, Philip, and Suh Jimoon, eds, *Remembering the 'Forgotten War': The Korean War through Literature and Art* (New York and London, 2001)

Whelan, Richard, *Drawing the Line: The Korean War, 1950–1953* (London, 1990)

CHAPTER NINE: POST-WAR KOREA

Abelmann, Nancy, *Echoes of the Past, Epics of Discontent* (Berkeley, CA, 1996)

Anthony of Taizé, Brother, and Young-moo Kim, trans., *Back to Heaven, Selected Poems of Ch'ŏn Sang Pyŏng* (New York and Paris, 1995)

Blix, Herbert, *Hirohito and the Making of Modern Japan* (New York, 2000)

Cumings, Bruce, *Korea's Place in the Sun: A Modern History* (New York and London, 1997)

——, *North Korea: Another Country* (New York, 2003)

Gills, Barry, *Korea versus Korea: A Case of Contested Legitimacy* (London, 1996)

Hesselink, Nathan, ed., *Contemporary Directions: Korean Folk Music Engaging the Twentieth Century and Beyond* (Berkeley, CA, 2001)

Howard, Keith, '*Juche* and Culture: What's New?', in *North Korea in a New World Order*, ed. Hazel Smith et al. (Basingstoke, 1996), pp. 169–95

Kang U-bang, 'The Charm of Anomaly in Korean Art', *Koreana*, XII/3 (1998), pp. 16–21

Kang Young-Zu, 'Hong Myŏng-hŭi: Korea's Finest Historical Novelist', *Korea Journal*, XXIX/4 (1999), pp. 36–60

Kim Byong-ik, 'Modern Korean Literature: Its Past, Present and Future', *Koreana*, X/2 (1996), pp. 4–9

Kim Youngna, 'Korean Arts and Culture at the End of the Twentieth Century', in *Korea Briefing, 1997–1999*, ed. Oh Kongdan (New York and London, 2000), pp. 101–22

——, *Modern and Contemporary Art in Korea* (Seoul, 2005)

Kim Young-uk, Lee Doo-shik and Yu June-sang, 'Korean Art on the World Stage: Where Does It Fit In?', *Koreana*, IX/2 (1995), pp. 34–41

Lee Hyangjin, 'Ch'unhyangjon: Cinematic Texts of the Era of Division', *Review of Korean Studies*, III/2 (2000), pp. 139–65

——, *Contemporary Korean Cinema: Culture, Identity and Politics* (Manchester, 2001)

Lee Jaehyuck, 'Rational Renderings of Confucian Relationships in Contemporary Korea', *Korea Journal*, XLIII/2 (2003), pp. 257–88

Oberdorfer, Don, *The Two Koreas: A Contemporary History* (New York, 1998)

O'Rourke, Kevin, 'Demythologizing Mŏt', *Koreana*, XII/3 (1998), pp. 34–41

Pak Yong-suk, 'What Makes Korean Paintings Korean?', *Koreana*, X/3 (1996), pp. 56–61

Petrov, Leonid, 'Restoring the Glorious Past: North Korean *Juche* Historiography and Goguryeo', *Review of Korean Studies*, VII/3 (2004), pp. 231–52

Portal, Jane, *Art under Control in North Korea* (London, 2005)

——, and Beth McKillop, eds, *North Korean Culture and Society* (London, 2004)

Rozman, Gilbert, ed., *The East Asian Region: Confucian Heritage and Its Modern Adaptation* (Princeton, NJ, 1991)

Wells, Kenneth, ed., *South Korea's Minjung Movement: The Culture and Politics of Dissidence* (Honolulu, 1995)

Discography

This discography is by Keith Howard.

Anthology of Korean Music 1–6 (1996) [Recordings of court and folk music by the Seoul Ensemble]. M People HPTD-0001-6

Anthology of Korean Traditional Folksongs (Han'guk minyo taejŏn) (2000) [12 compact discs; 336-page book, in Korean (213 pages, including song texts) and English (123 pages)]

The Deep-Rooted Tree Sanjo Collection (Ppuri kip'ŭn namu sanjo chŏnjip) (1989) [Wonderful recordings by senior musicians, many of whom have now died, of *sanjo* schools for *kayagŭm* (12-stringed zither), *kŏmun'go* (six-stringed zither), *taegŭm* (transverse flute), *p'iri* (oboe), *ajaeng* (bowed zither) and *haegŭm* (fiddle). Accompanied by a 256-page illustrated book containing complete musical transcriptions and introductory articles in both Korean and English]. Reissued on CD in 1994 and 1996, *The Deep-Rooted Tree*/King Records CDD-001-9

From Korea: P'ansori, the Art of the Cosmic Voice (1999). World Music Gallery L382 (CD)

Kayagŭm Masterpieces by Hwang Byung-ki (1993) [Hwang's compositions]. Originally issued on LP in 1978, 1979 and 1983. Sung Eum DS0034–7 (four CDs)

Kimsohee Chunghyangka (Kim Sohŭi Ch'unhyangga wanch'ang) (1995) [Reissues of LPs of a complete repertory performance. Kim was the greatest female *p'ansori* singer of the twentieth century]. Seoul Records SRCD-1293-8 (six CDs)

Korean Court Music (1969) [Recordings and notes by John Levy featuring musicians from the National Center]. Lyrichord LL7206. LP. Reissued as LYRCD7206 (CD)

Korean Social and Folk Music (1969) [Recordings and notes by John Levy]. Lyrichord LLST7211 (LP)

Korean Traditional Music (Han'guk ŭi chŏnt'ong ŭmak) (1992 and 1994) [Subtitled 'Music for the 21st Century', assorted repertory including court, folk and new compositions]. Korean Broadcasting System KIFM-001-9 and Hae Dong 110–119 (19 CDs)

Acknowledgements

I am grateful to the British Academy and the Korea Foundation for generous grants that contributed to the funding of my research. Many individuals have also been generous and patient in giving me help, and I particularly thank Brother Anthony of Taizé (An Sonjae), Prof. Bill Callahan, Ms Choi Eunju, Chu Sangon, Pastor Hahn Manyoung, Dr James Hoare, Kwon Huh, Prof. Hwang Byungki, Ms Khayoung Kim, Prof. Yersu Kim, Prof. Youngna Kim, Prof. Lee Chae-suk, Lee Chul Soon, Ms Green Lee, Lim Ju-Youn, Prof. Sang-Oh Lim, National Assemblyman Dr Park Jin, Jane Portal, Prof. Shin Bok-ryong, Ms Son Kyung Nyun, Chang-kee Sung, Yim Hak Soon and Yeoik Yun. Professors Donald Baker and Donald Clark have read the whole text and made valuable comments and corrections, and Drs Keith Howard, Hyunsook Lee, James Lewis, Richard Rutt and Peter Dent have done the same for sections in draft, but I alone am responsible for any errors that remain. Keith Howard generously supplied the Discography (above).

Quotations on the following pages are reproduced with thanks to the appropriate publishers and/or copyright holders: p. 79, Peter H. Lee, *Anthology of Korean Literature: From Early Times to the Nineteenth Century* (© University of Hawai'i Press, 1981); pp. 91, 101–2, Peter H. Lee, ed., *Sourcebook of Korean Civilization*, vol. 1 (© Columbia University Press, 1993); p. 109, Richard Rutt, *A Biography of James Scarth Gale and His History of the Korean People* (© Royal Asiatic Society, Korea Branch, Seoul, 1972); p. 246, Brother Anthony of Taizé, *Midang: The Early Lyrics of So Chong Ju* (Forest/UNESCO, 1993); pp. 256–7, Philip West and Suh Ji-moon, eds, *Remembering the 'Forgotten War': The Korean War through Literature and Art* (M. E. Sharpe, 2001); p. 300, Brother Anthony of Taizé and Young-moo Kim, *Back to Heaven: Selected Poems of Ch'ŏn Sang Pyŏng* (Cornell/UNESCO Publishing, 1995). In some instances, despite strenuous efforts, I have been unable to contact authors and possible copyright holders, and to them I apologize.

The author and publishers wish to express their thanks to the below sources of illustrative material and/or permission to reproduce it: photo C. H. Ahn: p. 83; photos courtesy of the author: pp. 75, 156, 188, 289; British Museum, London: pp. 166, 294; courtesy of the Design and Imaging Unit, Durham University: maps on pp. 8, 9; Kansŏng Museum, Seoul: p. 113 (Nat. Treas. no. 68); photo T. B. Kim: p. 99; Korean Overseas Information Service: pp. 110, 142, 186, 214, 281, 288; Leeum Museum of Art, Seoul (formerly the Hoam Art Museum): pp. 230, 259; National Museum of Denmark, Copenhagen (Ethnographic Collections): p. 204; National Museum of Korea, Seoul: pp. 53 (Nat. Treas. no. 195), 55 (Nat. Treas. no. 275), 57 (Nat. Treas. no. 154), 61, 71, 93, 123, 162 (Nat. Treas. no. 527), 171; Seoul National University Museum: p. 149; photo Yonhap News Agency: p. 261; photo Hwang Yŏngyŏp: p. 284.

Index

The suffix –sa (Jap. –ji) indicates Temple.
A more detailed index may be obtained on request from the author: keith.pratt@durham.ac.uk

academies, 38, 64, 76, 88, 106,
    128–9, 202
  Kukcha-gam, 88
  Sŏnggyun-gwan (Confucian),
    88, 98, 124, 139
  T'aehakkam, 76, 88
agriculture, 10, 30, 36, 120, 121,
    174, 195, 211, 213, 220, 223,
    272
Akhak kweibŏm, 124, 125, 188
Allen, Horace, 11, 167, 199, 202
America, 11, 179–80, 193, 194,
    195, 198, 209–10, 216, 231,
    237, 238, 240ff., 247–63
    passim, 266, 271, 277ff., 279
American Military Govt, 11, 215,
    243, 246
An Ch'angho, 211, 236–7
An Chunggŭn, 198, 236
Anapchi, 69, 70, 87
Andong Kims, 153, 169, 172,
    173, 174, 178
Annexation, the (1910), 11, 21,
    209, 211, 212–18 passim, 219,
    222, 237
April 19 Uprising, the (1960),
    264, 276, 299
Arirang, 232–3, 303
Armistice, the (1953), 12, 15, 21,
    251, 252–3, 261, 269, 272–3,
    275, 277
armour, 35, 38, 49, 51, 54, 105,
    132
art exhibitions, 229, 293, 296
  Hyŏpchŏn, 229
  Kukchŏn, 256
  Kwangju Biennale, 293
  Mijŏn, 229, 239
  Modern Artists' Invitational,
    282
  National (1961–), 282
  Senten (Kor. Sŏnjŏn), 229,

    230, 256, 297
Autumn Harvest Uprising, the
    (1946), 12, 242, 245–6

Beijing, 25, 102, 103, 132, 138,
    145, 164, 169, 193, 242, 273,
    278; see also Dadu
bells, 32, 49, 72, 73, 77, 81–3,
    199, 293
Bethell, Ernest, 212
Bishop, Isabella Bird, 185, 190,
    206, 306
Bohai, 30, 32, 67, 95, 102;
    see also Parhae
books, 19, 23, 47, 64, 66, 91, 95,
    97, 107, 119, 121, 122, 124,
    128, 138, 144, 147, 160, 165,
    188, 211, 219, 224
brick, 44, 45, 47, 56, 72, 143
bronze, 31, 32, 43, 45, 46, 50, 51,
    54, 57, 69, 74, 81, 121, 134,
    281, 297
Buddhism, 39, 41, 44, 56, 69, 76,
    78ff., 87, 89, 107, 112, 114,
    118, 124, 126, 140, 154, 159,
    165, 169, 175, 217, 222–3, 290
  introduction of, 10, 39, 108
  Lamaist, 111
  persecution of, 119
  schools of, 78–9, 89, 95, 124
burial customs, 30–31, 35, 45–6,
    50, 60; see also tombs

calendar, the, 40, 75, 76, 91, 158,
    159
calligraphy, 25, 38–9, 108, 146,
    148, 169, 228, 298
Capitol Building, the, 49,
    214–15, 245, 280
Censorate, the, 89, 129, 130
chaebŏl, 14, 220, 265, 266, 268,
    269, 287, 291, 305

Chajang, 72, 82
Chang Myŏn, 264
Chang Pogo, 67
Chang Woosung, 228, 296
Changdŏk Palace, 164, 165
Changsu, King (Koguryŏ), 37,
    40, 50
Cheju island, 63, 103, 169, 175,
    193
Cheju Rising (1948), 11, 242, 246
Chijŭng, King (Silla), 45
Chin, polity, 36
China, 10–11, 13–26 passim,
    (pre-Han) 30–32, 33, (Han)
    34–6, 205, (Northern and
    Southern dynasties) 38–41,
    44, 45, 50–51, 56, 58, (Sui-
    Tang) 38, 41–3, 60, 62–7
    passim, 68, 70, 72, 73, 74–5,
    76–9, 82, 85,
    (Song/Liao/Jin/Yuan) 90,
    91, 94–7, 98, 103–5, 106, 109,
    112, 115, 126, (Ming) 117,
    119, 131, 133, 136–9 passim,
    (Qing) 175, 180–83, 190, 192,
    193, 194–7, 202, 203,
    (Republican) 224, 227, 233,
    237, 245, (People's Republic)
    173, 238, 248, 250, 251ff. 253,
    254, 260, 262, 266, 270, 275,
    277, 278, 282, 294, 297
Chindŏk, Queen (Silla), 43, 47,
    50, 63
Chinhan, confederation, 10, 36,
    37
Chinhŭng, King (Silla), 52, 53,
    58
Chinkam, 77
Chinul, 79, 95
Chiphyŏn-jŏn, 120, 121, 122
Cho Mansik, 243, 244
Chŏn Hyŏngp'il, 227, 228, 239

Chŏng Mongju, 106–7, 118, 126
Chŏng Sŏn, 146, 148–9, 230, 295
Chŏng Tojŏn, 100, 118, 119, 126
Chŏng Yagyŏng, 131, 143, 168–9
Chŏng Yakchŏn, 168, 169
Chŏngjo, King (Chosŏn), 11,
    131, 139, 140–41, 143, 144,
    145, 147, 154, 166, 168, 171,
    173, 174, 188, 189
Chosŏn Ilbo, 219, 234, 282
Christianity, Christians, 132, 202,
    216–17, 238, 244, 290; see also
    missionaries
    and post-1953 ROK politics,
    290
    in DPRK, 290
    in Korea 1945–53, 244
    introduction of, 11, 153
    Korean Roman Catholics,
    141, 168, 176, 193, 290
    Korean Protestants, 202,
    290–91
    persecutions and martyrs,
    153, 168, 173, 193–4, 223,
    244, 290
    under Japanese colonialism,
    223, 225, 226
Chun Doo Hwan, 12, 266, 267,
    268, 276, 286, 288
Ch'oe Chegong, 142, 144
Ch'oe Cheu, 175–6, 181
Ch'oe Chiwŏn, 77
Ch'oe dictatorship, the, 10, 101ff.
Ch'oe Namsŏn, 33, 217, 219,
    221, 234, 235, 239
Ch'oe Sŭngno, 88, 89, 115
Ch'ŏlchong, King (Chosŏn), 153,
    171, 173, 175, 176, 178
Ch'ŏn Sang Pyŏng, 300, 304
Ch'ŏndo-gyo, 198, 217, 219, 222,
    227
Ch'ŏnt'ae-jong, 79, 95
Ch'ungyŏl, King (Koryŏ), 104
Ch'unhyang, 160–61, 232, 303,
    304
clans, 62, 66, 68, 72, 97, 101, 125,
    171; see also Andong Kims,
    P'unyang Chos, Yŏhung Mins
commanderies, Chinese, 10, 34,
    44, 48; see also Lelang
communism, communists, 14,
    23, 221, 224, 244, 246, 248,
    249, 250–55 passim, 262, 263,
    264, 265, 270, 271, 300
Company Law, the (1910), 213,
    219
Confucian Classics, the, 76, 88,
    120, 126, 127, 130, 141, 154,
    165, 188
Confucianism, 38–9, 40, 44, 76,

87, 88, 89, 125, 126, 233, 235,
    238, 274–5, 290, 291, 303,
    305; see also Neo-
    Confucianism
constitutions
    DPRK, 270
    Meiji, 216, 266
    ROK, 265, 266
    Yusin, 12, 266
copper, 39, 65, 67, 100, 109, 118,
    211, 281
cotton, 118, 144
Court Music Office , the (Yi
    Wangjik Aakpu), 189, 232,
    255
crowns, 46, 51, 56–7, 69, 87
curfew, 24, 198–9, 266

Dadu, 103, 104, 105, 118
Daewoo Corporation, the, 287
daggers, 31, 43, 45, 51, 247
dance, 46, 48, 70, 76, 77, 90, 121,
    150, 158, 161, 168, 189, 286,
    307
    Ch'ŏyong, 90, 92, 147, 156,
    189
    masked, 78, 92, 147, 150, 160,
    279, 297, 298, 305
Declaration of Independence,
    the (1919), 21, 217, 227, 234
DMZ, the, 15, 21, 86, 261, 306
dolmens, 31, 51
DPRK, 12, 13, 21, 33, 35, 46, 84,
    86, 87, 174, chap. 8, passim,
    269–72, 291, 293, 296, 299,
    305, 307; see also juche
    cultural policy, 279, 280, 282,
    286, 294–5, 296–7, 299, 301
    economic development, 271
    famine in, 12, 272
    foreign policy, 21, 271–2, 275,
    277
    foundation, 242, 245
    nuclear development, 12,
    271–2
    political system, 270, 274ff.
dress, clothing, 38, 41, 48, 64, 91,
    94, 95, 97, 105, 157, 158, 159,
    181, 189, 295, 297, 303
drugs, 65, 95, 101

Eighth Army, US, 247, 250, 254
Elite Patrols, 102, 103

factionalism, 11, 114, 129ff., 139,
    171, 267, 276
factions, 88, 131, 141
    Dogmatist; see Principle
    Easterners (Tongin), 130, 132,
    174

Lesser Northerners, 130
New Teaching (Soron), 130,
    139
Northern Learning (Pukhak),
    141, 169
Northerners (Pugin), 130
Old Teaching (Noron), 130,
    139, 140, 148
Principle (Pyŏkp'a), 130, 140,
    141, 143, 144, 154, 173
Realist (Sip'a), 130, 131, 140,
    176
Southerners (Namin), 130,
    144, 148
Westerners (Sŏin), 130, 132,
    174
festivals, 50, 90, 92, 159–61, 279
filial piety, 91, 127, 141, 156, 173,
    188, 287, 290, 291, 303
film, 233, 283, 286, 293, 301,
    302–3
folk art, 148, 166, 167, 203, 206
folk religion, 46, 159, 181, 212,
    223; see also festivals
food, 65, 82, 95, 138, 140, 165,
fortresses, 34, 41, 51, 95, 138, 175
Foulk, George, 181, 195, 196
Four-Seven debate, the, 128, 130

games, 69, 72, 161, 205, 283, 303
Gaozong, (Tang) Emperor, 43,
    47, 63, 66
genealogies, 154, 172
Germany, 183, 195, 231, 249,
    262, 292
ginseng, 65, 118, 167, 198
glass, 44, 46, 70
gold, 35, 38, 39, 43, 44, 46, 54,
    56–7, 65, 69, 74, 81, 95, 118,
    211, 212, 281
Great Britain, 190, 191, 195, 245
Great Han (Taehan) Empire, the,
    11, 15, 185, 190, 245

Haein-sa, 108, 110–11, 287
Hague Peace Conference, The
    (1907), 11, 209, 210, 212
Hamel, Hendrik, 193
han, 257, 304
Han river, 30, 34, 35, 36, 41, 97,
    103, 119, 194, 252
Han Sŏrya, 235, 270, 301
han'gŭl, 21, 24, 121, 122, 130,
    145, 185, 187, 200, 212, 217,
    219, 233–4, 280, 305
Hansŏng (Seoul), 39, 41, 51, 94,
    100
Hideyoshi, Toyotomi, 11, 17, 51,
    118, 131, 132, 133, 136, 137,
    138, 146

Hŏ Hŏn, 243, 244
Hodge, Lt-Gen. John, 243, 244
Hong Kyŏngnae, 11, 174
Hong Yŏngsik, 180, 199
Hong-giltong-jŏn, 145, 303
Hŏnjong, King (Chosŏn), 153,
    171, 173, 175, 178
hostages, 42, 66, 138, 211
Hulbert, Homer, 164, 200, 210,
    212
Hunmin chŏng'ŭm, 121, 122
Hwabaek, the, 63, 125
Hwang Yŏngyŏp, 235, 256, 282,
    284–5, 291, 292, 293
Hwangnyŏng-sa, 39, 70, 72, 73,
    78, 103
Hwaŏm-jong, 78
hwarang, 59, 77, 92
Hwasŏng castle, 141, 142–3, 188
Hye Ch'o, 79
Hyegyŏng, Lady, 140, 143, 173
Hyundai Group, the, 272, 287,
    305

Ich'adon, 39
Imjin Waeran (Imjin wars,
    1592–8), 11, 80, 131–9, 143,
    164, 192, 278
Imo Incident, the (1882), 180,
    181, 195
Independence Club, the, 21, 185,
    190, 197, 198, 238, 240
Independence Gate, the, 185,
    186–7, 201
Injong, King (Koryŏ), 88, 96,
    101, 107
Inoue Kaoru, Count, 183, 184,
    197
iron, 10, 35, 36, 45, 51, 54, 58,
    86, 109, 132, 134, 135, 211
Iryŏn, 17, 18, 78, 81, 108, 115
Itō Hirobumi, 180, 181, 210, 236,
    237

Japan, 10–12, 13–26 *passim*, 33,
    (Yayoi) 35, (Kofun/Yamato)
    36, 38, 39, 40, 41, 42, 45, 50,
    54, 56–7, 58 (Nara) 63, 64, 67,
    68, 72, 73, 85, 92, (Heian) 95,
    (Kamakura) 97, 103–5,
    (Ashikaga) 106, (civil
    war/Tokugawa) 117–8, 120,
    122, 124, 125, 131–9, 275,
    (Meiji) 180, 181ff., 194ff.,
    199, 202, 204, (post-Meiji)
    chap. 7, *passim*, 241, 242, 245,
    248, 249, 250–51, 254, 258,
    262, 265, 267, 269, 272, 274,
    276, 277, 278–9, 280, 289,
    291, 294, 296, 297, 305; *see*

    also Imjin Waeran, Wa
Jiandao Incident, the (1920), 218,
    223, 236
juche, 262, 271–2, 277, 278, 285,
    290, 295, 297, 299, 301, 305
June 10 Incident, the (1926), 222
June Uprising, the (1987), 267
Jurchen, the, 10, 95, 96, 126

Kabo reforms, 21, 155, 183–4,
    196
Kaehwadang, 179, 180, 194–5,
    240
Kaesŏng, 10, 84, chap. 3 *passim*,
    118, 119, 144, 147, 164, 251,
    297
Kang Sehwang, 147, 170
Kanghwa island, 86, 103, 106,
    109, 111, 138, 184, 194, 236
Kapsin coup, the (1884), 11,
    180–81, 182, 195
Kaya, 10, 37, 38, 41, 45, 51, 52,
    54, 56, 62, 108
Khitan, the, 10, 64, 85, 86, 91,
    94, 95, 96, 111, 126
Kija, 18–19, 20, 119, 235
Kim Chŏnghŭi, 169–72
Kim Chŏngp'il, 265, 267, 268
Kim Chunggun, 203, 204–5
Kim Daejung, 12, 14, 21, 131,
    266, 267, 268, 273, 283, 287,
    302
Kim Hongdo, 147, 162–3
Kim Hongjip, 183, 184, 194
Kim Il Sung, 12, 21, 35, 174,
    242, 244, 248, 249, 250, 251,
    253, 261, 263, 269, 270, 273,
    274, 276, 277, 278, 280, 290,
    294, 297, 301, 305
Kim Inmun, 43, 63, 66
Kim Jong Il, 14, 33, 269, 271,
    273, 274, 279, 295, 297, 302,
    305
Kim Kichang, 228, 292, 297
Kim Kisu, 194
Kim Ku, 216, 237, 244
Kim Kyusik, 244
Kim Okkyun, 179, 180, 182, 195
Kim Pusik, 17, 96, 101, 107–8,
    115
Kim Sakkat, 174, 301
Kim Sohee, 161, 232, 297
Kim Sŏngsu, 219, 220, 221, 227,
    239, 244
Kim Ŭnho, 228, 229, 239
Kim Whanki, 229, 258, 284, 291
Kim Young Sam, 131, 179, 266,
    267, 268, 273, 278, 280, 283
Kim Yusin, 42, 59, 272
kisaeng, 133, 150, 157, 158–9,

    160, 168, 205, 226
Ko Hŭidong, 170, 229
Koguryŏ, 6, 10, 25, 32, 34, 35ff.,
    37–58 *passim*, 59, 62, 63, 66,
    67, 86, 87, 96, 101, 107, 108,
    109, 170, 245, 258, 296
Kojong, King (Koryŏ), 103, 104,
    111
Kojong, King and Emperor
    (Chosŏn), 11, 15, chap. 6, *pas-
    sim*, 209, 210, 217, 231, 240
kolp'um, 41, 54, 62–3
Konishi Yukinaga, 132, 133, 137,
    193
Korean Central Intelligence
    Agency, the (KCIA), 265, 266,
    282, 300
Korean Communist Party, the,
    174, 221, 244, 246
Korean Conspiracy Trial (1912),
    216, 237, 239
Korean People's Army, the, 12,
    270, 275
Korean People's Republic, the,
    242, 243, 244
Korean Proletarian Artists'
    Federation, the, 229, 235, 256,
    282
Korean Provisional Govt, the,
    11, 218, 236, 237, 238, 243,
    244
Korean Repository, The, 182, 185,
    197, 203
Korean War, the, 12, 14, 15, 21,
    51, 137, 239, 247–63 *passim*,
    275, 282, 291, 300, 302, 303
Korean Workers' Party, the, 243,
    270, 275
Koryŏsa, 103, 119
Kublai Khan, 103, 104ff.
Kŭmgang-san, 14, 147, 148, 167,
    295, 297
Kungnaesŏng, 35, 37, 40, 46, 58,
    163
Kungye, 10, 85, 86
kwangdae, 90, 92, 150, 154, 161
Kwanggaet'o, King (Koguryŏ),
    40, 235, 247, 272
Kwangjong, King (Koryŏ), 87,
    88, 91
Kwangju Incident (1929), 11,
    221–2
Kwangju massacre (1980), 12, 22,
    267, 276, 292
kye, 174, 304
Kyo-jong, 124
Kyŏn Hwŏn, 10, 72, 85, 86
Kyŏngbok Palace, 145, 164, 179,
    182, 184, 200, 214, 233, 280
Kyŏngju, 10, 37, 39, 45, 51, 54,

chap. 2 *passim*, 85, 86, 87, 88, 101, 137, 193, 287

Lee Oyoung, 283, 300
Lee Ufan, 292, 296
Lelang, 10, 34, 35, 36, 37, 44, 48, 50, 54, 108, 227
Li Hongzhang, 180, 181, 195, 196
literature, 19, 23, 76–7, 109, 118, 121, 145, 174–5, 233–5, 239, 280, 287, 299–301; *see also* poetry

MacArthur, General Douglas, 240, 243, 249, 250, 251–2, 253, 256, 262
Maeil Sinbo, 212, 217; *see also Taehan Maeil Sinbo*
Mahan confederation, 10, 36, 37
Manchuria, 6, 10, 11, 17, 20, 25, 31, 33, 34, 36, 39, 40, 63, 64, 84, 85, 86, 94, 95, 96, 107, 114, 153, 183, 190, 191, 211, 217, 220, 223, 235, 237, 244, 246, 265
Manzhouguo, 224, 225
Mao Zedong, 242, 248, 249, 250, 270, 294
March First Movement, the, 11, 217ff., 233
markets, 88, 94, 100, 139, 144, 203, 265
Marxism, 125, 267, 290
medicine, 100, 118, 121, 140, 142, 167, 169, 194, 202, 223
Mencius, 65, 76, 128, 131, 240, 276
merchants, 36, 37, 81, 94, 97, 100, 120, 127, 139, 144, 161, 174, 181
Min, Queen, 11, 177, 178, 179, 180, 182, 183, 184, 191, 195, 196, 199, 210, 237, 276, 278
Min Yŏngik, 180, 195, 199
Minami Jirō, 225, 229, 235
minjung, 22, 174, 235, 256, 285, 286, 290, 292, 303
minjung movement, 276, 280, 298
missionaries, 209, 212, 223, 225
  Catholic, 14, 153, 193, 194
  Jesuit, 13, 131, 132, 138, 166, 200
  Protestant, 164, 193, 199, 200, 202, 205
Mo Yunsuk, 256
Mongols, the, 10, 72, 100, 102ff., 110–11, 126, 138
monks, 80, 81, 89, 91, 103, 111, 113, 124, 133, 141, 150, 157,

170; *see also* names of individual monks
Munmu, King (Unified Silla), 59, 62, 63, 64, 68, 69, 74
Muryŏng, King (Paekche), 40, 41, 45, 51, 56–7
museums and galleries, 227, 228, 247, 280
  Central Historical Museum (P'yŏngyang), 245, 280
  Chōsen Sōtokufu Museum, 227, 245
  Hoam, 287
  Kansŏng, 227, 239
  National Art Gallery (P'yŏngyang), 296
  National Folk Art Museum, 280
  National Museum for Contemporary Art, 187, 293, 296
  National Museum of Korea, 43, 49, 77, 80, 81, 105, 112, 215, 227, 245, 280, 282, 287
  Whanki, 288–9
music, 24–5, 46, 47, 50, 52–3, 70, 76, 77, 95, 96, 108, 109, 114–15, 121, 123, 131, 146, 147, 156, 158, 168, 189, 195, 203, 205, 231–3, 270, 283, 286, 297–9, 303, 306, 307
  aak, 98, 121, 189, 232
  court, 121, 168, 231–2, 297
  hyangak, 77, 98
  minyo (folk), 168, 231, 232, 286, 299
  nong'ak (farmers'), 298, 305
  p'ansori, 157, 160–61, 168, 231, 232, 297, 298, 305
  sanjo, 168, 203, 232
  tangak, 77, 90, 98, 121, 189
musical instruments, 31, 50, 74, 77, 82, 91, 94, 96, 98–9, 105, 145, 166
  kayagŭm, 24, 52, 168, 189, 297, 298
  kŏmun'go, 24, 50, 52, 150, 189, 232, 298
Myoch'ŏng, 96, 101, 107, 272

Na Un'gyu, 233, 303
Naisen Ittai, 224, 225, 226–7, 239
National Security Law, the (1948), 12, 242, 262, 268, 269, 276
nationalism, 17ff., 21–6 *passim*, 185, 192, 202, 215, 216, 218ff., 234, 235ff., 243, 245, 280, 283, 285, 291, 295
Neo-Confucianism, 10, 62, 82,

92, 100, 106, 114, chap. 4, *passim*, 155, 156, 165, 166, 169, 170, 172, 274, 290
newspapers, 203, 211, 212, 219, 221, 224, 265

O-gyo (Five Teachings), 78, 79
Old Chosŏn (Ko Chosŏn), 10, 18, 32, 34, 108
Olympic Games, the, 12, 225, 237, 267, 274, 276, 277, 300

Paekche, 10, 20, 32, 36, 37–58 *passim*, 59, 62, 63, 66, 72, 92, 107, 108
Paektu, Mount, 14, 18, 33, 295, 297
Paik Nam-june, 292–3
painting, 46–7, 87–8, 117, 146ff., 167–8, 169, 203, 228–30, 291–7, 306; *see also* folk art
  abstract, 228, 229, 256, 284, 289, 291
  avant-garde, 258, 282, 289, 291, 302
  ch'aekkori, 166–7
  Chinese styles, 118, 146–8, 203
  figure, 44, 170, 228
  flower-and-bird, 117, 147, 203, 296, 297
  Four Gentlemen, 169
  genre, 45, 150, 157, 169, 170, 203, 204, 292
  ink, 285, 291, 292, 295, 296, 298
  landscape, 117, 146–7, 148–9, 169, 203, 228, 295, 296, 297
  murals, 45–6, 47, 48–9, 156, 163, 258, 296
  oil, 171, 203, 229, 285, 289, 291, 295
  portrait, 45, 48–9, 117, 120, 147, 150, 167, 170–71, 297
  p'yŏngsaeng-do, 150, 167
  sehwa, 146
  Socialist Realism and, 229, 282, 294–5, 297, 305
  sweet dew (*kamno-jŏng*), 156–7, 170
  symbolism in, 88, 146, 166, 167, 282, 284, 289
  'true view', 147, 148–9, 170, 203, 230, 295
  t'aenghwa, 156–7, 203
Pak Chega, 140, 144, 169
Pak Hŏnyŏng, 221, 244, 270
Pak Yŏnghyo, 179, 183, 195
paper, 66, 74, 75, 92, 108, 144, 291, 295

Parhae, 63–4, 65, 66, 67, 85, 86, 170
Park Chung Hee, 12, 21, 24, 134, 238, 246, 264–5, 266, 274, 276, 277, 278, 279, 280, 283, 285, 286, 290, 292, 305
Park Sangkwang, 292
Park Seobo, 241, 256, 292, 293, 296
Park Seugun, 256, 284, 292
People's Committees, 243, 244, 246, 270
poetry, 25, 47, 77, 97, 109, 158, 174–5, 234, 299–300
  hyangga, 77
  sijo, 145, 175, 239
police, Japanese military, 211, 213, 215, 218, 219, 225, 226, 239, 244
Pŏphŭng, King (Silla), 40, 41, 62, 73
porcelain, 51, 97, 110, 112–13, 165, 166, 203, 227, 281
  celadon, 97, 101, 165
  inlaid celadon, 109, 112–14
  meibyŏng, 112, 288
  white, 109, 165
pottery, 35, 46, 50–51, 56, 203
  chŭlmun, 30, 31
  mumun, 30, 31
  punch'ŏng, 165–6, 203
  wajil, 50
printing, 73, 74–5, 108, 110–11, 115, 121, 144, 287
Pulguk-sa, 72, 73, 74–5, 80, 84, 137, 287
Pusan, 132, 136, 147, 193, 211, 220, 249, 250, 252, 254, 256, 258, 293
Puyŏ, 20, 35, 37, 68, 108
Pyŏnhan confederation, 10, 36
p'ungsu, 40, 200, 214, 288
P'unyang Chos, 153, 169, 173, 178

railways, 190, 191, 198, 202, 211, 220, 227, 273
Rhee, Syngman (Yi Sŭngman), 12, 22, 185, 198, 218, 235, 237, 238, 240, 243, 244, 245, 248, 249, 253, 262, 264
rice, 30, 36, 95, 100, 118, 142, 175, 213, 220, 223, 226
rites, ritual, 19, 30, 31, 38, 41, 46, 64, 65, 88, 89, 95, 98, 100, 113, 121, 126, 129, 145, 188–9, 202, 232, 286, 307
  ancestral, 127, 154, 156, 172, 183
  capping, 127, 158

domestic, 155, 159
Four Rites, 127
nectar (namjangsa), 156–7
Roh Moo-hyun, 238, 269
Roh Tae Woo, 12, 131, 267–8, 278, 283, 288
ROK, 12, 13, 215, 238, 239, chap. 8, passim, 264–9, 271, 274, 275–6, 291, 296, 305, 306; see also constitutions, Korean War
  cultural development, 279–89 passim, 299–301, 305
  cultural preservation policy, 256, 279–80
  democratic era, 267–9, 275–6, 286
  economic crisis (1997), 12, 14, 268–9, 283, 287, 291
  economic development, 21, 265
  elections, 264, 265, 266, 267, 268
  foundation, 242, 245
  military dictatorship, 22, 264–8, 275, 286
  relations with America, 21, 248, 249, 277–8
  relations with China, 26, 278
  relations with DPRK, 267, 269, 272–3, 283
  relations with Japan, 26, 265, 267, 277–9
Roosevelt, Franklin D., 243, 262
Russia, 181, 183, 184, 185, 190, 191, 192, 195, 196, 198, 209; see also USSR
Russo-Japanese War, the (1904–5), 11, 190–91, 198, 212
Ryūkyū kingdom, 117, 118, 120, 124, 159, 192

sadae, 65, 222, 240
Sadaedang, 180, 195
Sado, Crown Prince, 11, 130, 140–41, 143, 178
Saemaŭl Undong, 12, 24, 266, 274, 276
Saitō Makoto, 218, 222, 235
Samguk sagi, 17, 41, 42, 47, 74, 108
Samguk yusa, 17, 68, 77, 78, 82, 90, 108, 115
Samsung Corporation, the, 67, 287
schools, 106, 119, 199, 202, 211, 217, 218, 219, 220, 222, 225, 265, 266, 287; see also sŏwŏn
  English Interpreters', the,

196, 203
Paejae, 186, 203
  Royal English School, the, 186, 199
Sejo, King (Chosŏn), 122, 125
Sejong, King (Chosŏn), 11, 120–25, 132, 186
shamans, shamanism, 32, 36, 37, 39, 41, 45, 56, 87, 90, 100, 114, 127, 154, 157, 158–9, 175, 199, 217, 223, 285, 290
Shin Sang'ok, 302, 303
Shintō, 125, 223, 225
shrines, 72, 119, 134, 159, 160, 223, 225, 241, 280
  Confucian, 232
  Royal Ancestral, 98, 183, 232, 287, 297
silk, 35, 36, 44, 45, 52, 65, 100, 144, 295
Silla, 10, 35, 37–58 passim, 59, 63, 66, 69, 92, 107, 108, 125
sillok, 119, 120, 122, 124
silver, 35, 38, 43, 44, 45, 55, 56, 65, 69, 74, 94, 95, 118, 281
Sin Ch'aeho, 33, 235
Sin Yunbŏk, 150
Sin'ganhoe, 221
Sinminhoe, 211, 216, 236, 237
Sinmun, King (Unified Silla), 63, 64, 76
Sino-Japanese War, the (1894–5), 182–3, 191, 196, 197
sirhak, 11, 18–19, 122, 130, 141, 144–5, 147, 153, 160, 168, 169, 171, 178, 192, 194, 200, 202, 240
slaves, slavery, 67, 87, 97, 101, 102, 103, 106, 115, 120, 124, 133, 136, 140, 154, 183, 192
Sŏ Chaep'il, 179, 180, 185, 186, 197, 244
Sŏ Chŏngju, 246
Sŏn, 65, 79, 108, 124, 133, 169
Sŏng, King (Paekche), 39, 74
Sŏngdŏk, King (Unified Silla), 60, 64, 75, 76, 81, 84
Sŏngjong, King (Koryŏ), 88–9, 91, 100, 115
sŏwŏn, 88, 128, 129, 139, 178
Stalin, Joseph, 242, 244, 247, 248, 249, 250, 251, 261, 262, 269, 294
students, 22–3, 66, 76, 91, 180, 218, 220, 221, 222, 232, 234, 252, 264, 265, 271, 278, 282, 299, 307
Suh Seok, 292, 296
Sunjong, Emperor, 11, 210, 221, 235

Taehan Maeil Sinbo, 212
Taewŏn'gun, the, 11, 129, chap. 6, *passim*
Taft-Katsura Memorandum (1905), 191
Taizong, (Tang) Emperor, 42, 66, 115
Tan'gun, 17, 20, 32, 33, 108, 114, 159, 219, 235, 245, 280, 295
tanch'ŏng, 73, 164, 292
Ten Injunctions (Ch'oe Chunghŏn), 101
Ten Injunctions (Wang Kŏn), 87, 89, 90
Terauchi Masatake, 213, 216, 218, 236
Tohwa-sŏ, 146, 147, 150, 167, 170, 188, 200, 228
Tŏksu Palace, 120, 133, 164, 185, 187, 191, 199
Tokto islands, 6, 26, 278
tombs, 41, 44–6, 48–9, 51, 54–5, 56–7, 60, 68, 69, 141, 170
Tonga Ilbo, 219, 220, 225, 239, 305
Tonghak Rebellion, the (1894–5), 23, 175, 181–2, 195, 196
Tongnip Sinmun, 21, 185, 195, 198
Treaties, 11, 195, 196
  of Amity and Commerce (1882), 11, 195
  of Annexation (1910), 11, 209, 212, 240
  Basic Relations (1965), 12, 265, 278
  Chemulp'o (1882), 195
  Hansŏng (1885), 195
  Kanghwa (1876), 194, 198
  Portsmouth (1905), 191
  Protectorate (1905), 11, 191, 209, 210, 240
  Protocol (1907), 211, 240
  Shanyuan (1005), 94
  Shimonoseki, (1895), 183, 186, 190
  Tianjin (1885), 11, 180, 181, 195
tribute, 36, 38, 39, 43, 64, 65–6, 91, 94, 119
tribute system, the, 16, 38, 65, 76, 110, 117–18
Tripitaka, the, 109, 110–11, 114, 287
Truman, Harry S., 242, 247–8, 249, 252, 263
Tsushima, 13, 16, 132, 191
turtle boats, 133, 134–5

T'aejo, King (Chosŏn), 119, 122, 147, 164, 170, 179
T'aejo, King (Koryŏ), 86, 89, 90, 91, 115
T'ongni-gimu Amun, 194, 196

Ugaki Kazushige, 224, 235
ŭibyŏng, 23, 184, 211, 218, 234, 236, 237
Ŭich'ŏn, 95, 111
ŭigwe, 147, 188–9
Ŭisang, 78
Ŭlchi Mundŏk, 42, 236
United Nations Organization, the (UNO), chap. 8, *passim*, 271–2, 273
  UNESCO, Korean National Commission for, 286–7, 304
  UNTCOK, 242, 245
universities, 199, 221, 225, 228, 234, 266, 278, 280, 283, 295, 298, 300
US–Soviet Commission, the, 244–5
USSR, 12, 21, 241, 242, 243, 245, 248, 249, 253, 260, 265, 270, 277, 294

Vietnam, 256, 260, 263, 265, 266, 271
von Möllendorff, Paul-Georg, 195, 196

Wa, 36, 37, 41, 45
Waeber, Karl, 196
Wang Kŏn, 10, 70, 85–6, 101, 107, 115
Wanggŏmsŏng, 18, 34
War Memorial, the National, 134, 236, 247, 255, 260
weapons, 31, 35, 45, 51, 95, 97, 105, 132
Wiman, 18–19, 20, 22, 34
Wiman Chosŏn, 10, 34, 35, 108, 235
women, 43, 66, 87, 97, 112, 121, 124, 127, 155, 157, 159, 170, 204, 221, 228, 295, 297, 299, 302; *see also kisaeng*
  comfort women, 226, 303
Wŏn Buddhism, 223
Wŏnhyo, 72, 76, 78
Woo, Kyu Sung, 288
Wu, (Tang) Empress, 64, 74–5

Xianbei, 32, 39, 54
Xiongnu, 32, 34
Xu Jing, 96–7, 100, 109, 144, 164
Xuanzong, (Tang) Emperor, 64, 77, 115

Yalu river, 10, 13, 14, 29, 32, 34, 35, 36, 41, 64, 94, 133, 182, 191, 224, 250, 252,
Yan, state, 18, 32, 33, 34, 35, 48
Yang Kit'ak, 212, 216
yangban, 114, 117, 120, 124, 125–6, 138, 139, 144, 145, 146, 150, chap. 5, *passim*, 178, 199, 203, 204, 217, 222, 235, 305
Yejong, King (Koryŏ), 96, 98, 114, 161
Yi Cha'gyŏm, 96, 97, 101
Yi Chungsŏp, 257, 258
Yi Hwang, 127, 141
Yi I, 128, 141
Yi Inhwa, 141, 301, 306
Yi Insŏng, 230
Yi Kwangsu, 217, 219, 220, 221, 234, 239
Yi Kyubo, 77, 108, 300
Yi Munyŏl, 257, 300, 306
Yi Saek, 106, 118, 126
Yi Sangbŏm, 228, 229, 239
Yi Sŏnggye, 10, 18, 100, 106–7, 117, 118, 119, 126, 272
Yi Sunsin, 133–9 *passim*, 166, 241, 278, 280
Yi Wanyong, 184, 185, 211, 212, 240
Yŏ Unhyŏng, 221, 237, 243, 244
Yŏhung Mins, 178, 179, 180
Yongbi ŏch'ŏn ga, 122, 124
Yŏngjo, King (Chosŏn), 11, 139, 140, 141, 144, 145, 146, 170, 171, 173
Yŏngju-sa, 141, 147
Yŏsu–Sunch'ŏn Rising, the (1948), 242, 246
Yu Kilchun, 183, 184
Yu Sŏngnyong, 132, 133, 135, 136, 143
Yuan Shikai, 180, 181, 182, 196
Yul-jong, 82
Yun Ch'iho, 185, 197, 198, 216, 231, 238–9
Yun Isang, 231, 232, 239, 282, 302

Zhou Wenmu, Fr, 153
Zhu Xi, 106, 126, 127, 128, 130, 141
Zo Za-yong, 167